WALKING WITH THE POOR

WALKING WITH THE POOR

Principles and Practices of Transformational Development

Revised and Expanded Edition

Bryant L. Myers

ORBIS BOOKS

Maryknoll, New York 10545

Fourth Printing, January 2015

Founded in 1970, Orbis Books endeavors to publish works that enlighten the mind, nourish the spirit, and challenge the conscience. The publishing arm of the Maryknoll Fathers and Brothers, Orbis seeks to explore the global dimensions of the Christian faith and mission, to invite dialogue with diverse cultures and religious traditions, and to serve the cause of reconciliation and peace. The books published reflect the views of their authors and do not represent the official position of the Maryknoll Society. To learn more about Maryknoll and Orbis Books, please visit our website at www.maryknollsociety.org.

Copyright © 2011 by Bryant L. Myers.

This is a substantially revised and updated edition of the same book originally published in 1999 copyright © World Vision International.

Published by Orbis Books, P.O. Box 302, Maryknoll, NY 10545–0302.

Scripture verses taken from the HOLY BIBLE, NEW INTERNATIONAL VERSION, copyright © 1973, 1978, 1984 by International Bible Society.

Manufactured in the United States of America.

Manuscript editing and typesetting by Joan Weber Laflamme.

Library of Congress Cataloguing-in-Publication Data

Myers, Bryant L.
    Walking with the poor : principles and practices of transformational development / Bryant L. Myers. — Rev. and updated ed.
       p. cm.
    Includes bibliographical references and index.
    ISBN 978–1–57075–939–0 (pbk. : alk. paper)
    1. Church work with the poor—Catholic Church. 2. Poverty—Religious aspects—Catholic Church. I. Title.
    BX2347.8.P66M94 2011
                              261.8'325—dc22

To the triune God
who found this book in me and
helped let it emerge, and

To my wife and lifelong
mentor and love, Lisa,
who encouraged me to believe
that God could do such a thing.

Contents

Figures

Foreword

Paul G. Hiebert

This book is a masterpiece of integration and application in thinking about Christian ministry. The author draws widely on the best Christian and scientific sources on introducing changes in human societies and forms solid conclusions based on what we have learned from experience in development ministries around the world. He develops a solid, scripturally based framework, or theoretical structure that challenges the spiritual/natural dualism which pervades our Western worldview and that offers a consistent biblical worldview in its place. He shows how the vision of Christian ministry can be implemented in transformational development that is truly *transformational* in the full sense of the world, and *development* in that the transformations are lasting and profound.

Myers's focus on relationships and stories is particularly helpful in developing a holistic view of ministry. This approach brings people together and builds bridges of understanding and communication, whereas abstract analytical categories often separate them. Relationships and stories also help us see that the kingdom of God is central to God's plan for the universe, for peoples and for individuals.

Myers does more than give us a new vision of what Christian ministry might be like. He provides guidelines for implementing this vision in life and ministry in ways that are consistent with the vision, and he reminds us that the life and relationships of Christians are the most powerful testimonies to the transforming power of God. In this, Myers points out that those who serve and those who are served must both grow spiritually in encounters of ministry.

The book is written for those involved in Christian development programs and challenges them to move toward holistic ministries. It is of equal importance for those involved in evangelism and church planting. It is a "charter" for a new way of doing mission, and the implications of its vision are far-reaching for all who serve Christ in the world. Too often in church planting we have relegated God's transforming work to spiritual realities and assigned earthly matters to science and technology. The result is a schizophrenic Christianity that leaves the everyday problems of human life to secular specialists and limits God to matters of eternity. A truly holistic approach to mission rooted in biblical truth is as essential in planting vital churches that remain Christ-centered over the generations as it is in Christian ministries of compassion.

Probably the greatest reward to many readers will be the way the author challenges our own distorted worldviews that have blinded us from understanding what it means to be living witnesses and servants in a world in desperate need. Such challenges are often costly, for they call us to experience radical transformations in our own lives and ministries.

Acknowledgments

For this second edition, I must begin by acknowledging and thanking my readers. When I wrote the first edition of *Walking with the Poor*, I was pretty sure my wife and my mom might read the book but was uncertain as to its wider acceptance. You have surprised me. I have been blessed by letters and emails from practitioners all over the world who have indicated this book was somehow helpful to them. I am also grateful to those who volunteered their time and treasure to translate the first edition of *Walking with the Poor* into Korean, Old Chinese (Taiwan), Spanish, Portuguese, and Arabic. Low-cost versions were produced in the Philippines to assist its dissemination in the South. I am deeply grateful to and honored by the many professors at Christian and secular universities, seminaries, and Bible schools who used the book in their classes. Without such encouragement, a second edition would have been an unattractive option.

ANTECEDENTS

No book such as this one is the work of one author. A lifetime of relationships and a great deal of lived experience form the raw material from which an author tries to pull together an articulation of what he or she has learned and hopes that others will find worth reading. For me, this is even more the case, since I am a person who creates by synthesizing, by pulling things together and fitting them into larger frameworks. I learn in community, listening to others, reading widely, brainstorming with enthusiasm, knowing that in time I will tumble on a frame that fits the many and disparate pieces together. Yet few of the pieces are mine: they are the faithful and precious work of others. I may refine or even extend them, but I always begin with the offering of others. This is what makes thanking others an important place for me to start.

GENERATIVE IDEAS

This book draws and builds on two powerful sets of ideas: Paul Hiebert's description of the Western worldview and its excluded middle, and

Jayakumar Christian's understanding of the nature of poverty as relationships that do not work for well-being and the cause of poverty as being fundamentally spiritual. I am deeply indebted to the creative work of these two men and for their friendship and counsel over the years.

Drawing on his experience in India, Paul Hiebert has had two significant insights that have proved very helpful to me and others in Christian mission. The first is his formulation of the Western worldview in terms of two separated realms—material and spiritual—with a gap between the two, the "excluded middle." Linking this with the thinking of Lesslie Newbigin provides the explanation for many of the dichotomies with which Western Christians struggle: faith and reason, evangelism and development, church and state, and values and facts. These dichotomies are major hindrances to finding a genuinely holistic Christian approach to human transformation.

Hiebert's second important insight is that the Western worldview, with its separated spiritual and material realms, has a particular kind of impact when it encounters the holistic, spiritist worldview of traditional cultures. Those of us carrying a Western worldview take it for granted that the location of cause and effect is in the material world. In contrast, traditional cultures believe that the cause of things is located in the unseen world of spirits and gods. The absence of a "middle" in the Western worldview means that we have no way to make sense of or respond to the very active and important "middle" of traditional cultures. This framework has proved to have a great deal of explanatory power when one comes to the work of development promoters and their tool kit of technological interventions, as well as our thinking as to how Christian witness and development intersect.

Jayakumar Christian is a World Vision co-worker and a personal friend of almost twenty years. Jayakumar has offered a family of ideas about the nature and causes of poverty that break us free from the material language and definitions that tend to dominate conversations about poverty. In his Ph.D. work Jayakumar offered the idea that poverty is experienced most fundamentally by the poor as a marring of their identity and that this is caused both by the grind of being poor and also by being captive to the god-complexes of the non-poor. I found these ideas liberating and highly generative. They provide the platform on which I frame my understanding of transformational development done by Christians.

I employ Jayakumar's ideas liberally in this book and then build on them. To the idea that playing god in the lives of the poor results in a marring of the identity of the poor, I add that it also mars the identity of the non-poor. They cannot play god and be who they are in God's sight. To Jayakumar's proposal that transformation is the work of helping the poor recover their true identity as made in the image of God, I add the idea that vocation or calling is also part of true identity. Our identity in biblical terms is both who we are and what we do. The poor and the non-poor need God's redemptive help to recover their true identity as children of God made in

God's image and their true vocation as productive stewards, given gifts by God to contribute to the well-being of all.

FORMATION

As a practitioner, I am indebted to many people. I began my journey in transformational development with Hal Barber and his relief and development innovation in World Vision in 1976. Our journey began with a stimulating three weeks with James Yen and Juan Javier at the International Institute of Rural Reconstruction in the Philippines. Over the years I have been influenced and enriched by a family of development professionals who have attended conferences, hosted me for field visits, and written papers that have influenced me. These include Mulegeta Abebe, Mulatu Belachew, Bruce Bradshaw, Rebecca Cherono, Ben Chitambar, Frank Cookingham, Helen Eversole, Judy Hutchinson, Bob Linthicum, Ken Luscombe, Eric Ram, Paul Peterson, Christina Lee Showalter, John Stewart, Morris Stuart, Bryan Truman, and Corina Villacorta.

In particular, I am deeply indebted to Ravi Jayakaran, Nora Avarientos, Sarone Ole Sena, and Jayakumar Christian, all of whom were willing to invest many hours in telephone interviews as a way of contributing to this book. Ravi Jayakaran is an expert in Participatory Rural Appraisals (PRAs) and has done pioneering work on enabling this method to allow the spiritual side of the traditional worldview to be heard. Nora Avarientos, together with Malcolm Bradshaw, developed the Scripture Search methodology for using the Bible in the context of community development in the Philippines. Sarone Ole Sena, a Masai anthropologist, along with Dirk Booy, a Canadian, were the World Vision pioneers in applying Appreciative Inquiry to development planning in Tanzania.

As a lay theologian, I am particularly thankful for those who shared in my theological formation, as ad hoc as it may have been. My introduction to thinking theologically about development began with Vinay Samuel and Chris Sugden and their workshops with World Vision in Asia in the early 1980s. I am also indebted to Sam Kamaleson, who mentored me patiently over his years in World Vision. I also recall, with some chagrin, a challenging and stimulating evening at Wheaton '83, when a kindly and learned man spent four hours patiently answering my simple questions about missiology: his name was David Bosch. I learned to think biblically and to trust that the word of God always has something to say to the world from Tom Houston, when he was the international president of World Vision.

In addition, the International Fellowship of Evangelical Mission Theologians (INFEMIT) has provided a family of friends who have nurtured my understanding of theology and development from the perspectives of cultures other than my own. These friends include Valdir Steuernagel, Tito Paredes, René Padilla, Kwame Bediako, and Miraslav Volf. From the United States I am indebted to Ron Sider and my co-workers in MARC, Saphir Athyal and Tom McAlpine.

Frank Cookingham, the chief evaluation officer of World Vision International, and I have carried out an ongoing dialogue about how the framework for transformational development of this book, including Christian witness, might be monitored and evaluated in the real world of development programming. Frank has pursued a long-time exploration of how spirituality and discernment should become part of any Christian attempts to monitor and evaluate holistic programming. I am indebted to Frank for helping me rework and ultimately write Chapter 9.

For this book I must say a special thanks to my friend Bill Dyrness for his willingness to review, and then review again, my chapter on the biblical story both in the original and the second editions. Bill and I also taught a course together on theology of poverty and development during which I learned a great deal. For the second edition Howard Loewen and Doug McConnell at Fuller Theological Seminary and Bill Burrows, my editor from Orbis Books, gave the theology chapter a close review. Of course, all the lousy theology that remains in the chapter is my responsibility.

Steve Commins, a long-time friend and an instructor in international development at UCLA, was kind enough to read the new chapter on the evolution of the idea of development. I am also indebted to two master's-degree students, whose final papers for my poverty and development class introduced me to material that was new to me and highly relevant to the second edition. Monica Felix, of Fuller's School of Psychology, wrote an intriguing paper that linked descriptions of chronic poverty expressed in the World Bank "Voices of the Poor" study to a theoretical construct used in post-traumatic stress studies in psychology. Gareth Mayhew introduced me to the Positive Deviance approach of public health as it was adapted to a variety of poverty settings by Save the Children. Finally, I must pay tribute to my Ph.D. students who have suffered under my academic inexperience, had to listen and react to most of the new material in this book, and gave me feedback on some of the chapters: Nathan Penner, Josh Smith, Bobby Lynch, and Isaac Voss.

MEANS

The chapter on Christian witness draws on research made possible by the Dellenback Initiative of World Vision US in the late 1990s. Field research into Christian witness in the context of relief and development in West Africa and other parts of the world and several small consultations with practitioners and theologians were made possible through this initiative. I am very grateful to the leadership and commitment of Bob Seiple and Ron Vander Pol, whose vision made this possible.

This second edition would not have been possible save for my vocational shift from World Vision International to the School of Intercultural Studies at Fuller Theological Seminary. While I had never anticipated leaving active ministry for an academic setting, and still wonder why an "agency guy" might be attractive as a potential faculty member, I have felt welcomed, respected, and supported here. I am particularly grateful to the dean of the School of Intercultural Studies (now provost) Doug McConnell, who has coached, nurtured, and encouraged my transition and who was a major source of prodding to get this second edition written. Howard Loewen, dean of the School of Theology, has been a continual source of theological and personal support, somehow convincing me that there is enough theology in my thinking so as not to be an embarrassment to an ancient professional tradition. My fellow faculty members have been welcoming, encouraging, and challenging.

My five years at Fuller made this second edition possible. The pace of seminary life allowed me to expand my reading beyond what could be done on long plane flights. Access to a first rate academic library has allowed me to explore areas of the literature in development studies and development research that were largely inaccessible and hence unknown to a busy, always traveling, senior administrator. In an academic setting one is actually given time and rewarded for writing and teaching, both ways to extend one's thinking and learning.

PERSONAL GRATITUDE

In the Bible we are told that the last is really the first. And so it is with these acknowledgments. I am indebted to my mother, Patricia Myers, for setting aside her loft, enduring my bewildering pile of papers and books, and making my lunch during the months that I wrote the first edition of this book in her home. She prayed for a lost and hopeless son for many years before God finally relented and dragged me into his kingdom at the age of thirty-one. I am deeply grateful that she is alive to see the book that summarizes why she and God went to all that trouble.

I am also deeply grateful to Tom and Hazle Houston, who turned over their home in Oxford to the Myers clan for five weeks in the summer of 1997. The first manuscript of this book was born in Tom's study, and our family became closer to each other and to God in his sitting room.

I must also thank Dean Hirsch, the international president of World Vision, and the International Board of World Vision for allowing me the time to complete the research and write the first edition of this book.

Bill Burrows of Orbis Books had the vision to see the potential of the first edition of this book and the ecumenical spirit needed to fight for a joint publishing arrangement between Orbis and World Vision, an unusual partnership at that time. With grace and patience, Bill pushed me to do this revision even as he was retiring and was trying to slow down. I am grateful to Bill for his friendship and seeing something of value that I could not see.

Finally and most important, I must acknowledge the unpayable debt I owe my family. My children, Brooke and James, of whom I am exceedingly proud, have taught me more than I ever taught them. There is no better or harsher corrective to one's thinking about human transformation and development than one's children.

There are not enough words to convey my appreciation, affection, and love for my wife, my longtime mentor, my friend, and my deepest love, Lisa. At great sacrifice to her own aspirations, she has encouraged, nurtured, and supported me. I can only pray that this all proves worthy of her sacrifice.

As Lisa read the first edition, she kept exclaiming, "This is my stance in spiritual direction. This is how I help people hear and see God in their lives." Only then did we discover that walking with the poor and walking with those who seek a deeper and more personal spirituality employ similar frames and tools. Transformation is transformation; we should have known. As a result of this discovery and her quarter century of experience of spiritual direction and innovations in group direction, Lisa helped write two important contributions to this second edition.

Abbreviations and acronyms

ADP	Area Development Program (World Vision)
AI	Appreciative Inquiry
ARVIN	associate, resources, voice, information, and negotiation
CA	*Centesimus annus*
CBPM	community-based performance monitoring
CV	*Caritas in veritate*
DEEDS	Development Education Services (India)
DFID	Department for International Development (UK)
DME	design, monitoring, and evaluation
EFICOR	Evangelical Fellowship of India Committee on Relief
EN	*Evangelii nuntiandi*
GDP	gross domestic product
HDI	Human Development Index
IDS	International Development Society (UK)
IMF	International Monetary Fund
INTRAC	International NGO Training and Research Centre (UK)
J-PAL	Jameel Poverty Action Lab (MIT)
LEAP	learning through evaluation with accountability and planning (World Vision)
MDGs	millennium development goals (UNDP)
MSC	Most Significant Change
NGO	nongovernmental organization
PD	Positive Deviance
PLA	Participatory Learning and Action
PP	*Populorum progressio*

PRA	Participatory Rural Appraisal
PRSP	Poverty Reduction Strategy Paper (World Bank)
QA	*Quadragesimo anno*
RN	*Rerum novarum*
SRS	*Sollicitudo rei socialis*
TDI	Transformational Development Indicators
UNDP	United Nations Development Program
USAID	US Agency for International Development
WTO	World Trade Organization

1

Charting the course

The purpose of this book is to describe a proposal for understanding the principles and practice of transformational development (positive material, social, and spiritual change) from a Christian perspective. It is my intention to try to bring together three basic streams of thinking and experience. The best of the principles and practice of the international development community needs to be integrated with the thinking and experience of Christian relief and development nongovernmental organizations (NGOs). Then these two streams of experience need to be informed and shaped by a theological framework for transformational development.

Throughout this book I will struggle to overcome problems presented by the persistent and insistent belief in the West that the spiritual and physical domains of life are separate and unrelated. This assumption has invaded and controlled almost every area of intellectual inquiry, including development theory and practice as well as much of Christian theology. I will seek an understanding of development in which the physical, social, and spiritual dimensions of life are seamlessly interrelated.

Origins

The pilgrimage that this book represents had its origin in 1975, the year World Vision received a Development Program Grant from the United States Agency for International Development (USAID) for the purpose of helping World Vision begin its relief and development ministry. I was part of the original team. We went to Washington DC, took a three-day course in development planning, and were then released to help World Vision's seven offices in Asia begin planning their first development programs. God forgive us for our sins.

1

The 1970s and early 1980s were interesting times for Christian relief and development agencies. It was a time full of argument and sometimes divisive discussions among evangelicals as to whether or not Bible-believing Christians ought to do development. Some were deeply concerned that including social action in the Christian agenda blunted the church's commitment to evangelism. Evangelism must be primary, went the argument. The modern assumption that the spiritual and the material were unrelated areas of life had infected Christian mission thinking.

Throughout this pilgrimage, many of us in the World Vision family shared a deep-seated concern that, for a Christian agency to be Christian, development programming had to be holistic, by which we meant that development and Christian witness should be held together in a creative tension. In these early days we simplistically and incorrectly understood this to mean that Christian witness was something one added to the development program mix to make it complete, just another sector, a wedge in the development pie.

In time we realized that this conceptualization was flawed. It implied that all the other development sectors had nothing to do with spiritual things and that we were treating spiritual work as a separate sector of life. This meant that, in the very communities where we wanted to be good models of the Christian faith, we were in fact witnessing to the fact that the material and the spiritual realms of life were separate and unrelated. Our struggle to escape this modern assumption led us to a great deal of inquiry concerning both the theology and the worldview of development.

The 1990s were a decade of seeking professionalism. Good intentions were no longer enough. The poor deserved better than gifted amateurs with their hearts in the right place. The world had learned a great deal about development and Christian organizations needed to take this on board. The social sciences were studied and our staff members were sent off to England, Canada, and the United States, to learn from centers of development learning in the West.

The first edition of *Walking with the Poor* was written in 1998. A lot had happened in the intervening twenty-three years since we set out to "do development." Much had been learned. As a cadre of long-time friends, we had shared our successes and wept over our failures. Hundreds of workshops have been celebrated or endured. Hundreds of papers have been pored over, and many books have been read. Thousands of hours of discussion, anguish, and discovery have taken place in long rides on dusty roads and over the dinner tables in featureless hotels. The outworking of all of this is the source of the thinking for the first edition of this book.

It is now 2011. I left World Vision to become a professor of international development in the School of Intercultural Studies at Fuller Theological Seminary five years ago. Still in touch with World Vision friends and colleagues, I continue to see a steady stream of position papers, evaluations, and white papers. I do a bit of consulting from time to time.

But my major source of new material and insights comes from the world of development studies and development research, a product of the professionalizing of the international development community that began in the 1990s. Today, there is a wide variety of academic journals, a number of serious schools of development studies and thousands of "fugitive documents"—research papers, evaluations, empirical studies—hanging on the websites of most development agencies, a number of development studies centers in Europe and the United States and the World Bank. By virtue of leaving the hectic life of an agency executive for the life of an academic, I finally have time to read and graduate students to exploit. Much of the new material in this book is a result.

Definitions

I will use two phrases over and over in this book: *transformational development* and *Christian witness*. It may help the reader if I define them here in the beginning.

Transformational development is the term I use as an alternative to the more traditional *development*. There are two reasons for this. First, the term *development* is heavily loaded with past meaning, not all of which is positive. When most people think of development, they think of material change or social change in the material world. Second, *development* is a term that many understand as a synonym for Westernization or modernization (Escobar 1995). For some, development is understood as simply having more things. Many in the development business, including many of us in the West, are not sure that this kind of development is good for people or for this planet.

I use the term *transformational development* to reflect my concern for seeking positive change in the whole of human life materially, socially, psychologically and spiritually. The adjective *transformational* is used to remind us that human progress is not inevitable; it takes hard work. There is an adversary who works against our desire to enhance life. True human development involves making choices, setting aside that which is not for life in us and in our community, while actively seeking and supporting all that is for life. This requires that we say no to some things in order to say yes to what really matters. Transformation implies changing our choices.

Transformational development is a lifelong journey. It never ends. There is always more before us. Everyone is on this journey: the poor, the nonpoor, and the staff of the development agency. The transformational journey is about finding and enjoying life as it should be, as it was intended to be. In this book I suggest that the goals for this journey of transformation are to recover our true identity as human beings created in the image of

God and to discover our true vocation as productive stewards, faithfully caring for the world and all the people in it.

Christian witness is the second phrase that I use frequently. Understanding what I mean by this requires a short introduction. Everyone believes in something and what we believe in shapes what we do and how we do it. This is no less true for those who are concerned for the poor and wish to help the poor on their development journey. This ideological center is a matter of faith, whether we are Christian, Muslim, Buddhist, agnostic, or atheist. These core values and beliefs are where we get our understanding of who we are and what we are here for. These guiding principles shape our understanding of what a better human future is and how we should get there.

I am a Christian, and I have been working among Christians in the development business for over thirty years. My Christian identity and my understanding of my faith shape my view of what development is for and how it should be done. Part of that understanding is my conviction that the best news I have is the knowledge that God has, through his Son, made it possible for every human being to be in a covenant relationship with God. We need only say yes to this offer. To not share this news, to not yearn that everyone might share what was given to me through no merit of my own, would be wrong in the deepest and most profound sense. *Christian witness* is the term that I use to describe my being compelled by love to share this news.

I deliberately chose the phrase *Christian witness* over the word *evangelism* for several reasons. First, like the term *development*, *evangelism* is a loaded phrase. Images of street evangelists yelling through megaphones and of crusade evangelists exhorting stadiums full of people come to mind, neither of which fits the idea of transformational development very well. Second, and more important, evangelism tends to be used in the limited sense of referring to the verbal proclamation of the truth of the gospel of Jesus Christ. I need a phrase that includes proclamation, but that is not limited to it.

I understand Christian witness to include the declaration of the gospel by life, word, and deed. By *life* I refer to the fact that Christians are the message. We are the sixty-seventh book of the Bible. People read our lives and our actions and listen to our words as their way of determining what being a Christian means. By *word* I refer to the need to say what the gospel story is and to invite others to make it their story. By *deed* I refer to the fact that the Christian faith, at its best, is an active faith, engaged with the world and seeking to make it more for life and for the enjoyment of life.

There is an important nuance here. There is no such thing as not witnessing. Christian development promoters are witnessing all the time. The only question is to whom or to what? Their deeds, both what they do and how they do it, declare in whom or in what they place their faith and also demonstrate the moral content of that faith. The way they live their lives declares whom they love and on whom they depend. And, if they are truly living lives that demonstrate their love of God and their neighbor, then questions will come to which the gospel is the answer and they will witness with the words that provide this answer.

THE PROBLEM OF THE MODERN WORLDVIEW

I have already mentioned that one of the primary characteristics of time in history has been the belief in the West that the spiritual and material domains of life are separate and unrelated. This dominating assumption controls almost every area of intellectual inquiry, including development theory and practice. The result is a tragic pair of reductions. First, poverty is reduced to a merely material condition having to do with the absence of things like money, water, food, housing and the lack of just social systems, also materially defined and understood. Second, development is reduced correspondingly to a material series of responses designed to overcome these needs.

Since the search for a genuinely biblical and holistic understanding of poverty and transformational development is the focus of this book, I believe it may be helpful to explore the nature of this modern blind spot more fully before going on. Why do we need the word *holistic* in the first place? What is the nature of the problem we are trying to solve by using such a term? There must be something that is not holistic.

The great divorce: Separating the spiritual and material realms

The place to begin is the way we understand and interpret the world in which we live, something anthropologists call our worldview. Our modern worldview is like a pair of glasses through which we see and make sense out of our world. Unlike glasses, however, our worldview also includes our assumptions about how the world works. Our need for holism has its roots in our modern worldview.

As the foundational paradigm shift of the Enlightenment has worked itself out in Western culture, one of its most enduring features has been the assumption that we can consider the spiritual and physical realms as separate and distinct from one another. On the one hand, there is the spiritual or supernatural world where God lives and acts, along with other cosmic Gods like Allah. This is the world of religion. On the other hand, there is the real world—the material world where we hear, see, feel, touch, and smell. This is the world of science, technology, and development.

Sadly, this is not just a problem for Western folk. This dichotomy, or absolute separation, between the spiritual and the physical is a central tenet of what some call modernity, and modernity is rapidly becoming a dominant overlay on the world's cultures. Modernity is deeply embedded in the modern economic system and in contemporary information technology, both of which are being extended wherever Coca Cola is sold. This same culture of dichotomies is taught in every classroom where the curriculum is based on Western educational models. Thus, every non-Western professional has imbibed this worldview as an unspoken part of his or her professional training.

This framework of separated areas of life is also deeply embedded in the Western part of the Christian church, in its theology, and in the daily life of its people. On Sunday morning or during our devotional or prayer life, we operate in the spiritual realm. The rest of the week, and in our professional lives, we operate in the physical realm and, hence, unwittingly act like functional atheists. Simply being Christian does not heal our dichotomous understanding of our world.

The dichotomies of the modern worldview

Lesslie Newbigin (1989) has shown how the modern separation of the physical and spiritual realms explains a wide range of the modern dichotomies that are prevalent in the modern worldview. For example, the spiritual world is the arena of sacred revelation, in which we know by believing. The real world where we hear, see, feel, and touch is where scientific observation allows us to know things with certainty. Faith and religion are part of the spiritual world, while reason and science provide the explanations in the real world. The spiritual world is an interior, private place; the real world is an exterior, public place. This means that values are a private matter of personal choice, having no relevance in the public square where politics and economics reign alone. Publicly, we only need to agree on the facts. Sadly, the church has also succumbed to this modern worldview and has allowed itself to be relegated to the spiritual world, while the state and other human institutions assume responsibility for what happens in everyday life.

Spiritual	Material
Revelation and believing	Observation and knowing
Faith	Reason
Religion	Science
Private and personal	Public
Values	Facts
Church	State

Figure 1–1: The dichotomies of the modern worldview.

Separating Christian witness and social action

Modernity's separation of the physical and spiritual realms is part of the explanation for how we have come to understand Christian witness, and specifically evangelism, as being unrelated to community development. Loving God is spiritual work, and loving neighbors takes place in the material world. So evangelism (restoring people's relationship with God) is spiritual work, while social action (restoring just economic, social, and political relationships among people) is not. In the final analysis this false dichotomy leads Christians to believe that God's redemptive work takes place only in the spiritual realm, while the world is left, seemingly, to the devil.

This two-tiered understanding of the world explains another curious phenomenon. As carriers of modernity, Western governments and most secular development institutions separate religion from development. They accept modernity's assertion that church and state must be separate because they deal with separate realms. Because the church understands evangelism as an activity appropriate to the spiritual world, while social action—if it is an appropriate activity for the church at all—is the appropriate response in the physical world, the church goes along with this imposed separation of what the gospel suggests is inseparable.

The Christian development agency is not immune to the phenomenon. We express our captivity to a modern worldview when we say that holistic ministry means combining evangelism (meeting spiritual need) with relief and development (meeting physical need) as if these were divisible realms and activities. Then we make it worse by insisting that the church or the evangelism part of our organization do the former, while the development agency does the latter. A number of serious and thoughtful Christian groups are organized this way. By so doing we declare development independent of religion, something most of us do not really believe.

Separating word, deed, and sign

Paul Hiebert has developed a very helpful framework that compares the worldviews of modern and traditional cultures. He portrays the modern worldview as two-tiered, with the physical and spiritual worlds completely separated. The traditional worldview is holistic, with the spiritual and material worlds interrelated in a seamless whole. The world of high religion is occupied by the great gods that should not be bothered or disturbed. The interrelationship between the seen and unseen worlds is mediated by shamans, sacred books, spirits, and others who have access to both worlds. This is the world of curses, amulets, charms, and other attempts to bargain with or "handle" the unseen world.

While the modern world has something to say about high religion and about the physical world, we have nothing to say to the world of folk religion. We suffer from what Hiebert calls "the excluded middle."

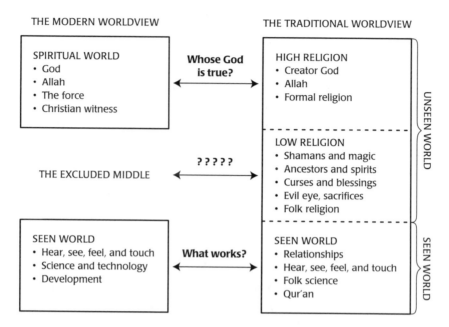

Figure 1–2: Modern and traditional worldviews.
(Adapted from Hiebert 1982)

We in the West no longer believe in ancestors, spirits, demons, and unseen actors. That's all superstition and ignorance, after all. Yet, most traditional cultures spend a lot of time being concerned about this unseen world and locate cause and effect there. The impact of this excluded middle from a development perspective is a blind spot. We fail to hear the community's story about the unseen world, and we fail to have answers that, in their minds, adequately take this world into account.

For Christians, it should be humbling to note that, while in no way the same, the worldview of the Bible is closer to the worldview of traditional cultures than it is to the modern worldview. The biblical worldview is holistic in the sense that the physical world is never understood as being disconnected or separate from the spiritual world and the rule of the God who created it. Moreover, Christ—the creator, sustainer, and redeemer of the creation—is both in us and interceding for us at the right hand of God the Father. The fact that the Word became flesh explodes the claim that the spiritual and physical can be separated meaningfully.

A clarification is needed. Having noted the holism in the biblical worldview and the fact that most traditional worldviews are holistic is not to say that the biblical worldview is animistic. The biblical and animistic

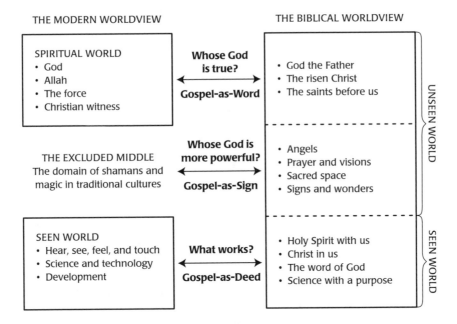

THE MODERN WORLDVIEW   THE BIBLICAL WORLDVIEW

Figure 1–3: Contrasting modern and biblical worldviews.

worldviews are quite different, as a comparison of Figure 1–2 and Figure 1–3 makes clear. There is only one God in the biblical worldview; all other spiritual beings are both part of the created order and fallen, just like human beings.

This worldview comparison also calls attention to the fact that the critical questions change depending on the level at which one is functioning. The gospel addresses the question of truth with gospel-as-word, the truth about God. The gospel addresses questions of power with the gospel-as-sign; the power of the Holy Spirit. At the material level of empiricism, the biblical worldview answers the question "What works?" with good deeds that express the love of God.

This reveals another level of the problem modernity poses to Christian mission. When we separate the spiritual from the physical, not only do we separate evangelism from development, but we separate gospel-as-word from the gospel-as-deed, and provide no home for gospel-as-sign. In the spiritual realm, the critical question is, Whose God is the true God? and the answer is an idea. This frame allows us to reduce the gospel message to truth in the form of propositions, even a set of "spiritual laws." Christian witness is reduced to words and speaking.

At the level of the physical world, the question is, What works? The answer comes in the form of effective methods and good technology. Deeds are the real thing. We then reduce the gospel message and evangelism to working for justice or saving God's creation.

Separating gospel-as-word, gospel-as-deed, and gospel-as-sign has serious consequences. In cultures in which words have lost their meaning, as is often the case of the West, deeds are necessary to verify what the words actually mean. Saying we are Christian is ambiguous, since almost everyone in the West claims to be Christian. If we want to know what people mean when they say they are Christian, we look at the quality of their lives. The way we live and act declares to others what we mean when we say we are Christians.

In other cultures deeds can be ambiguous. Whether we speak or not, people receive a message. Discovering water in the desert is a miracle, and animist cultures often interpret the technology that finds it as magic and witchcraft. Research done by Bruce Bradshaw (1993) has discovered this repeatedly in World Vision's development work. In the view of local villagers World Vision has outstanding diviners and powerful shamans on its staff. Development technology, without accompanying words to interpret its good deeds, can result in glory being given to clever or "magical" soil scientists and hydrologists, rather than to God.

We should also note the inadequate way the modern worldview deals with signs. Because there is no place for the appearance of the supernatural in the physical world, there is no home for signs and miracles. For most animists, the existential question has little to do with truth; it has to do with power. Since cause is located in the unseen or spiritual world, the critical question is, Whose god is more powerful? The fact that charismatic and Pentecostal folk have an answer for this question is a major part of the reason they are the fastest growing expression of the church today. The inability of the modern to deal with signs and miracles makes it very difficult for carriers of modernity, such as development practitioners, to carry out meaningful conversations with people who hold a traditional or animist worldview. The development practitioner thinks people are sick because of germs and dirty water, while the people believe they are sick because of curses and witchcraft.

Therefore, in dealing with the gospel message, we cannot separate word, deed, and sign without truncating our message. Words clarify the meaning of deeds. Deeds verify the meaning of words. Most critically, signs announce the presence and power of One who is radically other and who is both the true source of all good deeds and the author of the only words that bring life in its fullest.

Limiting the scope of sin and the gospel

Because we have tended to accept the dichotomy between the spiritual and the physical, we sometimes inadvertently limit the scope of both sin and the gospel. If God's concern is only for the spiritual, then we reduce our understanding of sin to something personal that separates people from God. This in turn tempts us to reduce the scope of redemption to the spiritual or personal realm alone. This makes it hard to understand the impact of sin in the material world of economics, politics, culture, and the church as an institution, and even harder to believe that God's salvific and redemptive work extends to this messy, sinful world. Yet this is the world in which the Christian development agency works.

By limiting the domain of sin to a person's soul, we inadvertently limit the scope of the gospel as well. We need to transform this way of thinking. God's rule extends to both the spiritual and material; the redemptive work of Jesus Christ is needed wherever sin has penetrated. This means we must redefine our understanding of salvation to be more inclusive or holistic without losing its meaning in terms of restoring our relationship with God.

Revelation and observation

The dichotomy in the modern worldview creates problems in terms of how we know things. Revelation is the way we know things in the spiritual realm, while observation and reason are the accepted ways of knowing in the physical realm. The modern dichotomy between revelation and observation conceals some interesting things.

First, the source of knowing is different. Revelation comes from God to us. Observation and reason we do for ourselves and, if we are not Christian, without any reference to God. Christians who separate the physical and spiritual realms tend to be God-centered in their spiritual lives and human-centered when they think and act in the physical world. For our spiritual work, we turn to the church and our bibles; for development work, we turn to the social sciences. This goes a long way in explaining why development practices of Christian development agencies often feel "secular."

Second, prayer, fasting, meditation, and other forms of spirituality are spiritual activities relegated to knowing things about the spiritual world. We then fail to see spirituality as a tool for knowing or working in the real world. Few Christian development workers understand that spiritual discernment is a key element in program planning and in monitoring and evaluation. Few development workers understand prayer and fasting as tools for human transformation or for working for justice. At best, prayer is either a personal, inner communion with God or a request to God for an extracurricular, "hit-and-run" intervention in the real world. On the other side, God and God's revelation is not considered germane to our social analysis, and we are left to interpret our world for ourselves.

Having explored the problem that modernity presents for the Christian practitioner who seeks to promote transformational development, it should be easier to understand why this book follows the path that it does. In every chapter, from the biblical account to principles and practice, I have attempted to overcome this blind spot and either suggest answers or point to further work that needs to be done.

THE PATH OF THIS BOOK

The evolution of the idea of development

Chapter 2 begins by tracing the emergence of the idea that our world is something that we can improve. There was very little change in the world in terms of population, wealth and health until the beginning of the nineteenth century. Life was hard. The world was an unsafe place where survival was daily task. Almost everyone was as poor as those in the poorer parts of the South today. The idea of improving the material part of the human condition did not exist.

With a radical change in the trajectory of economic history around 1800, a wide range of new ideas emerged—creating wealth, markets as systems, ordinary people as creative contributors, and the idea that God's world could be improved by human creativity. Science and technology emerged as ways to create wealth and increase human well-being. In the West, material improvements in the human condition were rapid. More recently, China, India, Brazil, and Indonesia have assumed this same trajectory. Sadly, this is less the case for Africa and Central Asia. While this process was wildly uneven and some benefited a great deal more than others, the fundamental historical shift that took place at the beginning of the nineteenth century is a historical fact that resulted in the creation of the idea that we now call development or poverty eradication.

The idea of development as poverty eradication directed at poor nations emerged in the aftermath of World War II, largely a product of Western nations facing a Cold War world. For decades, development meant becoming like the "modern" West and was measured in terms of economic growth. By the 1990s this economic model of development was being enlarged to include social development as well.

Chapter 2 then summarizes the current major voices in the development conversation as it is taking place within the United Nations and among governments and international NGOs. The stage is currently dominated by the predominantly modern frame of Jeffrey Sachs and his *End of Poverty* (2005), the more postmodern frame of William Easterly and his *White Man's Burden* (2006), and the more eclectic and pragmatic package of solutions offered by Paul Collier in *The Bottom Billion* (2007). I also present three important voices from the South. Amartya Sen, a Nobel Prize–winning development economist is responsible for shifting the global development conversation from economic growth alone with his book *Development as*

Freedom (1999). Hernando de Soto is an influential Peruvian economist who has written two seminal books: *The Other Path* (1989) and *The Mystery of Capital* (2000). Muhammad Yunus is a Nobel Prize winner for his pioneering work in microcredit and author of *Creating a World without Poverty* (2009). These offerings provide approaches for the eradication of poverty that are secular and materialistic, resting on the assumption that human beings can save themselves. Nonetheless, they are shaping the development conversation today and influencing donor priorities, and so we need to be aware of them.

The biblical story

Before getting to a conversation on poverty and then development, we stop for a chapter on theology. If transformational development is to be biblical, then we need to develop a biblical framework that informs the following discussions on development theory and practice.

Chapter 3 begins with a reprise of the conversation relating to poverty, development, and social justice in two Christian traditions—evangelical and Roman Catholic. The evangelical conversation—mostly American—on social justice and the poor is marred by an almost fifty-year silence between the modernist controversy of the 1920s and the reemergence of evangelicalism's historical concerns for the poor in the 1970s. On the other hand, the Roman Catholic Church's tradition of Catholic social teaching began in 1891 with Leo XIII's *Rerum novarum*. Over twenty documents, mostly papal encyclicals, have been written over the last 120 years as Catholic theologians have updated and extended their thinking in a rapidly changing world. There is a wealth of wisdom that we evangelicals need to know and appropriate.

The chapter then shifts gears in search of an evangelical theology of poverty and development. Traditional approaches to theology of development have tended to be propositional in nature, drawing on the Exodus account for an understanding of oppression and liberation, the psalms and the prophets for evidence of God's concern for the poor, and the gospels for examples of how Jesus responded to the poor and taught his disciples. All of this is very helpful and is still important.

In this book, however, I attempt to shift the perspective to a narrative account of the biblical story. I have done this because this perspective better fits and supports what I believe is a very helpful framework for setting the context in which development takes place: the convergence of stories.

The poor already have a story before the development agency arrives. It is both their immediate story and the story of their people. Furthermore, God has been active in their story since its very beginning, whether the people have recognized God's involvement or not. When development promoters arrive, they bring their story, both their personal story and the story of their development agency. Then, for the life of the program, the community and the promoters share a story.

Viewing the transformational development process as a shared story invites us to question what our stories are for, where they are going, and whose story is the true story. The biblical story provides a very helpful framework for seeking answers to these questions. The biblical story explains how every community's story began and why their stories are full of pain, injustice, and struggle at the same time that they are full of joy, loving relationships, and hope. The biblical story provides the answer to how the stories of the community and the development promoter may need to reorient themselves to the story intended by their Creator and describes, in the metaphor of the kingdom of God, what the best human story is like. The biblical story also tells us how all our stories will end. Most important, we can learn what our stories are for: the worship of the one true God.

What is poverty?

The way we understand the nature of poverty and what causes poverty is very important, because it tends to determine how we respond to poverty. Articulating what poverty is and what causes it helps us determine the source of much of our understanding of what transformational development is and how it should be practiced. The purpose of Chapter 4 is to try and integrate the best of what people have been thinking about the nature of poverty and its cause.

We must begin with ourselves. We need to work hard to discover our assumptions and our preconditioning regarding poverty and the poor. This is particularly true for Christians, because there have been a variety of views of the poor, depending on one's Christian tradition.

Chapter 4 then reviews the changing views of poverty as a way of showing that understanding poverty is a never-ending task. In the early days of development many assumed that poverty could be explained by the absence of things. This was followed by adding the absence of ideas or knowledge to the mix, and then, as the systemic nature of poverty became clear, absence of access to power, resources, and choices became part of our understanding of poverty. In the 1980s a systems view of poverty emerged with Robert Chambers's proposal that poverty is a system of entanglement. In the early 1990s John Friedmann added to the discussion by describing poverty as the lack of access to social power. Later in the 1990s Amartya Sen argued that poverty is more the result of a lack of freedom than the lack of money. More recently, community psychologists Isaac Prilleltensky and Geoffrey Nelson have argued that poverty is the result of oppression that diminishes personal and relational well-being.

Weighing in from a Christian perspective, Jayakumar Christian, building on Chambers and Friedmann, describes poverty as a system of disempowerment that creates oppressive relationships and whose fundamental causes are spiritual. Finally, I introduce Ravi Jayakaran's holistic framework of poverty as a lack of freedom to grow.

The chapter then explores the causes of poverty. I look at the interplay between the physical and social causes of poverty as causes largely external to the poor. I then explore the largely internal contribution to poverty resulting from mental and spiritual causes. Drawing heavily on Jayakumar Christian, I propose that the nature of poverty is fundamentally relational and that its cause is fundamentally spiritual.

The poor are poor largely because they live in networks of relationships that do not work for their well-being. Their relationships with others are often oppressive and disempowering as a result of the non-poor "playing god" in the lives of the poor. Their relationship within themselves is diminished and debilitated as a result of the grind of poverty and the feeling of permanent powerlessness. Their relationship with those they call "other" is experienced as exclusion. Their relation with their environment is increasingly less productive because poverty leaves no room for caring for the environment. Their relationship with the God who created them and sustains their life is distorted by an inadequate knowledge of who God is and what God wishes for all humankind. Poverty is the whole family of our relationships that are not all they can be.

The relationships of the poor don't work for the well-being of the poor because of spiritual values held by others and by the poor that do not enhance and support life. Selfishness, love of power, and feelings of ordained privilege express themselves in god complexes. Loss of hope, opportunity, and recognition mar the identity of the poor. Racism, ethnocentrism, and ostracism erode the intended blessing of having many cultures. Fear of spirits and belief in gods that cannot save obscure the offer of the God who desires to save. At the end of the day, the causes of poverty are spiritual.

The final section of Chapter 4 focuses on the poverty of the non-poor. They too suffer from a marred sense of identity and vocation, only in a different way than the poor experience.

Perspectives on development

Having developed a holistic framework for thinking about poverty, Chapter 5 surveys a number of ways of thinking about what development is and how it should work.

I begin by exploring where our ideas of development come from. The central question is, Who will save us? This is important because there are competing stories in this century, all of which offer salvation. Some believe we will be saved by science and technology. Others rest their faith on free markets and globalization. Still others put their faith in human ingenuity and the idea of inevitable human progress. The Christian view of salvation points to the cross and the resurrection as the only framework that can truly bring us home.

I explore a range of proposals for thinking about development. For evangelicals, the conversation started at a Lausanne consultation, Wheaton '83, at which theologians and practitioners moved beyond the debate as to whether evangelism and social action were both legitimate Christian activities and began the search for a biblical framework for understanding development. Of particular note was a paper by Wayne Bragg, then of the Wheaton Hunger Center, in which he proposed the phrase *transformational development* as a holistic biblical alternative to Western modernization.

I describe the *people-centered development* proposal of David Korten, in which he calls into question economic growth as an engine for sustainable development and insists that the environment and the limitations of "spaceship earth" become more central to development conversations. I explore John Friedmann's view of an "alternative development" that focuses on expanding the political and social power of poor families by supporting grassroots democratic practices and building civil society. I describe the proposal of Isaac Prilleltensky and Geoffrey Nelson, two community psychologists, that views development as enhancing personal, collective and relational power. I summarize Robert Chambers's proposal of development as responsible well-being, built on the principles of equity and sustainability and pursued by means of increasing the livelihood, security, and capabilities of the poor. Finally, I introduce Amartya Sen's proposal that human freedom is both the goal and the means to development.

I then spend a fair amount of space exploring the work of Jayakumar Christian and his idea of development as a kingdom response to the powerlessness of the poor that exposes the web of lies about the identity and worth of the poor and the god complexes of the non-poor to the transforming truth and demands of the kingdom of God.

Toward a Christian understanding of transformational development

With these three pieces in place—a biblical framework, a holistic understanding of poverty, and a survey of development thinking—Chapter 6 attempts a synthesis that pulls many of the pieces together into a proposal for a Christian understanding of transformational development. My proposal begins by stating the obvious: the transformational development journey belongs to God and to those who are on it, not to experts, donor agencies, or development facilitators. Whatever our framework or our methods, we must be willing to set them aside and let the poor discover their own way, just as we have done.

The first question a development program must answer is, What is the better future toward which it is pointing? This presumes that we have answered the more fundamental question of what human well-being is. The biblical narrative and our theology provide the answer. The best of human futures lies in the direction of the kingdom of God and toward Jesus Christ as the person who offers the way to become part of God's kingdom. Because poverty is fundamentally relational, I then articulate the twin goals of transformational development as changed people and just and peaceful relationships. By "changed people" I mean people who have discovered their true identity as children of God and who have recovered their true vocation as faithful and productive stewards of gifts from God for the well-being of all.

These twin goals of development transformation apply to the poor, the non-poor, and development facilitators as well. The human search for meaning and purpose is a universal and never-ending quest. It is only the nature of the struggle that is different. The poor suffer from marred identities and the belief that they have no meaningful vocation other than serving the powerful. The non-poor, and sometimes development facilitators, suffer from the temptation to play god in the lives of the poor, and believe that what they have in terms of money, knowledge, and position is the result of their own cleverness or the right of their group. Both the poor and the non-poor need to recover their true identity and their true vocation. Everyone is poor in God's world, and everyone is in need of transformation.

I then explore the implications of these twin goals for transformational development in terms of framing a process of change. Neither revolution, nor evolution, nor accepting the status quo is acceptable. I describe a process of change that affirms the joint roles of God and human beings, the need to focus on restoring relationships in all dimensions, and the need to keep the end in mind and to recognize that there is an adversary who actively works to defeat any genuine transformation. I point out the importance of seeking truth, justice, and righteousness, and also beauty, art, and celebration. Finally, I address the importance of addressing the causes of poverty, of expressing a bias toward peace, and of affirming the local church or churches as critical and indispensable partners in the process of seeking sustainable change.

The chapter closes with a brief exploration of the four dimensions of sustainability—physical, mental, social, and spiritual—and some reflections on the different ways in which we need to think holistically about transformational development. In particular, the section on social sustainability explores the dynamics of oppression by proposing a new synthesis of Christian's idea of disempowering systems and Ann Cudd's proposal for understanding the dynamics of oppression.

Principles and practitioners

Chapter 7 moves to the practice of transformational development with a focus on the kinds of principles and the characteristics of people that will be needed to pursue the Christian understanding of transformational development proposed in the foregoing chapter.

I begin by reiterating the basic affirmation that the ownership of the development process lies with the people themselves. They have a history that we need to hear and respect, while still affirming that God has also given us something to offer them. We need to overcome our modern blind spot in terms of the spiritual world so that we can hear their whole story, including the fact that they believe that many of the causes of their current situation and the dominant influence in terms of their future lie in the unseen world of spirits, gods, and ancestors. I also remind us that they already know a great deal and that this indigenous knowledge needs to be allowed to surface and to be respected. The poor already know how to survive. Any journey of transformational development needs to begin with this significant fact.

The chapter continues with a discussion about moving from participation to empowerment. Participation is not an end in itself, and hence the quality of participation matters. When people change by becoming less passive and more the primary actors in their own development, participation has become empowerment. It is changed people who change people. Finally, participation that fails to build a stronger sense of community is also flawed.

The chapter then moves from the principles to the practitioners of transformational development. Development is mediated through people and relationships. The attitude, knowledge, and behavior of the holistic practitioner are all critical to any chance of seeing any genuine transformation. The mindset of the practitioner must be holistic for the program to be holistic. If the holistic practitioner treats people as if they are made in the image of God, then the people can come to believe that they are truly children of God and are not god-forsaken. If the holistic practitioner believes people have gifts and a contribution to make, then people will make this discovery, too.

A profile for holistic practitioners is offered. Holistic practitioners must be Christians with a truly biblical worldview. They must have Christian character—acting, thinking, and working as holistic disciples. Holistic practitioners must be development professionals who are able to take advantage of the best the profession has to offer. Holistic practitioners must know the whole of the Bible and be lay theologians who understand that there is a fine line between doing development and doing theology. Finally, holistic practitioners must themselves be part of an ongoing process of professional and spiritual formation.

Designing programs for transformation

Chapter 8 begins with a discussion about how a development program is designed. The traditional role of design, monitoring, and evaluation tools to complete a logical and linear program plan packaged neatly in a Logical Framework is described. I then explain why this traditional management-by-objectives approach to development program planning is not well suited to planning change in social systems. Social systems are counter-intuitive and dynamical (a technical term meaning non-repeating and nonlinear). Social systems do self-organize, but they are not particularly amenable to management and control. I conclude by arguing that, rather than "planning our way to transformation," we and the people with whom we work will be better served by "learning our way toward transformation." Thus the emphasis is less on goals and milestones (except in the short term) and more on vision, values, and regular monitoring and evaluation. The role of the spiritual disciplines in this process is briefly explored with the help of my wife, Lisa Myers, who has been doing group spiritual direction for more than twenty-five years.

The chapter then moves on to some thoughts about what happens to our development response when we move from needs analysis to social analysis. It describes the way this is done using the vulnerabilities and capabilities analysis of Mary Anderson and Peter Woodrow. The Livelihood Security approach is introduced as a program-design framework followed by a brief introduction to community organizing. The chapter then focuses on one of the major development research and planning tools of the 1980s and 1990s: Participatory Learning and Action (PLA). The tools in the PLA toolkit "put the stick in the hands of the community" so that the research, analysis, and planning method itself becomes potentially transformational. The chapter goes on to introduce Appreciative Inquiry, a more recent development in participatory research and planning based on the work of David Cooperrider of Case Western Reserve University. Appreciative Inquiry's assumption of health, vitality, and life-giving social organization in even the poorest communities holds particular promise for helping the poor recover their identity and discover their true vocation.

The chapter then reports on some research investigating how development programs might end in a transition to sustainability. A framework for program transitions is introduced as well as proposal for critical success factors for successful transitions. One of the changes that occurs as programs mature is that issues of advocacy, policy, empowered citizenship, and good governance tend to emerge as central concerns of the community. This is explored briefly.

The chapter closes with a brief exploration of a number of other program-design concerns. What is meant when we speak of the community, and who is speaking for it? How do we ensure that we are listening to women and children? What is the appropriate pace for a program, and who decides? How do we let the spiritual worldview of the poor come through?

Learning toward transformation

This chapter, written with the expert help of Dr. Frank Cookingham, chief evaluation officer of World Vision International, begins by defining monitoring, evaluating, and reflecting. We observe that in today's development world monitoring is undersold, evaluating is oversold, and reflecting is ignored.

We begin with the fact that, if development programs aspire to change the dynamical social systems of the poor that do not lend themselves to neat, linear, and logical plans and actions, then the unexpected is the norm and possibly most important. Communities carrying out programs do unexpected things and change their minds. Bed nets given away free to prevent malaria end up being used as window screens; a new water supply goes unused out of a fear of the spirits of the old water supply. So monitoring and evaluation that tries to assess faithfulness to the original program design embodied in its Logical Framework will cost money and miss much that is important. If we must learn our way into the future in a development program, then impact evaluations become significantly less important, while consistent monitoring and reflecting on the expected and unexpected become the keys to this social learning.

Chapter 9 examines other critical questions relating to monitoring and evaluation. What is it for? Who is it for? What changed? Who changed? What do we observe and measure?

The question, Will it last? speaks to the concern for sustainability. Mental and social sustainability are explored briefly. Because this book seeks a Christian perspective on poverty and development, I spend more time on the topic of spiritual sustainability and explore what can be observed and measured that speaks to the quality of our Christian witness.

Again with the help of Lisa Myers, the chapter ends with a brief reflection on how spirituality and the spiritual disciplines must shape the assessment of development programs

Christian witness

The book closes with a chapter on Christian witness as it is seamlessly expressed in the context of doing transformational development. It begins by exploring both the necessity and the problem of Christian witness for the Christian relief and development agency. We must witness because witnessing is a central feature of our faith commitment; it is not an option. Yet how we witness raises a difficulty and a challenge. The difficulty is that everyone—Christian or non-Christian—is witnessing all the time anyway. The only question is to what or to whom are they witnessing? There are no "value-free" development facilitators. The challenge is to discover a framework for thinking about Christian witness in a way that is consistent with the principles of transformational development.

The chapter presents a framework derived from the work of Lesslie Newbigin. Doing development and living our lives in ways that result in the community or some of its members asking questions of us to which the gospel is the answer unites gospel-as-life and gospel-as-deed with gospel-as-word. This approach places the initiative for inviting witness with the people and the onus of responsibility for effective witness where it belongs—on the Christian. Our witness depends on our living lives so that the Holy Spirit may evoke questions to which our faith is the answer.

Using this framework of provoking the question, the chapter then discusses issues relating to holistic witness, including the need to tell the whole biblical story; the interrelationship of life, word, deed, and sign; and the need to avoid making a dichotomy between evangelism and discipleship.

The chapter goes on to explore issues relating to ensuring that our understanding of Christian witness is consistent with our framework for transformational development. It begins by pointing out that the goals of Christian witness are the same as the goals for transformational development: changed people and changed relationships. The only difference is that primary emphasis of Christian witness is on people's relationship with God. This convergence of goals is evidence that we have overcome the dichotomy between the physical and the spiritual.

This section goes on to present an organic or integrated understanding of the gospel as *being with* Jesus so that we may *witness by deed, word, and sign*. The Christian message is an embodied message, carried by living witnesses. The clarity and attractiveness of this message is dependent on the quality of our life with Jesus and our willingness to give expression to that life through word, deed, and sign. A warning is then presented that we must avoid separating evangelism and discipleship. This is a false dichotomy, and overcoming it is critical to overcoming our concern for the kind of Christians that are resulting for our witness. The section concludes with a call to be sure that, when we witness, we do so in a way that sooner or later shares the whole biblical story. It is the whole biblical story that carries the account of who we are and what we are for, that declares the lordship of Christ over all of creation and all our relationships.

The chapter moves to the issue of how we must witness. It begins with a call for Christians to live eloquent lives, the key to provoking questions to which the gospel is the answer. It goes on to remind us of the importance of carrying out our Christian witness with a crucified mind, not a crusading mind. I take note of the importance of helping the community—and ourselves—discover the fingerprints of God in our history, in creation, and in development interventions. I point out that questions about meaning and purpose hold the most promise for changing worldview and changing the view the poor have of themselves and their future. This section includes a brief discussion of how we can interpret technology so that it points not to its own efficiency but to the activity and character of the God who made it possible. This section concludes with a reminder that we need to avoid being apologetic for being Christian and thus be willing to say what we believe.

At this point the chapter shifts to the importance of the Bible to the process of transformational development. The argument is made that the Bible, as the living word of God, must be released from its spiritual captivity to Sunday morning and personal devotion and be allowed to be active in the development process. The chapter challenges us to find ways to let the Bible speak for itself. The Roman Catholic frame of the Pastoral Circle is introduced. I then share the examples of Scripture Search and the Seven Steps in which the Bible is being used in development programming. I also briefly describe the New Tribes Mission innovation of Storying the Bible and make a suggestion as to how it could be made more holistic and thus more applicable for use in the development process.

The chapter on Christian witness closes with discussion of the focus of Christian witness. The central focus for Christian witness must be on the twin goals of transformation: changed people and changed relationships. The poor, non-poor, and the development practitioner (and his or her agency) must work together in seeking their true identity and recovering their true vocation within the context of just and peaceful relationships. The section then discusses how this can happen as a result of Christian witness and worldview change. The section closes with the question, Who changes? The answer is that everyone must change. Transformational development is a journey that everyone is on and that everyone must seek.

2

Development—The origins of an idea

The idea of development in terms of helping a nation escape from poverty dates to the immediate aftermath of World War II. The underlying idea that societies can change and that living circumstances can be improved is a modern idea that slowly emerged in the seventeenth century and that did not take hold widely in the West until the late eighteenth century. Understanding the emergence of the idea of human and national development will help us better understand where we are in terms of poverty and development today. After a brief historical review, the chapter introduces some of the major contemporary contributors to the global conversation on poverty eradication. While their theories are global in scope and thus not especially helpful to development practitioners, their ideas are influencing contemporary development research and how donors and development implementers function today.

LOOKING BACK

The changed trajectory of history

The seminal work on the world's economic history by Angus Maddison has called our attention to how significantly the world changed around the beginning of the nineteenth century (2003). From the time of Christ until the early 1800s the human condition didn't change very much. The wealth of the world didn't change; the world's population didn't change; and life expectancy never rose above forty years.

As was the case from the beginning of time, almost everyone lived in a world of scarcity and insecurity. The entire world lived on the equivalent of $1.25 a day for a thousand years after the time of Christ. From 1000 to 1820, that figure only grew to $1.80 a day (Maddison 2003). Almost everyone lived and worked at home, and work was not something one did for a wage but rather something the family did to stay alive. While there were always a few with relative wealth, almost everyone was poor, roughly as poor as much of the poor in the South today. The ideas of creating wealth or the concepts of a market system, selling one's labor, or land as capital simply didn't exist (Heilbroner 1999, 18–19). Then, at the dawn of the nineteenth century, a stunning historical shift introduced a radically new trajectory of global wealth and human well-being (Figure 2–1).

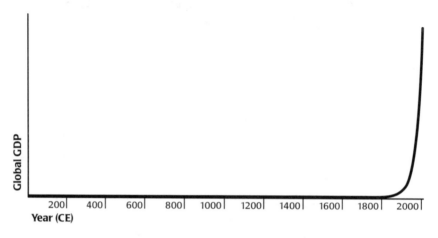

Figure 2–1: Global GDP estimates.
(Adapted from Maddison 2003)

Over the last two hundred years the world's wealth has increased over fifty times and the world's population has grown sixfold. The per capita wealth of the world increased an incredible nine times in this short two-hundred-year period (Maddison 2003, 256, 259). Life expectancy in Europe almost doubled over the same time period (Maddison 2001, 29). More people, more wealth per person, better health. What on earth happened?

A lot of things changed, and many of the changes were fundamentally radical in nature. As the new idea of a secular nation-state began to become a concrete reality in Europe, Adam Smith wrote his *Theory of Moral Sentiments* (1759) and then *Wealth of Nations* (1776) with a new set of ideas that we now call political economy. Driven by a desire to explain what was happening in Britain as a result of the Industrial Revolution and his concern for protection of the common good, Smith proposed two major new ideas (Heilbroner 1999, 20). First, wealth—the annual production of the land and labor of a society—could be created (increased) through innovation and investment in a market system; economies need not be zero-sum games. Second, economic life no longer needed to be organized around cultural tradition or authoritarian command. "The great chariot of society, which for so long had run down the gentle slope of tradition, now found itself powered by an internal combustion system," namely, the market system and its "hidden hand" (Heilbroner 1999, 33). Without this paradigmatic shift in how we understand economics, the idea of development—improving the human condition—is unintelligible.

As we are all aware, this change was accompanied by the Industrial Revolution, which itself was driven by a flood of technological inventions that extended human physical power dramatically. For the first time in human history the amount of work a person could do was not limited to the strength of his or her back. At the beginning of the seventeenth century Francis Bacon had challenged the Scholastic scholars of the academy of his day to shift their focus from deducing everything from first principles—God's revelation—and called instead for a shift in focus to reading God's other book—nature. Bacon's motivation for this shift to observation and deduction was to improve the lives of the ordinary people (Anderson 1960, 23, 78). By the beginning of the eighteenth century this shift in mindset had resulted in a stunning variety of human inventions and the emergence of modern science in the West. Modern medicine and modern agriculture emerged. Transportation and communication were transformed. All of this joined the new understanding about economic growth.

The most fundamental change, however, was in how human beings understood their world and in their ability to change it. From a traditional sense of resignation in the face of an inhospitable world, human beings discovered a new sense of human agency and began to think new ideas and to take actions to improve their circumstances. Deidre McCloskey, a professor of economics, history, and English, has argued compellingly that rapid takeoff of innovation and economic growth in the early nineteenth century was driven by a shift in the view of ordinary people and their self-understanding. From poor serfs, who knew and accepted their immutable place in the world, a new middle class began to emerge that was treated with increasing respect and given the freedom to innovate and enjoy the rewards of their efforts (McCloskey 2010, 11–12). Liberty and increased human agency released human creativity and a corresponding hope that a better future was possible, an idea that resurfaces in this book when we talk about healing the marred identity of the poor. This was a radically new idea:

> Since Plato, being had been understood as timeless, unchanging presence. Change was always falling away from being, degeneration. . . . If change is not simply degeneration then some change may be progressive. Change guided by an enlightened humanity may produce good. Progress is opened up as a human possibility. (Gillespie 2008, 36)

A stunning wave of human creativity led to new inventions and, more important, to new conceptualizations and ideas. All this was sustained by a growing commitment to universal education, because everyone had the potential to become an actor in history.

Taken together, this view of human beings as rational, creative actors in history; the possibility of economic growth through a market system; and the enabling contributions of science and technology changed the trajectory of the world. A world of scarcity began to undergo a profound transition into a world of surplus and, some would say about the West, ultimately into a world of indulgence and overconsumption.

As people and society changed, another shift in ideas took place that is relevant to development. While the idea of charity *(caritas)*—feeling compassion for and caring for those who are suffering—is as old as the major world religions, it was not until the mid-nineteenth century that the idea of compassion began to include the moral idea that suffering was both wrong and should be prevented or ended, if possible (Sznaider 1998, 122ff.).

For the first time the idea of organized helping through institutions emerged.

> Modern humanitarian movements arose in the eighteenth and nine-teenth centuries . . . to abolish slavery, cruelty to prisoners, animals and children; factory, sanitary and prison reform were organized during that time and continue today. (Sznaider 1998, 120)[1]

During this same period the first humanitarian agencies appeared in Europe with the founding of the International Committee of the Red Cross (1863) and German Caritas (1867).

This fundamental shift in the trajectory of increasing wealth and well-being began in Europe and has spread unevenly and sometimes hesitantly around the world, usually accompanied by Western colonialism. Although China, India, and Brazil are now experiencing this new trajectory for the first time, this change was slow to benefit the poor and often made them victims. A competing vision of economics arose—Marxism—claiming to address these very human concerns. But, for all the unevenness and continuing struggle to figure out how this all works, the idea that poor nations and poor communities can *develop* is now commonly accepted. The story of transformational development begins with this radical change in the trajectory of history.

The evolving idea of development

Development—used as a word to describe efforts to improve the well-being of the poor—was used for the first time in the early 1950s in the

---

[1] Sznaider is well aware of the ministry of charity of the medieval religious orders but notes that they were not developed exclusively for what he calls organized helping. Social institutions organized solely for a charitable mission were a new thing in nineteenth century.

West. In the aftermath of the devastation of the World War II, Europe had been rebuilt and was taking off economically. The postwar pressure to award independence to former colonies was under way.

At the same time, soldiers and war correspondents, who had been all over the world and seen things previously unreported, were returning home with stories of far-off places and seemingly exotic non-Western cultures. Radio and then television began to beam the words and images of very poor, distant places into the homes of people in the West. The gap between a rich and developed West and the rest of the world began to come sharply into focus.

The idea of development and the possibility of eradication of poverty became the norm in the West and was "often spoken of as a quasi religious mission: as the moral duty of Western industrialized countries to take active steps to help those who are more backward technically (and culturally) to advance along the road of progress" (Tyndale 2006, 156).

But what did these Western altruists mean by the term *development?* We do not always remember that, while the West understood itself as developed, it was not entirely clear how this development had happened. Furthermore, the West was still shaken by the fact that its development had included two world wars, a global economic depression, and a holocaust. Nonetheless, the underlying assumption was taken as a given: The underdeveloped world should develop by emulating the development path of the West.

In the 1960s Walt Rostow's "non-Communist manifesto" and his five stages of economic growth became the blueprint for Western development strategies of the time (1960). The goal of development was understood as modernization (Westernization) and the measure of development was the size of a nation's economy. Making economies grow by following Rostow's five stages of economic growth was the means of development.

The basic assumption of what came to be known as modernization theory (see Figure 2–2) was that the traditional culture and values of poor societies needed to change and would change as they encountered a modernizing world of urbanization, public education, and integration into the Western

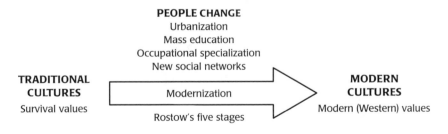

Figure 2–2: Modernization theory.

market system. Traditional values, judged as not conducive to economic growth, would fall away and "modern" values would take their place. This change in values would lead to a "modern" economy.

We need to remember that Rostow's path to development was also part of the Cold War strategy of the West. Sometimes this meant guns and proxy wars; sometimes the strategy took the form of development aid. Helping poor nations in the South was seen as a way of keeping them out of the Soviet orbit. The idea of development in the 1960s was not altogether altruistic.

This growing commitment to development aid required a development delivery system. Western governments founded foreign aid departments such as USAID in 1961 and the British Ministry of Overseas Development (now the Department for International Development or DFID) in 1964. The United Nations set up the United Nations Development Program (UNDP) in 1965. Regional development banks were established in Latin America (1959), Africa (1964), and Asia (1966). During this same period many secular and Christian organizations, originally founded to do humanitarian relief, began to add development activities to their ministry portfolios. These included Oxfam, CARE, Catholic Relief Services, Caritas, Church World Service and, in the 1970s, Action Aid, World Vision, and Tear Fund.

While modernization theory held sway for a while, it eventually lost its luster as the culturally and economically myopic creation that it was. Other theories of development emerged. Dependency theory, with its neo-Marxist and Latin American roots, argued that the West was the source of the underdevelopment of the South and that modernization theory and development aid were just a "fig leaf" to cover up this unchanging, neocolonial, capitalist reality. The goal of development for both theories was still economic growth, but the means of development was now a choice between Marxist or capitalist economics. Some even began looking for a third way, as exemplified by E. F. Schumacher's *Small Is Beautiful* (1973) and his attempt to formulate what he called Buddhist economics.

In the 1980s development practitioners, weary of the arguments about global economic history and theories, began articulating an approach they called people-centered development that was derived from what they had learned on the front lines working among the poor. Alternative, small theories, limited by time and place, began to emerge, and increasingly the idea of development as economics alone was called into question.

Robert Chambers, a research associate of the Institute of Development Studies at the University of Sussex with long field experience in rural India and Africa, argued for an understanding of poverty as entangling systems calling for a systems response focused on encouraging "responsible well-being" (Chambers 1983, 37; 1997, 10). John Friedmann, a professor of urban planning with extensive Latin American urban experience, insisted that, while the kind of grassroots development programming that Chambers argued for was needed, it was not enough (1992). For Friedmann, the poverty of poor households was a result of not having enough social and political power to develop themselves and insist on the services they deserved from the state. What was needed was to organize the poor into associations and networks that would make them increasingly hard to ignore as important players in civil society; only then could the poor push back against the political and economic systems that limited their initiative. While issues of access, vulnerability, and social power became more central to the development conversation, the central measure remained the size of the national economy. We will take a much closer look at Chambers and Friedmann in Chapters 4 and 5.

Amartya Sen—Development as freedom

Finally, in the 1990s there was a shift in the measures of development. A development economist from India, Amartya Sen, began working with the Mahbub ul Haq, a Pakistani economist in the UNDP, to create a new index for assessing development with the declared purpose of moving development economics from its focus on gross domestic product (GDP) to a more people-centered approach. The resulting Human Development Index (HDI) added life expectancy as an indicator for health and literacy as an indicator for knowledge and education to GDP as a measure of standard of living. In time, this shift in the measurement of development began to change the way development projects were designed. Development was no longer focused only on economic growth.

Sen had also studied the relationship between famines and democracy. There has never been a major famine in a functioning democracy (Sen 1999, 16). This discovery led to *Development as Freedom*, in which Sen announced his conclusion that poverty is better understood as being the result of deprivation of human freedom. Things like low income, lack of education, ill health, and lack of access to services make people less free, as does lack of freedom in the form of restrictions on political and civil liberties and participation (Sen 1999, 4). "What people can positively achieve is influenced by economic opportunities, political liberties, social powers and the enabling conditions of good health, basic education, and the encouragement and cultivation of initiatives (1999, 5).

For Sen, human well-being is best understood not by what people consume (economics), but by what people *are* and *do*, such as being literate, healthy, economically active, and participating in the life of their community. Sen calls these "functionings." Functions are the basic stuff of human life, such as having enough to eat, living in adequate housing, breathing clean air, and drinking clean water, as well as higher-value ideals such as possessing self-respect, having enhanced dignity, participating in community life, and feeling safe. The human rights tradition insists that all human beings have the right to function in this way. So does the biblical account. For the prophets, the test of the functioning of society and governing of the powerful was the well-being of widows, orphans, and aliens. If the poorest can function, the society is functioning too. But surely there is more than just survival in God's intent for human beings.

Sen argues that we must go beyond just the idea of functionings—what people are and do—and extend our development concerns to include human *capabilities*, which he describes as what people are *able* to do or *choose* to do. Sen argues that to experience human well-being we must be have the freedom (capability) to choose what we wish or are called to become and have the means to get there. Human beings are intended to develop, not just to survive. Sen defines capabilities as "a person's ability to do valuable acts or reach valuable states of being" (1999, 30). Sen is arguing that human well-being needs to be understood as people having the capability (freedom) to seek functionings in their world that the people themselves deem valuable. Surely this is consistent with God's call for human beings to survive, be productive, and act as co-creators after God.

Freedom is both the goal and the means to human development. The goal of development is to create the environment and conditions within which all people have the freedom to seek the better human future they desire. Freedom is the means of development in two ways. First, the poor themselves must be the actors if their capability is to be increased. Second, we must support the poor in removing impediments to their being actors and making choices, things that Sen calls "unfreedoms." For the first time an ethical standard has become central to assessing development theory and practice. If people are more free, they are experiencing positive change; if they are less free, the development policy or process is suspect. Increasing human liberty and agency is now central to the development task, and economic growth is just one domain among others. For this work Sen was awarded the Nobel Prize in development economics.

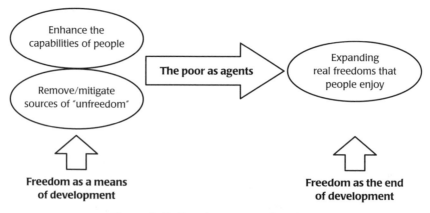

Figure 2–3: Development as freedom.
(Developed from Sen 1999)

Evaluating development as freedom is conceptually simple. The evaluative logic is "Are freedoms enhanced?" The effectiveness logic is "Are people more free to act?"

Sen's view of the importance of human freedom and human agency echoes a Christian anthropology to a significant but not complete degree. While Sen is not working from a Christian frame, the biblical idea of the image of God lies at the heart of understanding the central importance God gives to human agency—the freedom and responsibility to act and create. Sen's view and the Christian view part ways with the further Christian understanding that the freedom that God grants to human beings—including freedom not to believe in God if that is our choice—is not the unlimited freedom of the autonomous Western self. It is a freedom to give up some of our freedom because we can better love God and our neighbor when we do. This perspective on human freedom and agency represents a point at which the Christian development community has something to offer to the larger development community. More on this a little later.

With the broad acceptance of Sen's approach in the 1990s, the size of a country's economy was correctly made a means, not an end. Economics had found its proper, more incidental, place in a new multidimensional understanding of development that now includes ethical values and empowered human agency. The purpose of wealth is not to have wealth but to enable a person or household to pursue the kinds of capabilities they have reason to value (Sen 1999, 14). No longer is the development ideal that of Western modernization. The understanding of and pursuit of well-being is to come from the poor themselves.

The general acceptance of Sen's argument has transformed the development conversation. From a model of development based on emulating the West and measured by the size of a nation's economy, the development community is in a very different place. In the first decade of the twenty-first century the language of human well-being and increasing human and communal capabilities became normative.

The struggle now is to figure out what human well-being actually is and how one goes about increasing it. The development conversation may now be ready to join the other conversations on human flourishing, including religious conversations.

Voices of the poor

Well-being is a full stomach, time for prayer, and a bamboo platform to sleep on.
—A POOR WOMAN IN BANGLADESH
(NARAYAN-PARKER ET AL. 2000, 234)

The post–World War II conversation on the evolution and reframing of the idea of development had been primarily among academics from the

North who were eventually joined by academics and then practitioners from the South. It was not until the late 1990s that some began to wonder if listening to the poor articulate their own descriptions of poverty and human well-being might be a useful counterpoint.

After a decade of hectoring by NGOs and development academics, the World Bank began to accept the idea that its staff of economists, funded by the world's wealthiest countries, might be a little too far removed from the real world of the poor. Working with the advice of Robert Chambers, a team of researchers was sent out to listen to over sixty thousand of the world's poorest people. In the early 2000s the Voices of the Poor project published three books with the team's findings (Narayan-Parker et al. 2000).

In addition to listening to the poor speak about how poverty, oppression, and injustice were negatively affecting their lives, questions were also included about what the poor believed human well-being might be. As one might expect, more food, better health, and access to education made the list. Human well-being without the basics of survival is impossible to imagine. More surprising was the finding that having enough materially for a good life does not mean asking for very much. The material desires of the poor are modest: "At least for each child to have a bed, a pair of shoes, a canopy over their heads, two sheets—not to sleep like we do on the ground" (Narayan-Parker et al. 2000, 25).

But the conversation quickly moved beyond these more obvious material desires. Many of the expressions of well-being were relational; social well-being seems central to human well-being for the poor (Narayan-Parker et al. 2000, 26). The desire to be able to take care of one's family, harmony within the family and community, having friends, and helping others showed up regularly in the interviews.

Less expected by the researchers, many of the manifestations of well-being were psychological in nature (Narayan-Parker et al. 2000, 26–27). A desire to feel better about oneself and a wish for a sense of dignity and respect were heard. Peace of mind, lack of anxiety, being God-fearing, and being happy or satisfied with life were named as elements of human well-being. Somewhat to the surprise of the Western researchers, "a spiritual life and religious observance are woven into other aspects of well-being" (Narayan-Parker et al. 2000, 38).

Reflections on this conversation on development

First, let me begin by stating the obvious. The Western development conversation and its contemporary explorations of human well-being are products of modernity more than anything else. Faith in the idea of human progress seems untarnished in spite of the continuing presence of violence and poverty around the world. There is no need for the transcendent, it seems. We clever human folk just need to apply our reason and our scientific observations to the problem of poverty, and its solution is within our grasp. With the exception of what the poor say about their vision of human well-being, God is not part of the Western vision. The issues I raised in Chapter 1 remain serious and in need of attention.

Second, it seems pretty clear that the development conversation is not over and that there is a growing space for Christians to contribute. The distance the development conversation has traveled in sixty years and the continuing reinvention of ideas and approaches suggest there is more to learn about both the purpose and means of development. The development conversation has not generally involved the domains of psychology and religion/spirituality until very recently. Often religion was considered part of the problem of poverty and thus surely could not be part of the solution. This is changing, and the door is opening to allow people to speak from a religious perspective. Let me share a few examples of this.

The international development community, a generally secular and modern lot with suspicions about religion, has begun to reach out to talk to those representing faith-based institutions. The first step occurred when *World Development*, the journal of the Society of International Development, devoted a special issue to the relationship between religion and development in 1980 and then proposed a new research agenda (Clarke 2006). Almost twenty years later, inspired by James Wolfensohn, then president of the World Bank, and George Carey, the archbishop of Canterbury, the World Faiths Development Dialogue was launched in 1998. This led to a multi-year process of dialogue and continuing exploration (Marshall 2001; Marshall and Van Saanen 2007). Subsequent research called attention to the fact that faith-based civil society organizations were the major, if not the largest, contributors to social welfare in much of the South (Clarke 2006, 837, 841).

In 2005 a five-year Religions and Development Research Programme was launched by a consortium that includes the Universities of Birmingham and Bath in the UK along with other British institutions and partners in the South. Funded by the UK government's Department for International Development, the program has already completed a series of interesting working papers on religion and development from the perspective of sociology, anthropology, and economics (available on the rad.bham.ac.uk website).

Most recently, a serious challenge has been articulated from within the secular development studies community itself. Séverine Deneulin from the University of Bath and Masooda Bano of Oxford have called for a "rewriting of the secular script" of development (2009). Pushing the development community to go beyond an instrumental view of religion *and* development—the idea that religion may somehow be good for development—to a more embracing view of religion *in* development, Deneulin and Bano explore Christian and Muslim understandings of human development and demonstrate that working for development is intrinsic to religious experience and purpose. Deneulin and Bano drive home the point that for these religious traditions "there is no separation between religion and development. Development is what adherents to a religion do because of who they are and what they believe in" (2009, 4–5).

Deneulin and Bano point out that there are significant "overlaps between the religious and secular traditions on development issues" in the areas of human dignity, social justice, poverty, relief, concern for the earth, equality, and freedom (2009, 10–11). While there are also areas of significant and possibly irreconcilable differences, Deneuline and Bano wonder if there is potential for a dialogue between these two perspectives on development and even propose using interfaith dialogue as a model for carrying out such a dialogue.

As a final reflection, it is important to note that the topic of development or human well-being is the focus of conversations in a variety of heretofore disconnected domains. Within the realm of psychology, research on human flourishing, positive psychology, and community psychology are now explaining the role of social institutions and the community as a whole in terms of the mental health of human well-beings. Happiness—in the sense of having a positive view of one's life—is now a topic of growing interest in economics (Kenny and Kenny 2006), philosophy (S. Bok 2010), and political science (D. Bok 2010). The continuing extension of Amartya Sen's work with Martha Nussbaum is focusing on a holistic or comprehensive view of human well-being (Nussbaum and Sen 1993). Finally, development researchers are creating tools to measure well-being in development practice (White 2009).

Even theologians are getting into the act. Inter Varsity held a conference on human flourishing in 2008. Miraslav Volf, David Kelsey, and John Hare are overseeing a research project at Yale on God and human flourishing. Nicholas Wolterstorff's recent book *God, Justice, and Love* makes useful distinctions between the contemporary utilitarian idea of an "experientially satisfying life," the "life well lived" of Aristotle and others of ancient Greece, and what Wolterstorff calls "the life that is both well lived and that goes well" (Wolterstorff 2008). This formulation of human well-being unites the human capabilities and agency dimension—humans should be able to enjoy a life worth living and to pursue the ends of that life that they desire—and to be the recipient of the conditions that allow such a life—right and just kinds of relationships. More on this later. There is an urgent need for multidisciplinary conversations among these traditional academic silos. The poor require it of us.

CONTEMPORARY THINKING ON DEVELOPMENT

From the foregoing discussion of the evolution of development thinking, something significant has changed—a shift from global theories about economics to practice based on empirical research. Over the last fifteen years, a great deal of development research has been done by the World Bank, governmental development agencies, and academics. While we are far from a state of comprehensive knowledge, the research agenda is driving development thinking in a way that was not the case not too long ago.

Further, there is a lot more inter-agency cooperation and coordination. Christian development practitioners are far more likely to find themselves at the table with other development practitioners from secular and government agencies. A basic working understanding of contemporary development thinking and the research that lies behind it may make such conversations easier. Furthermore, I think we Christians need to expect that God may be working in our secular friends and their commitment to helping the poor and thus assume that God may well have gifts for us in their work. We need to get out of our Christian ghetto and see what God has for us.

Speaking to development from a global perspective and as a global problem, there are three major voices: Jeffrey Sachs, William Easterly, and Paul Collier. We also need to take note of the reincarnation of one aspect of modernization theory—the link between culture and development. Finally, there are two important voices that are adding Southern perspectives to the conversation—Hernando de Soto and Mohammad Yunus.

Jeffery Sachs—The big push

Sachs is the director at the Earth Institute and professor of sustainable development at Columbia University. From 2000 to 2006 he was the UN special adviser on the millennium development goals (MDGs), the internationally agreed goals to reduce extreme poverty, disease, and hunger by the year 2015.

In *The End of Poverty* Sachs argued that there are nations—representing one-sixth of humanity—that are locked in a poverty trap created by disease, geographical isolation, and a limiting environment. These countries cannot escape from this trap without outside help; they simply do not have the resources or the capability. All the other factors that exacerbate the impact of the poverty trap—demographics, governance, culture, innovation, fiscal, and geo-political—can be managed over time, but only if the poverty trap is broken (Sachs 2005, 56ff.). Thus these countries will need significant external help—a big push (ibid., 19, 208).

Sachs calls for a "global compact to end poverty" that sets a goal for rich countries to invest 0.7 percent of their GDP in the MDGs. This would provide up to US$175 billion annually in development assistance (2005, 218). This aid would be coordinated through a revamped aid system that includes the World Bank, IMF, UN agencies that support development, and government agencies for development (2005, 255ff.).

Using clinical medicine as a metaphor, Sachs creates what he calls "clinical economics" to diagnose and then propose solutions for differing local poverty situations (2005, 74ff.). Sachs, through the Earth Institute at Columbia University, has established a group of Millennium Village programs in Africa that combine health, education, agriculture, and infrastructure development to illustrate his approach (2005, 238–41). Evaluation of the villages is built around demonstrating the feasibility of achieving the MDGs.

William Easterly—Bottom up

Easterly is professor of economics at New York University, co-director of its Development Research Institute, and was an economist for the World Bank from 1985 to 2001.

Easterly's fundamental question is strategic. During the sixty years of development that we've just examined, over US$2.3 trillion has been spent on foreign aid. While some progress has been made, it has been very uneven, and the number of people living in abject poverty is distressingly close to one billion. Yet, those countries that have shown the most progress in economic growth—the Asian Tigers in the last forty years and China and India more recently—have neither followed the development formulas of the West nor received all that much in foreign aid. Intrigued by this, Easterly seeks to shift the question from Sachs's "How much foreign aid do we need to eradicate poverty?" to "What is the best use of foreign aid for development?" (2006, 4,11).

Easterly sees the world of development differently from Sachs in a number of important ways. First, Easterly does not believe in top-down, global planning for development. He sees this as a holdover from the colonial era, reflecting the idea that "the West knows best." Contrasting "planners" with "searchers," Easterly believes social problems are better solved as close to the action as possible by innovators who try and fail and try again (searchers). Planners, on the other hand, live in Washington DC, London, and Peking and assume they know enough to be able to figure out global solutions and then determine what needs to be supplied. Searchers know they will never know enough and instead look for what is being demanded and try to meet that need. Planners provide solutions that are developed a long way from the front line; searchers look for what is working locally and try to make it better (Easterly 2006, 14–19).

Second, Easterly's theory of social change is fundamentally different from that of Sachs and many Western development agencies. Top-down master plans betray a modern worldview that assumes there is a unified global theory of everything, including poverty and development. Discovering such a theory should then inform all development action in all contexts. Easterly does not believe this to be the case. A fan of Edmund Burke and the British Enlightenment, Easterly opts for a bottom-up, discover-what-works, and learn-your-way-into-the-future approach that assumes that incremental discovery is a better fit in a complex, dynamical world about which we can never know enough. We will pick up this theme of learning your way when dealing with complex social systems in Chapter 8, as it is highly relevant to the design of a development program.

Easterly's focus is on modest plans, local searching, and a lot of energy spent on evaluation (2006, 53, 193, 375). Take small steps, do things in several ways, and see what happens. Feed those things that are working, and starve those that are not. Esther Duflo, a French economist, professor of poverty alleviation and development economics at MIT and co-founder of the Poverty Action Lab, has picked up on this and is making some re-markable progress in development by testing and evaluating the way to success (Duflo and Kremer 2008).

Finally, Easterly does not believe that development research supports Sachs's idea of a poverty trap—conditions that nations cannot get free from without a big infusion of outside help. Easterly cites Angus Maddison's eco-nomic research to show that "eleven out of the twenty-eight of the poorest countries in 1985 were not in the poorest fifth in 1950. They got into pov-erty from declining from above" (Easterly 2006, 41). Easterly places geog-raphy, disease, and environment—the elements of Sachs's poverty trap—alongside conflict and the "resource curse"[2] as a set of conditions that interfere with poverty eradication but do not prevent it. Easterly goes on to add three additional factors that support poverty eradication: a positive in-stitutional environment, democratic institutions, and being connected to the global economy (2006, 36–55).

Paul Collier—The bottom billion

Paul Collier, professor of development economics at Oxford, comes to the development conversation from a different angle altogether. He begins by asking which countries are languishing in terms of economic growth and then asks what is distinctive about them compared to countries that are growing economically. He discovered that about one billion people live in fifty-eight countries that have suffered from negative economic growth since 1970, while all other nations are experiencing economic growth, albeit at

---

[2] The "resource curse" phrase was coined to refer to the paradox that poor coun-tries rich in natural resources often do not grow economically. The temptation to-ward rent seeking in contrast to building a modern economy, mismanagement, cor-ruption, and exploitation is very high.

differing rates. Seventy percent of these countries are in Africa, and most of the rest are in Central Asia (2007, 6–7). Examining the common issues these countries face, Collier identifies four poverty traps: experiencing chronic conflict, suffering the negative impact of natural resources (the resource curse), being landlocked with bad neighbors, and bad governance (2007, 5–6). These four traps may mean that these countries will be left behind by the globalization that is lifting people out of poverty in places like Brazil, India, and China. Furthermore, Collier notes that none of these traps will be overcome solely by a large input of foreign aid (Sachs) or by bottom-up problem solving by searchers (Easterly).

Collier's diagnosis leads him to an interesting family of proposed solutions. Like Sachs, Collier believes foreign aid can help, but only if it is used selectively (2007, 100ff.). Development aid injected into a conflict situation is clearly a formula for misuse or ineffectiveness. Aid that allows governments to continue misusing revenue from its natural resources also seems unwise. Collier argues that aid should be targeted at programs that encourage the reduction of conflict and/or that reward improved governance. Two of Collier's proposals have to do with creating a policy environment at the international level that encourages economic growth and good governance. Because many of the current trade policies of the developed world prevent Southern countries from gaining access to Northern markets, especially for agricultural products, Collier calls for changing trade policies in the North to enable local countries to become connected to and benefit from international markets (2007, 157–58). His second proposal calls for creating international laws and charters that encourage transparency and that discourage corruption. He calls for international charters or rules for budget transparency, managing post-conflict situations, and international investment (2007, 135–36).

Collier's final proposal is the most surprising in terms of development assistance. Where conflict is an endemic barrier to development, Collier wonders if military or police intervention may be a necessary development measure to create the security necessary to enable the other elements of his development proposal to be effective (2007, 124–25). Needless to say, this unusual suggestion has not been welcomed in the fields of development studies and practice. But it is unclear what else might help with the problem to which Collier has so aptly called our attention.

Banerjee and Duflo—Economics of the poor

Most recently, a new perspective for understanding poverty and development has been offered by Abhijit Banerjee and Esther Duflo, co-directors of MIT's Jameel Poverty Action Lab (J-PAL). Eschewing theories—large and small—of what causes poverty and the corresponding strategies for eradicating poverty as overly simplistic, optimistic, and insufficiently fact based, Banerjee and Duflo shift their focus to the poor in a particular location and ask the question: Assuming the poor know what they are doing and have a reason for acting the way they do, what kind of research would help us understand their actions and aspirations? "To progress, we have to abandon the habit of reducing the poor to cartoon characters and take the time to really understand their lives, in all their complexity and richness" (2011, viii).

Carrying out wide-ranging grassroots research in over eighteen countries in poor communities where development programming is being carried out, Banerjee and Duflo's findings are dismantling a whole series of common beliefs that drive development programming based on simplistic assumptions of what a program can do for the poor or get the poor to do. They call into question the idea that there are simple answers like bed nets, immunizations, or educating mothers to chlorinate their water as solutions to the complexity of providing effective healthcare to poor. They show that while microcredit meets one financial need of the poor, managing risk through insurance and establishing a safe way to save are equally important (Banerjee and Duflo 2011, 41–42, 133–34, 183–84). Furthermore, the idea that over one billion poor people are entrepreneurs and thus the solution to poverty is the provision of microcredit is called into question for two reasons. First, most of the poor who run their own farms and businesses are doing so because they have no choice; the research suggests that many would avoid this life of risk and challenge if they could (ibid., 205–6), just as most of us in the West choose to do. Second, there is no compelling evidence that micro businesses develop into small businesses, which are the key to providing jobs for those who are not themselves entrepreneurs (ibid., 157–58).

In another interesting example Banerjee and Duflo provide empirical information that suggests that is not true that there is a nutrition trap that keeps the poor malnourished and weak and hence unable to work, thus not being able to earn enough money to solve their nutrition problem (ibid., 19). The assumed solution to this trap is to increase the income of poor households. Banerjee and Duflo's research shows that when the poor receive additional income, the extra money is spent of festivals, TVs, medical emergencies, alcohol, tobacco, and better tasting but not more nutritious food. It seems that "the basic human need for a pleasant life might explain why food spending is declining" in many poor households (ibid., 37). Lest we criticize the poor for such choices, Banerjee and Duflo remind us that we in the West often make unexpected and seemingly irrational choices when it comes to how we spend money on food and other things. Our spending choices are not always consistent with what we know is best for us; why should we expect the poor to be any different? (ibid., 68).

In light of this unpredictable behavior on the part of most humans in terms of what is best for their future and the fact that there is a substantial limit to what any outsider can know about a given context, Banerjee and

Duflo encourage us to avoid simplistic diagnoses and their corresponding single-answer development programs. Instead, they have adapted the idea of randomized control trials—an approach most commonly used for the testing of new drugs—and applied it to developing program plans. For example, in an area of India with very low immunization rates in spite of free immunizations available at government health huts, the villages in the area were divided into three groups. The first group comprised villages that received no program intervention; they were the control group. The second group of villages became the site of a monthly village fair at which the government health workers gave free immunizations. The third group of villages was also visited by the monthly health fair, but in addition, the mothers were given a kilo of dal (beans) and a set of metal dishes when their children completed their immunization series. Based on empirical results, the third option proved the most effective. This is an example of learning the way into the future—something we will turn to in Chapters 8 and 9—and echoes Easterly's concern for the importance of evidenced-based monitoring and evaluation.

Bangerjee and Duflo conclude with an admonition that is a helpful corrective to many of the theories we explore in this book.

> If we resist the kind of lazy, formulaic thinking that reduces every problem to the same set of general principles; if we listen to poor people themselves and force ourselves to understand the logic of their choices; if we accept the possibility of error and subject every idea, including the most apparently commonsensical ones, to rigorous empirical testing, then we will be able not only to construct a toolbox of effective policies but also to better understand why the poor live the way they do. (Banerjee and Duflo 2011, 272)

Lawrence Harrison—Culture matters

With the necessary and appropriate dismissal of the original version of modernization theory and its thesis that traditional cultures are poverty cultures while modern Western cultures are not, it became inappropriate to discuss culture and development for quite a long time. Harrison, a former USAID office director and now director of the Culture Change Institute at the Fletcher School of Tufts University, has resurrected the idea that culture and poverty may have connections that need to be taken seriously. His major work, *Underdevelopment Is a State of Mind*, used case studies from Latin America to support his assertion that culture has been one obstacle to economic development in the region (1985).

In an edited volume from the Cultural Values and Human Progress symposium at Harvard University in 1999, the culture and development question was posed this way: "If culture is important and people have studied culture for a century or more, then why don't we have well developed theo-ries, practical guidelines and close professional links between those who study culture and those who make and manage development policy?" (Harrison and Huntington 2000, xvi). While the idea of connecting culture and poverty still makes some folks very nervous, this question is important. Setting aside Harrison's particular views on culture and development for a moment, the idea that anthropology might have a contribution to make to development theory and practice is a good one, even though anthropolo-gists needed a lot of encouragement from within their own discipline to reengage with development (for a useful summary, see Sillitoe 1998).

Harrison's first thesis is that cultural values and practices can help or hinder economic development and thus need to be part of social analysis before development programs are designed. On this he is right, and we will see more on how anthropology has engaged and enhanced participatory development methodologies in Chapter 8.

Harrison's second thesis provokes more controversy. It rests on his con-clusion that economic development in the last fifty years is geographically uneven and that culture provides a significant part of the explanation in two ways. First, Harrison believes that "the society that is most successful at helping its people—all its people—realize their creative potential is the so-ciety that will progress the fastest" (Harrison 1985, 2). Echoing McCloskey, this means that those cultural values that encourage people to be creative and productive; that reward merit, risk taking, and saving; and that encour-age trust and transparency tend to support economic growth. Cultures and values that limit any or all of these are simply less supportive of economic growth.

Second, Harrison argues that these same cultural values have a profound influence for good and for ill on the effectiveness of social, and particularly economic, institutions (Harrison 1985, 2–3). Douglass North has made a compelling case for the importance of such institutions in contributing to the economic growth in the West (North 2005).

The contemporary conversation on poverty and culture has several weak-nesses. First, the idea that people live within a single cultural frame is not true. We all live and move within a complex and fluid set of cultural and sub-cultural realities. Second, modern values are not exclusively located in outsiders, with the traditional values finding expression only among insiders. Thus, the conversation gets complicated and muddy in the real world.

More important, while the new conversation affirms that cultural change needs to come from within and not from without, the culture and develop-ment conversation naively ignores how little we really understand how cul-tures actually change. There is no agreement as to whether economic growth changes cultural values, as Sachs suggests (2005, 317), or whether cultural values enable economic growth, as Landes claims (1999, 516).

Nonetheless, as Vijayendra Rao and Michael Walton make clear in *Culture and Public Action*, we must take the issue of culture and development seriously, if carefully. "A focus on culture is necessary to confront the difficult questions of *what* is valued in terms of well-being, *who* does the valuing, and *why* economic and social factors interact with culture to unequally allocate access to the good life" (2004, 4).

There is a related question that brings the issue of cultural values down to the domain of the practitioner. One of the controversies that emerged in the Cultural Values and Human Progress symposium (from which the book *Culture Matters* developed) had to do with the extent to which "cultural change should be integrated into conceptualizing, strategizing, planning and programming political and economic development" (Harrison and Huntington 2000, xxx). Jeffrey Sachs, Hernando de Soto, and Amartya Sen view the desirability of making cultural change a goal of development with considerable suspicion. Cultures do not appear to change at the pace of a development program and its lifetime. There is simply not enough data to support the claim and too great a temptation to enable prejudice and even blame the victim. In light of the history of Western colonialism and assumptions about the superiority of things Western, the step of trying to change culture seems a bridge too far for many.

Hernando de Soto—The poor as entrepreneurs

De Soto is a Peruvian economist who has made two very important contributions to the development conversation. In 1989 his first major piece of research from the Peruvian context demonstrated three things about the poor that may be relevant elsewhere. First, he demonstrated the vitality, creativity, and entrepreneurial nature of Peru's urban poor. De Soto's research demolished the prejudice that the poor are lazy and stupid. Second, de Soto demonstrated the highly negative impact on the poor of being relegated to the informal or non-formal economy with its crime and its lack of the rule of law, legal protections, and social services. While the poor are risk-taking entrepreneurs nonetheless, de Soto showed that the informal businesses of the poor cannot grow in the informal sector and are vulnerable to theft, extortion, and natural disaster (1989, xix).

Finally, de Soto called attention to the exclusionary nature of the formal economy in Peru (and in other Latin American countries) resulting from the mercantile arrangement by which the government is kept in power as long as the government protects the economic advantage of the oligarchies that control the economy (1989, 201–2). De Soto documented the raft of rules, fees, and procedures created by government regulation that make the legal registration of a local market or vendor's license a time-consuming and costly nightmare. These convoluted processes can involve more than fifty different steps, dozens of different government ministries and departments, and two to four years' worth of income to complete (1989, 131–32). The purpose of these regulations is to protect vested economic interests from competition. Friedmann calls the "persistence of the poor in the face a hostile state . . . an act of civil resistance" (1992, 23).

In 2000, de Soto's second important contribution came as a result of his exploration of what he called the mystery of capital and why capitalism works in the West and not so well elsewhere (De Soto 2000). The first part of his discovery was that we in the West have changed the way we think about property. Land or any physical asset has become more than just some plot of ground to be owned; an asset that has value as capital and thus can be leveraged. One can keep the land, take out a loan based on its value, and start a new business to create new wealth. Thus, property was transformed into capital. De Soto estimates that the world's poor are sitting on assets worth forty times more than all the foreign aid delivered since 1945 (2000, 4). But the poor cannot turn this property into capital; it is "dead capital," described in his second discovery.

De Soto traced the history of the development of capital in the West and realized that the key to being able to take out a loan on an asset one owns is being able to prove that one owns it. The emergence of a system of property rights in the West provided this kind of proof to a lender, and so property became capital that could be leveraged. A system of property rights and the legal means to enforce them are largely missing in many parts of the world where the poor live. Systems of communal ownership, government ownership, or conflicting or undocumented ownership make for what de Soto calls dead capital, because no one will loan money on something a person cannot prove he or she owns (De Soto 2000).

Muhammad Yunus—The right to access to credit

Yunus is a Bangladeshi professor of economics and founder of the Grameen Bank and its related enterprises. In the midst of a serious famine in the 1970s, Yunus met a poor woman bamboo stool maker on the streets outside his university and wondered if his economics had anything to offer her for her poverty. To his surprise, he learned that she was not looking for a handout. She wanted to make things that people would buy, but she was being limited by the high interest rates of the moneylenders and the fact that no bank would loan money to someone with no address and no assets.

Free from any experience in banking, Yunus had a series of liberating insights. The poor did not have access to affordable credit. The poor might be good credit risks under the right conditions. And the amount of credit the poor needed to become productive parts of the local economy was relatively small. The result is the widely known story of the Grameen Bank, which today has over 5.6 million members (Dowla and Barua 2006, 29).

Like de Soto, Yunus has a very positive view of the poor's willingness to work hard under difficult circumstances.

One of the key contributions Yunus made to thinking about development was his idea that simply transferring money from the non-poor to the poor through a non-profit charitable arrangement might not always be the best thing to do. It has two weaknesses. First, this approach tends to create dependency and has not always helped the poor find a sustainable role in the local economy. Second, the scale and sustainability of such an approach are limited by how much the non-poor would give and how long they would give. Will there ever be enough charity to help two billion people living on less than US$2 a day? Yunus set out to create what he called social businesses that are able to recover their costs through affordable interest rates and two-tiered pricing (one subsidized price for the poor and another higher price for the middle class) for their services. The net result is a family of twenty-five Grameen companies that provide services like microcredit, health and welfare services, sales and distribution of handmade products, small-business loan guarantees, information technology training, and mobile phone service (Yunus 2009, 78–79).

Yunus's latest proposal is for what he calls social businesses. These are businesses that create a social good and that are managed with business principles just like a for-profit companies—no subsidies and able to pay the cost of capital to grow. Like the Grameen business models, the cost of doing business is recovered through fees and interest payments, and now includes the cost of new capital in order to fund future growth. The only difference from a for-profit business is that creating a social good replaces profit maximization. Investors recover their investments but do not receive dividends. Yunus calls these non-loss, non-dividend companies and offers the idea as the missing element of capitalism (Yunus 2009, 21–25).

SUMMING UP

As we look back on this account of the history and current thinking about development from a global perspective, there are profound contradictions, a common and flawed perspective, an irony, and an opportunity.

The contradictions are obvious. The good news is that the percentage of people living on less than US$2 a day has dropped from over 95 percent in 1820 to about 43 percent in 2008 (World Bank 2008). In the almost twenty-five years between 1981 and 2005, the absolute number of people in the world living in absolute poverty has dropped from 1.9 billion (52 percent of the world's population) to 1.4 billion (25 percent), with the largest declines in China, India, and, more recently, Brazil and Indonesia (World Bank 2010).

Almost a billion people in fifty countries are deeply mired in poverty, and it is unclear how development as we now understand it can take place (Collier 2007, 5–7). The good news is that development assistance is at its highest level in history. The not-so-good news is that we are unclear on how best to use this foreign aid to facilitate effective and sustainable development (Easterly 2006, 4, 11; Banerjee and Duflo 2011). The good news is that we know a great deal more about economic policies, participatory methods, good governance, and useful cultural values that enable development. The not-so-good news is that the development goal is "in the service of expanding the human ability to produce and have more—more stuff, more freedom, more years, more control" (Hoksbergen, Curry, and Kuperus 2009, 30). Finally, the good news is that the number of non-poor in the world is also the highest in history. The not-so-good news is that they are struggling with obesity, consumerism, and a deteriorating natural environment.

Although the development proposals of Sachs, Easterly, Collier, de Soto, and Yunus have led us beyond simple models of economic growth and the historical tendency to have negative views of the poor and their potential, all of these contributors and their varied approaches share a common perspective: the modern worldview. All are materialistic, often technocratic, and reflect a firm belief in human reason, technology, and money as the keys to solving the problem of poverty. Their biggest common gap lies in the absence of religion and things spiritual in their explanation for why people are poor and what can be done to help them.

The deep irony in this story of the emerging idea of development is that the development conversation has forgotten its roots, roots that were embedded in a Christian view of the world and how the world works (Stark 2005; Gillespie 2008). The irony is deepened by the fact that the same modernity that birthed the ideas and conceptual frameworks that led to the idea that human beings could change history and that development or poverty eradication was possible also led to the problems presented by modernity to Christians who wish to do development (described in Chapter 1).

The opportunity is that the so-called secular development conversation is rediscovering religion and its importance to any idea of human and social change (Deneulin and Bano 2009). This product of the postmodern challenge means that Christians, and their religious perspective on development, may be in a place to make an important contribution to the development discourse, providing we are willing to take our development practice and thinking into the larger development community.

We Christians need to be willing to come out of our self-imposed exile, stop being apologetic about being Christians, and begin to contribute the material that our faith tradition has to offer, which is considerable.

3

Theology, poverty, and development

WHY DO WE NEED TO DO THEOLOGY?

Why does a book on transformational development need a chapter on theology? Some people think that development is a practical activity of the material world, something done in the real world of human life. They think that theology is different, assuming that theology is thinking about God, about otherworldly and spiritual things. These very assumptions are part of the problem this book is addressing.

Since God is at work in God's world redeeming and restoring it, this means that development, understood from a Christian perspective, is a theological act every bit as much as it is a technical or problem-solving act. One's vision of a better human future and how one works toward that future are grounded in one's theology and understanding of the biblical narrative. This means the Christian development practitioners must take time to develop their theological skills just as they develop their technical skills.

This chapter summarizes the history of American evangelical thinking on poverty and development. This is a story with a big gap from 1920 until the 1970s. We will then look at Catholic social teaching—a robust conversation dating back over hundred years.

I will then take a narrative approach to scripture to sketch out an evangelical theology for thinking about poverty and development. By the end of this chapter I hope the reader will understand that because God is working now in the concrete world of space and time, doing transformational development must be a form of acting theologically.

A LOOK BACKWARD

Evangelical theology

This book is written from an evangelical perspective, with the word *evangelical* understood as affirming the uniqueness of Christ, the need for personal conversion, the importance of Bible as a guide to life, and a commitment to doing mission in the world. I do not use the term to imply a conflation with conservative politics that has sadly become all too common in the United States.

The evangelical mission movement has a lot of catching up to do when it comes to thinking theologically about social action, social justice, poverty, and development. There was a time—much of the nineteenth century—when evangelicals and social action were words often uttered in the same sentence (Dayton 1976). But then, for understandable reasons, most evangelicals took their eye off the ball.

In the 1920s American evangelicals took a holiday from history when it came to the thinking and doing of social action. Deeply wounded by the modernist-fundamentalist controversy, our conservative forbearers retreated behind the fundamentals of the faith and the singular importance of evangelism and stayed in a defensive posture for almost fifty years.

In 1947 Carl H. Henry, the leading conservative evangelical theologian of that era, stirred the waters when he wrote *The Uneasy Conscience of Modern Fundamentalism*, in which he recalled the evangelical involvement with social issues at home and on the mission field throughout the nineteenth century (1947, 109). Henry wondered if losing sight of the social side of the gospel of Jesus Christ might have been an unintended consequence of the "battle for the faith" in the 1920s.

It took almost another quarter century before this question was raised again with the emergence of the Lausanne movement at its inaugural meeting in 1974. As the Lausanne Covenant (Stott 1975)—still the most widely accepted contemporary affirmation of evangelical beliefs—was being drafted, some courageous evangelicals from the South insisted that no statement of evangelical beliefs could be complete if it did not include action on behalf of the poor and the oppressed. Today we stand indebted to Samuel Escobar and René Padilla for reminding evangelicals who we really are.

During the 1980s a new but related disagreement emerged. It was agreed that social action and concerns for social justice were in the Bible. But were evangelism and social action equally important? Wasn't evangelism primary? This led to a series of meetings in the early 1980s in Grand Rapids, Michigan (Nicholls 1986) and at Wheaton College (Samuel and Sugden 1987). Discussions ranged over issues relating to justice, social action, eschatology, and the importance of reaching the unreached. Evangelism and social action were described as two sides of the same gospel coin or two wings on the gospel bird. In the midst of this discussion Wayne Bragg of the Wheaton Hunger Center introduced a new word: *transformation*. The gospel was about change—material, social and spiritual change—and the theological concept for this was transformation. The word stuck.

By the early 1990s a strong movement of evangelical social action emerged that grew increasingly self-confident. A variety of labels emerged for this integration of evangelism and social action: holistic mission, holistic development, integral mission, holistic ministry and transformational development. Evangelical agencies like Food for the Hungry, World Relief, World Vision, World Concern, and others moved forward to the next questions: What does holistic mission or transformational development look like in practice? How does one do it well?

During the 1990s this was the question that evangelical relief and development agencies and practitioners met to talk about. Ted Yamamori and others organized meetings where practitioners shared holistic mission case studies. This was done in Africa, Latin America, and Asia; there was also a meeting on holistic ministry in the cities (see Yamamori et al. 1995, 1996, 1997, 1998).

Among evangelicals today the issue of social action versus evangelism is largely a historical footnote. Over half of the incoming master's students to the School of Intercultural Studies at Fuller Theological Seminary in 2009 enrolled to study international development, children at risk, and urban ministry. Allen Hertzke has documented the increasingly normative engagement of contemporary evangelicals with human rights and advocacy work (2004). Operation Blessing is an outgrowth of Pat Robertson's ministry; Campus Crusade has its Global Aid Network (GAiN). Small evangelical missions are simply getting on with transformational development, like Mission Moving Mountains and its discipleship for transformation-training programs.

This is all well and good, but it is important to say what has *not* happened in evangelical thinking about development. No case studies have been published in the last ten years. There are very few serious evaluations that are genuinely holistic. There is very little, if any, serious research by Christian practitioners—very few Ph.D. studies and almost no evidence-based research into transformational development.

Of relevance to this chapter, there is very little new theological reflection. We seem to be resting on the theological work done in the 1980s. We have a biblical and theological rationale for doing evangelism and social action, but almost nothing has been done theologically on how this transformational work might be done. We have largely failed to draw on and form Christian perspectives that take into account recent work in the rapidly changing fields of anthropology, sociology, community psychology, and development studies; nor have we engaged the burgeoning amount of development research. We are not even all that significantly involved in the religion and development conversation that has changed so dramatically in the last ten years.

There has been little fresh thinking on development ecclesiology. Yet the question of the relationship between the Christian relief and development agency and local churches remains both unclear and problematic. The proclivity of Northern churches to seek partnerships for development with Southern churches has created a new set of theological questions and a larger number of practical challenges. Little has been said about the right and proper role of local churches in the development of their communities: Are churches mini-development agencies, members of civil society, or something else altogether?

The bottom line is this: For the last twenty years, we evangelical activists have done what we tend to do best—we have acted. We've gone out and done transformational development. Doing is good, of course. But there is more to doing than just acting. We need to begin thinking and pick up the theological side of our work once again.

Catholic social teaching

The Roman Catholic Church took a very different trajectory to thinking about the social issues of justice and peace. It has had on ongoing conversation that started in 1891 and continues to this day. While we evangelicals need to restart our theological conversation, we do not have to reinvent everything. There is much in the Roman Catholic conversation to which we can profitably listen.

In the aftermath of the radical changes during the eighteenth and nineteenth centuries, the Roman Catholic Church faced a very different kind of world in which the role of the church—and Christian thought—was being questioned. The emergence of the secular nation state, capitalism, industrialization, urbanization, and the radical disruption and suffering these created in the lives of ordinary people had led to a deep suspicion of capitalism. Modernity, and particularly the fruits of the French Revolution, had led to a faith in the supremacy of human reason, and the resulting critical philosophies were pushing religion off the public stage. The effectiveness of science and technology was having the same effect. The materialistic and critical voices of Marx, Darwin, and Freud made religion seem less and less important. Modernity was in full bloom, and religion had been relegated to the spiritual realm and was expected to eventually go away altogether.

Into this context of a diminishing role for the church and religion in society, Pope Leo XIII wrote *New Things (Rerum novarum)* in 1881. The encyclical addressed the new ideas about the role of reason, labor, capital, private ownership, and the modern state. It went on to focus on the importance of the family, the relationship between employee and employer, and roles of both the church and the state when it comes to the poor. *Rerum novarum* criticized both socialism, dismissing it on the grounds that it "subordinated individual liberty to social well-being without respect for human rights or religious welfare," and capitalism, which in the pope's view had "released the individual from social and moral constraints" (O'Brien and Shannon 1992, 13). This encyclical also made it clear that the church's concern for the spiritual well-being of human beings must not be used as an excuse to neglect the well-being of the poor (RN, no. 23).

Avoiding the modern temptation to dismiss the old in our enthusiasm for new thinking and discoveries, Catholic social teaching became a serious conversation of reaffirmations and reinterpretations of earlier encyclicals within the social teaching tradition. Pius XI extended the conversation in 1931 with *After Forty Years (Quadragesimo anno)*, as did Paul VI in 1971 with *A Call to Action on the 80th Anniversary of* Rerum novarum *(Octogesima adveniens)*. John Paul II wrote *On the Hundredth Anniversary of* Rerum novarum *(Centesimus annus)* in 1991. Each spoke to the ideas that were unchanging yet responded with fresh theological insight to the changing historical context of poverty and injustice during this one-hundred-year period.

With Vatican II, additional theological thinking became part of Catholic social teaching. Of particular interest to those working with the poor are *On the Development of Peoples (Populorum progressio*, 1967), written by Paul VI; *On Social Concern (Sollicitudo rei socialis*, 1987), by John Paul II; and *Charity in Truth (Caritas in veritate*, 2009), by Benedict XVI. In addition to its concern for the well-being of the poor, Catholic social teaching never lost sight of the need to share the good news of the gospel. *Evangelization in the Modern World (Evangelii nuntiandi*, 1975) by Paul VI specifically reaffirmed this fundamental commitment. *Caritas in veritate* echoes this ongoing concern: "Without the perspective of eternal life, human progress in this world is denied breathing space. Enclosed in history, it runs the risk of being reduced to mere accumulation of wealth" (no. 11).

Overall, there are seventeen to twenty documents that make up this living tradition of social thought. Together they provide a consistent yet adapting Christian moral perspective on poverty, inequality, injustice, and human well-being (Groody 2007, 94–95). They also provide a consistent view of the role of the church in the world when it comes to social concern. In *Populorum progressio* Paul VI accepted the idea that the church and the state (and presumably he would agree to include the market) are different powers and thus each is supreme in its own sphere of competency (no. 13). This brings the work of Abraham Kuyper and his concept of sphere sovereignties to mind.

The *Pastoral Constitution on the Church in the Modern World (Gaudium et Spes)*, a product of Vatican II, is the conciliar text on the issue of the church's responsibility to speak to social issues. In *Caritas in veritate* Benedict XVI echoes this sentiment while adding a critical caveat: "The Church does not have technical solutions to offer and does not claim 'to interfere' in any way with the politics of States. She does, however, have a mission of truth to accomplish . . . for a society that is attuned to man, to his dignity, to his vocation" (no. 9). So while the state and the market have their own responsibilities, the church has a moral obligation to speak to the world about the truth about God and about humankind:

The church's social doctrine is not a "third way" between liberal capitalism and Marxist collectivism, nor even a possible alternative to other solutions less radically opposed to one another: rather, it constitutes a category of its own. . . . Its main aim is to interpret these realities, determining their conformity with or divergence from the lines of the Gospel teaching on man and his vocation, a vocation which is at once earthly and transcendent; its aim is thus to guide Christian behavior. It therefore belongs to the field, not of ideology, but of theology and particularly of moral theology. (SRS, no. 41)

There are seven key themes that emerge consistently in Catholic social teaching:

1. Truth about God and about humanity
2. Charity and justice
3. Human dignity
4. Common good
5. Subsidiarity
6. Solidarity
7. Option for the poor

The truth *about God and about humanity* forms the basis for a Christian anthropology. The truth about God is that God is the creator, sustainer, redeemer, and restorer of creation, and that God chose to make humankind in God's image. The truth about us is that we were made as moral actors responsible for the well-being of one another and the created order. We are to act in ways that make the world conducive to human well-being, and this implies that human well-being starts with directing ourselves toward God. Christian anthropology draws heavily on the biblical creation account.

The linking of *charity and justice* is a more recent clarification within Catholic social teaching and is closely linked to idea of the truth about God and about humankind. Charity has been seen by some as simple almsgiving disconnected from the idea of justice. Sometimes charity has been described as indifferent to or even supporting injustice. Some in liberation theology were critical of Mother Teresa on these grounds. In *Caritas in veritate* Benedict XVI argues forcefully against this alienation of charity from justice. Charity or love in truth requires that human beings receive what they are due because of who they are. The result is that "charity demands justice" (no. 6). But charity as love goes beyond justice and gives human beings what they are not due as evidenced by God's act of love in the form of the birth, death, and resurrection of Jesus. "Thus charity transcends justice and completes it" (no. 6). This echoes recent thinking by Miraslav Volf (2009) and Nicholas Wolterstorff (2008).

The idea of *human dignity* rests on the fact that God made every human in God's image and that God's son died for the redemption of every human being. This expression of love means that every human being has inherent worth, value, and a singular identity in God's sight. The chief concern of Catholic social teaching is to speak for those for whom this is not the case: "Catholic social teaching pays particular attention to those in society whose dignity is diminished, denied or damaged or those who, when they are no longer deemed useful, are rejected and discarded or those who are dehumanized in their jobs" (Groody 2007). This affirmation of human worth and dignity also means that all social institutions must be assessed in terms of their contribution to enhancing (or not) the dignity of all humankind. The identity and agency of human beings are ultimately derived from their being in the image of God. We are the image of God, not of our country, our race, our gender, or our religion.

Common good rests on two related biblical ideas. First, a God of love intends a life for those made in God's image that is life giving and good without regard for our productive value or any other secondary identifier. Second, being fully human means being in relationships, and thus relationships must work for the well-being of all. No autonomous modern self here. Together, these expressions of common good speak to living a moral life that is for others as well as for us. It follows that it is a moral requirement that all social institutions—the state, the market, the church, and civil society—work to create a set of social conditions within which everyone and every group can flourish. Taking a step further, Catholic social teaching on the common good is also "built around the vision of a peaceful society. . . . Here it is enough to note that peace is a fruit of justice and integrally related to the development and empowerment of poor people and poor countries" (Groody 2007, 108).

Subsidiarity is an awkward word but an important idea. The focus is on the fundamental importance of human liberty before God. In *Quadragesimo anno* Pius XI asserted: "It is a fundamental principle of social philosophy, fixed and unchangeable, that one should not withdraw from individuals and commit to the community what they can accomplish by their own enterprise and/or industry" (no. 79). The idea of subsidiarity, combined with that of human dignity, establishes human agency and human freedom as principles that should not be encroached upon or eroded by higher social institutions—the state, the market, and any part of civil society, including the church. Subsidiarity validates the idea of voluntary civil society in which people may freely associate to work for policies, ideas, and programs that they deem important. There is an echo of Amartya Sen at this point.

Solidarity as a principle of Catholic social teaching is more recent and is generally associated with John Paul II. Some have called this the principle of civic friendship (Weigel 2008, 7). It reflects the simple biblical idea that we are all part of the human family and that we are all responsible for the well-being of all (1 Cor 12:25–26). The incarnation was Jesus coming close to those whom he loved and who could not help themselves. Jesus' call to love our neighbor as ourselves defines the meaning of solidarity, especially when there is no limit as to whom our neighbors might be (Luke 10:25–37). This is not a call for a warm and fuzzy sense of concern but a command to stop, cross over to the other side of the road, and change the circumstances of someone who has been wronged (SRS, no. 38).

Solidarity is deeply connected with the idea of the *option of the poor*, a term that arose with Vatican II and developed particularly in the liberation theology in Latin America. The idea draws on the central ethical focus that Jesus declared in the Beatitudes. It notes that Jesus chose to carry out the great majority of his ministry in Galilee, that marginal place inhabited by the marginalized of Jewish life. This idea called into question the location from which we do our theological thinking and acting:

> It became clear that my own theological reflection needed to move to the other side of the cognitive wall, from the comfortableness of my own room, my own library and my own ideas about God to the uncomfortableness of the world, the living "texts" of the poor and the challenge of the living God. (Groody 2007, 182)

Furthermore, this shift in social location causes two things: a different view of the poor, and an undeniable call to act on their behalf:

> Love for others, and in the first place love for the poor, in whom the Church sees Christ himself, is made concrete in the promotion of justice. Justice will never be fully attained unless people see in the poor person, who is asking for help in order to survive, not an annoyance or a burden, but an opportunity for showing kindness and a chance for greater enrichment. (CA, no. 55}

Vatican II and its aftermath (1960s–1970s) represented a transition moment for the Roman Catholic Church as well as an important moment of emerging ecumenical cross-fertilization. It was at this point that the Roman Catholic tradition of social teaching connected with the mainline Protestant concerns for justice and peace. Since evangelicals were still on the social-action sidelines at this time, this convergence was mostly unnoticed.

Now that ministries of social action, justice, and peace are becoming mainstream for evangelicals, and since I have already said that we need to add theological thinking to our evangelical being and doings, it would seem that we evangelicals would be served by exposing ourselves to this rich tradition of Christian social teaching. In doing so, one must always take into account the differing social-historical contexts within which the documents of Catholic social teaching were written. Ideas and contexts have substantially changed, and this living tradition has adapted to reflect the differing signs of the times. But having shown some respect for this living tradition, evangelicals also have to do the hard theological work of thinking about social teaching from within their own tradition.

TOWARD A NARRATIVE THEOLOGY OF TRANSFORMATION

Why does God care about how we think about poverty and development? I understand the Bible to say that God is the creator of this world. Furthermore, the Bible asserts that in Christ all things hold together through the work of the Holy Spirit. The text of the Bible suggests that there is a beginning and an end to God's creation. This suggests that God is actively at work in the world, working for God's purposes. No disengaged watchmaker here. If this is so, then God has a stake in what we are making in the world. This means that God is very interested in our thinking and our practice of transformational development, because it either supports or works against what God is doing.

Why a narrative approach to this inquiry? The development process is a convergence of stories. The story of the development practitioner is converging with the story of the community, and together they will share a new story for a while. Because the development promoter is a Christian, and because God has been active in the community since the beginning of time, the biblical story is the third story in this confluence of stories. This brings the development practitioner back to theology and the biblical account.

Every community needs a big story, a story that frames our lives and our understanding of the world. Everyone must have some kind of transcendent narrative that gives answers to questions of meaning and provides moral direction and social purpose. We need to know who we are (identity and purpose), where we are (location in the world and the universe), what went wrong (making sense of the poverty, pain, and injustice we see), what we must do (what must change and how it can be changed), and what time it is (how our past, present, and future fit into this picture).

Development practitioners need a big story too. At its heart transformational development is about seeking a better human future. Any vision of a better human future must have its roots in the story that makes sense of our lives. Sadly, there is more than one story competing for the allegiance of most development workers. First, we all live within the story of our culture. Second, all of us who have been educated in Western schools or schools using Western curriculum also carry the story of modernity. Finally, if we are Christian, we carry the Christian story as well. These three stories shape our view of the better future and how to get there. Therefore, before we set out to accompany the transformation of others, we need to be sure we are clear on the biblical story that has the final say on our individual stories.

COMPETING STORIES

The modern world has a number of competing stories. Some are age-old stories rooted in the great religions of the world. Others are the products of the Western Enlightenment and the emergence of modernity in the nineteenth century. Marxism was a comprehensive narrative about what the world is like, how it got that way, and a seductive promise of a better human future. It lasted almost a century, and its idolatry claimed the lives of millions of people. Capitalism and globalization are related stories that proudly assert that they "won" the battle of economic stories and now are the sole path to a better human future.

Science and technology, the siblings of capitalism and globalization, also continue to demand our faith and allegiance. Theses "isms" are gods that we are often quick to worship. Koyama tells us that these gods "are fascinating because they claim to give us our identity and security more directly and quickly than our crucified Lord. . . . The selling point of these gods is directness and security. . . . They give us instant service" (Koyama 1985, 259). Yet at the end of the twentieth century the authority of these modern stories is fraying in the face of broken promises.

Science claims to understand how the universe works and promises the power to master nature, but it does not provide answers to some pretty important questions. How did the world begin? By accident? How will it end? By accident? Why are we here? What moral guidance does your story have to offer us? Science is silent. (Postman 1997, 31).

Technology speaks only of power, offering mastery of nature to all. Technology offers convenience, efficiency, and prosperity here and now with its benefits available to rich and poor, or so it claims. Technology is a jealous god; those who follow must "shape their needs and aspirations to the possibilities of technology" (ibid., 31). Worshiping any other god or good means slowing down or frustrating the benefit of technology. Yet the technological god is a false god: "It is a god that speaks to us of power, not limits; speaks to us of ownership, not stewardship; speaks to us only of rights, not responsibilities; speaks to us of self-aggrandizement, not humility" (ibid., 31).

Capitalism today asks for faith in a god called "the hidden hand" and seems to have forgotten the goal of the original story. Adam Smith, capitalism's original storyteller, "wrote that the ultimate goal of business is not to make a profit. Profit is just the means. The goal is general welfare" (Wink 1992, 68). Instead, the view of capitalism in play today tends to reduce people to economic beings driven by utilitarian self-interest toward the goal of accumulating wealth. What is wealth for? What are we for if we do not have wealth? Who are we if we do not have wealth? No answer.

Finally, even the human story (history) is not a big enough story. The human story can explain the story of my people and even my personal story.

The human story also contains the stories of science, technology, and capitalism. It fails, however, to provide the answers to the questions of identity and meaning for which we search. Only God's story, the story that is outside human history but containing human history, can do this. Yet you can't get there from here. Beginning from the human story only leads to the smaller stories, the story of my people, my story, and the story of my atoms and molecules. You cannot get from the smaller stories to God's story. The only point of departure that works is to begin with God's story, even if our various Protestant traditions have differing renderings of that story.

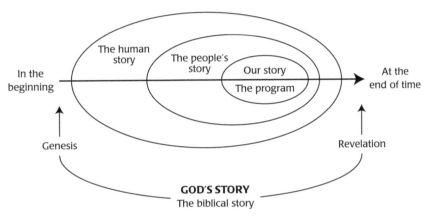

Figure 3–1: The constellation of stories.

In the latter years of the twentieth century, it is becoming clear that the modern world is discovering that it has lost its story. Part of the malaise in the West is the sense of loss and confusion that the absence of a true story brings. There is no widely shared story that makes sense of our lives, nor is there any promise of a better human future that compels belief. Modernity has failed to create a story line, and it has failed because it has no storyteller. "If God does not invent the world's story, then it has none" (Jenson 1993, 21).

Christians do have a story, however. The Bible is the narrative of God's creative and redemptive work in the world; thus it also contains the story of the Christian community. It is God's story about what God is doing. This Christian story was received; we did not make it up. It is not our story about God. Nor is it the sum of our individual stories, even though God holds these stories in high regard; after all, God sent the Son to die for our stories so that they might be restored to God's story.

It is this story of what God wants and is doing that compels us to care for the poor and to work for human transformation. God's story is the source of our motivation, our vision, and our values of being, thinking, and acting in God's world.

The biblical story also puts our stories in their place. We learn that it is not my story, or your story, or our story that is the main story, the story that gives all other stories their true meaning. Meaning and a moral frame only comes from the story of God's project in history. To pursue human transformation as Christians means understanding where humanity is coming from, where it is going, and how it can get there. To do the work for transformation, we have to embrace the whole of the biblical story, the story that makes sense and gives direction to the stories of the communities where we work, as well as to our own stories.

God's project in history is at heart a simple one. It is the story of creation and redemption by the God of Israel and Father of the risen Christ working through the Holy Spirit. God's story tells us how things started, lost their way, can be redirected, and how God's intention for God's creation is restored in the end.

But the biblical story is also a very unusual story. We are told the beginning, the middle, and the final chapter of the story. But the piece between Jesus and his work on the cross and the final chapter when Jesus comes again is still being written. God's story is not just about what God has done, but also about what God, through his church, is doing now. God is still writing the story, and incredibly, God has invited us to participate in the completion of God's project.

Because God is still doing things in our world, we must begin our theology with the storyteller. The storyteller of the biblical story is a unique storyteller, because the storyteller is also the main actor in the story. Before there was any story, there is God. And now, in the chapters just before the end of the story, this same God is working in this world through the church, doing what God has been doing since the fall: working for the redemption, transformation, and restoration of human beings, their relationships, and the creation that God made and in which they live.

THE STORYTELLER

We have to begin with God because he is the storyteller and the author of the story as well. Who is God? must be the first question. This is the question "that frames and anticipates all other questions" (Leupp 1996, 89). We must know who God is before we can answer the question about who we are and what we are supposed to be doing.

The Christian response is that God is three in one, Father, Son, and Holy Spirit. While we affirm this in worship, we don't use this trinitarian formulation very much in thinking about issues of daily life. In the last twenty years, however, a lot of theological work has been done to help us recover and make use of the trinitarian understanding of God. Some of this thinking is important to developing a framework for thinking about human transformation or well-being.

Who is God? The question must be carefully put. One of the recent developments in philosophy is that being must not be separated from doing when addressing the question of identity. Catherine LaCugna, a Catholic feminist theologian at the University of Notre Dame, suggests that the more correct questions are who is God and what is God doing? (1991, 1–3). If we focus only on who God is, God's being and character, then we struggle when pressed with hard questions: Can we believe in a God who seems to allow the poor to be poor in an unjust world? Can we believe in a God in the face of the genocides in Cambodia in the 1970s and in Rwanda and Bosnia in the late 1990s? Does belief in God hinder human development? To answer that God is all-powerful, all-knowing, and all-caring fails to provide a believable response to these questions. If there isn't more to God, then there isn't enough.

To find a more satisfactory answer, we have to go beyond who God is and also talk about what God is doing. The trinitarian formulation informs us that God is saving the world through Christ in the power of the Holy Spirit. The question of who God is in an unjust and violent world can only be answered adequately by talking about an all-powerful and all-knowing God who is acting to save a fallen and failed world in a particular way. Thus, God is not the God who permits a genocide; rather, God is the God who is hard at work trying to prevent future ones.

Jesus provides another example of the importance of keeping who God is and what God is doing together in our thinking. Knowing that Jesus is God is not enough to know fully who Jesus is. We also need to know that Jesus emptied himself of his prerogatives as God and, in obedience to the Father, died for the sins of all humankind and provided for our forgiveness by his resurrection. Jesus is God (being) and Jesus became like us, died, and in so doing saved us (doing). This provides a more complete account as who Jesus is.

Why does this trinitarian formulation of being and doing matter to the development worker? Three reasons are important to our thinking about development. First, not to be trinitarian in our thinking is dangerous. LaCugna reminds us, "A non-Trinitarian theology of God opens the door to every kind of ideology or idolatry, whether it comes in the form of a self-sufficient, masculine Father-God, or a plenipotentiary God who perversely wishes children to die, or an apathetic God who does not mind if people are always poor, or a violent, vengeful God who enjoys wars fought in his name" (1991, 395). Also, a non-trinitarian view of God leads to a view of humankind "that is derogatory and detrimental because one human being is put forward as normative for another" (ibid., 396).

Second, a trinitarian view of God frames our mission response as Christians. We must be Christians, think in a Christian way, and do Christian work. Doing transformational development is acting out who we truly are. If there is no dichotomy between being and doing in God, then there can be none in us.

Finally, this trinitarian view leads to another helpful conclusion: we need to think of God as a loving, self-giving community; three, yet one. The Christian God is a relational God, and this defines God's character: self-giving love. "Trinitarian theology could be described as *par excellence* a theology of relationship, which explores the mysteries of love, relationship, personhood and communion within the framework of God's self-revelation in the person of Christ and the activity of the Holy Spirit" (LaCugna 1991, 1).

A lot follows from this for the development worker. First, if human beings are made in the image of this triune community, then our understanding of the individual must be very different from the autonomous, self-determining individual of Western culture. Development cannot be reduced to simply empowering individuals with new choices. Second, if God is in God's very essence relational, then our understanding of the impact of sin must also be relational and this will shape how we understand poverty (more on this in the next chapter). Third, if this triune God is saving the world by inviting people to join the movement toward the best of human futures in God's kingdom, then our view of the better future of transformational development must be fundamentally relational too. Finally, as Leupp points out, "Christian ethics that hope to be triunely grounded must be an ethics of relationality" (1996, 159). Thinking in trinitarian terms "is practical because it is *the* theological criterion to measure the fidelity of ethics, doctrine, spirituality and worship to the self-revelation of God and the action of God in the economy of salvation" (LaCugna 1991, 410).

THE BEGINNING OF THE STORY

Creation

In the beginning was God, the triune God. The biblical story begins by God making something out of nothing. This relational God created the earth and everything in it. Genesis tells us that the triune God spoke the creation into being (Gn 1:1). God's first action was to create a material world that could be seen, heard, felt, and touched. John tells us that Christ was God's Word in the beginning (Jn 1:1–2) and that through Christ all things were made (Jn 1:3). The Holy Spirit hovered over the deep (Gn 1:2). The whole person of God was creating and active from the beginning of time. The world was God's act, not God's thought or dream. And the result was very good, according to the one who created it.

The trinitarian formulation of who God is helps us understand another implication of the creation account. God is God, and the world is the world, distinctly separate and yet personally related. Creator and creation are in continuing relationship, distinct yet inseparably linked together in a relationship of love. God transcends creation, yet through Christ is actively involved in sustaining it (Heb 1:2–3). The creation account is neither the work of the distant high god of traditional religion nor the blind clockmaker of the modern West.

Image of God

Because human beings were made in the image of the triune God, we are meant to be in loving, self-giving relationships with one another. We must never forget that our identity and vocation are embedded in a system of relationships: with God, with self, with community, with those perceived as "other," and with our environment. Our relational identity is the foundation of our understanding of the common good and our motivation for solidarity. From this base the commandment of Jesus that we are to love God and our neighbor as we love ourselves follows directly. This is a relational understanding of whom we were created to be. But, as we've said before, identity is more than being; it also includes thinking and doing. So what is the other part of human identity?

God created male and female in God's own image and directed them to "be fruitful and increase in number, to fill the earth and subdue it" (Gn 1:27). The idea that God made human beings in God's image and then gave human beings the power to name (organize), rule over, and make the creation productive has a stunning implication. Human beings are to be God's co-creators in the world—with a very large assignment. In creation we are to use our God-given power to observe, reason, and then act on that new knowledge. Remembering that we are not God, and so cannot create out of nothing, we are empowered by God to create out of everything that God created in nature as long as we remember that the purpose of our creating is to enable the well-being of all human beings and natural world.

Richard Middleton, professor of Bible and culture at Northeastern Seminary, boldly asserts that "the human calling as *imago Dei* is itself developmental and transformative and may be helpfully understood as equivalent to the labor or work of forming culture or developing civilization" (2005, 89). Thus the Genesis account declares the centrality of the human role in development and in seeking human well-being. You and I are more than simply alive (being). Our purpose or vocation as human beings is to make the earth fruitful for human well-being (thinking and doing).

Being an actor with a purpose in God's creation has another implication when it comes to thinking about human development. In *Populorum progressio* Paul VI concluded that being made in the image of God, and having been given gifts by God to contribute to the well-being of creation, implies that "every human life is called to some task by God. . . . By developing these traits (gifts and skills) . . . the individual works his way toward the goal set for him by the Creator" (no. 15). Benedict XVI reinforces this idea in *Civitas in veritate*: "Precisely because God gives a resounding 'yes' to man, man cannot fail to open himself to the divine vocation to pursue his own development" (no. 18). The implication for development is that "it is always man who is the protagonist of development" (SRS, no. 30) not the development agency, the government, or the West.

But Benedict XVI also reminds us that there is a significant limitation to this call that we must not forget. While this call to enhance and improve the human condition is a vocation given to us by God, it is also true that human beings are nonetheless "incapable, on (our) own, of supplying its (life's) ultimate meaning" (CV, no. 16). We cannot develop ourselves by ourselves alone.

Implications of the creation account

In addition to establishing who we are, whose we are, and what we are called to do, the creation account also points to several other implications as we think of working for human development and well-being.

First, the trinitarian understanding of the one who created the world also allows us to understand that the rich diversity of creation and the human family in an important way. Cultural and ethnic diversity is not a mistake God made, nor is it the result of the fall. Diversity is a reflection of who God is. "The plurality in unity of the triune revelation enables us to do justice to the diversity, richness and openness of the world without denying its unity in relativist versions of plurality. It is this vision that trinitarian theology has to offer to the fragmented modern world" (Gunton 1997, 103). It is not by happenstance that when creation is finally restored to what God intended, John reports: "After this I looked, and there before me was a great multitude that no one could count, from every nation, tribe, people and language, standing before the throne and in front of the Lamb" (Rv 7:9). Human and cultural diversity is a gift of God and an asset for supporting human well-being.

Second, the creation account establishes the requirement for a Christian ecology. We are to be stewards. Everything belongs to God—humankind, the creatures of the earth, and the earth itself. The call to and promise of productivity and fruitfulness find their ground in the intent of the God who created them.

Finally, the repeated evaluation on God's part that who and what God created was good does not only mean that creation worked or that God liked it. It must also include the idea that the creation was beautiful. Genesis 2 speaks of "trees pleasing to the eye." We know that beauty of creation is itself a witness to God and reveals God's glory (Ps 19:1–4; Rom 1:20). Aesthetics is also part of the created order, and our human appreciation of beauty reflects the image of a God who created that beauty. Without art, music, ritual, and other aesthetic practices, worship would be impoverished, as would be human life. William Dyrness, a professor of theology and aesthetics, claims: "Since symbolic practices are fundamental to human flourishing, any project of human betterment will seek to appreciate and celebrate the aesthetic impulse that is already present in the community" (Dyrness 2011, chap. 9). More on this in Chapter 6.

Creation and social institutions

Going back to the story of creation, Gerhard von Rad reminds us that the account of creation in Genesis ends with the creation of the nations in chapter 10. Human institutions are also part of creation. The story of creation does more than explain how and why humankind was created, it also "provides a common foundation for all human enterprises we call culture—not just theology, but science, politics, ethics and art as well" (Gunton 1997, 98). This raises an important idea that will keep coming back to us in this book. We cannot separate people from the social systems in which they live.

Since the emergence of human institutions is part of God's intention for creation, we must not demonize them, as is often popular in liberal circles today. Human institutions are necessary for the right functioning of all but the simplest human societies. In this sense, social institutions are part of the original good of creation. The great change in the trajectory of human history at the beginning of the eighteenth century is an example of humankind creating good out of creation, including new ideas and new human institutions. But, then neither can we naively trust in these human creations. Our institutional creations fell, just as we did. More on this in the section on the fall.

An interesting set of implications for the development worker can be derived from the creation account. Since God owns the earth but has entrusted it to humankind, the critical metaphor for us is that of the steward and the principle of stewardship. From this, Wright develops four ethical principles (Wright 1983, 69–70):

Sharing resources: The land and natural resources are gifts to all humankind, not to only a few. While this does not mean there can be no private ownership, Wright argues that "the right of all to use is prior to the right to own."

Responsibility to work: Work is part of being fruitful. God is productive, and thus it is in our nature to be productive, too. Thus work is a vocation and a responsibility. The implication for development is straight forward. Every human being has a responsibility to work and to enable or allow others to work so that they can fulfill their purpose.

Expectation of growth: "Be fruitful and increase" applies to the number of human beings and to the means of supporting them. God has provided abundantly in creation so that this can be done, and God has given humankind the ingenuity and adaptability necessary to create this necessary increase.

This should give us pause when we too quickly and uncritically blame poverty on population growth. New babies are not simply empty stomachs or economic sink holes. They are also creative human minds and spirits, endowed with creative and productive potential. They, too, can be fruitful (Cromartie 1995, 282).

Shared produce: Being productive is also accompanied by the idea of being able to consume or enjoy the end-product of one's work. This is part of the biblical image of the better human future (Is 65:21–22). "We are as responsible to God for what we do with what we produce as we are for what *he* has given us" (Wright 1983, 70).

The fall

Sadly, the big story did not end with the fruitful garden where human beings are obedient stewards and God walks in the afternoon. Yielding to temptation from an adversary working against God, humankind, man and woman together, decided to disobey God. They acted as if they knew better than God (Gn 3). Being like God was apparently more attractive than listening to God and doing as God asked. The effect of this disobedience ensured that human identity would be marred and all dimensions of human relationships would work less well for human well-being. The impact of the entry of sin into the world proved very broad—very holistic, if you will. It led to widespread deception, distortion, and domination in all forms of

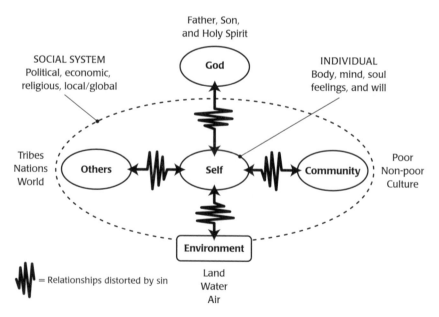

Figure 3–2: Impact of sin on all relationships.

human relationships—with God, within one's self (and family), within the community and between others, and with the environment.

I do not want to move past the issue of an adversary too quickly. Someone other than human beings created the temptation that triggered this first disobedience. Too often we dismiss the idea of a form of personal evil who actively works against God and God's intentions for human beings and creation. Yet, without Satan's role in the first part of the biblical story, there would be no need for the rest of the biblical story. We cannot read Satan out of the story and have it make any sense.

The direct consequences of the fall in terms of poverty and development are fairly obvious. A fruitful creation meant to sustain life does so reluctantly (Gn 3:17), and making the creation productive enough to sustain life now means struggle and hard work (Gn 3:19). Human life now has an end (Gn 3:19). The relationship between men and women became distorted and unequal (Gn 3:16). Violence and murder entered the human story (Gn 4:8), and the hunger for revenge entered the human heart (Gn 4:23). Complete human well-being is now a struggle and beyond the reach of human agency alone.

Yet God's love and God's continuing gift of grace remain in the human story even with the fall. God made us our first clothes and prevented us from making our condition permanent (Gn 3:22). God still speaks of human beings as being made in God's image (Gn 5:1) and, even after starting over with Noah, God's image in us is still there as is the mandate to be fruitful in creation (Gn 9:1, 6). The first humans cultivated the ground, raised families, made music and musical instruments, and created tools out of elements in creation to make the struggle for a human life easier (Gn 4:21–22). Cities were built, and humanity rose to the challenge of having to make themselves safe in a sinful world (Gn 4:17). Thus, our vocation of making God's creation fruitful for all and conducive to human flourishing remains. Sometimes we evangelicals focus too much what some call original sin and forget that God's original good continues as well. Human beings have made the world a better, safer, less threatening place to live, and abject poverty has been in decline since the beginning of the 1800s. Yet this improving world is still the site of genocides, wars, unjust social structures, greed, consumerism, and a host of other reminders that sin is alive as well.

Each of Wright's ethical domains in creation was affected negatively by the fall. Instead of shared resources, land and natural resources have become a universal cause of strife and violence. They are hoarded by some and squandered and abused by others. Land and natural resources have become the counters in games of domination and oppression (Wright 1983, 71–74).

Instead of a way of using our gifts for ourselves and others, work has been corrupted. It can be toilsome and frustrating (Gn 3:17). Work has become a commodity, something we sell and buy with the temptation to reduce the human being to an economic asset, a living machine. Work has become a tool for greed, and even an idolatry whereby one makes a name for oneself. For the poor, this distorted work is often not available and the poor are vilified as "not productive."

Production and growth have become pathologically obsessive in many parts of the world. Covetousness has replaced contentment. "I saw that all labor and achievement spring from man's envy of his neighbor" (Eccl 4:4). There is never enough. "The effect of the fall was that the desire for growth became excessive for some at the expense of others, and the means of growth became filled with greed, exploitation and injustice" (Wright 1983, 81). The result of this pathology is the systems of poverty that keep some people poor.

Finally, the product of work is seen as human property. Claims of ownership are privatized and made an absolute, ignoring the claim of God on all things in creation or the transcendent responsibility each has for the well-being of the larger community. Worse, those who create wealth use that wealth to influence the laws and the economic, political, and cultural system to protect their advantage. "A poor man's field may produce abundant food, but injustice sweeps it away" (Prv 12:23).

The bottom line of the fall is that the good creation of God became bent and no longer points at the purpose for which it was created. "The narrative of the Fall portrays the personal force of evil approaching man by means of the material creation and using the same material creation as a means of enticement to unbelief, disobedience and rebellion" (Wright 1983, 73).

Sometimes, evangelicals get so focused on the impact of the fall on the individual that they forget that the impact of the fall was on the whole of human society as well. Remember that the nations and their corresponding social institutions were part what Christ created in the beginning (Col 1:16–17) and thus were designed for the well-being of human beings. It was the fall that changed this original good. In *City of God, City of Satan*, a theology for the city, Robert Linthicum outlines the impact of the fall on these institutions (1991, 106–7).

The *economic system* was created by God to nurture responsibly and fairly natural and human resources and to encourage men and women to be productive, using the gifts God has given to create wealth. The goal is to provide every human being with both the means of living a life worth living and an opportunity to make contribution to society. Distorted by the fall, people occupying positions of power or influence within the economic system yield to the temptation to act more often as owners and less as stewards. They skew the system to enhance and protect their own self-interest and insulate themselves from the impact of these distortions on the less fortunate.

The *political system* was created by God to encourage kingdom ethics and to bring a creation order into the management of human affairs, an order based on justice and peace. Yet, as a result of the fall, the political system becomes captive to the economic order and begins to serve the powerful; its ministries of justice cease being either ministries or just.

Finally, the *religious system*, which was created by God to bring the nations and their institutions into relationship with God and to make them aware of God's will and commands, too often colludes with the fallen political and economic systems. The prophets of accountability are gradually seduced by money, power, and prestige, gradually becoming silent (Ezek 22:28).

The net result of the fall on the economic, political, and religious systems is that they become the places where people learn to play god in the lives of the poor and the marginalized. When fallen human beings play god in the lives of others, the results are patterns of domination and oppression that mar the image and potential productivity of the poor while alienating the non-poor from their true identity and vocation as well.

This malfunctioning of social systems as a result of sin led theologian Andrew Sung Park to argue that we need a theology of sin that does not just talk about sin and sinners, but also about the impact of sin on those who are being sinned against. Park argues that focusing only on sin, as has been the preoccupation of Western theology, makes the impact of social or structural sin invisible. To rectify this, Park has proposed a theology of the wounded (2004). Park uses the Korean idea of *han*, which emerged as part of *Minjung* theology in the 1970s, to refer to the deep wounding of the heart and spirit that results from being systematically and systemically sinned against. Park reminds us that Jesus came both to die for sinners and to care for and liberate the oppressed—the sinned against (Luke 4:18–19). He encourages us not only to talk about sin and salvation, but also to be concerned with the need for a gospel response to the impact of sin on the sinned against. Park calls the impact *han*, a mixture of "frustrated hope, a collapsed feeling of pain, a resentful bitterness, and a wounded heart" (1993, 31).

This idea of *han* being the impact of sin through social structures of power leads us to consider how the account of the creation and the fall sheds light on how the social power of these fallen institutions works. In the creation account human beings, by virtue of being in the image of God, are given by God the authority to name the animals. Naming, organizing, and rationalizing are the beginning of science. The ability to reason and to act is a form of social power. The way this organizing and naming is done implies judgments of value and worth. Sometimes it tends to predispose actions (Hunter 2010, 178). Sadly, while this assignment of social power was intended for the well-being of all and of creation, the impact of the fall results in this kind of social power being abused: "The capacity to define reality varies extensively and those individuals and institutions that have more engage in a kind of 'symbolic violence' against those who have less" (ibid., 178). This abuse of cultural and social power finds its expression most in the social institutions. More on this in Chapter 4 on the social causes of poverty.

We need to return to our earlier observation that human beings cannot be separated from the human institutions of which they are a part. In Ezekiel's examination of Jerusalem's sin, Linthicum (1991, 106) reminds us that the spiritual nature of the nation and its human institutions—families, businesses, temple and government—all created for good, have become increasingly anti-life, anti-kingdom, and evil (Ezek 22:1–13). At the same time, the people, embedded in these distorting, deceiving, and dominating systems, themselves become exploiters of each other (Ezek 22:29). Of this relationship between individuals and systems, Wink observes, "Human misery is caused by institutions, but these institutions are maintained by human beings. We are made evil by our institutions, yes; but our institutions are also made evil by us" (1992, 75). We will pick up on this theme when we talk about the god complexes of the non-poor in Chapter 4.

Because economic, political, and religious systems are so important to our understanding of poverty and therefore to the work of transformation, we need to look a little more closely at the underlying spirituality of these institutions. Walter Wink (1992, 65–85) has made a significant contribution in this regard. Wink proposes that Paul's "principalities and powers" are the "interiority of earthly institutions or structures or systems." Wink points out that Paul says that the powers are created in, through, and for Christ (Col 1:16–17), thus supporting the claim that social institutions were created by God and are not simply human artifacts. Social institutions were created by God because they are necessary to a full human life in community.

However, these powers—these social systems and their structures—were profoundly distorted by the fall. They became idolatrous, along with the people who inhabit them. "An institution becomes demonic when it abandons its divine vocation—that of a ministry of justice or a ministry of social welfare—for the pursuit of its own idolatrous goals" (Wink 1992, 72), usually by serving the powerful in the name of self-preservation.

Wink goes on to argue that the doctrine of the fall is essential to understanding ourselves in relationship to these principalities and powers. The doctrine of the fall affirms the radical nature of evil and frees us from any illusion that we or our social institutions are perfectible apart from the redeeming work of Jesus Christ and the full coming of the kingdom of God. This should save us from any temptation toward an optimistic belief in the ability of government or the free market or our own efforts at human transformation to change the reality of the poor in and of themselves. The relationship between this understanding of the fall and why people are poor will be developed in the next chapter.

The bottom line from the account of our first disobedience in terms of poverty and development is threefold. First, sin is the foundational reason that relationships do not work for the well-being of all, and thus dealing with sin through redemption in Christ is the beginning of development: "The principal obstacle to be overcome on the way to authentic liberation is sin and the structures produced by sin as it multiplies and spreads" (SRS, no. 46). Second, this understanding provides us an explanation for why the world is as it is without blaming its pain and suffering on God. John Paul II observed that

> Man, who was created for freedom, bears within himself the wound of original sin, which constantly draws him toward evil and puts him in need of redemption. Not only is this doctrine an integral part of Christian revelation; it also has great hermeneutical value insofar as it help one to understand human reality. (CA, no. 25)

Finally, since we too are fallen, the development promoter and the development agency both have the potential to either support or hinder human development.

The liberation story

To get from the fall to Jesus, God called a man, whom we know as Abraham, and made a promise to him: God would make through him a great nation that would be a blessing to all the nations (Gn 12:2–3). God kept his promise, and the Old Testament is the story of Abraham's nation, of its greatness and its flaws, of its loyalty and its betrayal of the God who called it into being. It is also the story of a promise-keeping God, who would not be diverted from completing the story that God began at creation.

For the development professional, the Exodus story is instructive because it is the defining narrative for the people of Israel. It is a story of their liberation and of their formation. The liberation was from the oppression of Egypt and its pharaoh, and the formation was God transforming them from a group of slaves into a people, a nation. This was hard work. It took a day to get Israel out of Egypt and forty years in the wilderness to get Egypt out of Israel.

The Exodus narrative highlights the holistic and relational nature of God's redemptive work. Spiritually, Exodus is the story of the one God revealing God's self and demonstrating God's power so that Israel would believe and be faithful. Israel was freed from Egypt's gods and invited into a covenant with an ethical God who did not belong to any one place.

Sociopolitically, Exodus is the story of moving from slavery to freedom, from injustice toward a just society (at least that was the intent of God's instructions for pre-monarchy Israel [Wright 1983]) and from dependence to independence. Economically, the Exodus story is about moving from oppression in someone else's land to freedom and a productive life in their own land, a land fairly distributed to all so that everyone could enjoy the fruit of his or her own labor. Psychologically, the Exodus story is about Israel losing its self-understanding as a slave people and discovering the new understanding that, with God's help, they could be a people and become a nation.

What is sometimes overlooked is the other intention of God in the Exodus account. Throughout, there was a twofold agenda. The one we all know is the one just described—liberating Israel from its slavery and taking it to the Promised Land. The second was so that "the Egyptians might know that I am the Lord" (Ex 7:5). God was not being capricious as God repeatedly hardened Pharaoh's heart. Pharaoh believed that he was God and thus fully justified in playing god in the lives of "his" slave people. This arrogance could not be ignored. "I have raised you up for this very purpose," God said through Moses to Pharaoh, "that I might show you my power and that my name might be proclaimed in all the earth" (Ex 9:16). This reminds us that the non-poor are also the subjects of the good news, although I am sure it was very hard for Pharaoh to see liberation from his god complex as such. The cost of discipleship is very high for those with wealth and power (see Acts 16:16–21). Jesus pointed out that the rich have a particularly hard time getting into the kingdom; this is part of the reason why.

The prophets

The history of Israel was not always consistent with the story God was attempting to create. Though Israel was God's chosen people and the people through which Jesus came into the world, Israel was also a source of pain for God. Hosea 11:8 reveals the "agitated mind" of God, whose emotions were always "jumbled up within him" (Koyama 1985, 220): loving Israel as a husband loves his wife and yet hating her idolatry and injustice, all at the same time.

Deuteronomy tells us that the prophet is "raised up" by God and set up over and against the priest and the king, taking on the character of God's own voice: "I will put my words in his mouth" (18:15, 17). The stories of the prophets tell us a great deal about how God views sin and its impact and serve to remind us of what God wants from us and God's creation as well as what God intends to do.

In the prophets we learn a great deal about how idolatry and injustice are related. When God, speaking through Isaiah, deplores "meaningless offerings" and "evil assemblies," Jerusalem is told, not to improve its worship in the temple, but to "stop doing wrong, learn to do right, to seek justice and encourage the oppressed, to defend the cause of the fatherless and plead the case of the widow" (Is 1:17). Loving God and loving neighbor are a seamless whole.

In Isaiah, we also see a strong message as to how God feels when the non-poor play God in the lives of the poor.

> Woe to those who make unjust laws,
> to those who issue oppressive decrees,
> to deprive the poor of their rights
> and withhold justice from the oppressed of my people,
> Making widows their prey and robbing the fatherless.
>   (Is 10:1–2)

Echoing Mary's Song (Lk 1:46–55), God will show the bankruptcy of power, privilege, and wealth (Is 5:8–10, 15–16). In front of a holy God it is made clear that there is no salvation in riches or power:

> What will you do on the day of reckoning,
> when disaster comes from afar?
> To whom will you run for help? (Is 10:3)

The prophets also alert us to the fact that idolatry, personal sin, and social sin are a seamless package. We all easily associate Sodom with sins of sexual impurity. Ezekiel speaks of their "detestable practices," when declaring Israel an "adulterous wife" who has become "more depraved than they" (Ezek 16:48). Then he surprises us when he describes Sodom's sin: "She and her daughters were arrogant, overfed and unconcerned; they did not help the poor and needy" (Ezek 16:49).

Ezekiel, interpreting the exile as God's punishment, condemns Jerusalem for a political system that "has eaten the people" and seized their wealth (Ezek 22:23), for an economic system that "bribes for shedding blood" and "robs your neighbor by extortion" (Ezek 22:27) and a religious system that draws no distinction between the sacred and profane and does not "teach the people the difference between clean and unclean" (Ezek 22:26).

Finally, the prophets keep reminding us of what God's story is all about, where God is going, what God is doing, and what God expects of us:

> He has showed you, O Man, what is good.
> And what does the Lord require of you?
> To act justly and to love mercy
> and to walk humbly with your God. (Mic 6:8)

The wisdom of the people

The wisdom literature is the accumulated wisdom of the people who have lived under and within the Old Testament part of the biblical story. This literature summarizes the learnings of the community of faith concerning right and just relationships and testifies to people's experience that God's rule is the only rule at the end of the day. The rich are warned, as are the poor. God's concern for just social relationships surfaces throughout Psalms and Proverbs.

This part of the biblical story also illustrates God's interest in the everyday things of life—eating, drinking, playing, and laughing. Our inability to see God active in and interested in daily life is a serious weakness. It is as if we believe that God is absent from or disinterested in this part of life. Robert Banks addresses this in his helpful book, *Redeeming the Routines: Bringing Theology to Life* (1993).

Apparently the wisdom of the people of Israel, or at least of their leaders, was worthy of being enshrined in God's revelation. This has implications for the development worker. The poor and their communities often embody their local wisdom in epic poems and large collections of proverbs. Are we willing to listen to this hard-earned wisdom and take it seriously? Are we willing to help them "write it down" as a way of helping them recognize how wise they truly are? Stan Nussbaum's *The Wisdom of African Proverbs* is an illustration of how the wisdom of the people allows us to engage local people in their own terms and in their own idiom (Nussbaum 1996–98).

THE CENTER OF THE STORY

The center of the biblical story is the birth, ministry, death, and resurrection of Jesus Christ, a Jew who lived in Palestine almost two thousand years ago. This part of the story begins in Nazareth in Galilee, a place far from the center of political, economic, and religious power. No one expected anything good from there: "Can anything good come from Nazareth?" (Jn 1:46). According to those in religious authority neither the messiah nor a prophet could come from Galilee (Jn 7:41,52). A son of ordinary people, living in an unremarkable place, Jesus "grew in wisdom and stature, and in favor with God and men" (Lk 2:52). We need to note the holistic and relational framework for human growth that this passage portrays: mind and body in relationship with God and humankind.

The Christ of the periphery

The Christ of God was very much the Christ of the powerless and despised on the geographical and social margins of Israel. The news that the Messiah had finally came was first announced by a lonely and strange man preaching in the desert of Judea. Jesus learned his true identity at his baptism in the Jordan River, far from Jerusalem and the Temple. Jesus then came to understand the fullness of his true vocation while enduring the desert wilderness. By struggling with the temptations and deceptions of the Evil One, the one who is against life and against God, Christ determined that he was called to be the Son of God and the Suffering Servant, both at the same time.

Much of Christ's ministry took place in Galilee, on the edge of Israel. For the most part, His work was done among the common people, those whom society labeled "publicans and sinners" or "unclean." Christ chose to do his work of preaching, healing, and casting out of demons in this backwater of the Roman Empire, without any political or religious prestige. An itinerant preacher, Jesus was supported by some faithful women (Lk 8:3). In a sense, the political and economic power of Jerusalem had only one benefit to Jesus. By acting out its role as the center of power, it would put him to death.

This strange location for the work of the Messiah of the whole world has implications. Koyama reminds us that since Jesus is the true center of the kingdom of God, where he is becomes the center (1985, 251–52). This means that Galilee becomes the weak center, outside the powerful center of Jerusalem. The powerful of Israel go to the periphery to see this person, this one who teaches with authority and who does things only God can do (Lk 5:17), this person who takes the center with him wherever he goes. Development workers must search their heart to see where they believe the center of power is that can transform the poor, where they believe Jesus will be found, where the "foolishness of God is wiser than man's wisdom, and the weakness of God is stronger than man's strength" (1 Cor 1:25). Perhaps the periphery is not god-forsaken at all. Maybe there is something there that will surprise us, too (see Figure 3–3).

This poses some interesting questions for the development practitioner, especially when involved in advocacy work. Where is the periphery today, and what does it mean to say that Jesus can make it the center of power? What is the proper location for advocacy work? What result is likely if we, go to the centers of power on behalf of the periphery? Are we willing to pay the price? Where are the real transformational frontiers? The ones that make foolishness into wisdom and weakness into power? Where are the places where the false wisdom of the world is unmasked and declared a lie?

The mission of Jesus

At the synagogue in Nazareth, Jesus said that the Holy Spirit had anointed him "to preach good news to the poor. He has sent me to proclaim freedom for the prisoners and recovery of sight for the blind, to release the oppressed, to proclaim the year of the Lord's favor" (Lk 4:18–19). Jesus' mission is a holistic mission to the poor.

Jesus preached the good news of the kingdom because this is what he was sent to do (Lk 4:43). While we can see no pattern of activity, no "model"

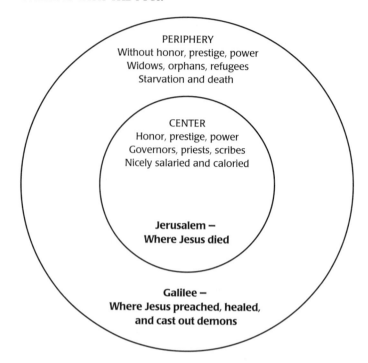

Figure 3–3: Center and periphery as the location of transformation.
(After Koyama 1985, 251–53)

for transformation, the gospel story is full of stories of preaching, teaching, healing, and casting out of demons—word, deed, and sign. Surely, Christian transformation should aspire to the same—word, deed, and sign. As for the kingdom, we will come back to this defining theme.

Jesus did not fulfill his mission alone

The triune God would not be expected to become an lonely individual savior. He chose twelve fairly ordinary people "to be with him" in order that he could send them to do what he had been doing—preaching, casting out demons, and healing the sick (Mk 3:13–15, 6:12). A company of women helped support him "out of their own means" (Lk 8:3). Transformation is the work of a community; it is not served well by lonely "cowboys." The gospel message is a way of living with Christ and each other that then enables the ministry of word, deed, and sign.

The greatest commandment

When asked what must be done to inherit eternal life, Jesus said that the greatest commandment was a twin affirmation: "Love God with all your heart and with all your soul and with all your strength and with all your mind and love your neighbor as yourself" (Mt 23:36). This is a commandment about relationships, not law and transgressions; about whom we must love, not simply what we must believe or do. This commandment must frame our approach to transformational development. It is both our motive for helping the poor and the point of departure for what a biblical understanding of transformation means: right and just relationships.

Jesus died alone on a cross

Outside the city gates, in the company of criminals, Jesus died on a cross, abandoned by everyone, even God. The physical pain of death was insignificant compared to the pain of being wholly alone. "My God, my God, why have you forsaken me?" (Mk 15:34). There is no greater loss, no greater pain for the three-in-one God than complete abandonment. This must shape our view of poverty. Poverty is about relationships that don't work, that isolate, that abandon or devalue. Transformation must be about restoring relationships, just and right relationships with God, with self, with community, with the "other," and with the environment.

The cross, Leupp tells us, is a great clarifier. The cross is the vantage point of the triune God—God's point of view. From its perspective, Jesus revealed "not tarnished human possibility, but divine forgiveness" (1996, 89). We are good, fallen, and redeemable, all at once. The downward spiral of the fall meets the radical possibility of redirection toward the kingdom in the cross and resurrection of Christ.

The cross clarified something else. On the cross, in addition to canceling our sin, Paul tells us that Christ disarmed the powers and authorities, making a public spectacle of them (Col 2:15). In Christ, we no longer have to accept the rule of oppressive structures or of deceiving and dominating social systems. Their transformation is also included in Christ's finished work. Wink says, "The final subjugation of the Powers under Christ's feet will happen (1 Cor 15:24–25), but it is already, in anticipation, experienced now (Eph 1:19–23) in the new reality of resurrection experience" (Wink 1992, 70). Like us, the powers are good, fallen, and redeemable all at the same time. Transformational development that does not declare the good news of the possibility of both personal and corporate liberation and redirection toward God is a truncated gospel, unworthy of the biblical text.

Finally, there is an important paradox in the cross. From the epistles we learn that Christ has the power "that enables him to bring everything under his control" (Phil 3:21) and that "God has placed all things under his feet" (Eph 1:22). Yet, Wink points out that this Jesus who subjects all things to himself also "did not consider equality with God something to be grasped" (Phil 2:6). Jesus emptied himself of all desire to dominate, and taking the form of a human, identified himself with the poor and suffered a criminal's death. "Subjection to such a ruler means the end of all subjugation. The rulership (of Christ) thus constituted is not a domination hierarchy but an enabling and actualizing hierarchy. It is not pyramidal, but organic, not imposed but restorative" (Wink 1992, 83). This non-coercive, upside-down turning, healing, releasing Christ has implications in terms of who must own the development process and how we must run our development institutions. More on this in Chapter 7.

Christ is risen

This is the transformation that begets all other transformations. Death to life. Something only God can do. Any work of human transformation that does not announce this incredibly good news is fatally impoverished. The cross and the resurrection are the very best news that we have.

The Jesus story does not end with an empty tomb outside the gates of Jerusalem, the center of power. Jesus, risen in power and glory, returns to the periphery, to Galilee. The center has nothing more to offer him. Also, Jesus is concrete again: "Touch me and see" (Lk 24:39). He eats in the presence of his disciples. He appears to them for forty days, speaking about the kingdom of God (Acts 1:3). His last reported instructions were to go, to make disciples, to baptize in the name of the triune God, and to "teach them to obey everything I have commanded you" (Mt 28:20). Teaching about the kingdom of God seems to be something important to the risen Jesus, and so it must be to those of us who follow him.

THE CONTINUING STORY

One of the many peculiar elements of the biblical story is that, after his resurrection, Jesus did not stay on earth to see his mission through, at least not in the way that anyone would have expected. After forty days of speaking about the kingdom of God, Jesus announced that the disciples would be his witnesses to the ends of the earth, once they received the power of the Holy Spirit (Acts 1:8). At Pentecost, the Holy Spirit reversed the story of Babel and those present heard them "declaring the wonders of God in our own tongues" (Acts 2:11). The biblical story was now a story for every language, for every person to hear in his or her mother tongue. The implications of this fact change history and make Christianity unique (Sanneh 1989).

The church

From the time Jesus ascended until now, you and I are the ongoing work of Christ in the world. In the form of the church we are his body, his hands, and his feet here on earth. Again this seems a strange choice: handing over the work of saving the world to people who, while redeemed, are yet flawed and struggling with sin. Yet, this is what Jesus chose to do. The church, the community of faith, is the bearer of the biblical story, the "cracked pot" that is to continue announcing the good news of the unchanging person and the unshakable kingdom until Christ comes again. At a deeper level the church is to be the body of Christ in the world living a life of sacrificial service as its way of bearing witness to its risen Lord. We bear this witness by word, deed, and sign. The witness of word means announcing the truth about God and humankind:

> The Church renders this service to human society by preaching the truth about the creation of the world, which God has placed in human hands so that people may make it fruitful and more perfect through their work; and by preaching the truth about the Redemption, whereby the Son of God has saved mankind and at the same time has united all people, making them responsible for one another. Sacred Scripture continually speaks to us of an active commitment to our neighbor and demands of us a shared responsibility for all of humanity. (CA, no. 51)

In understanding the nature of the church in the world we must again think in trinitarian terms. E. Stanley Jones helps us a great deal by describing the church in relationship to the triune God. Jones argues that the kingdom is the Father's, that Jesus is the embodiment of God's kingdom, and that the Holy Spirit is the first fruit of God's kingdom on earth, the assurance that there is more to come, and the one who helps us discover the truth and fullness of the kingdom. When it is at its best, the church is the sign, a witness, to the kingdom of God breaking into the world (see Figure 3–4).

This has two important things to say to development workers. First, God brings the kingdom; it is neither our task nor that of our transformational development. We must not put the weight of building the kingdom on our shoulders; we cannot carry it, nor are we expected to. Second, the sign of the kingdom is the church, the community of faith, not the development worker or the development agency. Somehow development workers must understand themselves as part of the church, not just an NGO or some "para-church" organization vaguely or disinterestedly related to the church. Development workers as Christians need to embrace the fact that their local community of faith is the local church wherever they work among the poor. Their work of transformational development needs to be seen as the sign of that church and not as some beacon of personal piety.

The body of Christ is a community. This seems obvious enough, but sometimes we forget it. If our life with Christ is our first call (Mk 3:14), then our church is our family in which this life is nurtured and our Christian

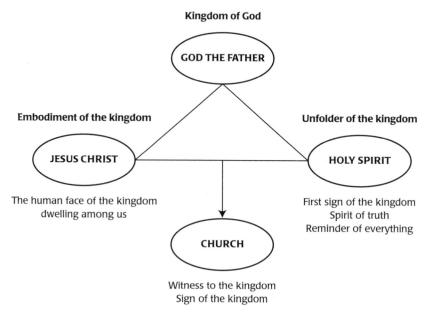

Figure 3–4: The triune God and the church.
(After Jones 1972, 26–29)

character is formed. Our worship and our experience of the sacraments are the practices that prepare us to fulfill our call to take the whole message of Jesus and the kingdom of God into the world. The church is also our hermeneutical community in two ways. First, it is a community of and around the word of God and of and around our fellow believers. Believers are to study and interpret the scriptures, doing so within the community as a correction against error. Every Christian community has the responsibility to read the biblical story in light of its own story for the purpose of shaping its vision of mission and repenting of its errors. Where else does the vision of human transformation come from? Second, the church is a hermeneutical community of believers who live life together with God and one another. Within this hermeneutical community we discover more about who God is and who we are. It is in the life of this hermeneutical community that we uncover how we are both gifted and flawed. Where else will development practitioners, who are whole and holy, come from?

Many in the development business, particularly internationally, have deeply ambiguous feelings about this church of which we are a part. David Bosch reminds us that "the church is both a theological and a sociological entity, an inseparable union of the divine and the dusty." He continues with an eloquent description of our contradictory feelings about the church:

> We can be utterly disgusted, at times, with the earthliness of the church, yet we can also be transformed, at times, with the awareness of the

divine in the church. It is *this* church, ambiguous in the extreme, which is "missionary by its very nature," the pilgrim people of God, "in the nature of" a sacrament, sign, and instrument, and "a most sure seed of unity, hope and salvation for the whole human race." (Bosch 1991, 389)

We must remember that the church, while it is to be sign of the kingdom, is not the kingdom itself. The kingdom judges and redeems the church. The church is successful in being a sign to the extent that the Spirit makes it so. The church is a true sign only to the degree that it lives up to the spirit and life of the kingdom. "The church is not the end of mission, the kingdom is the end" (Jones 1972, 35).

This has two implications for the development worker. First, it is a counter-balance to the earlier claim I made that the church is to be the sign of the kingdom, not the development worker. While true, the church is as fallible as we are and sometimes fails to be this sign. Our greatest pain comes when we wish our work to be part of the sign of the kingdom, expressed through the local church, and yet find ourselves engaged with a church that is unwilling or unable to be this sign with us. Such is the ambiguity of being in development work, especially if one works for a Christian NGO or so-called para-church organization.

Second, this means that church planting cannot be the final objective of mission, only the beginning. A church full of life and love, working for the good of the community in which God has placed it, is the proper end of mission. Transformational development that does not work toward such a church is neither sustainable nor Christian.

The church represents a special challenge to many involved in Christian development, since much of the work in the last quarter-century has been done by the so-called para-church agencies. Made up of Christians, these agencies go directly to Christians in the pews to solicit funds and then directly to poor communities to help the poor. The local church on both ends is too frequently ignored, or worse, seen as part of the problem. This is a seriously flawed view. I will address the role of the local church in the chapter on transformational development.

To summarize, the church is the bearer of the biblical story because it is Christ's body in the world. As Christians, we are part of this body, and that's the way it is. With all our warts and pimples, witnessing about Christ and doing his work within the context of the church is our mission. Fortunately, to carry out our role as the body of Christ in the world, the church has some additional help. We have been given a person and a book.

The Holy Spirit

The Holy Spirit is the third person of the Trinity. The Holy Spirit is the expression of God who accompanies the church on its fallible journey of witnessing to Christ and the kingdom. God's Spirit of truth reminds us of everything Jesus taught us (Jn 14:16, 26) and unfolds the meaning of the kingdom to us (Jones 1972, 38). The Holy Spirit is the actor of mission, the one who convicts the world, including the prince of this world, of its sin (Jn 16:8–10).

The Holy Spirit is the source of power (Lk 24:49) that transformed a fairly ordinary group of disciples, who had abandoned their Lord, into a fearless group of witnesses who would not surrender their mission even under threat of death (Acts 4:19). This Spirit is the source of our mission: "The same Spirit in whose power Jesus went to Galilee also thrusts the disciples into mission" (Bosch 1991, 113). The Holy Spirit initiates mission (Acts 13:2), guides mission (Acts 8:28, 16:9), and creates the response to mission (Acts 16:14). The signs and wonders of the Holy Spirit demonstrate the power of God in a way that demands an explanation so that credit is given to whom credit is due (Acts 14:8–18). Any transformational development that is not guided, empowered, and made effective by the Holy Spirit will not prove sustainable (see McAlpine 1995). Furthermore, expecting and praying for supernatural interventions by the Spirit must be part of the spirituality of Christian development workers.

The Bible

We were also given a book, the Bible. This book is the received story of what the author of the story has done, is doing, and plans to do. In this living word we have the whole story that makes sense of our stories. This book tells the only story that answers the questions that really matter: Who am I? Whose am I? Where am I? What's wrong? How can it be changed? What time is it?

We are to be the living illustrations of the truth of this story. Newbigin says, "We live in the biblical story as part of the community whose story it is, find in the story the clues to knowing God as his character becomes manifest in the story, and from within that indwelling try to understand and cope with the events of our time and the world about us and so carry the story forward" (1989, 99).

We also received the story in another way. The story of the church is the story of how the biblical story has been lived out in the two thousand years since Christ created his church and set it on its mission. The history of the church—its thinking and its actions in the world—is the lived-out story that we inherit. The flaws and failings we see in this history should remind us how fallible we are, create in us a deep-seated suspicion of our own righteousness, and lead us to humility. At the same time, this story of Christ's body also reveals many who have tried to live out God's story by caring for the poor and working to transform society. We need to know that, with all its imperfections, the church has been in the transformational development business since its beginning.

We must also take note of the fact that the Bible is more than a book. It is the living word of God, "sharper than any double-edged sword, it penetrates even to dividing soul and spirit, . . . judges the thoughts and attitudes of the heart. Nothing in all creation is hidden from God's sight" (Heb 4:12–13). The Bible is unique among books; it is "the only book that reads me" (Weber 1995, ix). Because it is the living word of the living God, it always has something to say to every situation, and it always has more to say than we can ever know.

For too long evangelicals have treated the Bible as a book for the spiritual world and have failed to give it the freedom to inform the material world of everyday life and everyday "non-spiritual" decisions (see Figure 1–2). One of the challenges of Christian holism in development will be to release the Bible and the biblical narrative to speak to all phases of the process of human transformation. One of the best gifts that we have for the poor and the non-poor is the living word of God. We need to share it with them and let the living word speak for itself. More about this in the chapter on Christian witness.

THE END OF THE STORY

The end of the biblical story is the end of history. John tells us that Jesus will come again in power and glory. This leads to the judgment of judgments, the one and true judgment, the one that ends in the eternal destruction of the Evil One and of those whose names are not written in the book of life (Rv 20:15). Then the first earth and first heaven pass away and a new earth and new heaven, in the form of the new Jerusalem, descend from heaven. The story that began in a garden ends in a city.

Once again the dwelling place of God is with men and women (Rv 21:3). There are no more tears, or death, or crying, or pain, nor is there famine or drought (Rv 7:16, 21:4). Everything is made new—the people and their city. There is no church in this new Jerusalem because it is no longer needed; God and the Lamb live among the people (Rv 21:22). The mission of the church as a "history-making force" (Newbigin 1989, 129) is completed. The unshakable kingdom of God stands alone at the end of time. It is the final reality; all other kingdoms have passed away.

The nations now walk by the light of the glory of God shone forth by the Son. The honor and glory of the nations, all their "artistic, cultural, political, scientific and spiritual contributions" (Wink 1992, 83), transformed and no longer a seduction away from the worship of God, are brought into the city (Rv 21:24, 26). The gates never shut.

The measures of value are turned upside down. Gold, the most valuable commodity in this world, the commodity that drives greed and violence, is so common that it is used to pave the streets. The foundations of the city are made with precious stones (Rv 21:20–21), because we have a new understanding of what is valuable. These gemstones are simply beautiful, no longer objects of greed in the eyes of fallen humankind.

Finally and most important, this new Jerusalem is a city of life, of life in all its fullness (Rv 22:13). The earth itself is redeemed and once again produces the fruit and the healing that human beings and their nations need. Our true vocation is once more within our grasp as "his servants will serve him" (Rv 22:3).

It is important for those concerned for human transformation to keep the end of the story in mind. This is where the triune God is going. This is how God's project will end. This is the best human future. Human well-being or flourishing are no longer aspirations; they just are. While this triumphant vision should guide us, it should also instill a sense of awe and humility in us. This end comes only at great cost, since Christ died and the saints suffered. There is a cross on the way to this triumphal end.

THE POINT OF THE STORY

By now, the point of the story should be clear. From the day our first parents walked out of the garden, estranged from God, each other, and the earth itself, God has been at work redeeming and reconciling the fallen creation, its people, and its social systems. God's goal is to restore us and God's creation to our original identity and purpose, as children reflecting God's image, and to our original vocation as productive stewards, living together in just and peaceful relationships.

This restoration project requires hard work, very costly work; work that could only have been motivated by the most profound, self-giving love. "The center of the New Testament lies in the narrative of the death and resurrection of Jesus Christ understood as an act of obedience toward God and an expression of self-giving love for his followers as well as a model for his followers to imitate" (Volf 1996, 30).

The goal of the biblical story, then, is the reconciliation and redemption of all things, on earth and in heaven (Col 1:19) with Christ as the head (Eph 1:10). Relationships are restored in all the dimensions distorted by sin. "The gospel is the news that distorted patterns of power have been broken; the reception of the gospel is the embrace of radically transformed patterns of social relationships" (Brueggemann 1993a, 34). This is the story into which every human being has been invited by God to be a participant. This goal must inform our understanding of transformational development.

THEOLOGICAL SUMMARY

Who are we?

This seems a simple question. Sometimes we move too quickly past it, assuming everyone knows the answer. We need to pause a moment and be sure that the Western understanding of the autonomous, self-directed individual has not distorted our Christian understanding of who we really are.

We are human beings made in the image of God. We all know this. What we forget sometimes is that the God in whose image we are made is the three-in-one God, the God who is communion, the relational God. This means that our individual self can never be itself apart from our being-in-communion with God and with other human beings. The trinitarian nature of God means that we are self-in-community when we are fully human. Our human selves are embedded in relationships, finding their fullest meaning in just and harmonious relationships or losing meaning and worth when these relationships do not work. This view of the human being is radically contrary to that of modern times, at least in the West.

This trinitarian view of the self does not mean that the self is submerged in the group. As Leupp clarifies, "Egocentricity is different from ego awareness" (1996, 100). Every person is unique and should be aware of his or her uniqueness, just as the Father, Son, and Holy Spirit are aware of their respective uniqueness. This uniqueness, however, does not lead to egocentricity but rather finds full expression in self-giving love. "The triune premise is that love is completed when it is invested in the other. Love that is given away does not impoverish, but enriches and perfects the giver" (ibid., 101). Thus the thrust for mission—for loving God and loving neighbor—is found first in God and then in us because we are made in his triune image.

This has practical implications. As Christians, we can no longer simply view the world as a collection of individuals. Instead, we need to view each individual is an encumbered self, embedded in families and communities as well as being participants in the whole gamut of social institutions—economic, political, cultural, and religious. All of this is what it means to be human, to be made in the image of God.

This view of the self is also helpful in terms of what the self is not. While no one can deny the importance of an assured and centered self, a trinitarian view of self will not validate metaphors like the lonesome, self-contained, "I don't need help from nobody" cowboy; the entertainer who "does it my way"; or the entrepreneur who gambles with shareholder's resources without regard for the people who work in his or her company and contribute to the value of the company. Self-actualization in any form will not create the full human self of the Bible.

Finally, just as we cannot understand who God is without reference to what God is doing, the same applies to human beings. We are made in the image of a God who is and who is acting. Thus, we must be who we are—bearers of the image of a relational God—and do what we were made by God to do—be fruitful and creative in self-giving relationships.

To be true to our identity as Christians, we must be in Christ and be doing mission, loving God, and loving our neighbor. We are not who we truly are unless we are doing both.

One final observation as to who we are. Human beings are located in a concrete place and at a particular point in time. We are material as well as spiritual. Our self breathes, eats, laughs, and walks through the bush. We are located in God's creation and are sustained by it. We are not disembodied ideas, thoughts, or spirits. We do not float above history or time. Our story and nature's story are inseparable.

What are we to be and do?

We are first of all to be with Christ. Being is the beginning. We cannot do what we are not. Furthermore, life in Christ means life in his Body; we are with Christ when we are in his church. As Christians, the church is our community because our being is being-in-community. There is no transformational development apart from people who themselves are being transformed and who live in the community that is the home of their transformation.

We are then to live the life that God gave us through Christ. We are to live the biblical story. We are to live from and for God, from and for others; we are to live a life of being, thinking, and doing. We do transformational development because this is what the biblical story tells us that God is doing.

> Living the trinitarian faith means living as Jesus Christ lived: preaching the gospel; relying totally on God; offering healing and reconciliation; rejecting laws, customs and conventions that place persons beneath rules; resisting temptation; praying constantly; eating with modern day lepers and other outcasts; embracing the enemy and the sinner; dying for the sake of the gospel if it is God's will. (LaCugna 1991, 401)

We are to do transformation in the Spirit since the mission is God's. The Holy Spirit empowers us for mission, leads us into mission, and is responsible for the results of mission. If there is to be any human transformation that is sustainable, it will be because of the action of the Holy Spirit, not the effectiveness of our development technology or the cleverness of our participatory processes (see Chapter 6). Because our role is to be faithful and obedient, in contrast to being successful, we must modify our ambitions and redirect our praise.

The chief actor in the historic mission of the Christian church is the Holy Spirit. He is the director of the whole enterprise. The mission consists of the things that he is doing in the world. (Taylor 1972, 3)

We are to embrace the "other," and this must include the non-poor as well as the poor. This is the heart of the gospel and the beginning of transformation. The open arms of the father embracing the son, who had made himself wholly other, and the healing embrace of the Jew by the Samaritan are the images that must shape our mission of transformation to the poor and non-poor alike. God has no enemies whom he does not love, and hence neither can we. The embrace is the necessary first step toward reconciliation and justice (Volf 1996, 29).

We must fulfill our mission by accepting the paradoxical location of every Christian (Walls 1996, 53). The gospel is infinitely translatable, available to everyone in every language. Therefore, as bearers of the gospel story, the Christian agent of transformation can and should be thoroughly local, at home everywhere, just as the gospel is. At the same time, however, the kingdom is not yet fully here and will not be until the second coming of Christ. Thus, we are also pilgrims, at home nowhere, because our real home is the transcendent Christian community moving toward a kingdom not yet here. This means we are in the world and not of it. This also means that we accept people where they are without judgment, while also knowing that the Spirit of God celebrates the good, unmasks the evil, and calls for the most fundamental change in everyone.

We are to see the world as created, fallen, and being redeemed, all at the same time. We must not separate creation and fall from redemption. As a story, the parts are inseparable, each giving meaning to the other. Wink reminds us,

God at one and the same time *upholds* a given political or economic system, since some such system is required to support human life; *condemns* that system insofar as it is destructive to full human actualization; and *presses for its transformation* into a more human order. Conservatives stress the first, revolutionaries the second, reformers the third. The Christian is expected to hold together all three. (1992, 67)

Our practice of transformational development must be informed by these three lenses for making sense of the human story. Understanding creation helps us understand what was meant to be. Understanding the fall helps us recognize what is working against life in poor communities and why. Understanding the redemption story helps us know what can be and who and what can help us get there.

Important theological themes

There are five theological ideas that seem useful for Christians working for transformational development: creation, incarnation, redemption, kingdom of God, and power.

Creation theology

We always need to begin where God began. A fully developed doctrine of creation is foundational to our thinking about human flourishing. We need to be clear on who human beings really are and why they are here. We need to remember that it is creation itself that supports human life and well-being with its air, water, trees, fruits, animals. God's creation declares the glory of God and inspires our understanding of beauty, poetry, and song. A substantial part of our ability to worship and celebrate has roots in the wonderful, beautiful, and sustaining world that God made for us.

We need to understand that creation is not just a stage on which God has us acting out the human story, with the stage being irrelevant at the end of time. Christ came to a real place on earth and walked its dusty roads for over thirty years. We need to remember that God's creation itself is good and is to be redeemed and restored. Creation is not a stage, but a living home.

Incarnation

One of the most incredible parts of this biblical account is the idea that the triune God would stoop to becoming flesh and dwell among us (Jn 1:14). For many inside and outside the faith, this is a stumbling block of major proportions. The incarnation is a powerful theological metaphor for those who practice transformational development for several reasons.

First, the incarnation is the best evidence we have for how seriously God takes the material world. The incarnation destroys any argument that God is only concerned for the spiritual realm and that the material is somehow evil or unworthy of the church's attention. God became concrete and real. It was possible to hear God's voice at the baptism of Jesus and touch Christ's wounds after the resurrection. Real people were healed; a dead man lived again.

This suggests that doing transformational development is a part of what God does. We are only following after God. This is the bottom line of the biblical story. This is why "Christians cannot, indeed they must not, simply believe the gospel; they must practice it so that by God's grace they might embody its reality—what the Christian scripture calls the down payment of God's future glory" (Dyrness 1997, 3). To declare that the mission of the church is solely about spiritual things ignores the incarnation.

Second, the incarnation provides a highly instructive model for how we must be willing to practice transformational development. God emptied himself of God's prerogatives. Are we willing to empty ourselves of ours? Jesus did not come as a all-knowing, problem-solving Christ. Jesus is not the quick-answer god Koyama warned us against (1985, 241). In the form of a man, Jesus was the God who was not able to save himself, and so he is able to save others. There are lessons here for development professionals who arrive with their check book in their pocket, their head full of technical skills and their abiding confidence that they bring "good news" for the poor. Any practice of transformational development must be framed by the cross and the broken Christ.

Finally, we must always remember that Jesus chose freely to empty himself of his prerogatives as God, making God's self nothing (Phil 2:7), so that every tongue might confess that "Jesus Christ is Lord" (Phil 2:11). The entire purpose of the exercise was to invite people to redirect their lives and to provide the means by which they might do so. Transformational development must have the same end in mind.

Redemption

The point of the biblical story is to redeem and thus redirect the trajectory of the human story after the fall. This was made possible by the finished work of Jesus Christ. We need to remember, however, that this act took place in the concrete world of Israel, at a particular point in real human history with the real death of a real man. Redemption is material as well as spiritual. Both our bodies and our souls are redeemed. The new heaven comes down to earth. The glory of all nations will enter the city at the end of the day, our cultures, our science, our poetry, our art, even our transformational development—all are redeemed and part of the end of the story.

For this reason we must remind ourselves constantly that the work of transformational development is part of God's redemptive work (Bradshaw 1993, 43). Don't misunderstand me. Transformational development, by itself, will not save. The charitable and transforming acts of Christians will never mediate salvation. But, having said this, it is also wrong to act as if God's redemptive work takes place only inside one's spirit or in heaven in the sweet by-and-by. This disembodied, wholly spiritualized view of redemption is not biblical. God is working to redeem and restore the whole of creation, human beings, all living things, and the creation itself. "For the creation was subjected to frustration, not by its own choice, but by the will of the one who subjected it, in hope that creation itself will be liberated from its bondage to decay and brought into the glorious freedom of the children of God" (Rom 8:20–21). It is in this sense that transformational development is part of God's redemptive work in the world.

Finally, because God is working out God's redemptive purposes in spiritual, physical, and social realms, this also means that we are God's agents of redemption, however flawed and unsatisfactory we may be in this incredible role. When we work for transformational development, we are working as God's hands and feet.

The kingdom of God

We need to spend a moment on the issue of Jesus and the kingdom of God. The kingdom of God is something Jesus talked about a great deal. Between 1920 and the 1980s, evangelicals could not talk about the kingdom of God as it was a theme associated with "being liberal" and the ecumenical movement, and it was thus an object of some suspicion. This was unfortunate, unhelpful, and not very biblical. After all, the kingdom of God was the subject of Christ's first sermon (Mk 1:14), was the only thing Christ called the gospel (Mt 4:23), and was the topic on which he focused his teaching to the disciples during his last forty days on earth (Acts 1:3). Jesus said that the kingdom is the key to understanding his teaching (Lk 8:10). In the Sermon on the Mount, Jesus said that the kingdom of God was the first thing we should seek and that everything else will follow (Mt 6:33). The coming of God's kingdom is the first petition in the prayer Jesus taught us to pray (Mt 6:10). Luke closes the book of Acts by telling us that Paul "boldly and without hindrance preached the kingdom of God and taught about the Lord Jesus Christ" (Acts 28:31). Jesus even said that "the gospel of the kingdom will be preached to the whole world as a testimony to all nations, and then the end will come" (Mt 24:14). The kingdom of God is an important idea for those who work for human transformation.

When we think about the kingdom of God, we have to be careful with our understanding of timing. The kingdom of God arrived on earth with the coming of Christ and was inaugurated with Christ's death and resurrection and the coming of the Holy Spirit. But the coming of the kingdom of God in its fullness awaits the second coming of Christ at the end of history. So the kingdom of God both is, and is coming. For the development worker, this is a relief. We are not the bringers of the kingdom of God, only witnesses to its arrival.

Recalling the importance of the interrelationship of people and the social systems within which they live, E. Stanley Jones, long-time missionary to India, makes an important contribution to kingdom theology when he presents the biblical metaphors of the "unshakable kingdom" and the "unchanging person" (Jones 1972). The kingdom of God is unshakable (Heb 12:28) because it is the true and ultimate reality, the way things really are. Christ is the unchanging person (Heb 13:8), the reality of the kingdom in human form, the only way to enter God's kingdom.

The kingdom of God, Jones says, is both radical and conservative at the same time. It is radical in that no one or anything is beyond the claim of God's kingdom. It is conservative in the sense that it "gathers up everything that is good (God's good creation peeking through the results of the fall) and fulfills the good, cleanses the evil, and goes beyond anything ever thought of or dreamed anywhere. This is the desire of the ages—if men only knew it" (1972, 27). Jones continues, the kingdom of God simply "is and you must come to terms with it" (ibid., 46).

Jones also rejects the reduction that limits the gospel to the individual alone. People and social systems are interrelated. While people create the political, religious, and economic institutions of their society, at the same time these institutions shape (create) the people who live in them. The impact of sin, and hence the scope of the gospel, includes both the personal and the social (see Figure 3–5).

If we reduce the gospel solely to naming the name of Christ, persons are saved but the social order is ignored. This is a "crippled Christianity with a crippled result" (Jones 1972, 30). If we act as if individuals are saved now and the kingdom is only in heaven when Jesus comes, then we in effect leave the social order to the devil. "Vast areas of human life are left out, unredeemed—the economic, the social and the political" (ibid., 31). Into this vacuum other ideologies and kingdoms move with their seductive and deceptive claims of a new humanity and a better tomorrow—socialism, capitalism, globalisms, nationalism, ethnic identity, and denominationalism—shakable kingdoms all.

Therefore, the scope of the gospel of the unshakable kingdom and the unchanging person is the individual, families, the social systems in which

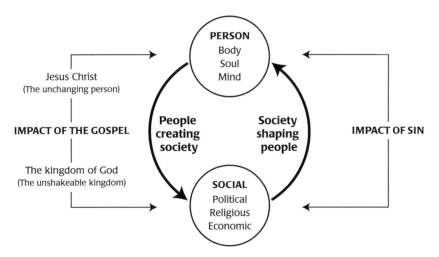

Figure 3–5: The inseparability of the person and the social order.
(After Jones 1972, 32–35)

we live, and the earth upon which we depend for life. Jones's argument anticipates Wink's work on the principalities and powers to a remarkable degree. The impact of the fall is on both the individual and the social system, and so the impact of the gospel of the kingdom must be on both. Wink makes this provocative claim, "The gospel is not [just] a message of personal salvation from the world, but a message of *a world transfigured, right down to its basic structures*" (Wink 1992, 83). Even the creation itself has "been groaning as in the pains of childbirth" waiting "in eager expectations for the sons of God to be revealed" (Rom 8:22, 19). To work for human transformation as a Christian means working for the redemption of people, their social systems, and the environment that sustains their life—a whole gospel for all of life. This is the kingdom of God.

We must never separate the person and the kingdom, Jones warns us (1972, 37). Jesus, the unchanging person, is the embodiment of God's kingdom. The best news is that God's kingdom is not just a theological phrase or an ethereal idea, but "is now a name with a human face" (Newbigin 1981, 32–33). Better yet, this person came and dwelt among us, "tempted in every way just as we are" (Heb 4:15). The kingdom of God has indeed drawn near in the form of the unchanging person: "Jesus is the kingdom of God taking sandals and walking" (Jones 1972, 34). Any Christian understanding of transformational development must keep the person of Jesus and the claims and promise of the kingdom central to the defining of what better future we are working for and for choosing the means of getting there.

Power

Power is a subject that no development practitioner can ignore. On the one hand, much of what contributes to people being poor has it roots in asymmetries of power and a resulting misuse of power among individuals, groups, and social systems. Addressing and coping with asymmetries of power and the abuse of power are unavoidable in development, if transformation is the goal. This is not just an issue for systems and structures of power external to the community. These kinds of power relations exist in the community and within each household (Friedmann 1992, 32). Furthermore, every development practitioner enters a poor community from a position of power, particularly in the eyes of those we come to serve. Therefore, some theological reflection on power is in order.

We need to begin, however, with an observation about asymmetries of power. Sometimes we in the modern West assume that asymmetrical power is a bad thing and that seeking to abolish such asymmetries is the ideal. Some Christian folk seem to think that powerlessness is the Christian norm. My reading of the creation account suggests we may need to think a little more about this.

Simply put, the created order does not appear to be equal everywhere. While we are all made in the image of God, everything else about us and our particular context seems to reflect an unequal distribution of gifts, talents, and resources. Furthermore, it is not at all clear that this is not God's intention. Jeffrey Sachs has called our attention to list of geographical inequalities. Some countries are landlocked and thus harder to connect with the world. Some countries have arid climates and thin soils, resulting in low agricultural productivity. Other countries are located in tropical settings that seem ideally suited for tropical diseases that do not create development issues for the cooler Northern climes (2005, 58). Jared Diamond, a bio-geographer, has observed that out of all the animals God made, only fourteen were susceptible to human domestication, and these fourteen were not equally distributed around the world (1997, 160). Diamond has concluded that "history followed different courses for different peoples because of differences among peoples' environments, not because of biological differences among peoples themselves" (ibid., 25). Apparently not all contexts are equal. But there are other inherent inequalities in God's creation.

We all know that some people are smarter or stronger or more relational than others. Not all of us have the gift of leadership. Only a few are called and equipped for a life of the mind. Not everyone has the skills and mental gifts necessary to build a home or an artificial knee. James Davison Hunter, a professor of religion, culture, and social theory at the University of Virginia, asserts that "this means that human relations are inherently power relations," and he further argues that this is a good thing (Hunter 2010, 178). Rather than being a problem per se, this unequal distribution of gifts and skills creates the imperative for interdependence.

> Human beings have differing capacities to act in the world and to influence the environment around them. It is for this reason that interdependency is built into human experience. We need each other and the abilities and talents everyone brings to make survival possible. (Hunter 2010, 178)

This suggests that the central concern for mission must not be trying to create or undo inherent or natural asymmetries of power. Asymmetries of power and structures of power just are, and they are not necessarily a bad thing. This leads to two additional important clarifications.

First, structural power in particular is simply unavoidable. A world of six billion human beings needs a wide variety of social structures in order to organize life, survive, and flourish, and social structures mean structures and positions of power. Presidents, members of parliament, heads of ministries, business leaders, chairs of community-development organizations, and coordinators of advocacy coalitions seem both natural and needed. We cannot avoid surrendering power to others, to people who can do things we need done or that we cannot do for ourselves. Some folks will necessarily have power relative to some of the rest of us. The real missiological issue is not "power over" but whether or not the exercise of power over us enhances or diminishes our well-being.

Second, we must avoid uncritically demonizing social structures and their power. While social structures can impoverish and oppress, they can also empower and care for people in ways that allow people to flourish. Voting in a transparent and honest election empowers. Having a voice at a village meeting with local government officials is empowering. Protection against criminals and having courts that work fairly and protect property rights are empowering too.

Thus, development concerns managing power relations for human well-being, not trying to make power relations go away. With this adjustment in perspective, let's look at the first and last stories of the Bible and think about power relations and social structures.

In his examination of the creation account Richard Middleton calls our attention to the intriguing fact that the understanding of the relationship between God and human beings in the creation account stands in stark contrast to that of the other religions and empires in the Near East at the time the Genesis account was written (2005, 204–12). In those settings the king was the only person made in the image of a god, and the king's purpose was to serve (worship) the gods. This starting point legitimated the king's exercise of power over all other human beings. Such power is exercised from above, while service, worship, and wealth flow up from the people. This leads to the conclusion that oppressive, one-way religious-political-economic systems of power are normative, ordained by the gods.

In the biblical creation account the relationship between God and humankind is fundamentally different. God makes all human beings in God's image; there is no mention of a king (this comes later). Carrying God's image empowers all human beings to be able to do the kind of productive and creative work in creation that God wants done. Thus all human beings have power. As Richard Middleton puts it, "The *imago Dei* designates the royal calling of human beings as God's representatives and agents in the world, granted authorized power to share in God's rule or administration of the earth's resources and creatures" (2005, 27). The creation account diverges from the understanding of creation and power of the surrounding Near Eastern cultures in that "there is no mandate for one human being to oppress another" (ibid., 204–5).

In the last book of the Bible, understanding the historical-cultural context of the church at the time is a key to understanding John's revelation. Richard Bauckham, professor of New Testament at the University of St. Andrews, reminds us that "Revelation portrays the Roman Empire as a system of violent oppression, founded on conquest and maintained by violence and oppression" (1993, 35). Summarizing Bauckham, the emperor was considered to be God, and Rome was called the Eternal City, the center of an empire of power. Revelation then speaks of two major symbols for Rome, representing different aspects of the empire. The beast of the sea (Rev 13—17) represents the military and political power of Rome and the emperor. In Revelation 17—18 we are introduced to Babylon, the harlot who rides the beast (Rev 17:3), to remind us that the imperial economic system of exploitation relies on the coercion of imperial armies. Revelation then speaks of those through whom the beast and the harlot work their power, coercion, and seduction. The beast of the sea works through the "kings of the earth" (Rev 17:2), who have committed adultery with the harlot (Rev 17:2, 18:9), who has also seduced the "merchants of the earth," who mourn her passing because no one buys their goods anymore (Rev 18:11).

This is the context against which Revelation announces the good news that, upon the return of the Lord of history, all of this apparently irresistible power is in fact shown to be powerless as history ends. Jayakumar Christian, a development practitioner and colleague in India, has also explored the reversal of power in Revelation (1994, 11–12). He points out that the lamb of God that was slain is the one worthy to open the scroll. The lamb, convicted by Pilate and sentenced to death as a criminal, sits on the only throne that matters at the end of time. The slain lamb, not the British lion, the Indian tiger, or the American eagle, is the symbol of power when history ends. The kingdom of the broken and humiliated Christ is the only kingdom standing at the end of time.

It does not require much of a leap of the imagination to get from the historical-cultural contexts of the oppressive systems addressed by Middleton and Bauckham to those of today's world. Not much has changed, it seems. The misuse of power and the price paid by the powerless seem to be an immutable part of human history. But the first and last stories of Scripture suggest that Christians may not accept this fatalistic view. Our mission calls for more than just an announcement that sin and evil is at work in the social structures of this world. We have power—by virtue of being made in the image of God—and thus are empowered as human agents by God and by virtue of having been adopted into the only kingdom that stands the test of time. The question is how we will use the power we have.

We need a theology of power that helps us understand power and how power is intended to be used from a Christian perspective. There really are two questions here. First, how should we respond to oppression, the misuse of power, especially as it affects the least of these? How should Christians respond in the face of oppressive systems? The work of Middleton, Bauckham, Wink, Yoder, and many others suggests that we are to confront the powers and the powerful. Critique of and resistance to such power is a Christian witness. God wishes that those exercising power would also hear and respond to the gospel of the kingdom. Wink reminds us that "the goal is not only our becoming free from the powers, however, but freeing the Powers; not only reconciling people to God despite the Powers, but reconciling the powers to God (Col 1:20)" (Wink 1992, 319). I will pick this theme up later when I deal with marred identity and how to understand the dynamics of oppression in Chapter 4.

The second question has to do how we should we think about power as Christians and understand the power we have as individuals and as a church. Said another way, what kind of theology of power should we derive from our theological reflections thus far? A couple of things come to mind.

First, our power to name, organize, create, and make productive as creative human agents comes from God; it is not something we create for ourselves. Thus, our power is not really ours other than as a gift. This has several implications. First, this power is given to us in the context of a creative act of a God who loves and, in particular, loves us. Our power as human agents is the product of an act of generosity on God's part (Middleton 2005, 278). Second, this power is given to us in the context of a moral order; it has limits and constraints imposed by God. We may not use power any way we wish.

In the case of social power, whether in its political, economic, cultural, or religious form, its purpose in creation is to order, sustain, and improve creation so that creation supports the well-being of all human beings. The creation account does not support making things better for just the powerful; that is how the world uses power. This is an important perspective. While social power is an essential element to organizing large societies, social power is intended by God as a means, not an end. The test of the use of social power is made clear in Psalm 72 in its prayer to God for a certain kind of king:

> Endow the king with your justice, O God,
> the royal son with your righteousness.
>
> May he judge your people in righteousness,
> your afflicted ones with justice.
>
> May the mountains bring prosperity to the people,
> the hills the fruit of righteousness.
>
> May he defend the afflicted among the people
> and save the children of the needy;
> may he crush the oppressor.

This are the measures of the degree to which a leader is being faithful to what God requires of the use of social power: righteousness, prosperity, and justice, which work together with the result that the most vulnerable are saved and those who abuse their social power are judged harshly. Psalm 82 echoes a similar set of measures of faithful exercise of social power as

God judges the "gods" or powers on the basis of what they have done: Did you defend the weak, uphold the cause of the poor and oppressed, and rescue the weak? The powers and powerful, who instead "defend the unjust," are found to know nothing, understand nothing, and walk around in darkness undermining the foundations of the world (Ps 82: 5).

In light of this understanding of the use of power, so radically different from that of the world itself, James Davison Hunter addresses the church: "The question for the church, then, is not about choosing between power and powerlessness, but rather, to the extent that it has space to do so, how will the church and its people use the power they have" (2010, 184). Searching for a way to answer his question, Hunter makes a proposal for what he calls the social power of the kingdom on which the church can draw. He draws his description of this relational power from the actions of Jesus in the gospels. Hunter makes four observations about how Jesus had power and used it. To summarize Hunter's comments:

- The social power of Jesus is derived from Christ's complete intimacy with and submission to his Father. (Jn 12:49–50; 8:28; 14:10; Heb 5:7–8; Mt 28:18)
- Jesus' understanding of the Father's power rejects the status and reputation, and the privilege that accompanies power. (Phil 2:6; Jn 13:3)
- Jesus' power is derived from compassion or love that reflects Christ's kingdom more than anything else—this is the source, means and end of Christ's power. (Mk 10:45)
- The exercise of power by Jesus was non-coercive—respecting of human liberty—in relation to those who are outside the community of faith. (see Hunter 2010, 187ff.)

This is an attractive synthesis of spirituality, humility, and love that should infuse actions of charity and justice. These are things the church can do without money or power or even with them. These are things we need no permission to do. And in the world in which the poor live, these very counter-cultural things unmask the difference between the gospel and the world. These are not the traditional activities associated with power seeking power as an end. They are the tools of those who plan to give themselves away and by so doing unmask the powers and the powerful and the idolatries they follow.

In the coming kingdom of God, what we believe to be the natural order of things is reversed (Kraybill 1978). This certainly applies to those for whom power is an end to be hoarded or increased. We were told by Jesus that this kingdom is peopled by those we think of today as powerless: the poor (Lk 6:20), the meek, and the persecuted (Mt 5:5,10). Finally, all expressions of human power, every tribe and language and people and nation, will stand in front of the lamb and acknowledge who he is and what he has done (Rv 7:9–10). So if this is the way things are at the end of history, we'd best get with God's program and act accordingly.

This understanding of power needs to inform our development work. Getting this right allows the people with whom we work to discover the power they were always intended to have and protects us as development workers from misusing our power in the name of trying to help the powerless.

But, like the cross and the kingdom, this weak and meek understanding of social power poses some hard questions for those who wish to enable transformational development. Where is the power that can help the poor? In whom or in what do we trust? What does the image of the slain lamb have to say to the development practitioner in the time before the second coming of Christ? Even more provocatively, what does this mean to the development agency? Are we willing to pay the price of being a "weak" social power in a world in which "hard" social power is the norm? Should the poor be expected to pay that price? Are we asking the poor to practice a form of social power that we are unwilling to practice in the modern West?

Weak and meek social power, a coming upside-down kingdom that is not yet here, a triumphal resurrection that is preceded by torture and death on a cross—this is a hard road, and we need not only think about this theologically but also determine if we have the courage to live it. I am still on the fence.

The biblical story and transformational development

Evangelistic intent

This biblical story, of which the Jesus story is the center, is a transformative story. The story of Jesus can heal our story and can heal the story of any community or society by giving it hope and life, if we will accept God's offer of redemption. Failure to share this story is to withhold the only story that Christians believe brings real hope. No other story leads to life and life eternal. This is the only story that has good news, transformative news, for human sin and for dominating human systems. There can be no better human future apart from this story. For this reason, transformational development done by Christians must include sharing the biblical story in a way that people can understand and that calls for a response. (More on this in the final chapter.)

Restoring relationships

The point of the biblical story is ultimately about relationships, restored relationships. "Living as persons in communion, in right relationship, is the meaning of salvation and the ideal of Christian faith" (LaCugna 1991, 292). Relationships must be restored in all their dimensions. First and foremost, in an intimate and serving relationship with God, through Jesus Christ. Second, in healthy, righteous, and just relationships with ourselves and our communities. Third, in loving, respectful, "neighboring" relationships with all who are "other" to us. Finally, in an earth-keeping, making-fruitful relationship with the earth. We will come back to this in the section on restored relationships as the goal of transformation in Chapter 7.

The integrating and focusing importance of relationships in the kingdom is a consistent biblical theme. The creation account, including the fall, is a relational account. The Ten Commandments are about relationships with God and each other, with a bias in favor of the well-being of the community. The covenant with Israel was about a relationship between God and God's people. Melba Maggay, a Filipina theologian and development practitioner, reminds us that "Israel was sent into exile because of idolatry and oppression, prophetic themes resulting from the laws of love of God and love of neighbor" (Maggay 1994, 69). Loving God and loving neighbor must be the foundational theme for a Christian understanding of transformational development.

Jesus made a radical extension to loving neighbor when he told us to love our enemies (Mt 5:44). This is not like us, but it is like God. God has no enemies who lie beyond the love of God, even the most vicious, grasping, greedy landlord. Therefore, we must love the poor and non-poor alike. This is not, however, a call to a warm and fuzzy, uncritical, "I'm OK you're OK" kind of love. God's love is often a very tough love. Egypt suffered greatly so that Pharaoh might know "that I am God" (Ex 7:5, 14:4). God sent his beloved Israel into exile, even to Babylon, and then did not speak to her for almost six hundred years. God's love of us and our neighbor can be a tough, truth-telling, there-are-consequences, your-soul-is-in-danger kind of love. But, there is never hate; the enemy is never demonized or declared hopeless. The offer of grace is always there.

We need to spend a moment exploring the nature of these relationships. What do we mean? How should such relationships be assessed? The biblical image of shalom is particularly helpful here. Nicholas Wolterstorff points out that *shalom* is usually translated by the word "peace," but that it means more than the absence of strife. First, shalom is a relational concept, "dwelling at peace with God, with self, with fellows, with nature." Then, Wolterstorff suggests, we must add the ideas of justice, harmony, and enjoyment to capture the full biblical meaning of the word. Shalom means just relationships (living justly and experiencing justice), harmonious relationships and enjoyable relationships. Shalom means belonging to an authentic and nurturing community in which one can be one's true self and give one's self away without becoming poor. Justice, harmony, and enjoyment of God, self, others, and nature; this is the shalom that Jesus brings, the peace that passes all understanding (Wolterstorff 1983, 69–72). Shalom is the biblical ideal for human well-being or flourishing.

The idea of shalom is related to one of the interesting ways Jesus described his mission: "I have come that they may have life, and have it in the full" (Jn 10:10). Life in its fullness is the purpose; this is what we are for and what Christ has come to make possible. To live fully in the present in relationships that are just, harmonious, and enjoyable, that allow everyone to contribute. And to live fully for all time. A life of joy in being that goes beyond having. While shalom and abundant life are ideals that we will not see this side of the second coming, the vision of a shalom that leads to life in its fullness is a powerful image that must inform and shape our understanding of any better human future.

A holistic story

Holism is an important word for Christian thinking about development. There are a variety of ways in which we must think holistically.

First, we need to remember the whole story from beginning to end. Sometimes we are tempted to shorten the biblical story and limit it to the birth, death, and resurrection of Jesus. While this is the center of the story, it is not the whole story. To think properly about human transformation, we must see the world of the poor and the non-poor in light of the whole biblical account. We must be clear on what was intended, how things got as they are, what God is offering to do to change them, and what we can and cannot do as participants in the story. We must have a holistic understanding of the whole story.

The whole story is also important because it helps those who have not heard the story to understand the gospel. It is hard to make sense out of any story if the storyteller insists on starting in the middle. For example, telling people that Christ died to forgive their sins can be hard to understand if people do not know which God you are talking about or understand the idea of sin. Folks that only tell the story of Jesus unhelpfully truncate God's story. We need a holistic view of the biblical narrative to create a complete framework of meaning for all the gospels have for us.

Second, we need a holistic view of time that includes eternity. God's project of redemption and restoration focuses on making life possible beyond the end of history. If we forget the eternal or relegate it only to the spiritual realm inside the church, we lose something critical to our thinking about development.

> Without the perspective of eternal life, human progress in the world is denied breathing space. Enclosed in history, it runs the risk of being reduced to the mere accumulation of wealth; humanity thus loses the courage to be at the service of higher goods, at the service of the great and disinterested initiatives called for by universal charity. Man does not develop through his own powers. (CV, no. 11)

Third, we need a holistic view of human beings. This brings us back to an earlier theme: God's redeeming work does not separate individuals from the families, communities and larger social systems of which they are a part. People come first, of course. Changed people, transformed by the gospel and reconciled to God, is the beginning of any transformation. Transforming social systems alone cannot accomplish this: "No arrangement of social cooperation, in which power controls power and anarchy is tamed, will produce human beings free from the lust for power" (Wink 1992, 77). Therefore, transformational development that is Christian cannot avoid giving the invitation to say Yes to the person of Jesus and the invitation to enter the kingdom. At the same time, however, this individual response does not fully express the scope of God's redemptive work.

Social systems are made up of persons, but they are also more than the sum of the persons involved in them. Corporations, government ministries, and even church structures have a character or ethos that is greater than the sum of the individuals who work in them. Wink explains this ethos or spirit in terms of the biblical concepts of principalities and powers: "The principalities and powers of the Bible refer to the inner and outer manifestations of the political, economic, religious and cultural institutions" (Wink 1992, 78). As I have said, this social dimension of human life is also fallen and is thus a target of God's redemptive work.

The Great Commission calls for making the nations into disciples, not just people. This commission of the living Christ instructs us to baptize the nations in the name of the triune God, "teaching them to obey everything I have commanded you" (Mt 28:20). What did Jesus command? To love God and your neighbor as yourself. Kwame Bediako, the Ghanaian theologian, articulates the full meaning of the Great Commission nicely:

> The Great Commission, therefore, is about the discipline of the nations, the conversion of the things that make people into nations—the shared and common processes of thinking; attitudes; world views; perspectives; languages; and the cultural, social and economic habits of thought, behavior and practice. These things and the lives of the people in whom such things find expression—all of this is meant to be within the call of discipleship. (Bediako 1996b, 184)

Recalling Hiebert's three-tiered worldview scheme in Figure 1–2 in Chapter 1, God's redemptive work addresses all three levels. God is the only true God, the God who is more powerful than all other gods, and the God who loves and works in the real world of sight, sound, and touch. His redemptive agenda works for truth (upper level), by power (the excluded middle of the West) and through love (the concrete world of science and the earth). A whole gospel for all levels of our worldview.

Finally, one other aspect of holism needs mentioning. The gospel of Jesus and his kingdom is a message of life, deed, word, and sign, an inseparable whole, all expressions of a single gospel message. Mark's account of the calling of the disciples says that Christ "appointed twelve -designating them apostles—that they might be with him and that he might send them out to preach and to have authority to drive out demons" (Mk 3:14–15). When the apostles are sent on their first solo ministry outing, Mark reports that "they went out and preached that people should repent. They drove out many demons and anointed many sick people with oil and healed them" (Mk 6:12–13).

Activists are quick to pick up on the preaching, the healing, and the casting out stuff. They too often overlook that Christ's call was first and foremost "to be with" Christ. Being must precede doing.

I find it helpful to picture the gospel message in the form of a pyramid. The top of the pyramid is being with Jesus, life in and with the living Lord. This relationship frames all that lies below it. Each of the corners of the pyramid are one aspect or dimension of the gospel: preaching—the gospel-as-word; healing—the gospel-as-deed; and casting out—the gospel-as-sign.

Each of these can be developed in turn. Gospel-as-word includes teaching, preaching, and the doing of theology. Gospel-as-deed means working for the physical, social, and psychological well-being of the world that belongs to God. This is the sole location of transformation for too many Christians. Gospel-as-sign means signs and wonders, those things that only God can do, as well as the things the church does as a living sign of a kingdom that is and has not yet fully come.

The metaphor of a pyramid is helpful because one cannot break off a corner and still claim to have a pyramid. This reminds us that for the gospel to be the gospel all four aspects—life, deed, word, and sign—have to be present. They are inseparable, and so is the holism of the Christian gospel (see Figure 3–6).

Technology and science have a place in the story

One of the increasingly clear features of the modern era is that science has lost its story (Postman 1997, 29–32). Science and technology do not, indeed cannot, provide the answers we need. Science helps us figure out how things work, but not why they work or what they are for.

> Science cannot create. Because science is assumed to be value free, it did not operate within a vision of what ought to be. It could relentlessly and efficiently disassemble; it could not construct an alternative whole. (Shenk 1993, 67)

It was not always this way; science was once part of a larger story. Postman reminds us that the "first science storytellers, Descartes, Bacon, Galileo, Kepler and Newton for example—did not think of their story as a replacement for

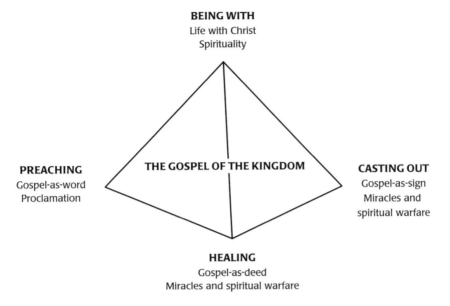

BEING WITH
Life with Christ
Spirituality

PREACHING
Gospel-as-word
Proclamation

THE GOSPEL OF THE KINGDOM

CASTING OUT
Gospel-as-sign
Miracles and
spiritual warfare

HEALING
Gospel-as-deed
Miracles and spiritual warfare

Figure 3–6: The gospel of the kingdom:
Being, preaching, healing, and casting out.

the great Judeo-Christian narrative, but as an extension of it" (1997, 31). Yet in the intervening centuries science and technology increasingly seemed to be able to explain themselves without need to include God as part of the explanation. God became increasingly marginal to their story and was ultimately dismissed as no longer needed. Today science and technology explain themselves: "We work, don't we? What else matters?" Relationships, ethics, and justice are pushed to the sidelines.

Yet technology and science are an inseparable part of working for human transformation. Immunizations, water drilling, improved agricultural practices, indigenous or folk science make positive impact in the lives of the poor. Any Christian understanding of transformational development must have space for the good that science and technology offer. Yet, to be Christian, this science and technology cannot be its own story, cannot stand apart from the biblical story that is the real story. We need a modern account of divine action in the natural order (Murphy 1995, 325). If we fail to recover a fully Christian narrative for science and technology, one that recognizes God at work through science in the natural order, and one that places science at the service of life and enhancing relationships, we will bring the poor the same story-less science that is impoverishing the West. This would not be good news. I will develop this more fully in the chapter on Christian witness.

The biblical story is for everyone

In our eagerness to be with and for the poor, we must not forget the biblical story is everyone's story, poor and non-poor alike. Both are made in the image of God, both experienced the consequences of the fall, and both are the focus of God's redemptive work. The hope of the gospel and the transformative promise of the kingdom are for both. The only difference is social location. The poor are on the periphery of the social system while the non-poor, even when living in poor communities, occupy places of preference, prestige, and power.

While God's story is for everyone, there are two ways in which human response to the story creates a bias that favors the poor. First, it is apparently very hard for the non-poor to accept the biblical story as their story (Lk 18:18–30). Wealth and power seem to make people hard of hearing and poor at understanding (Lk 8:14). Even Christians who are not poor have a problem living out the story. There is a strong temptation to domesticate the story in a way that uses it to validate their wealth or positions of privilege and power. For the Christian non-poor, there is a need to appropriate the whole biblical story as stewards, not owners. The church has lost its way in this regard from time to time.

Second, it is the poor who most consistently seem to recognize God's story as their story. The church has a long history of growing on its margins and declining at its center (Walls 1987). Furthermore, God has always insisted that caring for the widow, orphan, and alien is a measure of the fidelity with which we and our societies live out our faith (Ps 72, 82). No story in which the poor are forgotten, ignored, or left to their own devices is consistent with the biblical story. If the poor are forgotten, God will be forgotten too, it seems. Loving God and loving neighbor are twin injunctions of a single command, a command that is good for our well-being.

If the biblical story is for both poor and non-poor, then we must work to understand the poverties of both as seen from God's perspective. Furthermore, we must see how the poverty of both interact, reinforcing each other. Any theory or practice of transformational development must be predicated on an understanding of the whole of the social systems and those—both poor and non-poor—who inhabit them.

This leads us to explore the nature and causes of poverty. We need to understand who the poor are and why they are poor, as well as who the non-poor are and how their poverty contributes to the poverty of the poor. We are now prepared biblically and theologically to do so.

HELPFUL RESOURCES

Belshaw, D. G. R., Robert Calderisi, and Chris Sugden. 2001. *Faith in Development: Partnership Between the World Bank and the Churches of Africa*. Washington DC: World Bank.

Brady, Bernard V. 2008. *Essential Catholic Social Thought*. Maryknoll, NY: Orbis Books.

Holman, Susan R. 2008. *Wealth and Poverty in Early Church and Society*. Grand Rapids, MI: Baker.

Hughes, Dewi Arwel. 2008. *Power and Poverty: Divine and Human Rule in a World of Need*. Downers Grove, IL: InterVarsity Press Academic.

Hughes, Dewi Arwel, with Matthew Bennett. 1998. *God of the Poor*. Carlisle, UK: OM Publishing.

4

Poverty and the poor

Poverty is an important word for a relief and development agency. After all, we exist in response to the material poverty of our time. Helping the poor is what we do. *Poverty* is a word, however, whose meaning we tend to take for granted. Everyone knows what poverty is. When we see its images on television or hear its stories, we recognize poverty with ease. So, why define it?

Like so many of our ideas, the meanings we ascribe to an abstract noun reflect our way of looking at, thinking about, and making sense of our world. Therefore, we need to examine how we understand poverty as well as how we think and feel about the poor. We need to identify our assumptions and look for blind spots. In addition, sociologists have been studying poverty for a long time. Development academics have been doing field research and codifying what they have found. We need to take this in as well.

This chapter provides an overview of the problem of poverty and presents a series of different but related ways of understanding who the poor are and why they are poor.

WHERE DO WE BEGIN?

We need to begin by reminding ourselves that poverty is the condition of people whom we describe abstractly as "the poor." Referring to people by a label is always dangerous. We may forget that the poor are not an abstraction, but rather a group of human beings who have names, who are made in the image of God for whom Jesus died. The people who live in poverty are as valued, as important, as loved as those who do not.

Why is this reminder important? The world tends to view the poor as a group that is helpless thus giving ourselves permission to look down on them and even play god in their lives. The poor as a category are nameless, and this invites us to treat them as objects of our compassion, as a thing to which we can do what we believe is best. We, the non-poor, take it upon ourselves to describe the poor with words like *homeless, destitute, hopeless, working poor, marginalized*, and so on. Talking about the poor as an abstract noun invites well-intentioned people of compassion to speak for the poor and to practice the latest fads for "eradicating poverty." The poor become the custodians of the state, objects of professional study, or a social group to be organized, liberated, or developed. Whenever we reduce the poor from people with names to abstractions, we add to their poverty and impoverish ourselves.

Our point of departure for a Christian understanding of poverty is to remember that the poor are people with names, people to whom God has given gifts, and people with whom and among whom God has been working before we even arrived.

Who do you say that they are?

When Jesus asked his disciples, "Who do you say I am?" (Mk 8:29), he received a variety of answers. Most saw who they expected to see—Elijah or another of the prophets. Only Peter saw the Messiah, and we are told it was only because the Holy Spirit enabled him. Seeing what we expect to see is a common human weakness. Therefore, before we begin the work of exploring the world of the poor, we need to begin with ourselves.

We view the poor from a point of view—as Christians, as Westerners, as development professionals, as urban folk. We see them through the lens of our personality and the lens of the culture from which we come. We have a lot of different schema that determine what we see and what we don't in order to make sense out of what we observe. We need to make our assumptions explicit and to ask God's help to see the poor and the circumstances of the poor more truly.

One useful exercise is to make a list of all the adjectives that we have heard or that we use to describe the poor. This usually results in a list of negative labels: dirty, uneducated, lazy, hopeless, superstitious, oppressed, ineffective, marginalized, and so on. Then we can ask ourselves if these labels describe poor people we actually know, and of course they do not. One simple bias is exposed. We can do a similar exercise by making lists of why we think people are poor, what our agency advertising suggests are the reasons why people are poor, and what the culture from which we come believes are the reasons people are poor. Uncovering our biases is an important exercise. Only when we do this are we able to deconstruct the lenses we use to work for transformation. We need to remove the log in our own eye so that we have eyes to see and ears to hear.

Who are you?

This is especially important for development workers. We come with a full array of information and perspectives that affect how we view the poor and understand poverty. As Vinay Samuel has pointed out:

The development worker is shaped by a particular understanding of progress, health, modern education, family life, democracy, participation, decision making, market reality, economic principles and perspectives. (1995, 153)

Naming and owning these understandings is an important way of identifying the baggage we are carrying with us into the community.

As professionals, we can bring another level of bias that can be quite destructive, if it is unseen and unnamed. Robert Chambers (1997, 78–83) identifies four particular areas of concern:

Conditioning: Echoing Samuel, every development worker is a conditioned human being. The temptation to transfer our view of how things work and what will make things better is very powerful. After all, we have studied hard and have a lot of field experience, all done so that we could provide professional assistance to the poor.

Dominance: All of us have within us the desire to feel superior or dominant over others. This can be part of personality as well as culture. The fact that we can read, express ourselves clearly and effectively when we speak, write things down, reduce complex problems to diagrams, arrive in a car or a motorcycle, ask for a meeting with important people and get it, all communicate a position of power and privilege that we can unwittingly assume is part of who we are.

Distance: Development professionals often work at a distance, geographically and psychologically. When we are with the poor we are "in the field"; our office is in the city where we have access to email, telephone and our computer, where we can "get things done." In addition, the differences in language, food, customs, and ways of problem solving all serve to create distance. We "know" the poor only at a distance.

Denial: When the real world of the poor conflicts with who we are or how we are trained or what we believe, the reaction is too often denial. We simply reframe or recompose the discordant experience. This all-too-human reaction allows us to remain untroubled and unchanged, leaving the poor to adapt to us.

So we must begin where we are, with ourselves. "Know thyself" is a useful reminder for any development worker. Work spent articulating one's assumptions about how the world works, why it is as it is, and what might improve it is work worth doing. It will make life easier for the poor, and should make us more effective.

CHRISTIAN VIEWS OF THE POOR

Since this book addresses poverty and human transformation from a Christian perspective, the process of uncovering our views of the poor should begin with the ways Christians think about the poor. Richard Mouw (1989, 20–34) has proposed a simple typology of Christian perspectives that is helpful (see Figure 4–1).

Poor as made in the image of God: This view draws on the creation narrative and tends toward a romantic view of the poor. Their poverty is the result of lack of skills and opportunity. What they need is a "leg up."

Poor as people in rebellion: This view draws on the fall as the defining reason why the poor are poor. They are lazy and make bad choices. The poor need to accept the gospel, go to work, and make better choices. Personal responsibility is the key.

Poor as Christ incarnate: Drawing on Matthew 25, this view of the poor centers on the incarnation and, with Mother Teresa, "sees Christ in the distressing guise of the poor." The poor lack love and relationships; they do not belong. The poor need accompaniment; we should relieve as much suffering as we can.

Poor as God's favorites: This view draws on the prophetic literature and the Exodus account. The poor are the ones who are blessed, for theirs will be the kingdom. They are poor because they are oppressed by social systems that keep them poor for the benefit of the non-poor. The poor need justice and help in finding their voice and place in the economic and political system.

Poor as lost souls: This is a category that I am taking the liberty of adding to Mouw's typology. This view draws selectively on the gospels and reflects the dichotomy between the spiritual and the physical of the modern world. The poor are lost. The kingdom is coming when Jesus comes, and that will be soon. The poor need to be saved. Helping them is a misplaced priority.

Seen in this light, the conclusions are obvious. First, Christians can be selective in their use of Scripture and tend to favor a view of the poor that supports what they already believe or that they received from somewhere else. Second, it would seem more fruitful to develop an understanding of the poor that includes all and excludes none of these images. The poor are made in the image of God. They are fallen. Christ did use the poor as a metaphor for himself and our need to serve the less fortunate. There is a bias toward the poor and against the non-poor (see the end of the theology chapter), and the poor are often lost souls.

WHO ARE THE POOR?

This section attempts to integrate a family of definitions drawn from several sources. As we do this, we must keep in mind my opening admonition: any such definition is necessarily flawed because it describes real people using ideas and concepts. The following observations must be held lightly in the palm of our open hand. We must be ready to let our concepts,

View of the poor	Theological frame	Key biblical texts	Expressions	Why the poor are poor	Christian response
Poor made in the image of God	Creation	Genesis 1-2	Poor as creative. Poor as a work of art. See God's hidden glory.	The poor lack skills, knowledge, and opportunity.	Enable the poor to be fruitful and productive.
Poor as people in rebellion	Fall	Genesis 3 Proverbs	Poor as lazy. Poor make bad choices. God helps those who help themselves.	The poor are in rebellion and their culture keeps them poor.	Challenge the poor with the gospel and encourage them to make better choices.
Poor as Christ incarnate	Incarnation	Gospels	Christ in the distressing guise of the poor. What you did for the least of these...	The poor lack love.	Accompany the poor and relieve suffering as possible.
Poor as God's favorites	Prophetic Eschatological	Exodus Prophets	Blessed are the poor for theirs will be the kingdom. Liberation theology	The poor are oppressed by the non-poor. Poverty is structural.	Work for justice. Help the poor find their voice and place in socio-political-economic system.
Poor as lost souls	Salvation Soteriological	Matthew 28 Acts	The better future lies in eternity. Save as many as we can. The poor will always be with you.	The poor are lost from God, and the kingdom is coming soon.	Proclaim the gospel and encourage the poor to respond.

Figure 4–1: Christian views of the poor.
(Developed from Mouw 1989, 20–34)

theories and ideas go, when our experience with real poor people says otherwise.

The poor are people, and we must begin there. Our theological reflections in the last chapter tell us that the poor are whole, living people, inseparably body, soul, mind, and heart. Further, they are persons embedded in families, communities, and corresponding social systems. Like us, the poor are encumbered selves. Finally, the biblical narrative tells us that the poor are made in the image of God and thus have gifts, skills, and the potential to become kingdom-like, just as we do.

Households

The poor live in households, and some development thinkers believe that we need to view the household as the economic and social unit of importance, in contrast to the Western temptation to think only in terms of individuals. Each member helps and hinders, produces and consumes, yet all understand themselves as part of this social unit rather than thinking of themselves so much as individuals. Chambers' definition of the poverty as entanglement, which I will introduce later, assumes the household as the basic economic unit of society (Chambers 1983, 108). Maldonado reports on the power of Christian conversion for social transformation acting through and changing the culture of the household unit in Latin America (1993, 196). Friedmann sees the household as a living social unit with people in dynamic relationship located in a real place (1992, 46). Households are the building blocks of larger social systems. Friedmann's analysis is worth developing in greater detail.

Friedmann sees households as made up of three-dimensional moral human beings living in dynamic interaction with others. People have obligations to one another as well as needs and wants. Human needs, according to Friedmann, include the psychological needs for "affection, self-expression and esteem that are not available as commodities but arise directly from human encounter" (1992, 32). Each household forms a political structure and economy in miniature, the self-same image of the larger social structure of which it is a part. Households exercise three kinds of power:

- *Social power* dealing with access to information, knowledge and skills, participation in social organizations and access to financial resources.
- *Political power* dealing with access to the process by which decisions affecting their future are made.
- *Psychological power* dealing with a sense of individual potency or self-confident behavior. (ibid., 33)

Time is the basic resource of the household, according to Friedmann, not money. The household allocates the time of individual members to different tasks, areas of life, and domains of social practice in order to live. "Poor households . . . rely heavily on non-market relations both for securing their livelihood and pursuing their life goals" (Friedmann 1992, 45). The poor cannot rely on money to satisfy their needs. This often makes poor households invisible to economic research.

Using the household as the lens through which we see the poor also allows us to see the poor both as individuals and as embedded in social systems:

> Households are miniature political economies that have a territorial base (life space) and are engaged in the production of their own life and livelihood. Households are *political* because their members arrive at decisions affecting the household as a whole and themselves individually in ways that involve negotiating relations of power. Households have *a territorial base* because people have to have a place to live even if it is only a cardboard shack. . . . Finally, households are conceived as producers and thus as collective actor on behalf of their own (and sometimes others') material interests. (Friedmann 1992, 47)

Because households normally consist of people related to one another in some way, they manifest reciprocity and mutual obligation. Thus there is a moral economy of mutual exchange that operates by moral rules learned largely within the household (Friedmann 1992, 48). This moral economy operates, at least in part, outside the market economy and is an important way the poor maintain life and livelihood. Relationships are often more important to life than money.

The idea of the household as the central social unit also resonates with the biblical narrative. The Bible seems to see people in household units, too. Noah and his extended family were saved (Gn 7:1). God distributed the Promised Land fairly according to clans and household units (Wright 1983, 68). Joshua made commitments in the name of his family (Jos 24:15). Lydia and her household were baptized by Paul, as were the Philippian jailer and his family later in the same story (Acts 16:15, 33). One test of leadership is that a deacon "must manage his children and household well" (1 Tim 3:12).

Finally, understanding poverty in terms of a household sets the stage for thinking about the causes of poverty in terms of the larger social systems. I will say more about this toward the end of this chapter.

The poor among the non-poor

We cannot talk about who the poor are without pointing out the fact that they live among others who are not poor. Too often we oversimplify and use mental models that assume the poor live in poor communities and that the non-poor live somewhere else—a nearby community, in the city, in the North. This is not true. Even in the poorest communities, there are some who are less poor and who occupy positions of relative power and privilege. In any area, there is always a small group of communities that are not poor in relation to the other communities in the area. Even in the household unit this is true; there is usually a dominant man who is not poor in comparison to the rest of the household (Anderson 1996c, 8). Therefore, poverty and the poor can only be understood by keeping the relationships between the poor and the non-poor clearly in mind.

Who the poor are not

We must stop for a moment and deal with two things people sometimes say about the poor that are not always true. Some say the poor are lazy, fatalistic, and will not save for the future. Others say the poor are ignorant. Chambers debunks these claims and calls us to be more humble in our judgments. The poor may not save, but this may be for the very good reason that their survival today will not permit it. The poor may appear lazy, but what we may be seeing is their way of conserving limited physical energy. Fatalism may be an adaptation that is prudent, not a giving up. "The appearance of powerlessness, unawareness and acquiescence may be a condition for survival" (1983, 106).

The assertion that the poor are ignorant and stupid does not survive any informed knowledge of real poor people. The depth and breadth of their indigenous knowledge frequently astounds us (Chambers 1983, 106; Muchena 1996, 178–79; de Soto, 1989). Their knowledge of local ecology, traditional medicine, and survival skills is considerable. The poor can survive in conditions that would daunt the non-poor. Furthermore, Chambers reminds us that "apparent ignorance and stupidity are part of the strategy of lying low, a stance necessitated in the face of officials who demand obsequious behavior" (1983, 107).

The poor are no more lazy, fatalistic, improvident, stupid, or arrogant than anyone else. All people suffer from these problems, poor and non-poor alike. But only the non-poor can afford to indulge in these behaviors. "People so close to the edge cannot afford laziness or stupidity. They have to work and work hard, whenever and however they can. Many of the lazy and stupid poor are dead" (Chambers 1983, 107).

Which poor?

The poor are not a homogeneous category, and poverty is different for different groups. Poverty means different things to children and youth, to women, to the mentally and physically challenged, and to the old. To think and do well, we need to understand these differences and plan accordingly without increasing the poverty of the community through social fragmentation. Mary Anderson's book *Development and Social Diversity* helps open up this world of differences, while affirming that solidarity among these groups is equally important to effective development.

Children and youth are often an under-utilized development resource. Too often they are viewed as helpless, vulnerable, and in need of care. This reflects a mental model that says that the poverty of children is complete; they are simply poor and have nothing to contribute. This makes them all the poorer. We are always tempted to "do for" children, not recognizing the potential for transformation that children represent. I will come back to the potential transformational role of children in Chapter 8.

The poor are often women, and the poverty of women is both a special concern and a special opportunity. These UN statistics are now widely known: women perform two-thirds of the world's work, earn one-tenth of the world's income, are two-thirds of the world's illiterate, and own less than one-hundredth of the world's property (Williams and Mwau 1994, 100). There is a great deal of documentation that shows that women and young girls get less schooling, have poorer nutrition, and receive less health care. The poverty of women is physical, spiritual, and social. This must be an area of special concern for those working for human transformation. At the same time, there is another body of research that shows that female literacy is a positive predictor of many good things—lower fertility, lower child mortality, and successful micro-enterprise development. Thus, women offer a special opportunity if we simply keep them in sight and involved as part of the development process. Transformational development that does not include gender analysis and seek the empowerment of women will fail.

WHAT IS POVERTY?

Poverty has been described in various ways and with increasing sophistication. It is important to articulate our view of poverty because our view of poverty strongly influences what we think transformational development is and how we should go about doing it.

Poverty as deficit

In the early days of development thinking, people defined poverty as a deficit, things that were missing. Poor people do not have enough to eat, a decent place to sleep, or clean water. Their land is poor, there is no water for irrigation, roads are inadequate, and there are no schools for their children. This view of poverty encourages plans to provide the missing things: food, low-cost housing, and wells. The unspoken assumption is that when the missing things are provided, the poor will no longer be poor.

Another kind of deficit has to do with things people do not know or skills they do not have. Poor people may not understand the basics of nutrition, the need to boil water, the importance of child spacing, how to read the instructions on a packet of improved seeds. They don't know about sustainable agriculture, running small businesses, the importance of saving money. This view of poverty invites programming that features education and non-formal learning. It assumes that if the poor simply learn enough, they will no longer be poor. This is the classic response of modernity to social problems.

Christians tend to add another dimension to poverty as deficit: the non-Christian poor lack knowledge about God and the good news of Jesus Christ. To make their understanding of poverty holistic, Christians add knowledge of the gospel to the list of other things the poor do not have. Thus proclamation of the gospel is added to the development program.

A final extension of this deficit idea of poverty is that the poor lack access. They do not have access to good land, a health system, markets, or credit. The underlying assumption is that if someone provides this access, then the deficit is corrected and people will no longer be poor.

These views of poverty are true, and, as far as they go, they are correct. People *do* need things—clean water, safe housing, and sufficient food. They do need education, training, and a chance to hear the gospel. People do need access to resources that are not locally available or that are being withheld. However, limiting one's understanding of poverty to this deficit framework also creates some serious problems.

One problem has to do with the radical materialism of this view. Lack of things, ideas, and access focuses on things we can see, hear, and touch. While true, this is incomplete. The spiritual is left out altogether, and social issues of culture, religion, and power are obscured. This deficit frame invites a primarily materialistic view of poverty and people.

A second weakness resides in the kind of response that is invited if poverty is viewed as the absence of things, ideas, and access. The solution is to provide what is missing. This often leads to the outsider becoming the development "Santa Claus," bringing all good things from the outside: food, well drilling, education, a working health system. The poor are reduced to passive recipients, incomplete human beings whom we make whole through our largess. This unwitting attitude of superiority has two very negative consequences.

First, this attitude demeans and devalues the poor. Sadly, our view of them can become their view of themselves—they are defective and inadequate. We do not treat them as human beings made in the image of God. We do not look for the gifts that God gave them. We act as if God gave us the useful gifts and skills while neglecting the poor, as if we have something to contribute and the poor do not. This attitude increases their poverty and tempts us to play god in the lives of the poor.

Second, our attitude about ourselves can become messianic. We are tempted to believe that we are the delivers of the poor, that we make their lives complete. We can inadvertently harbor a belief that we are the ones who save. Such an attitude is not good for our souls. Sadly, this view of deficit and response is often the default option of wealthy churches in the North who want to help the poor in the South.

Robert Chambers—Poverty as entanglement

Robert Chambers, a respected development practitioner at the Institute of Development Studies at the University of Sussex with extensive rural experience in Africa and India, is a champion of participation in development (see Chapter 8). Using the household as his point of departure, Chambers describes the poor as being entangled in a "cluster of disadvantage." The household is poor in terms of assets and is physically weak, isolated, vulnerable, and powerless. Chambers describes these dimensions of poverty as an interactive system that he calls the "poverty trap" (1983, 103–39). Chambers's systems view of poverty has considerable explanatory power and aligns well with experience. Let's examine the respective parts.

Material poverty: The household has few assets. It has very limited or no savings or livestock. Its housing and sanitation is inadequate. It has little or no land, and, if it has land, it cannot prove title to it.

Physical weakness: The household members are weak. They lack strength because of poor health and inadequate nutrition. The majority of the household are women, the very young, and the very old.

Isolation: The household lacks access to social services and information. It is often remote—far from main roads, water lines, and even electricity. It lacks access to markets, capital, credit, and information. Children do not have access to quality education.

Vulnerability: The household has almost no buffers against emergencies or disaster as it cannot afford to save. They family is vulnerable to cultural demands, such as dowry and feast days, that soak up savings.

Powerlessness: The household lacks the ability and the knowledge to influence the life around it and the social systems in which it lives.

Spiritual poverty: With apologies to Chambers, I add this category in the interest of the holistic Christian perspective we are trying to develop. The household suffers from broken and dysfunctional relationships with God, each other, the community, and creation. Its members may suffer from spiritual oppression in the form of fear of spirits, demons, and angry ancestors. They may lack hope and be unable to believe that change is possible. They may never have heard the gospel or have only responded to a truncated version of the gospel that lacks transforming power (see Figure 4–2).

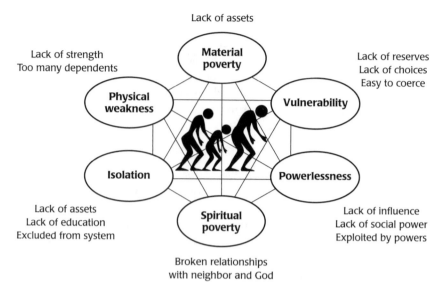

Lack of assets

Lack of strength
Too many dependents

Lack of reserves
Lack of choices
Easy to coerce

Material poverty

Physical weakness

Vulnerability

Isolation

Powerlessness

Lack of assets
Lack of education
Excluded from system

Spiritual poverty

Lack of influence
Lack of social power
Exploited by powers

Broken relationships
with neighbor and God

Figure 4–2: The entanglement of the household.
(Adapted from Chambers 1983, 110)

Chambers's systems approach to poverty is a powerful tool. The inter-connection among the six elements of his poverty trap is an important feature. Each is linked to and reinforces the others. A problem in one area means problems in another, and it is easy to see how the result can be greater and increasingly intractable poverty.

Two of Chambers's system elements—vulnerability and powerlessness—merit further descriptions. Chambers identifies four elements that contribute to the vulnerability of poor households (1983, 114–30). First, they are subject to *social conventions* such as dowry, bride price, feast days, weddings, and funerals. While these are examples of the importance of celebration and ritual, these social requirements may also deplete the assets of the poor by creating a permanent demand for moneylenders, whose usurious rates ensure permanent poverty. We must note that religious leaders often collude at this point by making such conventions part of religious life. Second, natural or manmade *disasters* expose vulnerability. The poor have no reserves, and disasters push them to do things they might not wish to do, such as sell land, livestock and sadly even their girl children. Third, *physical incapacity*—sickness, childbearing, and accidents—increases vulnerability as the physically weak cannot work. Fourth, there are *unproductive expenditures* for things like drink, drugs, unproductive assets (like radios, shoes, or clothes), and poor business investments. Finally, there is the *exploitation* that takes advantage of vulnerability. Exorbitant interest rates, trickery, coercion, intimidation, and blackmail are used by the powerful (often the non-poor in poor communities) to take what little a poor household has—its assets and even its labor.

Chambers's examination of powerlessness (1983, 131–35) is particularly interesting in that it prepares us for the poverty interpretations of Friedmann and Christian that will follow shortly. Chambers points out that powerlessness is often overlooked because it is discomforting to the powerful, even to development practitioners. Powerlessness is an invitation to exploitation by the powerful. Chambers alerts us to three clusters of exploitation. First, the local non-poor often stand as *nets* between the poor and the outside world by trapping resources and benefits that were intended for the poor. "It is a notorious commonplace how, almost everywhere in the third world, credit and marketing cooperatives have been dominated by the larger farmers who have used them for their own benefit, at the cost of smaller producers" (1983, 131). Second, *robbery*. Local police, politicians, and landowners use deception, blackmail, and violence to rob the poor who, in turn, lack recourse to justice, "since they do not know the law, cannot afford legal help and fear to offend the patrons on whom they depend" (1983, 133). Finally, there is *unfair bargaining*. The assets of the poor are bought at prices far below market value because they must be sold in times of hardship and stress. The poor borrow at exorbitant interest rates, even when less costly options are available, because they fear that alienating the local moneylender may lead to a lack of credit in the future. The poor are particularly vulnerable to unfair bargaining when it comes to being paid for their labor. The power to withhold work without reason is a powerful bargaining tool.

One important feature is missing from Chambers's analysis of poverty: the impact of spiritual poverty. Each of the elements of his poverty trap has a spiritual dimension. Powerlessness is not just a problem the poor have with the material world and the non-poor who live in it. The poor often live in fear of the unseen spiritual world of curses, gods, demons, and angry ancestors, a world over which they feel powerless. Physical weakness is often associated with spiritual causes. Isolation from God and the Bible is as significant as not having access to government services, markets, and capital. The need to find money to lift curses and ensure the blessing of the spirits contributes to vulnerability in the same way that disasters and social conventions do.

There is another, more fundamental level at which we can see the lack of the spiritual. There is a spiritual reality that underlies the entire poverty entrapment system and its six interacting elements. This foundational spiritual reality provides the explanation for (1) the deceptive and dominating activity of the non-poor, (2) the contribution the poor make to their own poverty by destructive behavior within the household, and (3) the poverty of being (we are of no value and are unworthy) and meaning (there are no answers for important questions), especially among the poor. No systems account of poverty is complete without a holistic view of the spiritual and material at the level of people and the social systems within which the individual lives.

John Friedmann—Poverty as lack of access to social power

John Friedmann, a professor of urban planning with extensive experience among the urban poor in Latin America, is a promoter of what he calls "alternative development." Friedmann focuses on the powerlessness of the poor and defines poverty as lack of access to social power. Like Chambers, he begins with the household as the social unit of the poor and sees the household as being embedded within four overlapping domains of social practice: state, political community, civil society, and corporate economy (Friedmann 1992, 26–31). Each domain has a distinctive type of power: state power, political power, social power, and economic power.

Each domain also has its own set of institutions. The core of the state consists of the formal executive and judicial elements of government. The core of the political community consists of independent political organizations. In the overlap between the state and the political community domains, Friedmann places the legislative and regulatory bodies. The core of civil society is the household. Where the domains of civil society and the state overlap, we find churches and voluntary organizations. The central institution of the corporate economy is the corporation. This domain is also open to and profoundly interconnected with the global economy and transnational corporations. Where the corporate economy overlaps with the political community, we find political parties, protest movements, and environmental groups. Where the corporate economy overlaps with civil society, we find the non-formal economic sector and popular economic groups. These interacting domains are the system within which the poor household struggles to find space, location, livelihood, and influence (see Figure 4–3).

Friedmann then describes eight dimensions of social power that are available to the poor as avenues for creating social space, influence, livelihood and ultimately increased social power: social networks, information for self-development, surplus time, instruments of work and livelihood, social organization, knowledge and skill, defensible life space, and financial resources (1992, 67). When the levels of these eight dimensions of social power are so low that the household is unable to move out of poverty on its own, Friedmann defines this as absolute poverty (see Figure 4–4).

The bottom line for Friedmann is that lack of social organization and access to the political processes are the keys to understanding why people are poor:

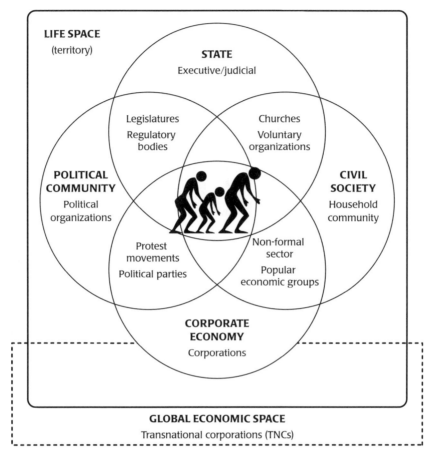

Figure 4–3: Life space of the household and the
four domains of social practices.
(Friedmann 1992, 27)

The (dis)empowerment model of poverty is a political variant of the
basic needs approach. It is centered on politics rather than planning.
. . . The starting point of the model is the assumption that poor households lack the social power to improve the condition of their members' lives. (1992, 66)

Friedmann's understanding of poverty as a lack of access to social power
is a more sophisticated understanding than that of poverty being simply a
lack of things or lack of knowledge. It also inserts poor households into a
social system that goes beyond the local setting. The role of government,
the political system, civil society, and the economy, integrated into the global economy, is now part of the field of play. Poverty is understood as a

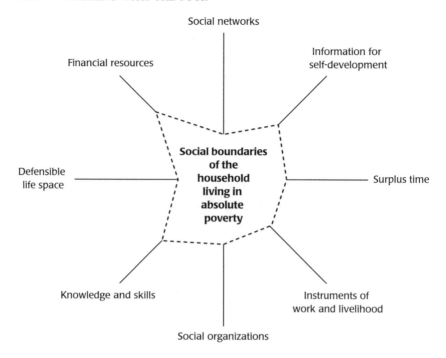

Figure 4–4: Eight dimensions of social power and the poor household. (Adapted from Friedmann 1992, 67)

state of disempowerment. In addition, Friedmann has introduced a psychological dimension to poverty and power. These are helpful developments.

Friedmann's understanding of poverty alludes to, but does not develop the spiritual dimension of life. There is no explanation for why social systems exclude the poor and become self-serving. A spiritual dimension is needed to account for the fact that social institutions frequently frustrate even the best and most noble intentions of the people who inhabit and lead them. Without a theology of principalities and powers, it is unclear why good people cannot make social institutions do what they were set up to do. Furthermore, there is no means to account for the destructive behaviors and poor choices of both the poor and the non-poor, nor for the fact that the poor often exploit each other.

Isaac Prilleltensky—Poverty as diminished personal and relational well-being

One of the intriguing ironies in development thinking is the absence of any contribution from the field of psychology until recently. There are two likely reasons for this. First, the disciplines of international development and psychology have emerged separately because they tend to focus on different geographical areas and occupy different locations in the academy. Second, at least in my case, there has been an unnamed assumption that psychology is largely focused on middle class, suburban folks in the West with personal issues and thus has little to offer the issues of the poor in the South.

A corrective to this bias began to emerge with the publication of the *Voices of the Poor* study by the World Bank. The researchers reported that the poor spoke of psychological dimensions of poverty such as personal "powerlessness, voicelessness, shame and humiliation as well as their manifestations in alcoholism, domestic violence and depression" (Sloan 2003, 308). More recently, the resulting focus on empowerment—increasing human agency—led to efforts to figure out how to measure empowerment and this included a new focus on subjective well-being and power (Narayan-Parker 2005, 123–76). Psychology has now joined the international poverty eradication conversation.

One of the major contributions comes from the field of community psychology. Originating in the 1960s community psychology developed in response to a desire by some mental health professionals to go beyond the mental health of an individual and take into account the complex relationships between the individual and his or her community and the wider social systems within which the individual lives. There was a growing recognition that the individualism of Western psychology can obscure or even validate the impact of oppressive social systems "by attributing problems to personal defects rather than to failures in social systems. The unjust status quo is thus reinforced" (Sloan 2003, 303).

The goal of community psychology is to try to understand the systemic political and economic factors that diminish human well-being and particularly the sense of identity. "From a critical or community psychology perspective, there is no (human) experience that is exclusively psychological or political; human phenomena always contain both (Prilleltensky 2003, 20–21). This stance forces community psychology to take into account and address issues of inequality and power.

Drawing on the work of Paulo Freire, community psychologists use participatory action research as a tool for enabling the poor to assess critically their social and cultural context with an eye toward creating social and institutional change. "This approach amalgamates the voice of the oppressed with the critical perspectives on what constitutes the good life, the good society, and what is the role of power in wellness and suffering" (Prilleltensky and Nelson 2002).

Isaac Prilleltensky, an Argentinean-born professor of community psychology, draws on Sen's development of freedom and the *Voices of the Poor* study to propose a model for understanding poverty that focuses on the impact of power on individual and communal identity and agency. His analytical frame consists of three interacting domains: personal, collective, and relational. The personal domain reminds us of Chambers's poverty as entanglement—ill health, malnutrition, and poor education, all limiting human agency or freedom (Sen). The collective domain includes the political and economic structures that limit well-being, bringing Friedmann to mind as well as Sen's instrumental freedoms (to be introduced in the next chapter).

The new piece that Prilleltensky adds, the relational domain, focuses on the psychological impacts of material poverty and of unjust and oppressive power relationships on the poor, especially their view of themselves and hence their potential for agency. Prilleltensky speaks of "human interactions being 'marred' by disrespect, exclusion, humiliation and erasure of identity" (2003, 19–34). This marring is both an individual and a communal reality. Interestingly, Friedmann also speaks of psychological power in terms of an "individual sense of potency" (1992, 33) and poverty as a lack thereof. Echoing Sen's idea of poverty as "unfreedom," Prilleltensky argues that deficits in these three domains result in a loss of "mastery and control" and thus lead to diminished identity and function (2003, 23) (see Figure 4–5).

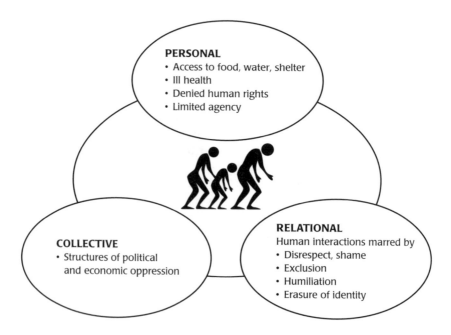

Figure 4–5: Poverty as diminished personal and relational well-being.
(Developed from Prilleltensky 2003)

This addition of the psychological dimensions of disempowerment experienced through "marred human interactions" will be highly relevant to the upcoming discussion of Jayakumar Christian's understanding of marred identity as the internalization of poverty and thus poverty's most fundamental impact on the poor.

Jayakumar Christian—Poverty as a disempowering system

Jayakumar Christian, a long-time Indian practitioner and World Vision colleague, codified his development experience in his Ph.D. thesis (1994) at Fuller Theological Seminary and his important book *God of the Empty Handed* (1999). Christian builds on Chambers and Friedmann while adding a spiritual dimension to his understanding poverty. Like Chambers and Friedmann, Christian sees the poor household embedded in a complex framework of interacting systems. For Christian, these systems include a personal system, which would include psychology; a social system similar to Friedmann's; a spiritual/religious system, which is both personal and social; and a cultural system that includes worldview (1994, 334). With apologies to Christian, I have added the biophysical system à la Chambers for the sake of completeness. A weak mind and body, resulting from malnutrition, illness, and hard physical labor, are obvious contributing factors to the rest of Christian's system of disempowerment (see Figure 4–6).

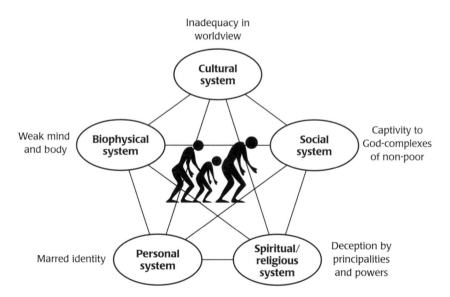

Figure 4–6: Poverty as disempowering systems.
(Adapted from Christian 1999)

The poor find themselves trapped inside a system of disempowerment made up of these interacting systems. Each part of the system creates its own particular contribution to disempowerment of the poor, including what Christian terms captivity to god complexes of the non-poor, deception by the principalities and powers, inadequacies in worldview, and suffering from a marred identity.

Captivity to god complexes of the non-poor— The social-economic-political system

Similar to Friedmann and echoing Wink, Christian argues that the social system reinforces the powerlessness of the poor by exclusion and exploitation, but Christian seeks deeper roots for this (1994, 178). The non-poor understand themselves as superior, essential, and anointed to rule. They succumb to the temptation to play god in the lives of the poor, using religious systems, mass media, the law, government policies and bureaucracies as tools. These people create the narratives, structures, and systems that justify and rationalize their privileged position. The result is that the poor become captive to the god complexes of the non-poor. According to Christian, the non-poor express their god complexes by

- Seeking to absolutize themselves in the lives of the poor.
- Citing the "eternal yesterday'" as the justification for influencing the "eternal tomorrow" of the poor. "It has always been this way."
- Influencing areas of life that are beyond their scope of influence (e.g., the landlord choosing the names of the children or deciding who will marry whom).
- Claiming immutability for their power over the poor. There will never be power sharing.
- Interacting with other non-poor in ways that safeguard and enhance each other's power. (1998a, 1–2)

This captivity finds concrete expression in the interactive workings of the social, political, economic, religious, and cultural systems, resulting in a web of lies and deceit (more on this shortly) that mediates power, often with no need of force. Furthermore, this systemic captivity has many levels. The local police, landowners, and religious leaders form the micro-expressions or the lowest level of this disempowering system. They, in turn, are linked to and usually subservient to business, political, and judicial leaders at the regional and national levels. This is the macro-level of the god complexes. These are embedded in global systems represented by transnational corporations, international financial institutions (the World Bank, IMF, etc.), the UN system, and the like, all of whom too often yield to the temptation to play god in the lives of the poor, albeit from a far distance. Structural adjustment and the Washington Consensus come to mind as examples. Finally, Christian follows Wink in reminding us that all these levels exist within a cosmic system in which the principalities and powers work out their rebellion against God and God's intentions for human life in creation through deception (see Figure 4–7).

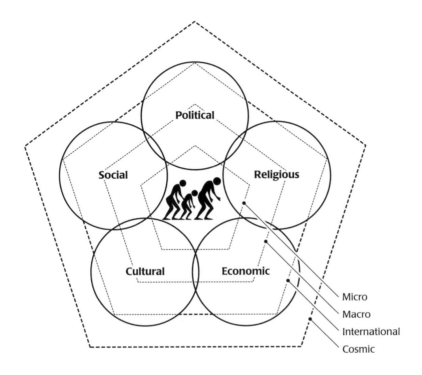

Figure 4–7: Systems framework for the god complexes
that disempower the poor.
(Adapted from Christian 1994)

Building on Walter Wink, Christian goes on to point out that these god complexes, especially at the level of systems and structures, have an ideological center, "an inner reality that governs and holds together the structures, systems and people who inhabit them. This inner reality provides the inner logic . . . and interpretations for ultimate values of life and events" (1998a, 3). Transformational development that does not assert God's truth over these self-justifying narratives leaves the structural side of poverty and its causes untouched.

This captivity to the god complexes of the non-poor becomes internalized as the poor acquiesce to what appears to be the normalcy and immutability of their captivity. This has been the case for a long time. Salvian, in the fifth century, wrote: "They [the poor] give themselves to the upper classes in return for care and protection. They make themselves captives of the rich, as it were, passing over into their jurisdiction and dependence" (in Oden 1986, 151). It took forty years to get the experience of Egyptian slavery out of the collective mind of Israel before Israel could be come a people and a nation. This is an expression of what Christian calls the marred identity of the poor (more on this shortly).

Deception by principalities and powers–The spiritual system

While acknowledging the impact of the fall and sin on individual human beings, Christian, drawing on Walter Wink, also includes the additional impact of the fall through the deception of the principalities and powers (1994, 252). The powerlessness of the poor is reinforced by fear and deceit created by the "god of this age that has blinded the minds of unbelievers" (2 Cor 4:4) and the "trap of the devil who has taken them captive to do his will" (2 Tim 2:26). Both the poor and the non-poor are "in slavery under the elemental spiritual forces of the world" (Gal 4:3).

The primary expression of this deception is through the ideological center or inner reality of the systems, structures, and legitimating narratives through which the non-poor play god in the lives of the poor. But there is a deeper truth as well.

Christian is also affirming that it is not simply human beings, and the systems within which they live, that create and sustain poverty. There is a cosmic adversary who is working against life. This adversary is "a liar and the father of lies" (Jn 8:44). Any account of poverty that ignores the reality of an Evil One lacks the full explanatory power that the Bible offers.

Inadequacies in worldview–The cultural system

For Christian, powerlessness is reinforced by what he calls inadequacies in worldview (1994, 199, 262). Writing within a Hindu context, Christian points to the disempowering idea of *karma*, which teaches the poor that their current state is a just response to their former life and something that must be accepted if they hope for a better life the next time around. When the poor are invited to try to change their present condition, their worldview tells them they are being invited to sin.

In another example of a worldview supporting oppressive social relationships, members of the Brahmin caste are taught by their Hindu tradition that they were made from the head of God and so are supposed to rule. The *harijan* are taught that they were made from the lower parts of god and thus are inferior by nature. This is not just a problem for a Hindu context. Every culture, including those of the West, has beliefs that disempower people, discourage change, and label oppressive relationships as sacrosanct and ordained.

Weakness in mind and body–The biophysical system

This expression of poverty corresponds to Chambers's category of physical weakness. The human mind and body is diminished by poverty and resulting from malnutrition, chronic illness and lack of education (1994, 200). Children who are undernourished for their first two years of life face permanent limits to learning. Sick and weak bodies and minds are easy homes for captivity to god complexes, deception, and inadequate worldviews.

The marred identity of the poor–The personal system

Christian concludes his explanation of poverty by pointing out that captivity to god complexes, deception by principalities and powers, inadequacies in worldview, and the strains of a diminished biophysical system result in a tragic marring of the identity of the poor. The identity of the poor is marred in three important ways.

First, the poor are systematically excluded as actors. Too often the voice of the poor is regarded as "damaged goods." The powerful do not expect the poor to have anything to offer, since they have been labeled (usually by the non-poor) as lazy, ignorant, or unworthy. Sadly, sometimes the development agency and its practitioners are so full of their own expertise that they treat the poor in a similar way.

Second, a lifetime of suffering, deception, and exclusion is internalized by the poor in a way that results in the poor no longer knowing who they truly are or the purpose for which they were created. This is the deepest and most profound expression of poverty. The poor come to believe that they are and were always meant to be without value and without contribution other than to serve. "Poor people feel nonexistent, valueless, humiliated" (Wink 1992, 101).

Internalization of poverty and the messages of non-value from the non-poor and social systems result in what Augustine Musopole calls a poverty of being: "This is where the African feels his poverty most: A poverty of being, in which poor Africans have come to believe they are no good and cannot get things right" (Musopole 1997).

Howard Thurman, the civil rights activist and dean of Marsh Chapel at Boston University, observed in 1949 that "there are few things more devastating than to have it burned into you that you do not count and that no provisions have been made for the literal protection of your person" (1996, 39). The bottom line is simple and frightening; marred identity is the perceived inability to act because individuals have come to believe that they have neither the right nor the social space to do so. The net result of this lack of freedom is the eradication of hope. Without liberty to act on our own and without hope, we are not human in any sense that God intends.

This idea of a diminished sense of identity and vocation resulting from grinding and chronic poverty and oppression has surfaced in a variety of studies in different disciplines. Mexican anthropologist Oscar Lewis was the first to describe the cultural accommodations the rural poor in Mexico made in the face of the oppression by the non-poor; he called the resulting sub-culture a "culture of poverty" (1959). Erving Goffman, a sociologist who investigated stigma, spoke of "spoiled identity" (1963, 15). Cameroonian priest Engelbert Mveng refers to this phenomena in Africa as "indigence of being" (1994, 156). Development economist Arjun Appadurai reports that poverty results in a "limited ability to aspire" (2004, 55–56). Liberation theologian Virgilio Elizondo describes this phenomena as "existential poverty" (2007, 159). Finally, we just looked at Prilleltensky's observations concerning the psychological response of the poor to power and oppression.

It is important to note that none of the foregoing authors is in any way blaming the poor for their poverty. Instead, they are reporting that the poor are making understandable, rational, and necessary emotional adjustments as a way of coping with the chronically oppressive and seeming immutable reality in which they live. The tragedy is that their children inherit these views and take them as normative, ordained, and unchangeable.

I would like to take this idea of marred identity a little farther. Who we are is a question of both being and doing. Christian eloquently calls our attention to the being part of the marred identity of the poor but does not speak to the issue of doing. I believe that poverty mars both parts of the identity of the poor. The result of poverty is that people who are poor no longer know who they are (being) nor do they believe that they have a vocation or gifts of any value (doing).

The web of lies

For Christian, the identity of the poor is distorted, and remains distorted as a result of a "web of lies" that entrap the poor in ways far stronger and insidious than physical bonds or material limitations (1994, 264). These lies are a result of god complexes, inadequacies in worldview, and deception by principalities and powers. Figure 4–8 describes this phenomenon as Christian found it in Indian villages.

Christian's idea of a debilitating web of lies can be used to show the impact of each element of Christian's disempowering themes in the way the poor view the social, political, and social systems within which they live (see Figure 4–9).

Christian's understanding of marred identity adds an additional dimension to the understanding of Chambers and Friedmann. Christian uncovers the internal nature of poverty, created and sustained by the social systems to which Chambers, Friedmann, and Prilleltensky are so sensitive. This inner

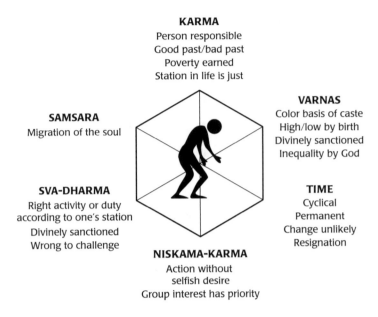

KARMA
Person responsible
Good past/bad past
Poverty earned
Station in life is just

SAMSARA
Migration of the soul

VARNAS
Color basis of caste
High/low by birth
Divinely sanctioned
Inequality by God

SVA-DHARMA
Right activity or duty
according to one's station
Divinely sanctioned
Wrong to challenge

TIME
Cyclical
Permanent
Change unlikely
Resignation

NISKAMA-KARMA
Action without
selfish desire
Group interest has priority

Figure 4–8: The disempowering themes in the
Hindu belief system.
(Adapted from Christian 1994, 241)

set of limitations, all lies, drives poverty deep inside, making it very hard to confront and change. As Christian stated in a telephone interview in 1997, "Poverty is the world telling the poor that they are god-forsaken."

This internalization of poverty in the form of lies about who one is can be so deeply embedded that even the good news of the gospel is no longer believable. Sitting at a campfire in the Kalahari Desert, I heard a San woman say, in response to hearing the news that the Son of God had died for her sins, that she could believe that God would let his Son die for a white man, and that maybe she could believe that God might let his Son die for a black man, but she could never accept the idea that God would let his Son die for a San woman. This is spiritual and psychological poverty of the deepest kind, the root of fatalism.

One final note. Christian's framework also provides a way of understanding what John Dilulio of Princeton University calls "moral poverty." In his studies of violent youth in American inner cities, Dilulio describes "the super-predators," teenagers who will kill without thought or remorse simply because they are inconvenienced. Dilulio says that moral poverty is what you get when people grow up

without loving, capable, responsible parents who teach you right from wrong . . . who habituate you to feel joy at other's joy, pain at other's

Theme	Social System	Lie
Captivity to the god-complexes of the non-poor	Social	You are outside the social system.
	Political	Your purpose is to serve us.
	Economic	You have no assets, nor should you.
	Religious	We will speak to God on your behalf.
Marred identity of the poor	Social	We are not worthy of inclusion.
	Political	We are not worthy of participation.
	Economic	We have nothing to contribute.
	Religious	We are not worthy of God's concern.
Inadequacies in worldview	Social	Our place in the social order is fixed.
	Political	They are supposed to rule over us.
	Economic	Our poverty is ordained.
	Religious	We sinned: God gives us what we deserve.
Deception by the principalities and powers	Social	Social systems are not for the likes of you.
	Political	Political systems are not for the likes of you.
	Economic	Economic systems are not for the likes of you.
	Religious	God is not for the likes of you.
Weakness of mind, body, and spirit	Social	I'm not smart enough.
	Political	I'm uneducated.
	Economic	I'm too weak to matter; I have nothing.
	Religious	I can't understand these things anyway.

Figure 4–9: The all-encompassing web of lies.
(Developed from Christian 1994, 264)

pain, happiness when you do right, remorse when you do wrong. . . . Poverty is growing up surrounded by deviant, delinquent and criminal adults. (1995, 25)

This suggests that in addition to internalizing negative, debilitating lies learned from the social system, poverty can also occur as a result of the chronic absence of any experience with love, responsibility, and righteousness. Apparently we also need to believe in a web of truth.

This is not a problem limited to the inner city of America. Young people in too many parts of the world are being denied this kind of poverty prevention when they are used in the sex trade, abused as child laborers, or sent to war as teenagers. We do not know what kind of adults we will encounter in ten years' time in places like Thailand, India, Rwanda, Liberia, and Sierra Leone—or in the inner cities of America.

When the poor accept their marred identity and their distorted sense of vocation as normative and immutable, their poverty is complete. As one's freedom diminishes, so does one's hope. The absence of freedom and hope erodes the human spirit. This is permanent unless this issue is addressed and the poor are helped to recover their identity as children of God, made in God's image.

Ravi Jayakaran—Poverty as a lack of freedom to grow

Ravi Jayakaran, an Indian expert in the use of the Participatory Learning and Action (PLA) methodology and a former colleague of Robert Chambers, describes poverty as a lack of the freedom to grow (1996, 14). Echoing Luke 2:52, Jayakaran pictures the poor wrapped in a series of restrictions and limitations in four areas of life: physical, mental, social, and spiritual (see Figure 4–10).

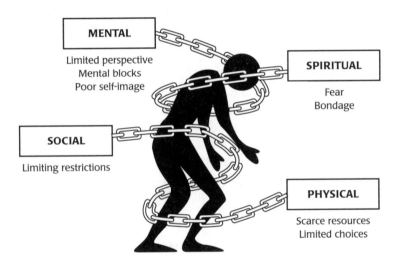

Figure 4–10: Poverty as a lack of freedom to grow.
(After Jayakaran 1996, 14)

Jayakaran's framework for poverty as limitation echoes Friedmann's observation that, while we do not know what a "flourishing human life" is, we "can know what inhibits it: hunger, poor health, poor education, a life of backbreaking labor, a constant fear of dispossession and chaotic social relations" (Friedmann 1992, 12). The response is to help the poor lose their limitations, a phrase that Ted Ward often used as he consulted with development agencies in the 1980s. This echoes Sen's proposal that the goal of development is to increase human freedom as both the means and the end of development.

Jayakaran goes on to point out that behind each of these "bundles of limitations" lies powerful stakeholders, people whose interests are served by the limitations and who have a stake in sustaining the illusion that such limitations can never be changed. We discover these limitations when we ask the critical diagnostic question: Who is doing what to whom? The micro-expression of these stakeholders is usually local and obvious: money-lenders, local traders and business people, police, government officials, and priests or shamans. The macro-expressions are often harder to name because they are located elsewhere, usually close to where decisions affecting the poor are made. In addition to being harder to find and identify, the higher-level stakeholders usually control the micro-level ones.

Jayakaran adds to our understanding of poverty in two important ways. First, he locates the causes of poverty in people, not in concepts or abstractions. This is important and is frequently forgotten. It is easy to blame greed, systems, the market, corruption, and culture, but these are abstractions and cannot be directly changed. People—the poor and the non-poor—have to change. Second, Jayakaran alerts us to the fact that these stakeholders, the sources of oppression, are often themselves operating within "bundles of limitations" kept in place by still-more-powerful stakeholders. The local non-poor are also the poor held in bondage by another group of non-poor who are operating at a higher level in the system. This staircase of oppression goes all the way from the village to the area, to the nation, and to the global level. Linthicum calls this "systems above systems" (Linthicum 1991, 19). This is the nature of poverty and oppression. Everyone is sinner and sinned against.

Summary

We have looked at poverty as deficit, as entanglement, as lack of access to social power, as diminished personal agency, as disempowerment and as lack of freedom to grow. All have added important elements to our picture. We can conclude that poverty is a complicated social issue involving all areas of life—physical, psychological, social, cultural, and spiritual. At some level, however, we must also conclude that poverty is in the eye of the beholder. We see what our worldview, education, and training allow us to see. We need to be aware of this and work hard at seeing *all* there is to see.

Having said this, I add a word of caution. I doubt there is or ever will be a unified theory of poverty. There is always more to see and more to learn. The corrective is to keep using a family of views to see all the things we need to see. We must work hard to be as holistic as we can be for the sake of the poor.

THE CAUSES OF POVERTY

Having explored the nature of poverty, we can now turn to the causes of poverty. Articulating our understanding of the causes of poverty is important since our understanding of the causes of poverty tends to shape how we respond to poverty. Our understanding of why people are poor shapes our understanding of transformational development, the better human future it seeks, and the methods we must apply to get there. The simple chart in Figure 4–11 illustrates the point.

View of cause	Proposed response
The poor are sinners.	Evangelism and uplift
The poor are sinned against.	Social action; working for justice
The poor lack knowledge.	Education
The poor lack things	Relief/social welfare
The culture of the poor is flawed.	Become like us; ours is better
The social system makes them poor.	Change the system

Figure 4–11: How cause shapes response.

Like our understanding of the nature of poverty, our understanding of the causes of poverty tends to be in the eye of the beholder. If care is not taken to understand our unwitting biases, our understanding of the causes of poverty tends to be an outworking of our place in the social system, our education, our culture, and our personality. Our understanding of the causes of poverty also depends on where we start looking at poverty, and more important, where we stop looking (see Figure 4–12).

For example, if we are only concerned with needs, we will only see lack of water. Without further thought, lack of water is the cause of poverty and providing water is the answer. However, behind needs are issues, such as ownership of the water. If this is the cause of the lack of water, then the response is to work on ownership or access. Yet behind issues there are structures, such as caste, which influence who gets access to water, and which often create insurmountable barriers to access. Behind structures are groups, people who inhabit and enforce the structures by insisting that "it is our water and our right to control its use." Behind these groups are the ideologies and values that inform the group and shape the social structure, the unspoken assumptions that "we are to be served and they are subhuman and aren't supposed to drink where we drink." This is the level at which cultural values are at work.

This kind of social analysis deepens our understanding of what causes poverty. It allows us to discover much of what Chambers, Friedmann,

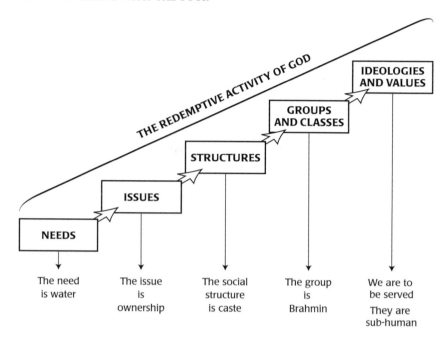

Figure 4–12: From needs to causes.

Prilleltensky, Christian, and Jayakaran say we must see. We raise our view from physical need and the individual person to the social and cultural systems within which the poor live. We are beginning to understand that ideas, values, and worldviews also need to change. This is good.

There is a downside, however, against which we must guard. Sometimes this kind of analysis results in the development practitioner ignoring the immediate needs of the poor and instead going single-mindedly after the underlying causes. While ideas and values must be addressed, leaving the poor without water or with even angrier custodians of water is questionable good news. There can also be a tendency to be caught up in the world of ideas—change the ideas or the cultural values and you will change the world. This can lead to depersonalization, forgetting that the web of lies and the value systems that created it are believed by human beings; they do not live in abstractions like "systems" or "ideologies" or "worldviews." At the end of the day, people are the cause of poverty, and it is people who must change for things to change.

Physical causes of poverty

There are physical causes to poverty. This is obvious. Chambers's categories of material poverty and physical weakness speak to this. People need food, shelter, water, and clean air. They need an environment that supports life. Money, land, and livestock are helpful assets to have. If these kinds of things are largely absent, poverty is the result.

There has been a recent addition to the physical causes of poverty offered by Jared Diamond, a physiologist with a background in linguistics, archeology, and ecology (Diamond 1997). Diamond looks not just at the biology of humans, but at the biology that surrounds humans. He is looking for an alternative to the kind of social Darwinism that explains the world map of development by implying that some ethnic groups are better than others. Diamond argues that *geography*, the quality of land, climate, and native plant species; *guns and capital*, which allow exploration and domination; and *germs*, carried by the urbanized and now immune explorers, hold more explanatory power for economic, political, and cultural progress, than the claim of superior racial characteristics.

Social causes of poverty

> *Our life is empty and we are empty handed.*
> *We are above the dead and below the living.*
> —POOR WOMEN AND MEN IN ETHIOPIA (NARAYAN-PARKER 2000 ET AL., 33)

The physical causes of poverty are intensified by the social causes of poverty. "There are large-scale social practices and a whole system of social roles, often firmly approved by the members of society generally that cause or perpetuate injustice and misery" (Wolterstorff 1983, 24). This social dimension is developed by Chambers, Prilleltensky, and more fully by Friedmann and Jayakaran. Christian's framework points to these systems as the tools and legitimating narratives of those who play god in the lives of the poor by creating the web of lies. Jayakaran identifies the social causes of poverty by pointing us to the stakeholders that stand behind each limitation to growth. But we need to go a little deeper in terms of understanding the dynamics of social systems that create and sustain poverty.

Ann Cudd, a feminist philosopher, discusses the dynamics of oppression in *Analyzing Oppression*. She describes how the cognitive revolution of the 1960s enabled for the first time the empirical examination of phenomena like stereotyping (2006, 68). The development of categorization theory and social-identity theory have shown how we use stereotypes to group and organize the complex social world in which we live by bolstering the self-identity of the group to which we belong; we do that by focusing on what is positive about our group. By itself, this is a helpful and necessary thing. But some observations from schema theory explain why we are tempted not only to think well of ourselves but also to devalue and demean others.

Role schemas provide a family of shorthand mental images of groups and their social roles. We develop these schemas as we grow up and are socialized into our group; in other words, they are socially constructed.

Role schemas allow us to fit a member of a group into a role category quickly, without having to make a thorough assessment of each individual. These role schemas often reflect the less-than-positive differentiating characteristics of the group being observed. Thus our role schema for homeless men is centered on dirt, smell, addiction, and an assumed unwillingness to work. For some men the role schema for women includes being weak, emotional, and only good for taking care of children. Sadly, when our role schemas join our stereotypes, we make our group superior by focusing on the weaknesses or shortcoming of all other groups (2006, 70). Thus our stereotyping is always good for us and not so good for "them" (see Figure 4–13).

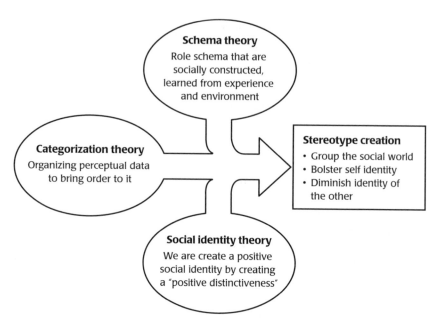

Figure 4–13: Dynamics of negative stereotyping.
(Developed from Cudd 2006, 68–77)

The natural outcome of this way of organizing our thought world allows dominant social groups to see themselves as justly privileged while viewing all other groups as less privileged, and rightly so. This sets up the potential for an oppressive system but does not explain what animates it. Cudd goes on to explain that stereotyping and the oppressive systems that result always have reinforcing coercive elements.

This coercion over the "other" can take the form of overt or threatened violence, since "violence directed against oppressed groups disables and impoverishes them, while enriching or empowering the oppressor or the indirectly privileged" (2006, 85). As an example, the *Voices of the Poor* study learned that the poor identified lack of physical safety and security (overt violence) as a major factor in their poverty. It is hard enough to live with high levels of crime, but such insecurity is often accompanied by police who "emerge not as sources of help and security, but rather of harm, risk and impoverishment" (Narayan-Parker et al. 2000, 278).

In addition, Cudd argues, the economic system reinforces oppression by creating incentives for the oppressed to behave according to their stereo-typical roles. The threat of withholding work or access to credit until there is peace or resigned acceptance to their inferior social role represents a common adjustment the poor have to make in order to survive. The net result over time is Christian's marred identity. As Cudd writes, "Oppressed persons often acquiesce to and accept their oppression because they come to believe in the stereotypes that represent their inferiority, are weakened by those stereotypes and even motivated to fulfill them" (2006, 80).

There is a second form of coercion that is hidden, subtle, and thus more insidious. Overt coercion by force, conscription, or economic incentives and disincentives can be replaced by what Pierre Bourdieu, a French soci-ologist who has focused on trying to understand cultural power, calls sym-bolic violence. Steve Swartz describes Bourdieu's understanding of sym-bolic violence in the following way:

> Bourdieu believes that even in the advanced societies the principal mode of domination has shifted from overt coercion and the threat of physical violence to forms of symbolic manipulations. This belief jus-tifies his focus on the role that cultural processes, producers and in-stitutions play in maintaining inequality in contemporary power. There is symbolic power as well as economic power. (1997, 82)

In other words, the rituals, explanatory narratives, art, the media, and so-cial institutions act together in communicating the nature of social roles and the correct behavior that accompanies them. For example, the bill-board advertising sugar in Brazil has a smiling white woman holding a bag of sugar against a backdrop of picturesque sugarcane fields with people of color working in them. The underlying message about roles and function is clear.

Now we can combine the disempowering system of poverty framework of Jayakumar Christian (1990) with Ann Cudd's proposal of the dynamics of oppression (2006) and make a proposal for the dynamics of marring of identity of the poor. Marred identity is a direct product of the psychologi-cal and biophysical wearing down of the poor as a result of chronic poverty and oppression, as Oscar Lewis (1957) has argued. But marred identity is also a direct outcome the poor being subjected to the oppressive dynam-ics that Cudd (2006) and Prilleltensky (2010) describe, with oppression reinforcement coming through the political and economic systems plus the impact of cultural power à la Bourdieu (see Figure 4–14).

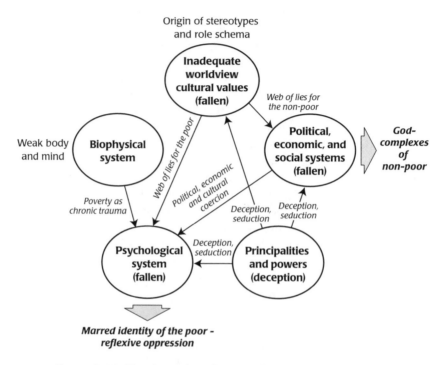

Figure 4–14: The dynamics of oppression and marred identity.
(Synthesis of Christian and Cudd)

This proposal begins with the work of deception and seduction by principalities and powers. This spirit of temptation and deception should remind us of the work of the deceiver in the garden in Genesis and again in the desert tempting Christ. Focusing on the poor, the first seductive invitation is for the poor to believe that they are diminished human beings, and that this is as it should be. Focusing on the non-poor, the second seductive invitation is for the non-poor to believe that they are superior human beings, gifted and ordained to lead. Focusing on worldview, and those whose worldview it is, the third seductive invitation is to adjust the worldview and its cultural values to reflect the two prior deceptions, thus making them culturally normative. The results of this third deception are the negative stereotypes and role schemas to which Cudd calls our attention and the inadequacies in worldview that Christian notes.

These believed and accepted deceptions create the foundation for oppressive social systems and the energy that animates them. The inadequacies in worldview that are directed at the non-poor take the form of a web of lies and delusional assumptions (see the end of this chapter) that the non-poor come to believe and that legitimates their power and authority. This web of lies provides the temptation for the non-poor to play god in the lives of the poor. This playing god is done by using their power to create tools and rules of political, economic, and cultural coercion (Cudd and Bourdieu), all done in the name of promoting the common good.

The poor are thus subject to a triad of disempowering and coercive influences, the first of which is the political, economic, and cultural coercion that wears them down and ultimately weakens their reason, will, and sense of identity. Second, chronic poverty is a form of chronic stress that weakens the poor physically, mentally, and psychologically (more on this in the next section). Finally, having been socialized into a worldview and a set of cultural values shaped by inadequacies in worldview in the form of Christian's web of lies, the poor come to believe that their powerlessness and poverty are normal, ordained, and immutable. The result of this cocoon of debilitation and deception is a form of reflexive oppression or what Jayakumar Christian calls marred identity. This system of deception and seduction is hidden and undeclared, especially for outside observers with a secular modern worldview.

Christian's framework of disempowering systems provides answers to questions that Cudd's analysis of the dynamics of oppression does not address. Why do social systems become oppressive? Why do worldviews have inadequacies that are harmful and debilitating? Why do the poor end up internalizing their poverty and oppression? The answer to these questions is that one element of these interacting systems is spiritual, and its function is solely to deceive toward the end of diminishing human well-being.

No understanding of the social causes of poverty is complete without a discerning social analysis that unmasks and decodes the functioning, deceptions, and impact of these oppressive systems. This must include naming the elements of the web of lies and unmasking the powers that lie behind them (Jayakaran 1996; Wink 1992).

Mental causes of poverty

Some of the causes of poverty have to do with the mental condition of the poor. At the simplest level it is obvious that poverty is caused in part by lack of knowledge and technical information. Poor nutrition during important early childhood years means permanent diminished capacity for learning. The existence of debilitated mental states as the result of poor nutrition, illness, alcohol, or drugs also creates and sustains poverty. But we need to go deeper in understanding the mental causes of poverty.

We have already explored the idea that sense of identity of the poor is marred on the inside. This is the deeper, more insidious, cause of poverty. Melba Maggay provides a highly literary description of this kind of poverty:

[It is] the spirit that always denies, the annoying yet darkly seductive doubt that constantly questions the best we believe. The result for some is a creeping disillusionment, an intemperate realism, that in the end takes away the spring and lightness in our step, stoops our shoulders and makes us bitterly huddle in corners. (1994, 97)

The question we need to explore is what causes this marring of identity. Three explanations come to mind

First, we've just explored the contribution made by the coercive effects of systems of political, economic, and cultural power that take root in the psychology and social psychology of the poor. This should remind us of Andrew Sung Park and his idea of *han* as the result of being sinned against by systematic and systemic disempowerment, violence, and deception. The result, he argues, is a deep wounding of the heart—a "wound to feelings and self-dignity." The result of this wounding is serious and debilitating: "Self-denigration, low self-esteem, self-withdrawal, resignation and self-hatred are conspicuous marks of passive *han* (1993, 20, 33). Furthermore, *han* is not just a personal or individual phenomena; it often finds communal expression. "Han can be described as *internalized collective memory of victims* generated by patriarchal tyranny, racial discrimination, economic exploitation, ethnic cleansing, massacre, foreign occupation, state-sponsored terrorism and unjust war" (Park 2004, 15). *Han* and marred identity seem deeply related.

Research done in World Vision development programs in Tanzania illustrates these internalized deceptions (Johnson 1998, 154–55). Examining the causes of poverty in an area development program, the view of the community differed considerably from the view of World Vision staff (see Figure 4–15).

Cause	Community view	WV staff view
Ignorance	Agree	Disagree
Laziness	Agree	Disagree
Lack of entrepreneurial spirit	Agree	Disagree
Lack of community spirit	Agree	Dasagree
Injustice	Disagree	Agree

Figure 4–15: Community *vs.* staff views.

In every case the community blamed itself for its poverty, having internalized the very descriptors of the poor that Chambers warns development workers to avoid (Chambers 1983, 107).

We need to be careful, however, lest we imply the poor make themselves poor. This is not the case. Wink reminds us that "powerlessness is not simply a problem of attitude. . . . There are structures—economic, political, religious, and only *then* psychological—that oppress people and resist all attempts to end their oppression" (1992, 102). This is also Cudd's position (2006).

Second, Christian suggests that this hopelessness has its roots in the distorted history of the poor and in the actions of the non-poor in making and writing history (1998a, 15). Describing what has happened or not happened in the past has the power to shape what we think can happen in the future. The way the poor remember their history shapes the day-to-day life of the poor today. In this way the past can become a limitation on the future. This is exacerbated by the fact that history is usually written by the non-poor, and they do it in a way that legitimizes their role, often writing the poor out of the story. Being dismissed to the sidelines of their own history increases the poverty of the poor. Those who "do not make history . . . tend to become the utensils of the history makers as well as mere objects of history" (Mills 1993, 162).

Poorly thought through development interventions can exacerbate this distorted view the poor have of their own history. Paulo Freire has exposed the negative contribution that educational systems can have when they teach the poor to understand their world and their past through the narratives of the powerful. An uncritical educational system, a form of cultural power, can reinforce an oppressive system. Freire's *conscientizacao* strategy for literacy and education was designed to allow "each man to win back his right to say his own word, to name the world" (1990, 13). History making and history telling are tools the non-poor can use to make the poor captive to their god complexes.

Finally, marring of identity can be a consequence of poverty as a chronic source of stress. A graduate student of mine compared the clinical definition of trauma with the definition of poverty that emerged from the World Bank *Voices of the Poor* study and noted that one could make a defensible observation that chronic poverty is a form of chronic trauma (Felix 2009). She then compared the evidence derived from the World Bank study to a proposal for a new psychology of trauma developed by Ronnie Janoff-Bulman (1992). The parallels were consistent and striking.

Janoff-Bulman argues that human beings, at least in the West, make three assumptions about themselves. First, we are good, capable, and moral; we have worth or value (1992, 11). Second, the world is more good than bad, and other people are basically good, kind, helpful, and caring; the world is or is supposed to be benevolent (1992, 6). Finally, people tend to get what they deserve, so they will act accordingly; the world is basically just (1992, 9). While most people believe that bad things can happen to good people and can cope with these events as anomalies, for those experiencing chronic trauma such as poverty, these assumptions are continuously contradicted and thus no longer tenable. The result is that adjustments are made in terms of how they understand themselves and how they relate to their world. This often includes blaming their own behavior for the problem or deciding that their flawed character is the cause and then adjusting to this sense of responsibility by what Janoff-Bulman calls "learned helplessness" (1992, 10). This should remind us of Oscar Lewis and his proposal for the subculture of poverty that the poor develop to cope with their oppressive circumstances and powerlessness (1959).

In another example of the relationship of chronic poverty and chronic stress, Tommy Phillips, examining the impact of economic poverty on the poor children and youth, has proposed that the interaction of chronic stress, social stigmatization, and limitations in terms of opportunity "conspire to place poor children and youth on different developmental trajectories (Phillips 2007). Attempting to understand the effect of poverty on how poor youth come to make sense of who they are—identity formation—Phillips identifies economic poverty as a source of chronic source of stress. He proposes that chronic stress interacts with two other pressures to distort and thus diminish a sense of personal identity or agency. The first is limitations in terms of opportunity, and the second is stigmatization and marginalization of the poor by the larger society. This proposal connects nicely with the work of Ann Cudd and the mental causes of poverty we just explored (see Figure 4–14).

Spiritual causes of poverty

While development academics and researchers are increasingly paying more attention to the role of religion in development, the spiritual causes of poverty are often overlooked or undeclared. I have already pointed out how Chambers, Friedmann, and Prilleltensky largely ignore the impact of the spiritual world, shamans, and witchcraft and their very significant contribution to making and keeping people poor. Money is spent on charms for protection and time is lost to feast days, all in an attempt to manage these power relationships. Technical improvements are refused for fear of the reaction of ancestors or the spirit world. Furthermore, while there are lots of references to oppression, deceit, malfeasance, corruption, violence, fatalism, alcohol, and broken and unjust relationships in the development literature, the spiritual dimension seldom surfaces in the explanatory schemes. As we have noted, Christian adds the principalities and powers and their active deception to his variation of Friedmann's framework for powerlessness as the cause of poverty. Melba Maggay supports this view:

> Social action is a confrontation with the powers that be. We are, ultimately, not battling against flesh and blood, nor merely dismantling unjust social systems; we are confronting the powers in their cosmic and social dimensions. (1994, 82)

Jayakaran actually names the spiritual as a cause of poverty. This is the reason I have adopted his framework for this section on the causes of poverty.

So, what can we say about poverty and its causes at the end of this review of major contributors to the conversation? First, poverty is a complex, multifaceted phenomenon. There are no simple answers. Second, understanding poverty requires that we be multidisciplinary; we need the tools of anthropology, sociology, social and community psychology, spiritual discernment, and theology, all nicely integrated. Third, the works of Chambers, Friedmann, Prilleltensky, Christian, and Jayakaran need to be seen as complementary views, each adding something to the other.

A HOLISTIC UNDERSTANDING OF POVERTY

I would now like to pull together material from the chapter on thinking theologically on poverty and development and this chapter's material on poverty and its causes. We need to look for an integrating frame that is both biblical and inclusive of the work of Chambers, Friedmann, Prilleltensky, Christian, and Jayakaran.

The nature of poverty is fundamentally relational

This is the point of departure: Poverty is a result of relationships that do not work, that are not just, that are not for life, that are not harmonious or enjoyable. Poverty is the absence of shalom in all its meanings. It is interesting to note that this view is consistent with the Hebraic worldview, in which relationships are the highest good, while alienation is the lowest.

All five poverty frameworks provide explanations that rest on the idea of relationships that are fragmented, dysfunctional, or oppressive. Chambers's poverty trap, Friedmann's lack of access to social power, Prilleltensky's proposal for poverty as diminished personal and relational well-being, Christian's framework for disempowering systems, and Jayakaran's lack of opportunities to grow all rest on the foundational idea of relationships that lack justice, peace, and shalom, that work against well-being, against life and life abundant.

There is an interesting confirmation of this in an account by Desmond D'Abreo, a leader of Development Education Services (DEEDS) in India. He led a series of exercises in exploring the root causes of what he calls underdevelopment by asking communities in rural India to develop a web diagram (a PLA tool) reflecting their understanding of the origins of some of the problems they had identified in an earlier exercise. In explaining the causes of both drunkenness and illiteracy, the underlying causes came out the same: selfishness and systemic injustice, both relational categories (1989, 107–9).

Understanding poverty as relationships that don't work for the well-being of all is consistent with the biblical story as well. The scope of sin affects every one of the five relationships that make up our lives: our relationship with ourselves, with our community, with those we call "other," with our environment, and with God. Each of these broken relationships find expression in the poverty systems we have covered earlier in this chapter. Jayakumar Christian is right when he asserts that, at its core, poverty is relational (see Figure 4–16).

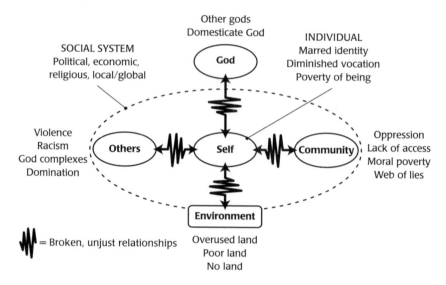

Figure 4–16: A relational understanding of poverty.

At the center of this relational understanding of poverty is the idea that the poor do not know who they really are. When people believe they are less than human or god-forsaken, their understanding of who they are is marred. Similarly, when the poor do not believe that they have the brains, strength, personhood, or right to contribute, that they cannot be productive, their understanding of their vocation is distorted as well. With marred identities and distorted vocations, the poor cannot play their proper relational role in the world, either within themselves or with those around them.

The cause of poverty is fundamentally spiritual

What causes this distortion and injustice in our relationships? What divides us inside ourselves into competing, conflicting voices? What separates us within our community, with some doing well and others suffering? What causes us to exclude and sometimes demonize the "other"? Why do we abuse the earth? What stands between us and God? What is it that works against life, against shalom? The answers to these questions provide us with the explanation of the causes of poverty. Any theory of poverty must have answers for these questions.

For the Christian, the biblical story provides an unambiguous answer. Sin is what distorts these relationships. Sin is the root of deception, distortion, and domination. When God is on the sidelines or written out of our story, we do not treat each other well.

Why does poverty entangle as it does? Why are the poor denied access to social power? What limits their sense of personal agency? What is at the root cause of the web of lies and the disempowerment that results? Why are there constraints to growth, with a group of people standing behind each limitation and restriction? It is because of deceptive and dominating relationships, because we are unable to love God and neighbor, because of sin. We work for what we think life is for. We try to provide our own abundant life. Without a strong theology of sin, comprehensive explanations for poverty are hard to come by.

One other point, a hard thing to say. If it is true that sin is the fundamental cause of our lack of shalom, of our world of dominating relationships, then there is good news and bad news. The good news is that through Jesus Christ there is a way out of sin toward transformation. The bad news is that if this news is not accepted, there is a sense in which those who refuse sit wrapped in chains of self-imposed limitations.

For the Christian development worker, there is an obvious implication. There can be no practice of transformational development that is Christian unless somewhere, in some form, people are hearing the good news of the gospel and being given a chance to respond. How one does this in a sensitive, appropriate, and non-coercive way is also very important and will be explored in Chapter 10 on Christian witness.

POVERTY OF THE NON-POOR

A chapter on poverty is not complete unless we make some comments on the poverty of the non-poor. After all, in God's sight all human beings are poor. The non-poor have a different set of problems to be sure, not the least of which is that God hates idolatry, injustice, oppression, and any attempt to play God's role in the life of anyone else.

We need to begin with the observation that the non-poor have a great deal in common with the poor from the biblical perspective. The non-poor are also made in the image of God, are also fallen, and are also being offered redemption. Sadly, it is harder for the non-poor to hear this good news than it is for the poor. This is true partly because they enjoy, knowingly or not, their privilege and playing god in the lives of the poor.

But there is a much deeper irony here. The non-poor suffer from the same kind of poverty as the poor. They too suffer from marred identity, but with a marring of a different kind. When the non-poor play god in the lives of other people, they have stopped being who they truly are and are assuming the role of God. Losing sight of their true identity leads the non-poor to misread their true vocation as well. Instead of understanding themselves as productive stewards working for the well-being of their community, they act as if their gifts and position are somehow rightfully theirs, or earned, and hence are solely for themselves and for their well-being. There is a sense in which the non-poor are also captive to a web of lies, only the lies are different from those of the poor (see Figure 4–17).

Interestingly, Walter Wink has described something similar in the form of "delusional assumptions," a term he uses to describe beliefs taken for granted by the powerful that justify their power (1992, 95). These deceptions are another kind of web of lies believed by the non-poor. As with Christian's web of lies, these deceptions are often undeclared and are accepted uncritically by the poor and non-poor alike. The non-poor are socialized into their dominant role through mythic stories, narratives, symbols, and rituals that make their position of power make sense, even seem ethically defensible. This is cultural or symbolic power as described by Pierre Bourdieu.

A partial list of Wink's delusional assumptions includes:

- The need to prevent social chaos requires that some should dominate others.
- Men are better at being dominant than women; some races are more naturally suited to dominate others.
- A valued end justifies any means.
- Violence is redemptive; it is the only language enemies understand.
- Ruling or managing is the most important social function.
- Rulers and managers are entitled to extra privileges and wealth.
- Those with the greatest military strength, the most advanced technology, the biggest markets, and the most wealth are the ones who will and should survive.
- Production of wealth is more important than production of healthy, normal people and sound human relationships.
- Property is sacred and property ownership is an absolute right.
- Institutions are more important than people.
- God, if there is a God, is the protector and patron of the powerful. (Wink 1992, 95)

Wink goes to the biblical account for an explanation of how the non-poor have been unwittingly deceived: "The rulers of the earth do not know that they too are held in thrall by the Delusional System. They do not know whom they serve" (Wink 1992, 97). Poverty cannot be addressed

Theme	Social system	Lie
Captivity to our own god complex	Social	We are the social system.
	Political	It is right that we be served.
	Economic	We are the key to successful economics.
	Religious	God has chosen us.
Marred identity of the non-poor	Social	We are better at running things.
	Political	We were made to make decisions for others.
	Economic	Having and winning is all there is.
	Religious	We are the blessed of God.
Inadequacies in worldview	Social	Our place in the social order is fixed.
	Political	We are intended to rule.
	Economic	It's a competition; some win, some don't.
	Religious	God has a formula for success, and they didn't follow it.

Figure 4–17: The web of lies of the non-poor.

fully unless these delusions on the part of the non-poor are exposed and their respective webs of lies confronted by God's truth. "The church has no more important task than to expose these delusional assumptions as the Dragon's game" (Wink 1992, 96, referring to the Dragon of Revelation 13). Yet Wink insists this must not be done by demonizing the non-poor because they too have been deceived by the rulers of this age.

The activity of the non-poor in safeguarding their privilege and power also creates a form of poverty unique to the non-poor. When we misuse a social system for our benefit, it is hard to believe that our friends are not doing the same. When domination is the goal, we have to keep winning in order not to lose.

> The more a rich man possesses the more worry he has. . . . He fears the failure of his revenues. . . . He fears the violence of the mighty, doubts the honesty of his household, and lives in perpetual fear of the deceptions of strangers. (Hugh of St. Victor, quoted in Oden 1986, 155)

When we get so far out of touch with what is real and true, when we believe in the delusional assumptions of Wink and think that the web of lies is a web of truth, we find ourselves alone, suspicious and fearful; we don't know what is real anymore.

There is another sense in which the poverty of the non-poor is the mirror image of the poverty of the poor. It seems as if having too much is as bad for us as having too little. Too little food makes us weak and susceptible to disease; too much food makes us overweight and susceptible to heart disease and cancer. The water in the Third World is dirty and unhealthy; the water in the West is bad for our health because it is increasingly polluted with chemicals. The poor have inadequate housing; the non-poor are often slaves to their houses. Octavio Paz observed that the rich have too few fiestas and are poor, while the poor have too many fiestas and are also poor (Parker 1996, 107). Koyama puts this "too much is poverty" idea nicely:

> Man cannot live without bread. But, man must not live by this essential bread alone. Bread-alone, shelter-alone, clothing-alone, income-alone, all these alones damage man's quality of life. Strangely, these good values contain danger elements too. Man is supposed to eat bread. But what if bread eats man? People are dying from over-eating today in affluent countries. Man is supposed to live in the house. But what if the house begins to live in man? . . . Man needs bread plus the word of God. (1979, 4–5)

The idea of too much or too little being two sides of the same problem reminds us of Proverbs 30:8–9:

> Give me neither poverty nor riches, but give me only
>   my daily bread.
> Otherwise, I may have too much and disown you and
>   say, "Who is the LORD?"
> Or I may become poor and steal, and so dishonor the
>   name of my God.

At the end of the day, the cause of the poverty of the non-poor is the same as that of the poverty of the poor, only differently expressed. The poverty of the non-poor is fundamentally relational and caused by sin. The result is a life full of things and experiences, but short on meaning. The non-poor simply believe a different set of lies. The only difference is that the poverty of the non-poor is harder to change. "A bank account and abundant diet somehow (I cannot explain it quite satisfactorily) insulate man from coming to feel the primary truth of history" (Koyama 1974, 23). This is what Jesus was trying to say when he compared a rich man getting into the kingdom as a camel trying to go through the eye of a needle.

5

Perspectives on development

To this point, we have described the biblical narrative as the normative story that frames our individual stories and the stories of the communities in which we live and work. We have also explored a number of perspectives for understanding the nature of poverty and its causes. Our next step will be to review how development is understood by some important Christian and non-Christian contributors to development thinking. As before, we will discover that there is much to learn from those who study development professionally as well as from Christian practitioners.

WHO WILL SAVE US?

This is another way of asking which story will inform our understanding of transformational development. It is important that the development practitioner and the community answer this question and not simply assume that everyone shares the same answer. After all, there are a number of competing stories claiming to provide the answer; some are quite subtle and seductive.

For most of the last two centuries modernity has put forth the claim that human progress is the inevitable outcome of applying human reason and modern science, the means by which "the fissures of the world could be repaired and the world can be healed" (Volf 1996, 25). What the myth of human progress ignores is that evil lies at the bottom of these fissures, and that evil bends human reason to other ends. The modern story of the West has no antidote for evil. Modernity sets its hopes "in the twin strategies of social control and rational thought" (ibid., 26), neither of which has power over evil.

At the beginning of the twenty-first century the four horseman of modernity—capitalism, globalization, science, and technology—still offer to save the poor. The claim is made that things are getting better, at least a little. The number of people living on $1.25 a day has come down significantly since 1990 (World Bank 2009, 2004). The decline in the numbers of poor people in China, India, and Brazil has been dramatic. Yet improving conditions are not enough to support the claim that modernity alone will save the poor.

Cristián Parker, a sociologist of religion in Chile, reflecting on the poverty of Latin America and the impact of modernity and unbridled capitalism from the North, argues that capitalism "carries within itself the limits of its own horizon, since it has no possible escape from its own golden calves and shatters on the ultimate unsatisfaction [sic] of vital human needs, including the deepest longings of the human being today" (1996, 256).

Parker goes on to note the continuing energy and staying power of popular religion in Latin America and wonders why this should be so.[1] He suggests that popular religion is answering questions and meeting needs that economic growth alone cannot. Parker argues that the worship of pragmatism, assessing everything only in terms of what works, and the ethic of freedom, understood as the right to be indifferent to others in your community, are reflections of a "crisis of civilization" (1996, 258). He goes on to say:

> It is a crisis because of the manner in which the dominant modern mentality unfolds in its relationship with nature—in the relation to human beings with one another, with things and with the transcendent. It is the crisis of instrumental rationality carried to its ultimate expression. . . . It is a sacrilegious, perverse conception . . . in view of the fact that it sets up reason as god of the intellect in order to legitimate actions oriented toward ends without any consideration of the value of the means, ultimately leading to the unscrupulous self-destruction of persons and their cultural and natural surroundings. It is modern human beings who are in crisis, since their relation with themselves and the ecosystem is in crisis. Human beings are splitting, have sundered, their original harmony (1996, 259).

The development practitioner must understand that the fundamental claim of capitalism, globalization, science, and technology is a lie: they cannot save. Saving is not within their power. Economic growth, modern medicine, agriculture, water development, and the technologies that support them are tools, provisions of a good God. We must use them sensitively

---

[1] This is the same question that Kwame Bediako (1992), Andrew Walls (1989), Augustine Musopole (1997), Cyril Okorocha (1994), and other African theologians and sociologists have been asking of African traditional religion, which, in spite of the significant inroads of Islam, Christianity, and modernity, persists as one of the most powerful forces at work on the African continent.

and appropriately. They can enhance life and make people more productive. But they do not save. "The unshakable hope the 1960s placed in development and freedom and expressed in the liberation projects of the 1970s has evaporated. . . . Latin America and the world . . . need to rethink . . . to reinvent hope on a different foundation" (Parker 1996, 248).

The wisdom of the cross offers a different basis for hope. The cross teaches us that salvation does not come from right thinking or right technique, but by divine action making right what we cannot make right ourselves. We are told that "the foolishness of God is wiser than man's wisdom and the weakness of God is stronger than man's strength" (1 Cor 1:25). Foolishness and weakness are the message of the cross, "the power of God" (1 Cor 1:18). The development worker must never forget this basic truth about who can save. The claims of modernity are seductive, and we encounter them every day in the things we read, listen to, and study. Our professional training as development specialists is predicated on the idea that the stories of the market, science, and technology can save others. This is not true, and we must guard against this deception. These things are tools and they can help, but they cannot save.

There is one other possible source of salvation that needs to be debunked, lest we do harm unwittingly. It is understandable that the poor may believe that the development worker or the development agency will be the one who saves. After all, we come in power with four-wheel drive vehicles, money, technology, and technical knowledge. We seem to understand why things are as they are and how to change them. Helping the poor set aside this perception is a significant methodological challenge for the development worker. I will come back to this important issue in the chapter on development practice.

SHAPING OUR VIEW OF TRANSFORMATION

Just as we saw with the causes of poverty, our point of view tends to determine how we think about human transformation. We need to make explicit our point of view and then see if we can enlarge it. There are several ways in which this takes place.

Transformation from what and to what?

One way to make explicit our assumptions is to take note of what we believe people are being transformed *from* and transformed *to* (see Figure 5–1).

If we see people as lost souls, then transformation is about saving souls. If we see people as suffering from hunger, then transformation is about feeding them. If the problem is unjust systems, then the tools of transformation

From what?	To what?	Which relationship?
Lost soul	Saved soul	With God
Dying body	Nourished body	With self
Sick body	Healed body	With self
Broken mind	Restored mind	With self
Unjust social system	Just social relationships	With community and others
Violence	Reconciled relationships	With community and others
Decaying creation	Sustaining world	With environment

Figure 5–1: Transformation from what? To what?

are community organizing, advocacy, or political activism. And so it goes—differing views of poverty drive us to differing approaches to transformation.

Each of these views is true, but each is also incomplete. If we can accept that biblical transformation addresses all these dimensions of human life, we can take another step toward a more comprehensive, holistic view of transformation. If we do not, we reduce transformation to evangelism to save the soul; to social work, medicine, or psychology to save the person; to political activism or peacemaking to restore the social system; and to environmentalism to save nature.

Levels of the problem

In the chapter on poverty and the poor, we discovered that our understanding of poverty depends on the level at which we examine any given situation. As we deepen our social analysis, our understanding of the causes of poverty changes. The way we understand the causes of poverty also tends to determine our response to poverty. If we see poverty as hungry children, the response is social welfare; we need to feed them. If we see poverty as lack of knowledge of nutrition and low agricultural production, the response is community development that teaches new skills and provides new seeds. If we go a level deeper and see poverty as an issue of land tenure and local marketing systems that favor cash crops over food, then the response is to work for policy change, government intervention, and community organizing. Once again, we need to resist the temptation to choose one view over the others. All call for a response. Transformational development takes each seriously.

WHAT IS DEVELOPMENT?

As with the section on understanding poverty, it is helpful to review several different perspectives on what development is and what's involved in causing it to happen. Each view has something to teach us and hence is important to our attempt to create a Christian framework for transformational development. The key will be to identify the transformational frontiers in each view. Transformational frontiers are those areas at which a transformational strategy might be focused to bring about sustainable change in the direction of the kingdom of God.

Wayne Bragg—Development as transformation

In the evolution of development thinking of evangelicals, the Wheaton '83 consultation entitled "A Christian Response to Human Need" was noteworthy. Wayne Bragg, former director of the Hunger Center at Wheaton College, wrote a seminal paper in which he argued that transformation was the biblical term that best fit a Christian view of development (1983, 37–95). While not a development theory per se, Bragg called for an understanding of development that went beyond social welfare by including justice concerns, something controversial for evangelicals at that time. Bragg listed what he called the characteristics of transformation, each a transformational frontier:

- *Life sustenance* or the meeting of human basic needs.
- *Equity,* meaning equitable distribution of material goods and opportunities.
- *Justice* within all social relationships, including democratic participation.
- *Dignity and self-worth* in the sense of feeling fully human and knowing we are made in the image of God.
- *Freedom* from external control or oppression; a sense of being liberated in Christ.
- *Participation* in a meaningful way in our own transformation.
- *Reciprocity* between the poor and the non-poor; each have something to learn from the other.
- *Cultural fit* that respects the best in local cultures and that treats them as creative.
- *Ecological soundness.*

Bragg added some important new ideas to the evangelical conversation about development. Just social systems and opportunities for all had not been on the evangelical development agenda. At the time they were deemed "too political," and most Western evangelicals had not yet formed a theology of political activism. The exceptions came largely from Latin America in the voices of Orlando Costas, René Padilla, and Samuel Escobar. In the United States, Ron Sider of Evangelicals for Social Action and Jim Wallace of the Sojourner Community were lone voices for a time.

The inclusion of freedom and participation were just gaining an understanding. Learning from the poor and seeing all cultures as made by God and being creative sources of transformation were also important. Ecology was a new issue for evangelical development thinking at that time.

Bragg's views had some weaknesses as well. There is a strong redistributionist undertone that is no longer viewed as positively as it once was. Bragg, like many evangelicals working in development at the time (including the author), also underestimated the importance of wealth creation. Finally, Bragg's view of the poor tended to be somewhat romantic. There was no space for the contribution the poor make to their own poverty; all sin, including the temptation to oppress others, seemed to belong only to the non-poor.

David Korten—People-centered development

David Korten, a development practitioner in the Philippines with the Ford Foundation and then USAID and now a leading critic of globalization, wrote *Getting to the Twenty-first Century*, an important book on development in the early 1990s. Korten contrasted what he called people-centered development with the economic growth-centered development promoted by many Western governments (see Figure 5–2).

Growth-centered development	People-centered development
Material consumption	Human well-being
Wants of the non-poor	Needs of the poor
Corporation or business	Household
Competition	Community
Export markets	Local markets
Absentee ownership	Local ownership
Borrowing and debt	Conserving and sharing
Specialization	Diversification
Interdependence	Self-reliance
Environmental costs externalized	Environmental costs internalized
Free flow of capital and services	Free flow of information

Figure 5–2: Two visions of development.
(Adapted from Korten 1991)

Korten believed the world at the end of the twentieth century was suffering from a threefold crisis: poverty, environmental destruction, and social disintegration (1990, 114). He defined development as "a process by which the members of a society increase their personal and institutional capacities to mobilize and manage resources to produce sustainable and justly distributed improvements in their quality of life consistent with their own aspirations" (1990, 67).

Korten's four key phrases were "process," "capacities," "sustainable and just," and "consistent with their own aspirations." Development is not something arrived at, an end point; it is a continuing process. This process, according to Korten, should be driven by three principles: sustainability, justice, and inclusiveness.

By "sustainable," Korten means that any good development must sustain and nurture the environment. By "justice and inclusiveness," Korten addresses the problem of the social disintegration and disenfranchisement that accompanies (and causes) poverty and the fact that governments and social systems are biased in favor of the powerful, who are also the major consumers.

Finally, for Korten, "consistent with their own aspirations" means that the people should decide for themselves what improvements are needed and how they are to be created. The development program must not come from the outside.

One of Korten's other major contributions is calling attention to the fact that a development agency must have some kind of philosophy of development and that this philosophy is primarily shaped by the agency's understanding of the nature and causes of poverty. He encourages agencies to make their assumptions about the nature and causes of poverty explicit and then review them critically in light of the agency's experience.

> In the absence of a theory, the aspiring development agency almost inevitably becomes an assistance agency engaged in relieving the more visible symptoms of underdevelopment through relief and welfare measures. The assistance agency that acts without a theory also runs considerable risk of inadvertently strengthening the very forces responsible for the conditions of suffering and injustice that it seeks to alleviate through its aid. (1990, 113)

Korten then creates a typology of development responses, each reflecting how the problem of poverty is understood (see Figure 5–3).

Korten's typology of problem definition moves from shortage of things to shortage of skills and local inertia, to failure of social and cultural systems, and finally to an inadequate mobilizing vision. The development response changes accordingly from feeding people to empowering communities, to developing sustainable social systems and finally to mobilizing people movements—the last two echoing Friedmann. Korten describes these responses as four generations of development strategy that move from responding to symptoms (relief) to addressing underlying causes (sustainable development).

Most development agencies began at Korten's first level and have moved to the second level of community development. A few have begun to work at the third level: working for sustainable systems. Korten's prophetic call is

	Relief and Welfare	Small-scale, self-reliant local development	Sustainable systems development	People's movements
Type of problem	Shortage of things	Shortage of skills and local inertia	Failure of social and cultural systems	Inadequate mobilizing vision
Time frame	Immediate	3-5 years	10-20 years	Indefinite
Scope	Individual and family	Neighborhood/village	Region and nation	National and global
Chief actors	Development agency	Development agency and community	All relevant public and private institutions	Networks of people and organizations
Role of agency	Doer	Mobilizer and teacher	Catalyst	Activist and educator
Management style	Logistics management	Community self-help	Strategic management and systems development	Linking and energizing self-managed networks

Figure 5–3: Korten's typology of development responses. (Adapted from Korten 1990)

to move to his fourth level—promoting people's movements. This is his answer to transforming the lives of the poor.

Korten's understanding of development has made some helpful contributions. Development as a process and not an end is an important idea. He also adds critical concerns for just social systems and for a sustainable environment. While there are things to argue about in Korten's view of people-centered development, its contrast with growth-centered development is helpful in disclosing the blind spots of this prevailing view.

Korten addresses the spiritual aspect of development in an interesting way by acknowledging a role for religion. He acknowledges that "questions relating to the uses of power, values, love, brotherhood, peace and the ability of people to live in harmony with one another are fundamental to religion and to the role of church in society" (1990, 168). After Charles Elliot (1987), Korten goes on to say that "the human spirit must be strengthened to the point that greed and egotism play a less dominant role" (1990, 168). Korten is struggling to find a way to help those who accept the growth-centered approach to development to change their view. How will the values of just distribution and sustainability be taught or caught? He concludes by noting that values formation, including reordering power relations, "has long been the essence of all great religious teaching" (1990, 168).

Korten seems to understand that value change is hard work and that it is the work of religion. He argues that, while religious institutions do not always have the best of records living out their own values in these areas, they are nonetheless the most likely candidates to help on this transformational frontier. Having bravely acknowledged the possible role of the faith-based organizations in the process, Korten stops short of declaring himself on the issue of evangelism and conversion. One gets the feeling that he would prefer faith-based value formation as long as that did not include asking people to change their religious perspective.

Korten leaves some other questions unanswered as well. He may be overly optimistic in expecting that a quality of life that is quality for all will emerge if its definition is left solely to local aspirations. Local aspirations are shaped by local culture, local worldview, and local social structures. As Jayakumar Christian has reminded us, accepting local worldviews uncritically is sometimes a source of poverty, not an answer to it. Finally, Korten's fourth-generation strategy calls for an adequate mobilizing vision but then is mute on the critical questions: Whose vision? What makes a vision adequate? Where does the vision come from?

Finally, while very helpful, there is also something worrisome about Korten's typology of development responses. He develops his four generations of strategy as a story of evolution, a social learning process whereby agencies move from symptoms to causes. Does he expect development agencies to cease working at the lower levels (symptoms) and focus solely on causes? Is the ideal development agency a fourth-generation agency? Or, does he expect development agencies to work at all four levels at once? Can any agency be effective working on this many fronts? Or should development agencies partner with relief agencies and advocacy groups, forming consortiums that together can work at social welfare, relief, community development, sustainable systems, and people movements? Finally, the evidence that people movements create sustainable societal change is limited.

John Friedmann—Development as expanding access to social power

John Friedmann's understanding of development follows closely from his definition of the cause of poverty: limited access to social power. Alternative development for Friedmann "is a process that seeks the empowerment of the households and their individual members through their involvement in socially and politically relevant actions" (1992, 33). Empowerment includes an emphasis on local decision making, local self-reliance, participatory democracy, and social learning. It pursues the "transcendent goals of inclusive democracy, appropriate economic growth, gender equality and sustainability" (1992, 164). Friedmann explains this using the schema developed in Chapter 4.

Recalling the eight bases for increasing social power (see Figure 4–4), Friedmann's view of transformation calls for working with the household so that it is empowered to increase the envelope of its social power outward along the eight lines of social power. He notes that the state and the economy can be limiting factors to expanding six of the eight lines of social power. Only by increasing social organization and social networks is it possible to pressure the state and economy to allow the other six lines of social power to expand. Thus, building, empowering, and nurturing social networks and social organizations is the key to expanding social power, according to Friedmann.

Social organizations include formal and informal groups to whom the household belongs, "including churches, mother's clubs, sports clubs, neighborhood improvement associations, credit circles, discussion clubs, tenant organizations, syndicates and irrigation associations" (1992, 68). Social networks, for Friedmann, "are essential for self-reliant actions based on reciprocity" and include family, friends, and neighbors. Indigenous movements are an example of what Friedmann has in mind.

Keeping in mind Friedmann's four domains of social practice (see Figure 4–3), Friedmann believes that, in the last part of the twentieth century, the domain of the state was shrinking because of the popularity of the neoliberal view of global capitalism—the Washington Consensus—which calls for smaller governments, free markets, freely convertible currency, and free trade. As the domain of the state shrinks, the domain of the economy expands because it is linked to and driven by the global economy. In

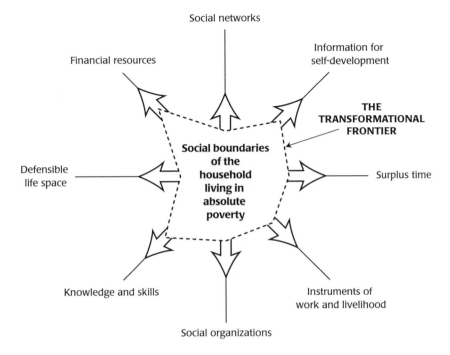

Figure 5–4: Transformation as expanding the frontiers of social power.
(Adapted from Friedmann 1992, 67)

Friedmann's view this leaves only two domains in which one can work to empower the household: the domain of civil society, and the domain of political community (see Figure 5–5). Alternative development works to expand these two domains, thus creating more life space for the poor.

Where civil society overlaps the domain of the state, Friedmann's goal is to expand household participation in democratic processes. Where civil society intersects with the economy, Friedmann sees the opportunity to increase household participation as productive citizens with a stake in society. Where political community overlaps with the state, the goal is to work for a more responsive, inclusive, and just legal system. Where political economy intersects with the corporate economy, work needs to be done to create an economic system that is more responsive to human and environmental costs.

Friedmann believes in a bottom-up approach to empowerment, in contrast to one mediated by government or even by the development agency. His logic works like this. The poor must take part in meeting their own needs. To do so, they must acquire the means to do this. The means should be the result of "the hurly burly of politics in which the poor continuously press for the support, at the macro level, of their own initiatives" (1992,

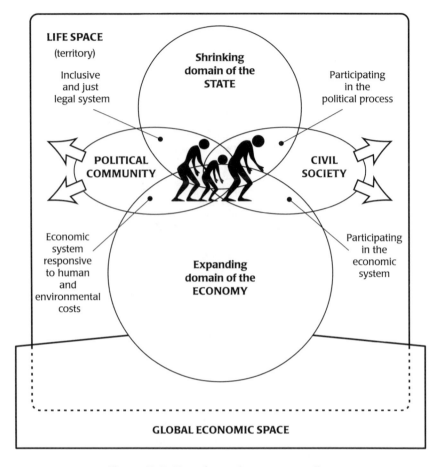

Figure 5–5: Transformation as expanding
the social and political power of households.
(Adapted from Friedmann 1992, 27)

66). However, he acknowledges that this is not enough: "Although an alternative development must begin locally, it cannot end there" (1992, 7).

The question is how one gets from a bottom-up, household-centered approach to development to increasing social power, especially political power. Friedmann suggests that this can be done by "scaling up" the micro development projects of the past. While small is beautiful, it is also often invisible and easy for the powerful to ignore, Friedmann argues. The key is to "expand the territorial scope of alternative projects" by linking projects into

networks, coalitions, federations and confederations of popular organizations and non-governmental organizations. These ensembles serve as vehicles for information exchange, technical and political support, and political lobbies, establishing the civil society of the disempowered as a significant actor outside the traditional system of party politics. (1992, 142)

Friedmann's view of alternative development is very helpful because it places social power—both economic and political—at the center of the development agenda. Locating the poor household in a social systems perspective, Friedmann makes clear the need for households to be able to participate in both the political and economic system if there is to be sustainable change. While Friedmann is focused on enlarging social power, he is not arguing against providing real help now to the poor. "If social and economic development means anything at all, it must mean a clear improvement in the conditions of life and livelihood of ordinary people" (1992, 9).

Friedmann's approach also gives considerable substance to what Korten calls "sustainable systems," but, unlike Korten, accepts the current global economic system as a given, rather than hoping it will somehow go away or that local realities can somehow act as if it were not there.

The objective of an alternative development is to humanize a system that has shut them [the poor] out, and to accomplish this through forms of everyday resistance and political struggle that insist on the rights of the excluded population as human beings, as citizens, and as persons intent on realizing their loving and creative powers within. Its central objective is their inclusion in a restructured system that does not make them redundant. (1992, 13)

This is why Friedmann makes a point of linking access to social power to the ability to use real political power. Without serious political power and the knowledge to employ it meaningfully, the open-ended local economy linked increasingly to the global economy becomes the only power that matters.

Friedmann's approach has some blind spots. He essentially takes a Western liberal stance that assumes that the good in people will somehow find a way to work in favor of good in social systems. This view does not explain why things are not working more justly and with more access now, nor is there a remedy for such poverty-sustaining behavior. The fact that social systems tend to become self-serving and that the non-poor are not troubled enough by the current state of affairs to seek remedies is not addressed. Nor does he mention the effect of worldview in perpetuating poverty and sustaining the privileged status of the non-poor.

The spiritual side of life is largely neglected in Friedmann's alternative development; life is more than access to social power. While Friedmann talks of "improving the conditions of life and livelihood"—and life and livelihood could include spiritual well-being—Friedmann's approach to development does not appear to extend this far. Life space must include the spiritual domain in addition to state, civil society, economy, and political community; the church is more than just a part of civil society. Access to spiritual power is as important to the poor as social and political power; this is illustrated by the explosion of Pentecostal churches in urban slums and rural areas of the South. While Friedmann does include the church in his understanding of civil society, the church is treated as a social institution, not as a sign of the kingdom. Perhaps Friedmann would include the spiritual in the category of household power he calls "psychological," but he does not say so, nor would this be fully adequate. In spite of this lacuna, Friedmann's contributions should not be down-played. In fact, his proposal should provoke us in a constructive way.

Friedmann poses a challenge to Christians, particularly evangelicals, who are for the most part nervous about political engagement. This needs to be overcome. If Christians cannot develop a truly Christian theology of political engagement on behalf of the excluded, then they will have nothing to offer the poor in this critical area of life.

The Old Testament is full of political stories, including God's proposal for the political and social life of pre-monarchy Israel (see Wright 1983). These accounts create no division between religious and political life. The challenge is to overcome the captivity to modernity on the part of the church (and its theology) and to rediscover a biblical approach to life in the public square. The consequence of this view of the world is twofold. Some believe that the work of the church is solely spiritual, and hence politics in the material world is of the devil and should be spurned. Others, believing in God's rule in the material world, nevertheless accept the dichotomy and express their Christian faith on Sunday morning and treat Monday through Friday political life as if their faith and the Bible had nothing to say. Either way, there is no biblically seamless spiritual/physical view of political engagement.

Isaac Prilleltensky and Geoffrey Nelson—Development as enhancing personal, collective, and relational power

We have looked at Prilleltensky's explanation of poverty as diminished identity caused by oppression caused by unequal power relations. The result is deficiencies in the personal, collective, and relational domains of life. The impact of collective and personal deficits on the relational domain allows us to integrate the psychological part of the life of the poor with the impact of their chronic poverty and their experience with unfair or unjust power structures of society.

In response to this three-domain understanding of poverty, Prilleltensky and Canadian psychologist Geoffrey Nelson have articulated a vision for increasing power as it relates to personal, collective, and, of particular interest to the argument of this book, relational well-being (2010, 60ff.) (see Figure 5–6). "Power refers to the capacity and opportunity to fulfill . . . personal, relational and collective needs" (Prilleltensky and Nelson 2002). While the focus is on well-being and power, Prilleltensky and Nelson are not naive. They acknowledge that a strategy of increasing power is ambiguous: "Power may be used to strive for wellness, oppress others and resist domination" (Prilleltensky 2003, 21). Sadly, without a kingdom understanding of power, this ambiguity is almost always fatal in a sinful world (Christian 1999, 181–82).

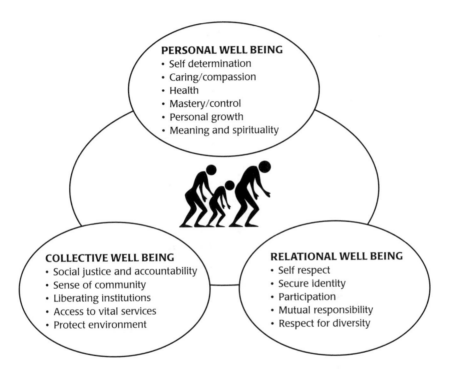

Figure 5–6: Transformation as increasing human agency.
(Adapted from Nelson and Prilleltensky, 2010)

Increased personal well-being includes unleashing a sense of agency, mastery, and potency combined with a spirituality that enables meaning-making in life (Prilleltensky 2003). The individualistic overtone of personal well-being is mitigated by the inclusion of caring, compassion, and concern for the well-being of others. Echoing Sen (who we will look at shortly), increasing collective well-being includes working for social justice and greater accountability expressed through a sense of community. Increasing collective well-being also means encouraging institutions to provide for fair and equitable distribution of resources, opportunities, and responsibilities. Increasing relational well-being means enhancing a sense of self-respect and identity that should remind us of Christian's idea of recovering from marred identity and forgotten vocation. Relational well-being also includes becoming a more effective actor in society and in one's personal and communal life, acting with a sense of mutual responsibility toward all and a respect for diversity (Prilleltensky and Nelson 2010, 60).

At the global level Prilleltensky's solution seems to echo David Korten, with an anti-globalization feel that targets the unregulated power of transnational corporations and the messengers of neo-liberalism such as the World Bank, IMF, and the WTO (Prilleltensky 2003, 34–35). At the national level Prilleltensky echoes Sen and Korten in dismissing the idea that development is only about economic growth and calls for a different approach to the provision of social services using Kerala, India, as an example. At the local level the focus, as with Friedmann, is on social organization and creating political and social power.

Robert Chambers—Development as responsible well-being

Fourteen years after Chambers published his idea of the poverty trap to help us understand how poverty entangles the poor, he published *Whose Reality Counts? Putting the First Last*, in which he proposes a framework for the outcomes of sustainable development. Taking note of the fact that development thinking has undergone a significant shift "from things and infrastructure to people and capacities" (1997, 9), Chambers presents a systems approach whose interactive framework points development toward what he calls "responsible well-being" (1997, 10) (see Figure 5–7).

For Chambers, the objective of development is *responsible well-being* for all. He describes well-being as quality of life and calls its opposite "ill-being." This moves him beyond the limiting categories of wealth and poverty. "Unlike wealth, well-being is open to the whole range of human experience, social, psychological and spiritual as well as material. It has many elements" (2005, 193). There is an intriguing echo of Jayakaran here. Chambers also makes the significant observation that while poverty and ill-being may be associated closely, wealth and well-being are not: "Amassing wealth does not assure well-being" (1997, 10).

Tipping his hat to the complicity of the non-poor in the problems affecting the poor, Chamber's phrase "responsible well-being" is also applied to the non-poor who need to change their behavior and behave responsibly toward the poor. Playing off of Freire's idea of a pedagogy of the oppressed as a way of liberating the poor, Chambers calls for a pedagogy for the non-oppressed that will work to enable the non-poor to become self-critically

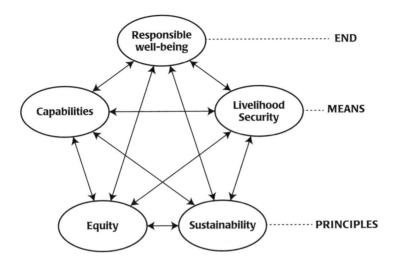

Figure 5–7: Transformation as responsible well-being.
(Adapted from Chambers 1997, 10)

aware of their roles and their potential for enabling a more inclusive well-being for all (2005, 184, 195).

There are two things that Chambers claims are basic to responsible well-being: *livelihood security* and the *capabilities* by which livelihood security and responsible well-being are achieved. Chambers defines livelihood security as

adequate stocks and flows of food and cash to meet basic needs and to support well-being. Security refers to secure rights and reliable access to resources, food and income and basic services. It includes tangible and intangible assets to offset risk, ease shocks and meet contingencies. (1997, 10)

Chambers's capabilities category is broad and rich and draws foundationally on the work of Sen. Intriguingly, he includes a concern for what people are capable of being as well as what they are capable of doing, and thus adds values formation to the conversation. People's capabilities are enlarged "through learning, practice, training and education," with the outcome being "better living and well-being" (1997, 11).

The two final categories of Chambers's interactive systems approach to well-being are the principles of *equity* and *sustainability*, both of which are to guide the process of increasing capabilities and ensuring livelihood security. Equity, for Chambers, means that the poor, weak, vulnerable, and exploited come first. Equity includes "human rights, intergenerational and gender equity and the reversals of putting the last first and the first last" (1997, 11). Sustainability is important as well: "To be good, conditions and change must be sustainable—economically, socially, institutionally and environmentally" (1997, 11).

All of this works within an interactive framework. Well-being cannot be achieved at the expense of some in the community because this violates the principle of equity. Well-being that is not environmentally sustainable is not well-being. Increasing capabilities must include the valuing of equity and sustainability as well as helping people define what well-being is for them. Overcoming the various elements of the poverty trap is the road to well-being and the guarantee of sustainability.

Chambers then explores the issue of the power and the will to make the changes necessary to move toward well-being for all. Responsible well-being is also the goal of development for the non-poor. Being responsible means a stance of sharing and generosity on the part of the non-poor. Chambers notes that there is considerable reason for cynicism but also points to some evidence for hope. The world is changing rapidly, modernity is waning, and some are making choices that are helpful. At the end of the day Chambers rests his framework for change on an optimistic view of personal choice.

> The actions of TNCs (transnational corporations), of currency speculators, of UN agencies, of governments, of NGOs are all mediated by individual decisions and action. The point is so obvious and so universal that it pains to have to make it. . . . People can choose how to behave and what to do. The assumption of pervasive selfishness and greed in neoliberal and male-dominated thought, policy and action supports a simplistic view of human nature. This overlooks or underestimates selflessness, generosity and commitment to others, and the fulfillment that these qualities bring. (1997, 13)

Chambers's well-being framework for development is helpful. It insists on basic needs being met and speaks to transformational training and the importance of sustainability He also makes space for both spiritual well-being and value change. His concept of equity is supported by the concept of the upside-down nature of the kingdom of God (Kraybill 1978). Chambers's focus on the importance of individual choice and holding people in positions of power accountable, rather than blaming unjust behavior on abstractions and systems, is also an important correction. There is much here that is fully consistent with the biblical narrative.

There are some contributions to poverty that are hard to find. Chambers's framework does not address the fear of spirits, shamans, and the like, yet these do suppress the will to change. The contribution of worldview to ill-being is not mentioned. The spiritual dimensions of powerlessness are also not addressed in any obvious way. Finally, like Friedmann, the underlying worldview is that of Western liberalism and its belief that there is enough good in people so that human political processes can correct themselves if we work at it long enough.

Amartya Sen—Development as freedom and rights-based development

We need to go a little deeper into Amartya Sen's idea of freedom as development, which was introduced in Chapter 2. Sen's central assertion is that development is less about increasing wealth, providing technical knowledge, and modernization, and more about increasing human freedom or agency in ways that allow people to pursue those ends that they deem important and valuable to them. Sen makes the bold claim that "free and sustainable human agency is the major engine of development" (1999, 4).

One of the major consequences of Sen's idea of development as freedom is that it opened the door for the two historically disconnected conversations about development and human rights to converge. The concept of the poor was enlarged beyond a view of the poor simply as victims (who need development assistance) to include a view that also sees the poor as rights bearers, human beings entitled to the possibility of living a truly human life. The underlying assumption is that society has a responsibility to create an environment that is supportive of everyone's search for well-being.

This conflation between human rights and development led to the emergence of the idea of *rights-based development*, which integrates advocacy and policy work into development with the new goal of helping the poor become effective, informed, and active citizens (Uvin 2004). Faith-based organizations have developed their own understanding of rights-based development from a faith perspective (Aprodev Rights and Development Group 2008). Rights-based development also opened up a new vista for the role of participation in development to go beyond just ownership of program design and implementation to the additional focus of empowering local citizens to press for good governance and the provision of their rights on the part of local governments and other local structures of power (Hickey and Mohan 2004).

While increasing human agency and promoting human rights for individuals and communities are important, in Sen's view they are not enough. Increasing human freedom also requires a supportive social environment. Sen identifies a family of *instrumental freedoms* that are necessary to support the expansion and exercise of *individual freedom*. People need to be free to participate *in the political process* in order have a say in "who should govern and on what principles" (Sen 1999, 38). People need the *economic facilities* that enable them to be productive and to exchange what they produce for what they need. They need the *social opportunities* created by education and health services that make it possible for people to live better lives. They need to experience a social world that is *open and transparent* and in which trust grows. Finally, Sen argues that people need *protective security*, by which he means a social safety net that protects people against unexpected shocks such as drought and other disasters, as well as the protection of the rule of law (see Figure 5–8). More on the impact of Sen's thinking in the sections on citizenship and good governance and PLA in Chapter 8.

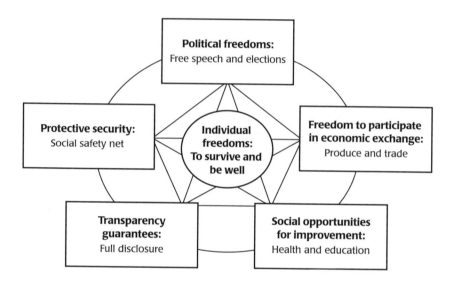

Figure 5–8: Instrumental freedoms and human well-being.
(Developed from Sen 1999, 6–11)

Jayakumar Christian–Development as a kingdom response to powerlessness

I now turn to the proposal of Jayakumar Christian. As we would expect, it reflects Christian's systems view of powerlessness (see Figure 4–6). Christian sees each area of his "web of lies" as a transformational frontier for which a web of truth is needed. The development response is to declare truth and righteousness while doing good works.

Christian's proposal rests on the assumption that the powerlessness of the poor is the "result of systematic socio-economic, political, bureaucratic and religious processes (systems) that disempower the poor" (1994, 335). The proper transformational development response must reverse the process of disempowerment with a kingdom of God response that includes three commitments:

1. Dealing with the relational dimensions of poverty "by building covenant quality communities that are inclusive . . . challenging the dividing lines . . . popular community organizing efforts that exploit issues and numbers . . . pointing toward the coming of the kingdom." (1994, 336)
2. Dealing with the forces that create or sustain powerlessness at the micro-, macro-, global, and cosmic levels.
3. Challenging the time element in the process of disempowerment by rereading the history of the poor from God's perspective, providing "a prophetic alternative to the distortions that the winners perpetuate . . . challenging the captivity of the poor to the belief that they cannot change their present reality." (1994, 336)

For each of the elements of the web of lies that entraps the poor, Christian outlines a kingdom response. For the *captivity of the poor to the web of lies*, Christian echoes Freire and calls for development processes that allow the poor to discover the lies they have been taught to believe and to discover the truth. This is not easy work.

> This web has several spiders. It includes the non-poor and the poor, the world views of persons in poverty relationships, the principalities and powers and the spiritual interiorities within structures and systems. (1994, 342)

Truth and righteousness must be established and the source of this truth is the "continuous study of the Word of God" (1994, 343). Development workers need to live lives that are consistent with that truth and that unmask the lies. The truth of the kingdom of God

> is the only thing that will reorder the relationship between truth and power. It will seek to establish truth with a capital "T," truth about self, truth in public and private life and truth about power. (1994, 343)

Responding to the *captivity to the god complexes of the non-poor*, the truth is declared that only God may act like God in people's lives and that the kingdom of God is the only alternative that promises liberation and human well-being. Wink would also add that one needs to expose the idolatry of the non-poor and unmask the powerlessness of their idols to provide well-being.

For the low self-confidence resulting from the *marred identity* of the poor, the kingdom response "clarifies and heals the marred identity of the poor. It goes beyond issues of justice and dignity to deal with the underlying marring of identity of the poor" (1994, 339). Christian proposes that we do our development work in a way that shows the poor that we value them. We need to work as "barefoot" counselors, listening, talking, and loving. Their history of exclusion and disrespect needs to be reversed. The poor need validation and respect. We need to proclaim the good news that the poor are made in the image of God, that God calls them his children, and that God values them as much as God values the non-poor.

For *inadequacies in worldview*, Christian insists that we must go beyond concerns for cultural sensitivity. There are elements in every worldview that are not for life or for the poor. As an Indian, Christian is especially concerned about religious sanctions that justify poverty (karma) and oppressive relationships (caste). The kingdom response is an "encounter of world view and religion, with the Bible as the basic frame of reference" (1994, 340). We in the West have our own inadequacies in worldview around sexuality, consumption, and violence.

For *deception by principalities and powers*, Christian calls us to the practices of prayer and fasting as important tools for social action. "There is a need to rediscover the potential of prayer and fasting to move mountains and cause the devil and his forces to fall from heavenly places (Lk 10:18)" (1994, 341). Grassroots development workers must have the spiritual disciplines necessary to equip them with the "whole armor of God" (Eph 6:10–12).

How does one establish truth and righteousness? Christian suggests the following. First, tools of social analysis can help the poor understand who is doing what to whom and to follow the money. The Bible can be used to assess the truth and justice of what they discover. The poor, then, need a chance to discover who they truly are by reflecting on the word of God and by being treated as valuable human beings with something to contribute. The truth of the kingdom also needs to be declared in public by the church, the community of faith that is supposed to be the sign of the kingdom. The truth also needs to be told about power: all power belongs to God and to God alone. This takes us beyond the idea of "power to the people." Finally, their worldview needs to be examined against the whole of the biblical narrative to see where it reinforces powerlessness and works against life and well-being (1994, 342–43).

How does all this relate to the models of development proposed by Korten, Friedmann, Prilleltensky, Chambers, and Sen? Has Christian spiritualized the whole exercise? No. This would be a profound misunderstanding of Christian's proposal. Christian is standing on the shoulders of Chambers, Sen and especially Friedmann, in particular. Christian's idea of marred identity anticipates Prilleltensky. Their frameworks all address the issue of disempowering systems and empowerment as a response. Powerlessness was one of the five interacting elements in Chambers's poverty trap, while Friedmann uses powerlessness (in terms of social power) as the central frame for his understanding of poverty and his response. Christian takes both views seriously and extends them.

As a people concept, powerlessness describes the experience of persons in households and communities. As a people concept, powerlessness is about real people living in real living space with micro, macro, global and cosmic dimensions. As a time related concept, it encompasses the forces in history, present realities and perceptions about the future. As a spatial concept, it includes geographical location, nature and environmental dimensions. (1994, 332)

Christian calls for a thorough mapping of the expressions of powerlessness, including those of Friedmann, and then goes beyond. For example, the time dimension of powerlessness as a transformational frontier is not part of either Chambers's or Friedmann's accounts of powerlessness. Understandably neither would include spiritual mapping.

What Christian proposes adds to Chambers and especially Friedmann. He does not take issue with them at any point other than to show that their analysis and proposals do not go far enough. Christian is attempting to fill in the spiritual blind spot in a broad and holistic way, and by so doing make their proposals more complete. Without addressing the web of lies, it is hard to see how any development process can be sustained.

What about Korten's development strategies? Or Friedmann's concern that development must lead to "clear improvement in the conditions of life and livelihood of ordinary people," and belief that the poor need greater access to social power? What about Chambers's sustainable livelihood and capacity building? Christian accepts or would accept these contributions; his work in development programs in India reflects this. If asked why he did not speak specifically to such things, he would argue that, as important as they are, they are means, not ends.

The end of development for Christian is true identity, the restored identity of the poor as "children of God with a gift to share" (Sugden 1997, 187). We are to be citizens of the kingdom on earth, people living in just and harmonious relationships with God, self, each other, and the created order. This is what being truly human means. This is what human agency or freedom is for.

Of Jayakaran's four dimensions of poverty, the spiritual and mental dimensions are the keys for Christian. In addition to the concern of Chambers and Friedmann for the material order and the structures of social power, the transformational frontiers for Christian are also inside the mind of the poor, where the disempowering deceptions have spiritual as well as social roots. In this he anticipates Prilleltensky to a degree. This concern for establishing one's true identity is shared by Kwame Bediako (1992) and is further developed by Vinay Samuel's theology of dignity (Sugden 1997, 183–201). See also the section on this in the next chapter.

There has been a great deal written in the last fifty years about eradicating poverty, mostly dealing with its physical and social dimensions. More recently the psycho-social dimension has been added. Korten, Chambers, Friedmann, Prilleltensky, and Sen are among the more recent contributors.

This is well and good. Christian development workers should and must take these ideas seriously and apply them to the physical and social dimensions of development. The poor are entitled to the benefits of this thinking. Christian would agree. He would go on to ask, however, what it is that believers in Christ bring to the conversation because they are Christian. His answer is the kingdom of God as the location of everyone's true identity: no more lies, a restored image, a transformed worldview, truth and righteousness established. In the next chapter I will come back to this question of recovering identity as one of the goals of human transformation.

There are two ways in which Christian's proposal could be extended. The first has to do with the vocation of the poor. In Chapter 3 we noted the importance of framing identity in terms of both being (who we are) and doing (what we do). Christian has correctly identified the marring of the identity of the poor, which has to do with being. To this I would add that the identity of the poor has also been marred with respect to their doing or their vocation. The poor have been taught to believe that they are supposed to be servants of others more worthy or that it is part of the scheme of things that they should do the work of untouchables or bonded laborers. They do not believe they are intended to be creative and productive stewards. To poverty of being we must add poverty of purpose.

Second, Christian expresses little sympathy for the non-poor because of the way they participate in the disempowering systems that create and sustain poverty when they play god in the lives of the poor. While this is appropriate and correct, it fails to take note of the fact that the non-poor also live in a web of lies that supports their sense of privilege. In this sense the non-poor also suffer from a marring of identity and vocation, only not in the diminished way experienced by the poor. The non-poor suffer from an overinflated view of who they are when they play god in the lives of the poor. They also have forgotten their true vocation—to love God and neighbor—when they use their gifts not to serve but to control and oppress.

Christian's approach is also ambitious. What is being proposed cannot be accomplished this side of the second coming of Christ. His vision is beyond human reach as long as there is sin in the world. We can respond to this in two ways. There is the danger of establishing expectations that permanently disappoint the poor and that become an intolerable burden for the development practitioner. On the other hand, committing oneself to an unattainable ideal, the kingdom of God, also creates an absolute demand for faith, since "faith is being sure of what we hope for and certain of what we do not see" (Heb 11:1). We know we cannot bring the kingdom, and yet we are committed to working alongside its coming. Living and working in the sinful here and now, while believing in the coming of God's perfect kingdom, is a uniquely Christian stance. Care needs to be taken that we understand that we are being asked by God to be obedient, not successful.

6

Toward a Christian understanding of transformational development

It is time to pull the material in the preceding chapters together and create a framework for transformational development from a Christian perspective. To do this we need to recognize who owns the development task and then place this task within the biblical narrative. I will then pose answers to the critical questions: What better future? What are the goals of transformation? What process of change? What is sustainability? In what ways do we need to think holistically? All of this will then be placed into a framework for thinking about and planning transformational development.

WHOSE STORY IS IT?

There is a sense in which every development program is a convergence of stories. We bring our story and join the story that is already there, the community's story. As Christians we bring more than one story. We bring our personal story and the story of the culture from which we come (which includes the story of our development institution) along with our understanding of the biblical story, the story of God at work in history. Within the community there are also two stories, the history of the community and the story of God at work in the community. If there are Christians there, the church or churches are the primary bearers of this story. If there are no churches, God has nonetheless been working in the community since the beginning of time, with God's story being hidden or only partially known or recognized.

This convergence of stories raises two very important questions: First, when we speak of the transformational development program, we must be clear as to whose story it is. Second, we must also affirm which story is to be the normative story among all the other stories that are converging in a particular time and place.

To whom does the program story belong? is simply answered but often hard to live out. The transformational development story belongs to the community. It was the community's story before we came, and it will be the community's story long after we leave. While our story has something to offer to the community's story, we must never forget that, at the end of the day, the program is not *our* story. We all know this and development literature affirms this consistently. It is in the day-to-day work of doing development that we are tempted to forget and compromise, all in the name of being helpful or efficient. Forgetting whose story it is means that we further mar the identity of the poor. When we usurp their story, we add to their poverty.

To frame the stories that are converging in a particular time and place, we must remind ourselves of the larger, foundational story of which all of these converging stories are a part. Transformational development takes place within the larger story of creation, fall, redemption, and restoration. Therefore, the community and everyone in it are facing a choice (see Figure 6–1).

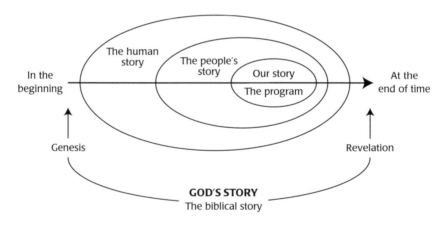

Figure 6–1: Development in the context of the biblical story.

They need to decide which narrative will have the final word as they decide on the important questions: What better future? and What process of change? Modernity's story? Their traditional story? The biblical story? By declining to choose, a choice is made for either modernity's story or their traditional story. As Christians we must share our belief that neither is the true story that addresses the whole of human life. Professional development work can improve material, mental, and social life within the lifetime of the community members without changing the ultimate outcome of the bigger story. Only by accepting God's salvation in Christ can people and the community redirect the trajectory of their story toward the kingdom of God. This is the bottom line of every community's story, poor and non-poor. No Christian development practitioner can ignore this bottom line. Yet, this is not our decision to make, nor can this story be imposed. It can only be shared in hopes that the Holy Spirit will elicit a "yes" to God's best offer of hope for the future.

WHAT BETTER FUTURE?

The quest for transformational development, therefore, begins with the need to articulate the better future the community decides it wishes to pursue. Making the better future clear requires a process that allows the community to clarify for itself what really matters and why it matters. What is human well-being? What is abundant life? What is the community for? What vision will beckon the community members toward becoming who they truly are? What claims does God make on the community? What claims do the members of the community need to make on one another? For what are human beings responsible? What will create joy at the end of the day?

In the section on the biblical narrative the answer became clear: The unshakable kingdom of God and the unchanging person of Jesus Christ (Jones 1972) are the best human future and the means to get there. This is God's best human future toward which everyone is invited to move. The kingdom of God is the future that has already invaded history and that is growing, albeit like leaven, in the present.

What does this mean in concrete terms? As we have developed the idea, the kingdom vision for the better human future is summarized by the idea of shalom: just, peaceful, harmonious, and enjoyable relationships with each other, ourselves, our environment, and God. This kingdom frame is inclusive of the physical, social, mental, and spiritual manifestations of poverty, and so all are legitimate areas of focus for transformational development that is truly Christian. Therefore, immunizing children, improving food security, and providing potable water can be part of a kingdom future if the community says they need to be. Reconciliation, peacebuilding, and values formation toward the end of including everyone and enabling everyone to make their contribution and to flourish is potentially part of the emergence of the kingdom in the community. Working to make social systems, and those who manage and shape them, accountable to work for the well-being of all can also be part of moving toward the kingdom. Simply listening to and being with those whose poverty resides in a broken heart or a defeated spirit is kingdom business too. Whatever heals and restores body, mind, spirit, and community, all can be part of the better future toward which transformational development should point.

Another way of saying this is that any better human future must be about life and life abundant. Jacque Ellul, the French philosopher and lay theologian, reminded us that "what matters is to live, not to act. ...In a civilization which has lost the meaning of life, the most useful thing a Christian can do is to live" (1967, 92, 94). The Mexican poet and essayist Octavio Paz puts it more sharply: "Progress has peopled history with the marvels and monsters of technology, but has depopulated the life of man (sic). It has given us more things but not more being" (1972, 8). Life abundant is about living, not simply having.

Abundant life means no limits to love, no limits to justice, and no limits to peace (Hall 1985, 99). Anything that is for life, that enhances life, or that celebrates life is pointing toward the kingdom. Africans pray for "life as well as the means to make life worth living" (Okorocha 1994, 79). Latin Americans are looking to a revitalized, celebratory view of life in which "space for spiritual quests is opened up" so that common people can find a God

> who walks with the human being in the latter's quest for a sound, gladsome, radiant well-being, a well-being in the spirit of the carnival—an individual and collective well-fare, from which the category of accumulation and worldly "success" is radically absent. (Parker 1996, 262)

The key to moving toward this better future of shalom and abundant life is the discovery that the community's story, and our story, can in fact become part of this larger story, the story of God's redemptive and restorative work in the world. Getting to a sustainable better future requires becoming part of the work that God is already doing. With God's help we can recompose our own stories so that we discover our true identity and true vocation, namely, being God's children journeying toward God's kingdom.

For example, World Vision in the Philippines, a Catholic country with a strong renewal movement emphasizing personal renewal and lay Bible reading, found that poor communities gravitated toward the biblical metaphor of Isaiah 65 as a way of visualizing the future that they believe God intends for them:

- A place of joy; there is no weeping.
- Children do not die. People live full lives.
- People build homes and live in them.
- People enjoy the product of their own labor.
- The community is restored and harmonious.
- The irreconcilable live in peace.
- God is in their midst, answering them before they call.

Both the poor and the non-poor need to respond to the only vision that promises life in its fullness and relationships that work for justice and peace.

This is a vision for transformation that is equally interested in being as well as having. Knowing who we truly are and pursuing our true vocation is the key to more life, not just more things or even more knowledge.

Being clear on God's better future is important to Christian development workers as they help communities develop their own view of the better future they wish to seek. Seeing the development story of the community as part of God's larger work in history "offers to all people the possibility of understanding that the meaning and goal of history are not to be found in any projects, programs, ideologies and utopia" (Newbigin 1989, 129). At its best, a ten-to-fifteen-year development project will bring limited good, none of which will be sustainable in the long term unless fundamental choices are made about redirecting the community's story.

Envisioning a better human future is hard work for both the poor and the non-poor. The web of lies believed by the poor has convinced them that there is no better future, at least not in this world. The act of getting the poor to believe in the possibility of a better future is a "prophetic act," in Jayakumar Christian's words. This is also hard work for the non-poor, for they believe they are already on the way to or part of a better future. It is very hard for them to believe that there is anything more, especially if it involves having less. It is even harder to get them to consider change—after all it is fun playing god in the lives of other people.

There is encouragement here. This vision of the best human future is not modernity's story of inevitable human progress or the mind-dulling, hope-destroying acceptance of the relativistic pluralism of post-modernity. The good news is that we do not have to create our own better future, nor do we have to accept that there is no better future. We do not have to accept a better future in which some have a lot and others are left at the side of the road, as if God didn't create enough to go around.

One final note. Any Christian vision of a better human future must include a vibrant, growing, living Christian community that is eagerly and joyfully serving God and its community. It is impossible to imagine a transforming community without a transforming church in its midst. Such a church is in love with God and with all its neighbors, celebrating everything that is for life and being a prophetic voice, telling the truth about everything that is against or that undermines life. More on the church later in this chapter.

THE GOALS OF TRANSFORMATION

Changed people: Recovering true identity and vocation

A central tenet in Jayakumar Christian's view of transformation is the recovery of the true identity of the poor. A web of lies results in the poor internalizing a view of themselves as being without value and without a contribution to make, believing they are truly god-forsaken (Sugden 1997, 183–201). No transformation can be sustainable unless this distorted, disempowering sense of identity is replaced by the truth. Healing the marred identity of the poor is the beginning of transformation.

Vinay Samuel takes us another step by pointing us beyond identity (Who am I?) to the importance of dignity (What am I worth?). Samuel's addition of dignity points us toward the idea of vocation in addition to that of identity (Samuel, in Sugden 1997, 183–97). Both identity and vocation are critical from a biblical perspective. We must know who we are and the purpose for which we were created. Therefore, restoring identity and recovering vocation must be the focus of a biblical understanding of human transformation. The transforming truth is that the poor and non-poor are made in God's image (identity) and are valuable enough to God (dignity) to warrant the death of God's Son in order to restore that relationship and to give gifts that contribute to the well-being of themselves and their community (vocation).

While the agenda for the poor and the non-poor are the same, the issues of each are different. The poor suffer from a marred or diminished identity and a degraded understanding of their vocation. The non-poor, on the other hand, suffer from an inflated sense of identity and of vocation. The challenge to the poor is to recover their identity as children of God and to discover their vocation as productive stewards, realizing that they have been given gifts to contribute to social well-being. The challenge for the non-poor, including the development agency, is to relinquish their god complexes and to employ their gifts for the sake of all human beings rather than using their gifts as a source of power or control (see Figure 6-2).

This is an important shift in the focus of transformational development. The point of greatest transformational leverage is changed people: "It is a transformed person who transforms his or her environment" (Musopole 1997, 2). Isaiah quotes God as saying that when the poor hear the good news and receive freedom and release, they become "oaks of righteousness

	Identity	Vocation
Poor	Believing that they are made in the image of God and are God's children.	Believing they have gifts to contribute and that they are called to be productive stewards of creation.
Non-poor	Laying down their god-complexes and believing that they are made in God's image and are not, themselves, gods.	Believing that their gifts are for sharing, not control, and that they are to lead as servants, not masters.

Figure 6-2: Identity and vocation for the poor and non-poor.

. . . that rebuild the ancient ruins and restore the places long devastated" (Is 61:3–4). People, not money or programs, transform their world.

The fulcrum for transformational change is no longer transferring resources or building capacity or increasing access, agency, and choices, as important as these things are. These are all means, after all. These things count only if they take place in a way that allows the poor to recover their true identity and discover the vocation God intends for them. This is important enough to say negatively to make the point. As good as transferring resources or building capacity or increasing choices can be, the process by which these changes are achieved can rob them of any goodness. A flawed process of change can make the poor poorer by further devaluing their view of themselves.

Transforming people begins with helping people discover that "their human dignity and identity are intrinsically related to God in Christ through his redemptive purpose in salvation history" (Bediako 1996a, 8). The moment people discover who they truly are is the moment in which their story takes on a new trajectory as a new reality breaks into their lives that cannot be contained, even by the cleverest of lies. With a recovered identity, the next step is the development of character, instilling and forming values that permit a better vision of the future and that allow the poor to love others as themselves, seeking to be life-enhancing for all. Finally, with a rediscovered identity and a character to match, transformational development works to empower people to live out these values in search of their new vision. This means teaching people to read, to understand and interpret their context, to figure out what and who is contributing to their current situation, and then to decide what they want to do about it. The launching point for increasing human freedom and agency is changed people. All other transformational frontiers are now more easily breached in a more comprehensive way with a greater hope of being sustainable.

We need to understand that helping people in this way means taking actions that are inherently a political, economic, and social. Increasing individual human freedom or agency in the absence of work to increase Sen's instrumental freedoms is naive. Not all governments, and certainly not most of the non-poor, those who benefit from things as they are, will welcome this kind of transformation. Transforming things can be acceptable; transforming people is often less so.

I do not want to overstate the importance of changing people. Having said that discovering one's true identity and vocation has the potential to enhance other kinds of transformative change, I must also say that identity and vocation are not enough. Newbigin reminds us that "no human project however splendid is free from the corrupting power of sin" (1989, 138). The continuing deception, distortion, and distraction resulting from sin at work in us, in the non-poor, and in the community means that all development programming will be flawed and fallible. This is simple Christian realism.

Finding that their story makes most complete sense and finds its best hope for the future in God's larger story opens up and invites a wide range of transformational responses. The web of lies is unmasked for what it is, an enormous deception serving the interests of both the Evil One and the non-poor. Bediako speaks of opening "the eyes of people and of societies to see those realities—personal and collective—in beliefs, world views and ethical choices, which continue to resist God" (1996a, 9). If poverty is the world trying to tell the poor they are god-forsaken, then transformation is the declaration that the poor are made in God's image, that God allowed his Son to die for them, and that God has given gifts to the poor so that they can fulfill God's creation mandate that they too may be fruitful and productive.

Helping people recover their true identity and vocation also requires that they learn to reread their history. God did not come into the life of the community with the arrival of the development agency. God has been active in the story of the community since the beginning of time. Although God is never without a witness (Rom 1:19), God was not always recognized for who God is or for what God has done. For the community to move into a new future, it must rediscover and recover its past, albeit understanding it in a different way. "The great travail of Christian Africa is over the conversion of the African past. Perhaps no conversion is complete without the conversion of the past" (Walls 1996, 53). This is important because the community needs to make the universal gospel story, the true story of history, its own story as well. "Once this basic, universal relevance of Jesus Christ is granted, it no longer is a question of trying to accommodate the Gospel in our culture; we learn to read and accept the Good News as *our* story. Our Lord has been, from the beginning, the Word of God *for us* as for all people everywhere" (Bediako 1994, 101).

For a Christian understanding of transformational development, restoring identity and vocation is the goal. This is the only path that leads toward life and that holds the promise of shalom. We must work alongside the poor and non-poor alike, helping them and helping ourselves uncover and accept our true identity as children of God. We must both work toward the recovery of our true vocation as productive stewards of God's earth, obedient to the claims and promises of Christ and his kingdom.

Just and peaceful relationships

Our identity and vocation are expressed through our relationships. Thus, recovering identity and discovering vocation require that transformational development focus on restoring relationships. From the chapters on the biblical narrative and the nature of poverty we have identified a relational framework that links everyone to God, to themselves, to their community, to those who are "other," and to the environment. This is an important framework for thinking about the goals of transformational development.

The central relationship in need of restoration is one's *relationship with the triune God*, the God of the Bible. The good news is that God desires this restoration and has already taken the step necessary for this relationship to be restored. There is very little for us to do except say yes to God's invitation to faith in Jesus Christ. I have already implied that restoring relationships with God, accepting God's story as the story in which ours finds a home and makes sense, is the transformational point of maximum leverage for change. If people are seeking God, many other good things will follow and become possible. If they are not, the horizons of change are more limited and difficult (see Figure 6–3).

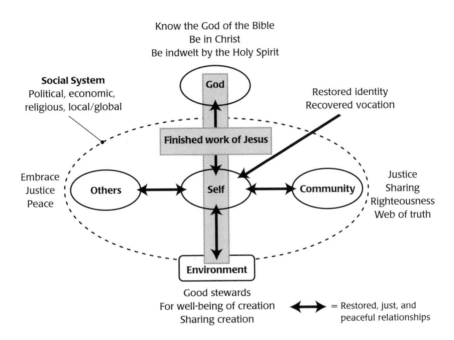

Figure 6–3: Transformed relationships.

Being in a healthy *relationship with oneself* is also an important transformational frontier. Many have suffered from the disempowerment that arises from a web of lies inside the mind, lies about oneself or one's group. Many of these lies arose externally and were internalized. Others are lies we told ourselves. These competing and conflicting voices inside ourselves are the root of the mental or psychological dimension of poverty. Seeking peace within ourselves requires truth and justice within ourselves. This is the task of Christian psychology. Finally, within oneself is the location of the formation of character and values. "Development has to start with the development of character that is according to the values of the kingdom of God" (Musopole 1997, 3).

The quality of *relationships within one's community* is also important. There are many things that need changing that can only be addressed by the community working together. It is hard if the community is divided or in conflict. Seldom can single individuals or households sustain change if they are working alone. The primary transformational divide within a community of people who share a common history and culture is between the poor and non-poor. Both are enmeshed in their own web of lies, and the non-poor have a great deal invested in rationalizing things as they are. In addition, the worldview of a cultural group can legitimate the current social location and identity of the both poor and non-poor, adding reinforcement to this separation. For example, in the Hindu context, the oppressive dimension of caste is reinforced by a religious worldview that says that *karma is* the just cause of both the wealth of the oppressor and the suffering of the oppressed (Sugden 1997, 184).

Healing the divide between the poor and non-poor is critical to significant long-term change. This means that the poor need help to recover their true identity and vocation while the non-poor need help to deal with the narratives and cultural artifacts that justify and reinforce their privileged position in relationship to the poor. The divide between the poor and the non-poor is exacerbated by the fact that, even though they share a common language, culture and place, the poor have nonetheless become "other" to the non-poor and vice versa.

Being at peace with *those who are "other" to us* means adding the ministry of reconciliation to the transformational agenda. Yet reconciliation is often very hard because the most frequent reason for declaring someone "other" is that they have done harm to you and your community. Miraslav Volf has made an important contribution to our understanding of identity, otherness, and reconciliation in *Exclusion and Embrace*. Volf explains that the beginning of reconciliation and hence the path to justice and peace is the embrace of the other, in spite of all that the other has done. "There can be no justice without the will to embrace." This call transcends the issue of who is right or wrong, who is righteous or unrighteous. We must embrace the other because this is what Christ did and continues to do. Yet, Volf explains, the embrace is not complete "until the truth is said and justice is done" (Volf 1996, 216).

This requires a particular kind of stance toward the other, a commitment to understanding them on their own terms. The will to embrace sheds light. The metaphor of embrace is the open arms of the father extended to the son who had made himself wholly other in the story of the prodigal son (Lk 15:11–31). The will to exclude creates blindness. Its metaphor is the clenched fist; there can be no good in the other, only evil. With the will to embrace comes the possibility of seeing that there is some good in the other, bringing hope that this may be a point of convergence, a way of coming together. This insight of Volf's may have particular value when we think about creating a new kind of relationship between the poor and the non-poor.

Volf would not have us be naive, however: "The initial suspicion against the perspective of the powerful is necessary. Not because the powerless are innocent, but because the powerful have the means to impose their own perspective by argument and propaganda . . . the groans of the powerless must disturb the serenity of their comforting ideologies" (1996, 219–20). Reconciliation is often very hard work.

Finally, the community must be in *a healthy and respectful relationship with the environment* on which it depends for food, water, and air. At the heart of our true vocation is the call to be stewards, caring for the world in which God has placed us so that it is productive and supportive of life. We need to transform our metaphor for our relationship with nature from one of being masters of nature to the idea of being stewards or caretakers of God's creation. Christians knew this once. In the Celtic tradition of the sixth and seventh centuries, "we find a holy intimacy of human, natural and divine. . . . We see everywhere . . . an abandonment to spiritual work and simultaneously a cultivation of the earth" (Bamford and March 1987, 19).

The focus of transformation of all of our relationships finds an echo in Daniel Groody, a Catholic theologian who describes the Catholic understanding of justice in these same relational terms. He speaks of internal justice, which addresses "being put in right relationship with God through the saving work of Jesus Christ," and external justice, which is our response to God's grace with good works and love of neighbor (2007, 26). "God's justice, in other words, is not principally about vengeance or retribution, but about restoring people to right relationship with God, themselves, others and the environment" (2007, 27).

In summary, to move toward a better human future we must encourage and develop relationships that work for the well-being of all, relationships that are just, peaceful, and harmonious. This is the heart and spirit of shalom and the only way leading toward abundant life for all. Thus transformational development that enhances life works to promote relationships that work as well as they can in a world of fallen people. Life and relationships are inseparable. "Development should aim at a blessed life, a life at peace with itself, others, the environment and with God" (Musopole 1997, 3).

WHAT PROCESS OF CHANGE?

Starting with the end in mind is not enough, however. The process by which we get there matters, too. This is because God has imposed some limitations on our choices. Some means are better than others. Some means actually help us live the future before it gets here. Some means have to be given to us; we cannot get them for ourselves. Therefore, we also have to answer the question: What process of change should we choose?

There is a variety of choices. Some look to governments as the driver of social transformation. Some believe that hard work, personal responsibility, and a free market are the best tools for social change. Others believe transformation depends solely on the work of God and the power of the Holy Spirit. Still others look to the efficacy of human reason and technology. Some believe the resources for change lie within us, while others believe change comes by taking the resources we need from others through government taxation or even more direct means.

The list of Christian elements of change that follows is not exhaustive. Our Bible and theology have a lot to say about how people and societies change. I have chosen a list of ten that seem particularly important in light of my experience. You will no doubt add some of your own.

Affirming the role of God

A Christian process of change must begin with the affirmation that, at the most fundamental level, transformation takes place because God wants change and is enabling change. At the end of the day, any transformation, justice, and peace will be because God has made it so. We are not the authors of change.

> It is the action of God, the triune God—of God the Father who is ceaselessly at work in all creation and in the hearts and minds of all human beings whether they acknowledge him or not, graciously guiding history toward its true end; of God the Son who has become part of this created history in the incarnation; and of God the Holy Spirit who is given as a foretaste of the end to empower and teach the church and to convict the world of sin and righteousness and judgment. (Newbigin 1989, 135)

Affirming the agency of human beings

Having said this, however, we must also go on to say that change takes place because human beings have a vocation of development (CV, no. 18) and thus must commit themselves to the process of change, investing whatever gifts and resources God has given them in the process (PP, no. 15). God gives us real choices over all elements of our lives, however limited our capabilities may be. Following God, we are actors in history. People must make the choice to seek transformation directed at what God intends and then invest themselves in making it happen. Thus, a Christian understanding of the process of change centers on the decisions and actions of human beings. This has several implications.

First, the change process belongs to those who are in need of change. If God will not impose change on us, then neither should we impose change on others. The beginning of healing the marred image of the poor is to accept that they alone have the right to describe their reality and to shape their vision of their better future. Second, since not all choices made by people are good ones, and since broken relationships and injustice are part of the problem, any Christian process of change must include processes for repentance and forgiveness. Finally, a process dependent on human beings can only go as fast as human beings can go. The pace must be set by the people, not the program. Koyama (1979) has spoken eloquently about the "three-mile-an-hour" God, who has graciously adjusted his pace to ours.

Focusing on relationships

This should not be a surprise. If the nature of poverty is fundamentally relational and the cause of poverty is relationships that do not work for well-being, then the transformational process must begin and end with different kinds of relationships. Yet sometimes we are unclear about the importance of beginning at the right place.

There is a temptation to begin with the problem or with the research that allows us to understand the problem. Getting on with the work of assessment, analysis, and planning is tempting to all of us. Yet we must not yield. Paraphrasing Koyama, we can know a poor person, but we cannot know poverty (1974, 129). Roberto Goizueta, a Catholic theologian who has proposed a Latino theology of accompaniment, observes correctly that "there is no such thing as an option for 'the poor,' only an option for *poor persons.*" Extending this, he argues that this must be an option of concrete love of particular poor persons "as members of our own family" (1993, 194–95). We must begin with people, not abstractions, research, analysis, or technique. Without transforming relationships there is unlikely to be much transformation.

Keeping the end in mind

When we focus on the process of change, there can be a temptation to value effectiveness over everything else. Donors seem to insist on this. Results-based management is a current fad. We need to remember that the goal of human transformation is the discovery of true identity and vocation, not simply meeting the goals, outcomes and outputs of a program on time and on budget. Meaning matters more than efficiency. Reflecting on Israel's making of the golden calf because Moses was too long on the mountain, Koyama tells us that Israel's pragmatism, driven by a sense of urgency, resulted in "theological impatience and technological efficiency." The result was "disfigurement of their own history and the loss of their own identity" (Koyama 1985, 139). Valuing efficiency or effectiveness over discovering meaning creates poverty.

Recognizing pervasive evil

With all the talk about God's role and a better human future pointing toward the kingdom of God, there is a danger that we may slip into a romantic optimism about the success of our efforts with the poor. While God will have the final say and the kingdom of God will prove to be the only unshakable kingdom at the end of time, getting there will not be easy. There is a Good Friday on the way to the joy of Easter morning.

The prince of this world works actively against life and shalom. The liar works through the sin in human beings, encouraging bad choices by promoting a web of lies. The Evil One also works a campaign of deception and domination through the political, economic, social, and religious structures of the world by subverting them in the pursuit of their intended missions. As I have already argued, Ann Cudd's dynamics of oppression (2006, 66) find their origins in the deceptions of the father of lies. No Christian process of change should underestimate this opposition or deny itself the spiritual tools with which to battle against this foe.

In societies in which fear of spirits and the unseen world is pervasive, the deception of the Evil One assumes a deeper, more pernicious role. People observe the actions of the gods and spirits, and those who claim to speak for them. The spirits who appear to respond to sacrifices are moved up the hierarchy of gods and receive more sacrifices, money, and attention. Those who prove less reliable or unapproachable are demoted. While wonderfully empirical, this is a framework of lies, a deceptive order that disempowers the poor and enriches and empowers those who claim to be the intermediaries linking this world to the next. Such a deceptive framework undermines human initiative and takes the place of the true God. This is evil at work against life.

Seeking truth, justice, and righteousness

If the most fundamental cause of poverty is the impact of sin, then dealing with sin must be part of any Christian process of change. While we must deal with the individual nature of this sin, we must also address its consequences as expressed in relationships that are based on a web of lies and that promote disempowerment of the poor and domination by the nonpoor. This means that a Christian process of change must center on truth-telling and the promotion of justice and righteousness (Christian 1994). The truth must be discovered about the way the poor contribute to their own poverty, and the truth must be discovered about how poverty is created by the god complexes of the non-poor, inadequacies in worldview, and deception by the principalities and powers. Only in repenting in the face of God's truth about human beings and about God can relationships be restored so that life, justice, and peace (shalom) can be restored. Thus, in a Christian process of change, every development action and process must be tested for its consistency with truth and its contribution toward peace and justice.

Care needs to be taken in how truth-telling takes place. People need to discover the truth about themselves and their reality for themselves. Facilitating processes that allow people to discover their own truth is itself transformative and liberating (Freire 1990). After all, it is the truth that makes us free (Jn 8:32). Simply announcing the truth about others can be violent and often counter-productive. It almost certainly blunts a transformative movement. We must also have the humility to remember that we can never be sure we understand the truth about others or their situation.

Seeking beauty, art, and celebration

Anyone who has worked among the poor can attest to the fact that, even in the poorest places, one always finds fun, celebration, art, and beauty. There are always fiestas that are venues for fun, nice clothes, celebration, and worship. Music is always present, no matter how simple the instruments. Many of the simplest homes have a border of rocks painted white and bright colors on the door frames. There is always someone who tells the stories or passes on the epic poems that affirm the history of the community. Kids make toys and soccer balls out of whatever scraps they can find.

Sometimes our development work is too narrowly focused on what is missing in terms of the material needs of a poor community. Clean water, primary schools, new agricultural methods, micro-credit, immunizations, and improved housing are usually high on the community's priority list. These are the material interventions necessary to stay alive. But if this is our sole focus, then we are missing something important, something fundamentally human.

Our reflections on the biblical account of creation informed us that all human beings are made in the image of God and are intended to live in a world where life is secure. But as we noted earlier, God's creation was also beautiful, echoing the nature of God and calling out a sense of awe and worship. Early in the creation account we learn of the creation of musical instruments. Worship of God emerges soon thereafter. Creation theology calls for a life that is secure but also a life worth living. Our explorations of the Hebrew idea of shalom added the ideas of joy and enjoyment to this understanding of life as God intends. This suggests that transformational development must also include a commitment to aesthetics, the word we use to refer to thinking about the nature and expression of beauty. Development that improves the water supply and lowers malnutrition is good, but it is not really adequate to meet the standard for having a life worth living.

In addition to art, music, and poetry, we need to think a little about what are called *poetic practices*, those things we do together that create excitement, make us happy to be alive, and give our lives form and meaning. Poetic practices are not a means to something else; they are good in and of themselves. Poetic practices are the means by which community is formed, social traditions are communicated, and hospitality and reciprocity are reinforced. But the value is deeper than this; poetic practices are the key to being fully human.

Roberto Goizueta uses the term "aesthetic fusion" to describe that moment in which we "lose ourselves" for a moment in the fun, the art, the celebration, the worship, and the sacraments. "Play, recreation and celebrating are the most authentic forms of human life precisely because, when we are playing, recreating and celebrating, we are immersed in, or 'fused,' with the action itself, and those other persons with whom we are celebrating" (1995, 94). We all remember those cherished moments when we "lost ourselves" in God or relationships with our family and others.

This means that we also need to give thought to the kinds of celebrations, art, and worship that might support and create this sense of being fully alive, of being fully human. Most development practitioners are not geared for this kind of thing. Most of us are not liturgists or artists. Frankly, many of us don't know how to celebrate very well under the best of circumstances. We are better at identifying problems and seeking solutions. We are doers, and our natural focus in our development work is on turning inputs into outputs and outcomes. Perhaps we are a little more Puritan than we should be. Perhaps the ability to have fun and to celebrate is something the poor have to teach us. Perhaps we need to figure out how to get our acts of worship out of our church buildings and into the streets or even our offices.

This call to focus on poetic practices does not mean encouraging fun, art, celebration, and worship uncritically. Some kinds of fun, art, and celebrations are not supportive of life. Chambers calls our attention to the fact that some celebrations are costly and are usually defined and led by elites who benefit financially to the detriment of the poor (1983, 114–30). When it comes to celebration and worship, we must also ask who or what is being celebrated and decide if this is something that a Christian can affirm. But even when it is not, we can offer alternatives. Ben Chitambar, an Indian rural sociologist working at an agricultural college in India, created Christian celebration booths that he set up alongside all the Hindu booths at Hindu festivals celebrating the harvest. He was creating an unusual kind of

Christian witness; Christians could have fun and celebrate the gifts of their God, too.

Addressing causes

No process of human and social transformation can be entirely defined locally. Every community is part of a family of social systems that are regional, national, and finally global. Alan Fowler, development specialist and co-founder of the International NGO Training and Research Centre (INTRAC) in the UK, has developed a helpful diagram (see Figure 6–4) that shows how the micro-level of transformational development is located within an international social system (1997, 13).

At the bottom of Figure 6–4 we find the transformational development that I have been describing: empowering communities, strengthening local institutions, and efforts to create sustainable well-being. Fowler links this micro level of development to the larger development environment of the national and ultimately the international economic and political orders. These are the locations of those who play god in the lives of the poor at a distance, such as the World Bank, IMF, and the WTO. These global institutions seem especially subject to Wink's "delusional assumptions."

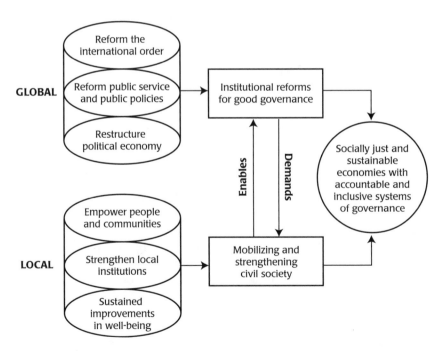

Figure 6–4: The micro and macro levels of development action.
(Adapted from Fowler 1997, 13)

Any understanding of transformational development that does not include concerns for reforming and restructuring at these higher levels is incomplete and somewhat naive. This is the point at which effective and discerning policy analysis and advocacy in all its forms must be included as part of the transformational development process. Fowler is right when he points out that the micro-level of development, where people are empowered and well-being is improved, must come together with the macro-level of development, where institutions are reformed for good governance, if we are to hope for "socially just and sustainable economies with accountable and inclusive systems of governance" (1997, 13).

Frances O'Gorman, a Catholic woman religious in Brazil, tells the story of her pilgrimage with poor women in *favelas* in Brazil and how their shared ministry evolved over time (1992). Her work began in the 1960s with a "band-aid" approach of social welfare that developed into a "patchwork approach" of program elements in the 1970s. Echoing Korten and Friedmann, O'Gorman's program approach then evolved into the "beehive approach" of educating the poor about human rights and then creating networks and social movements among the poor. The final stage was called the "beacon approach," which incorporated all the former approaches into a "transformational spiral" through which the poor emerge as actors and "become 'leadership citizens' forging a new kind of history for the whole world" (1992, 66). Development and advocacy are intertwined and mutually supporting.

Expressing a bias toward peace

Working for reconciliation and peace must be part of any Christian portfolio for transformational development. Mary Anderson has developed a useful planning framework whose goal is to enhance what she calls "local capacities for peace" (1999, 74). She argues that a key part of social analysis needs to include identifying the local institutions, cultural values, attitudes, experiences (history), symbols, and celebrations that tend either to unite the community or to divide it. Then the development program needs to be designed in ways that take advantage of the former and avoid or mitigate the impact of the latter.

Another way to express a bias toward peace can be found in how we use participatory methodologies for assessment and program design. We can insist that community committees include men and women, poor and non-poor, or representatives from every tribal group, church, and religious group in the village. Research into some of World Vision's area development programs in India, Ethiopia, and Uganda showed that insisting that local institutions involved with the development programming be inclusive of all groups in the community resulted in reconciliation and cooperative behavior (O'Reilly 1998).

In Bosnia, a community asked for help rebuilding a water system destroyed during the war. The request was for three independent water systems, one for each ethnic group. A peacebuilding bias demands that this request be rejected in favor of developing an agreement to create a single water system designed and managed by people representing all three ethnic groups.

Affirming the role of the church

In many communities living witnesses to God's larger story are already present in the form of the local church or churches. By *church* I mean the local body of believers that is doing its best to worship the God of the Bible—Father, Son, and Holy Spirit—and follow God's commands. Where there is more than one church, I am referring to all churches.

At the end of the day, the work of holistic mission belongs to the church, not the development agency or the development professional per se. Tim Chester, formerly of Tear Fund UK, points out that "the New Testament does not describe development projects or, for that matter, evangelistic initiatives. Its focus is on Christian communities, which are to be distinctive, caring, and inclusive. Integral (holistic) mission is about the church being the church" (2002, 7). This means that when the development practitioner or agency seeks to practice holistic mission, it needs to understand that it is only genuinely Christian when it carries out its mission as a member of the body of Christ. Christian activists and Christian agencies must be rooted in the larger church as well as its local expression.

I have already commented on the flaws that are part of every church. Yet, with all their flaws, local churches are nonetheless God's people and they were God's witnesses before we came and will be there long after the development intervention is over (Raistrick 2010, 137). This means that God's process of transformation toward the kingdom is already under way. Any Christian understanding of transformational development must take this fact seriously and accept that God has already put a living sign of God's kingdom in the community.

Too often Christian development professionals see the church as a distraction, or worse, an impediment to transformation. "The church has separated itself from the rest of the community." "Churches don't believe development is something they should be doing." "The church is not professional enough; it doesn't know what it is doing." Churches have been validating the current political and economic system; they are part of the problem." We know the litany well. Yet Newbigin insists that we must face one fact squarely:

It is surely a fact of inexhaustible significance that what our Lord left behind him was not a book or a creed, nor a system of thought, nor a rule of life, but a visible community. . . . He committed the entire work of salvation to that community. . . . The church does not depend for its existence upon our understanding of it or faith in it. (1954, 21)

Our goal must be to help the church be what it is intended to be, not to judge it or relegate it to the transformational development sidelines. Everyone is in need of transformation—ourselves, the poor, and the church(es). We are all on a journey. "Working toward a relationship of mutual spiritual accountability with local churches is part of what it means to be holistic in taking both the gospel and the context seriously" (Bediako 1996b, 187). If we are willing to love and accompany the poor toward transformation, why should we not be willing to love and accompany our brothers and sisters in Christ on their journey toward the same goal? Vinay Samuel offers a new development challenge:

What would happen if we apply the same principles of community participation to the establishment and building of the church as we do for the agriculture, health and school projects? How does the idea of building people's capacity to plan and manage their own development relate to the establishment and sustainability of a local church and the believer's spiritual life? (1995, 145)

We need a new development ecclesiology that helps us understand local churches as both the gatherers and caretakers of local Christians and also as the expression of God's holistic mission. "One of the greatest challenges we Christians have at the threshold of the third millennium is the articulation and practical implementation of an ecclesiology that views the local church, and particularly the church of the poor, as the primary agent of holistic mission (Padilla, in Chester 2002, 8). Our practitioners need to recover from their pride and professionalism and find a way to become part of the Christian community on the ground and thus function as part of the local body of Christ. Agencies must figure out a way to become engaging, supporting, and empowering partners of local churches, with each discovering and respecting their respective roles of the others in God's work of transformation. This should be important to the development practitioner and his or her agency for a very selfish reason. René Padilla in a workshop given to World Vision staff in Latin America left them with the bold warning: "The path to secularization is made straight if you lose sight of the local church."

SUSTAINABILITY

A great deal has been written in recent years about the need for development to be sustainable. There have been too many examples of development programming that seemed to be making a difference as long as the staff and the money of the development agency were present. Too many program evaluations, performed after the money and staff are withdrawn, reveal that the entire development enterprise has proven more than the community could sustain on its own. Within a year or two, it was hard to find evidence that there had been a program at all. In some cases, things actually got worse because the community had become dependent on external resources and now suffered from diminished capacity.

We need to be careful how we think about the idea of sustainability. First of all, we must recognize that even the poorest community already has some level of sustainability. If the community were not sustainable before the development agency came, it would not exist. There is considerable evidence that poor communities are quite sophisticated in developing sustainable survival strategies (Jayakaran 1996, 8) in terms of food, water, housing, and living within the constraints of a marginal natural environment (Chambers 1997, 24).

The second caution is that the ultimate source of sustainable life is not ours to control. It is God through Christ who sustains life. Psalm 104 reminds us of God's active role in making springs, giving drink, causing grass to grow, and "bringing forth food from the earth: wine that gladdens the heart of man, oil to make his face shine, and bread that sustains his heart" (Ps 104:14–16). Most communities are already sustainable in some manner because God has been and is at work through them.

Third, we need to ask whether the idea of sustainability is enough. If sustainable simply means things are being maintained or that the project activities and impacts continue after we leave, is this enough? Don't we really seek sustainable growth, learning, and continuing transformation? I think we do, but we need to say so.

Finally, we need to define sustainability in two ways. First, we do not want the transformational development process to be dependent on us. This is a negative definition, but it is essential that the development agency keep such a definition clearly in mind. Defining sustainability this way, however, is less helpful to the community. Not being dependent on us does not mean that the community and its story are necessarily sustainable on their own.

The community needs a different understanding of sustainability. To do this, we have to return to the same categories we used to frame our understanding of poverty. The community's understanding of sustainability must include the physical, mental, social, and spiritual.

Physical sustainability

This dimension of sustainability includes all the basics that people need to live: food, water, health, livelihood, and a sustainable environment. Adequate food and nutrition require sustainable agriculture, an approach to increasing agricultural production that is not dependent on chemicals that are costly or that damage the land and the water. Adequate water means sustainable water development that emphasizes more effectively managing rainfall run-off and ground water in ways that are sustainable (Serageldin 1995). As the examples of agriculture and water imply, physical sustainability implies enhancing the productivity and life-supporting capacity of the local environment in ways that ensure its future.

Physical sustainability also means people who are able to manage their own health care to the greatest extent possible. This means a community based approach in which people are empowered to do what they can for themselves, utilizing local indigenous knowledge and traditional sources of health care, with minimal dependence on the high-cost, expensive healthcare systems we are dependent upon in the West.

Physical sustainability means enabling the poor to create wealth. Microenterprise development programs that promote capital formation in poor communities and that teach the poor to run small businesses and to save money form the economic foundation without which sustainability is impossible. Micro-insurance provides buffers against shocks from bad weather and natural disasters that destroy the limited asset base of the poor.

Finally, we need to learn from the history of the so-called developed countries in their move toward material sustainability. They have developed the means to be sustainable (more or less) in terms of health, agriculture, water, and economics. However, this has often been done at the cost of environmental sustainability (Weaver, Rock, and Kusterer 1997, 233–58). We live in a robust and resilient world that has managed to contain several centuries of human creativity in the form of technological and economic development (see Figure 2–1). We must thank God for the resilience of creation. It seems, however, that there are limits both locally and globally to this singular creation God has given to us.

As Christians working for transformation, we must learn what these limits are and respect them as good stewards would. Francis Bacon, a Christian philosopher of the early 1600s and the father of natural philosophy (the breakthrough that opened the door to the development of science), said it well: "Nature can(not) be commanded except by obeying her" (Bacon 1620).

Mental sustainability

I've already made the case that the deepest form of poverty is poverty of being. Disempowering scars exist in the human and community consciousness of the poor. The web of lies is perceived to be the way things are— ordained, immutable, unchangeable. Transformational development that does not include restoring psychological and spiritual well-being is not sustainable. We must seek the healing of the marred identity of the poor. We must treat them as valuable human beings, made in the image of God, loved by God. We must listen to them as if they have something to contribute, because they do. They simply do not appreciate how much they know. We must encourage the belief that God is for them and that God has given everyone something to contribute.

A word of caution. We must take care as to how we approach a case of marred identity. Helping people understand the nature of their marring alone may not be as transformative as we would assume. There has been an interesting illustration of this from the Dalit Panchayat Movement in India. After years of focusing on the nature and dynamics of oppression of the Dalit (translated "broken to pieces" or "crushed") people, there has been a shift in focus. Now the Dalit are being helped to celebrate the strength and resilience of their culture and history, and this is creating pride, energy, and change. Drawing on Dalit history and culture is proving more transformative than repeating the tragic narrative of their victimhood. It appears that repeating a narrative of victimhood alone simply reinforces marred identity in oppressed people (Malanes 2009).

Releasing people's capacity to learn is also a critical element of mental sustainability. Helping people discover that they can study and make sense out of their world, that they can identify their capabilities and vulnerabilities, and that they can plan based on what they learn is part of a mental transformation that changes the people from the inside. Teaching people how to evaluate their efforts and to codify their experience is an empowering experience that sustains continuing transformation. At the end of the day, helping people learn how to learn is the key to increasing human agency—one of the most important parts of any transformative process.

Ultimately, the poor must come to believe in themselves—not in us, our development aid, or our development agency. If they believe we are the true instruments of development, then we have failed to create mental sustainability. Instead, we have created dependency and deepened their poverty.

Social sustainability

The need for sustainable systems takes us back to Korten and Friedmann. Korten's alternative development (1990, 218) seeks to return some level of control over local resources—by which he means both natural resources and the information people need to make informed decisions—to the people who live in the community in hopes that this will lead to sustainable choices on the part of the community. Korten calls for the development of sustainable development systems that include local NGOs, the local private and public sectors, and all the systemic links between the community and those whose decisions have an effect on the well-being of the community. This requires broadening local political participation, active mutual self-help, and empowerment. Because Korten believes that the earth cannot sustain unlimited economic growth and consumption, he argues against economic growth as the model of development (1990, 132). His view of an alternative development seems to hope for a future that operates apart from or that overcomes the neo-liberal economic globalization of today.

Friedmann's empowerment approach also places emphasis on local decision-making, local self-reliance, local participation in democratic processes, and social learning, but he accepts the inevitability of the constraints and influence of the "global economic forces, structures of unequal wealth, and hostile class alliances" (1992, viii). Therefore, sustainability, for Friedmann, requires sustainable social systems that are transformed into political power "to engage the struggle for emancipation on a larger—national and international—terrain." Sustainable social systems and helping the poor have a political voice of their own are integral parts of social sustainability.

Alex de Waal, director of African Rights in London and a frequent critic of humanitarian aid, argues that humanitarian assistance must support the incipient sense of political engagement and instinct toward political accountability that true development must bring. Social sustainability must include establishing or supporting the development of local organizations with social agendas (de Waal 1997, 219). People need to develop a sense that, as part of a larger political community, they have rights on which they should insist—to development, to a sustainable livelihood, to respect for civil and political rights. They have the right to expect that humanitarian law and human rights applies to them (1997, 8). If this is ignored or not supported, then humanitarian aid simply ignores the oppressive political and economic structures and thus sustains their illegitimacy.

Recently, social sustainability has come to include a concern for building *civil society*, a term used to refer to nonprofit groups or voluntary associations such as development agencies, environmental groups, service groups, sports clubs, church groups, peasant associations, self-help groups, and the like. Remember that Friedmann argues that social organizations and networks are the two primary means by which communities can expand social power (see Figure 5–4) (Friedmann 1992, 68–69).

Civil society is the point at which micro-enterprise development, political empowerment, and nurturing social organizations come together. These groups are the social capital that, along with economic and human capital, constitutes the productive capital of the community (Weaver, Rock, and Kusterer 1997, 208). Civil society can also be the bridge between the micro and macro levels of development action, between the work of the community and the regional, national, and global political and economic structures in which the community is embedded (see Figure 6–4).

Alan Whaites points out that this affirmation of civil society assumes a de Tocquevillian understanding of civil society in which civil society is a social good in that it acts as a defensive counter-balance against the strong (modern) state (Whaites 1996) and, I would add, the free market. The paradox is that most development NGOs operate in the context of weak states and economies. This means that NGOs must be concerned about usurping the right and necessary role of the state as NGOs provide social services to the poor. To fill in where the state should be providing services creates a new barrier to sustainability.

A Christian view of social sustainability will require a theology of civil society that defines the roles and responsibility that individual Christians, voluntary Christian groups, and churches should play in order to add value to the societies in which they live. Jayakumar Christian and Walter Wink provide an important additional insight. Social systems, including civil society, are the domains of what Paul called the principalities and powers. As a result of their fallen nature, principalities and powers work within the social systems to devalue or degrade life. They deceive by working against any recognition of God being at work in social systems or even that social systems have a spirituality. The result is a materialistic view of social systems and a distortion of their mission.

No Christian view of building civil society can neglect the fact that social systems have a spiritual interiority. Working for civil society and for extending social power will bring us up against spiritual forces that do not want the poor empowered or a role for the church in the "secular" social order. Thus, in addition to community organizing, institution building, and political action, building civil society that supports social sustainability is a spiritual task requiring spiritual tools.

Finally, enhancing civil society presupposes the "freedom to develop" (Weaver, Rock, and Kusterer 1997, 220). Transformational development that does not include concerns for peacebuilding, human rights, and democratic participation is very limited indeed. Development in societies in conflict must be done in a way that decreases tensions and that nurtures local capacities for peace (Anderson 1996c). While some argue that human rights and democracy are somehow uniquely Western concepts, the fact that they square fully with the biblical tradition (see Stassen 2008, 405; Wolterstorff 2008, 313–14) must move them onto the agenda for Christians involved in development. It is no accident that these concepts emerged in cultures that share the Judeo-Christian tradition. While one can discuss fruitfully the need to balance the rights of individuals with the rights of the community, it would be hard to imagine building civil society while ignoring the issues of freedom to assemble, freedom to speak, freedom to choose one's beliefs, and freedom to have a say in decisions affecting one's future.

Whaites argues against the universal and uncritical affirmation of all forms of civil society proposed by Jean-Francois Bayart (Whaites 1996, 242). Expressions of civil society that reinforce tribal, ethnic, or religious divisions within countries or communities would be hard to support in a Christian frame that assumes that every person is made in the image of God and that cultural diversity is a gift to the whole, not an excuse for division.

Spiritual sustainability

Spiritual sustainability begins with what seems to be a contradiction. While the community needs to believe that it is not dependent on the development agency, it must also believe passionately that it is dependent on God. No one is independent; we are all dependent on God, whether we acknowledge this fact or not. For centuries, contemplatives have opened their day with the prayer, "Thank you, O God, for waking me this morning, you didn't have to." Fortunately, most poor communities in the South believe this more deeply than most of us do in the West.

Another dimension of spiritual sustainability has to do with the contribution of faith-based organizations in the community. Churches, mosques, and temples are the location of value traditions without which human society cannot function. Decisions to include women in community decision making, to stop killing girl children, to work cooperatively with those formerly demonized as "other" all require a value change that most often finds its roots in the transformative power of faith traditions. At the heart of this kind of change is repentance and forgiveness, the twin foundations of reconciliation. At its best, this is the work of the religious community.

In spite of the uneven history of religions in terms of their contributions (or lack thereof) to human welfare, religious men and women concerned for the spiritual welfare of the community must play a role in the development of the community if it is to be transformational and sustainable. For Christians, this means surrendering a privileged place in the community and working alongside people who believe differently. This should not concern us. If our story is the true human story and if our God is the true God, then we need to become servants of all others and in faith believe that God is able to take care of God's self.

Finally, as Christians, it is hard for us to believe in sustainable transformation in a community in which the church is not acting as the sign of the kingdom, of God's better future. The church plays this role by what it does even more effectively than by what it says. The church is not so much the Christians gathered, although it is this too, as it is the place where Christians learn and are challenged to live the whole gospel in the fullness of the life of the larger community (see Figure 6–5).

There are several critical contributions to transformational development that only the church can provide. First, the role of the church in transformational development is the same as ours: to love the community and to serve it with a spirit of encouragement, not to be its judge.

> The church can be the servant of its community, harnessing the wind and wood and water into technologies that make the world a little more habitable, or singing with the rest of creation the wonder of existence, or working side by side with all people of good will toward

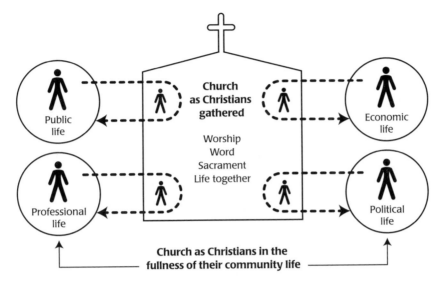

Figure 6–5: The church outside the building.

a better social order. If the church is to lead at all, it is in serving; in applying the creative energies released in Christ towards the steward-ship of creation and the bringing of fallen structures closer to God's original purposes. (Maggay 1994, 72)

Second, the church should be a source of holistic practitioners who are serving the well-being of the whole community. People who are reading and living the word of God under the discipling of the Holy Spirit should be a significant source of inspiration and perspiration working for life and shalom. The church may be more transformative as a source of loving people than as a source of instruction or prophetic word. Newbigin said it well:

The major role of the church in relationship to the great issues of justice and peace will not be in its formal pronouncement, but in its continually nourishing and sustaining men and women who will act responsibly as believers in the course of their secular duties as citi-zens. (Newbigin 1989, 139)

Third, the church can play a role as a civil society organization, working to enlarge people's access to economic and social power. In many parts of the world, and in the inner cities of the United States, local churches are the only functioning civil society there is. In Los Angeles some creative re-thinking concerning the nature of financial institutions and the role of the inner-city churches has led local churches to provide an interface between poor parishioners and financial-services companies that had heretofore shunned the idea of setting up their own offices in poor areas (Fondation, Tufano, and Walker 1999, 57).

Fourth, the church can be a pastoral presence. Transformational development is hard work; the road is not always easy. The poor and oppressed need love and care in the midst of their pain. The church is the one place they should always be hearing the message that they are loved by God, have been given gifts by God, and have a contribution to make. The non-poor need to be loved too, and part of "tough love" for them is being challenged by the word of God and hearing the truth about who they are really meant to be. Finally, the church can be the source of community and a spirituality that sustains those who are trying to facilitate transformational development.

Fifth, the church can be a prophetic voice addressing those who refuse to see and do not want to hear. The story of the effect of bad public policy as it is experienced in a poor village or slum is sometimes more compelling than World Bank economic research papers. Sometimes the prophetic voice needs to be directed at the non-poor in the community or elsewhere. Sometimes the church can be the institution that allows the stories of the impact of bad public policy on poor families to be told in those places where public policy decisions are made.

Finally, the church is the hermeneutical community that reads the biblical story as its story and applies this story to the concrete circumstances of its time, place, and culture. This is the community within the community from which the word of God is heard, lived, and revealed. This is the community that, because it knows the true story, can and must challenge the delusional assumptions and the web of lies.

THINKING HOLISTICALLY

The need for this way of thinking about and viewing the world should now be clear. As we take on the challenge of working for human transformation, we will have to learn to think and act holistically in a variety of ways.

The whole story

We have to keep the whole story in mind and avoid the temptation to reduce it to the four gospels only. The biblical narrative is a whole story that begins with creation and continues with the call of Israel, the exile, Jesus and his death and resurrection, the church, and the end of history with the second coming. The biblical narrative is a story of a world in which the material and spiritual are seamlessly related, a world of persons and social systems. If we truncate this story, we rob it of much of its life and meaning. The full story of Jesus begins at creation and ends with his second coming.

The whole gospel message

The gospel message is an inseparable mix of life, deed, word, and sign. We are to be with Jesus (life) so that we can preach the good news (word), heal the sick (deed), and cast out the demons (sign). This holistic gospel addresses all three of Hiebert's levels: the word of truth, the act of power, and the deed that works. Each dimension of the gospel message adds to the meaning of the others. Our life and deeds make our words intelligible; our words help people understand our life and deeds. Life, word, and deed are signs of the living presence of someone greater than ourselves.

While we should reveal the gospel message in whatever way best speaks to the immediate needs of our audience, over time all the dimensions of the gospel must be revealed for the good news of Jesus Christ to be understood in its fullness. Often the transformational development process begins with witness through good deeds. As relationships develop, the way we live our lives and treat people becomes a witness of life. Prayer, reminding people that God is the source of any good that is emerging in the community, and the occasional miracle are the witness of sign. When we answer the question "Why are you here?" or "Why are you making a sacrifice for the likes of us?" the answer is the witness of the gospel word. Limiting our work of transformation to only one aspect of the gospel message impoverishes the message and obscures the person of Jesus.

A holistic view of human beings

Remember Figure 6–3 above? It illustrates a holistic understanding of a human being. There can be no meaningful understanding of a person apart from his or her relationships—with God, self, community, those he or she calls "other," and the environment. People as individuals are inseparable from the social systems in which they live.

A holistic view of time

We need to understand time holistically and not separate past, present, future, and eternity. People's past can be a barrier to transformation. Inability to imagine a future that is different from today is a transformational frontier. Separating the time of our story (past, present, and future) from the time of God's larger story (eternity) is also a mistake. Transformational plans for the next fifteen years must be made in light of all of human history and its ultimate destination.

A state of mind

One final word on holism. Holism is for the most part a state of mind or an attitude. Holism must be in the mind of the practitioner as a habit—a way of living, thinking, and doing. Creating this mindset is very important since it is difficult to demand holism in the form of the program itself. No transformational development effort can do everything and work at every level of the problem. This means that the best test for holism is a negative test. If there is no work directed at spiritual or value change; no work involving the church; no mention of meaning, discovery, identity and vocation, then one should be concerned that the program is not holistic. The next step is to talk to the development promoter and the people. If they show no thinking that is holistic, then there is a problem.

A FRAMEWORK FOR TRANSFORMATION

Putting all of these ideas together, we have a framework for transformation that points us toward the best human future—the kingdom of God. This future is framed by the twin goals of transformation: changed people, who have discovered their true identity and vocation; and changed relationships that are just and peaceful. These goals are sought with a process of change that is principle centered. The development process belongs to the people; relationships are the critical factor for change; we need to keep the end of transformation in mind; we promote truth-telling, righteousness, and justice. These principles are expressed through persons or groups of persons working in the community: God, the church, the holistic development practitioner, and the Evil One. Three of these are working in favor of a better human future, while the mission of the fourth is to distract, divide, and destroy. Finally, these transformational development principles and positive active agents seek to move a community toward the goals of transformation in a way that is sustainable physically, mentally, socially, and spiritually (see Figure 6–6).

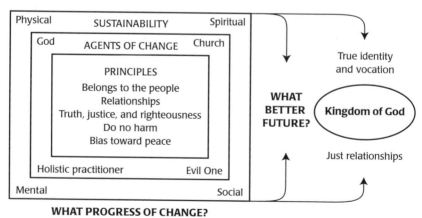

Figure 6–6: The framework for transformational development.

HELPFUL RESOURCES

Livelihood security

Livelihood Connect website in Eldis. Eldis is one of a family of knowledge services from the Institute of Development Studies, Sussex. Its mission is to support the documentation, exchange, and use of evidence-based development knowledge. http://www.eldis.org/go/livelihoods/

McCaston, M. Katherine, Kristina Luther, Timothy Frankenberger, and James Becht. 2002. *Household Livelihood Security Assessments: A Toolkit for Practitioners*. Washington DC: TANGO and CARE USA.

Sustainable agriculture

Altieri, Miguel. 1995. *Agroecolog: The Science of Sustainable Agriculture*. Boulder, CO: Westview.

Bunch, Roland. 1985. *Two Ears of Corn: A Guide to People-centered Agricultural Improvement*. 2d ed. Oklahoma City: World Neighbors.

Pretty, Jules N. 1995. *Regenerating Agriculture*. London: Earthscan

Scoones, Ian, and John Thompson. 2009. *Farmer First Revisited: Innovation for Agricultural Research and Development*. Rugby, UK: Practical Action.

————. 1994. *Beyond Farmer First: Rural People's Knowledge, Agricultural Research, and Extension Practice*. London: Intermediate Technology Publications.

Microenterprise development

Christian Economic Development Center at the Chalmers Center for Economic Development at Covenant College. Online and distance learning courses. http://chalmers.org/cedi/cedi.php

Consultative Group to Help the World's Poor (CGAP), hosted at the World Bank. Advances financial access for the world's poor. http://www.cgap.org

Hawtrey, Kim. 1990. "Oxford Declaration on Christian Faith and Economics." *Transformation* 7 (2): 1–8.

USAID program MicroLINKS (Micro enterprise learning, information and knowledge sharing). http://www.microlinks.org/

Virtual library on microcredit and microfinance of the Global Development Research Center. http://www.gdrc.org

Community-based healthcare

Rohde, Jon, and John Wyon. 2003. *Community-based Healthcare: Lessons from Bangladesh to Boston.* Boston: Management Sciences for Health Publications.

WHO. 2004. "Comprehensive Country and Home-based Healthcare Model." SEARO Regional Publication no. 40. http://www.searo.who.int/LinkFiles/Publications_Healthcaremodel.pdf

7

Development practice:
Principles and practitioners

To this point we have developed an understanding of what poverty is and why people are poor. To this we have added an understanding of what transformational development is from a Christian perspective. The next question that needs to be addressed is how we work with the poor and the non-poor in order to help them articulate a vision for transformation and the means by which they can attempt to move toward this vision.

Answering these questions takes some care. If we jump too quickly to development methodology, we can make some serious mistakes. There are some underlying assumptions that need clarification. Whose project is being planned? Who does the planning? What way of thinking about planning is best suited for development work? What requirements will we make of development-planning methodologies?

Finally, there are a whole series of considerations relating to the development practitioner. We need to address the mindset and characteristics of the holistic practitioner. What kind of formation and spirituality enables effective development promotion?

THE PRINCIPLES

Respecting the community's story

Earlier I described transformational development as taking place in the context of converging stories. The story of the development promoter and his or her agency is joining the story of the community and the individual stories of the people and groups in the community. It is important to be very clear as to whose story the transformational development project belongs. I have also pointed out that everyone is quick to say that the story belongs to the people, and that it is a great deal harder to live this out in practice. Too often development workers unwittingly assume that their story is a better story; after all, they know how to do sustainable agriculture and understand maternal child health. It is a difficult challenge to lay down our own story and not pick it up again until the poor ask us to do so (see Figure 7–1).

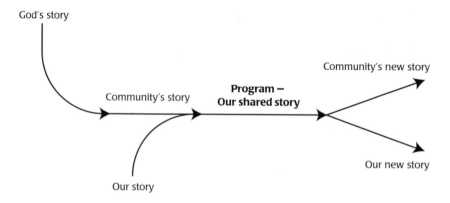

Figure 7–1: Convergence of stories.

At the same time, however, this convergence of stories means that the story of the community and the holistic practitioner will never be fully the same. Each story affects all the other stories. The poor will borrow from our story and we, if we are not too proud, will learn from theirs. There is no longer a single narrative in the community. This is why engaged, respectful relationships are so important to transformational development. Each story needs to engage all the other stories, and all need to engage the larger story of which all stories are part.

The history of the community

The community's story, up to the time the development practitioner arrives, is its history. The community comes from a past, and its memory of that past is the beginning of any new story. The community has been coping, adapting, and surviving. It has tried to innovate, sometimes with success and sometimes with failure. Good things have happened; the community has done things of which it is proud. As we know from appreciative inquiry, the positive elements of the past can be a source of vision and energy for the future. Leszek Kolakowski has reminded us that we study history, not to find out what happened, but to discover who we are. Thus, helping the community tell its own story is critical to understanding its present and its identity as well as getting a glimpse of a possible future.

When we take the time to listen to its story, we are signaling the community that we think its story is valuable.

There is also a need to help the community and us to recognize the activity of God in the story of the community. Whether the community is Christian or not, whether religious or not, our theology tells us that God has been doing creative and redemptive work in the life of the community, if only we look for it. Wherever a disaster was averted or a blessing was unexpected, God and grace were at work. Wherever things worked for life and against death, Christ's fingerprints can be seen—"All things were created by him and for him. He is before all things and in him all things hold together" (Col 1:17–18). Recognizing and naming God's activity in the story of the community is an act of discernment, a spiritual act. It is also an act of healing. Asking the community to locate God in its history is a way of helping its members to discover that they are not god-forsaken.

However, there is also a dark side to recovering this history. This dark side takes two forms. First, the history of the community is often told by those in positions of power, and they usually tell the history in a way that either supports their continuing claim to power or disempowers the community in terms of thinking about change (Christian 1998a, 15). Religious leaders sometimes reinforce fatalism by claiming that God wills the poverty of today or that the poverty today is a just response to bad behavior in the past. Political or economic leaders may justify their positions of power on the basis of having been blessed or being more virtuous or having served as the community's benefactors in the past. History is thereby distorted to serve an end. Illiteracy means the poor never have a chance to write their own history or read alternative views that subvert the stories of the powerful. But even the illiterate poor can remember their history and be helped to recover it and reread it. Any journey of transformation needs to begin by helping the community and its various sub-groups recover their own true stories.

Second, we need to be concerned about who made the community's history. Jayakumar Christian has pointed out that some people have more freedom to make history than others (1994, 201). Some have argued that if you are not a history maker, you become a passive participant in the hands of those who do make history. Thus, the very process of history-making can be a source of powerlessness and poverty. Knowing who participated in history-making in the past and why is critical to any effort to create a different kind of history making in the future.

Listening to the whole story

We must also remember to listen to their story in terms of both the seen and the unseen world. Hiebert, Shaw, and Tienou (1998) remind us that each level of worldview answers different questions. The top level of the unseen world is the domain of formal religion. Listening to people talk about this will reveal a community's understanding of the formal side of Islam, Christianity, or whatever belief system they believe. This is where we will hear stories and propositions that answer questions about ultimate origins, about the purpose and identity of the universe, our community, and ourselves (see Figure 7–2).

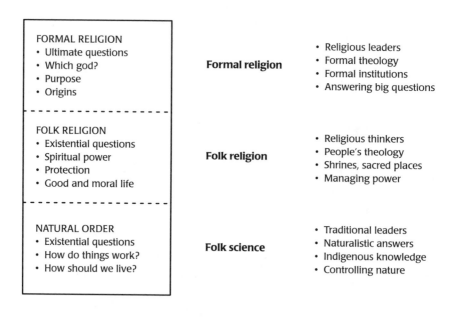

Figure 7–2: The three-tiered story of the community.
(Adapted from Hiebert, Shaw, and Tienou 1998)

The middle level of the worldview, while still spiritual and unseen, is the world of folk religion. There is a folk version of everything—folk Islam, folk Buddhism, and even folk Christianity. This level addresses questions about managing power in everyday life. Who has the power over this or that area of life? What do they demand of us? How can we be prosperous or avoid failure? What do we need to know about our past? How can we make the future more secure? What is the right moral and social order for us? The answers point to the interdependence of all things, to the sources of power and the management of power.

The lower level of worldview is the natural order, the material world. This is the world of science in both its modern and folk expressions. Nomadic people understand why and when to move their herds. Village healers have extensive knowledge of local herbs, barks, and leaves. The community has rules for how to live and work together. This is the world of hearing, seeing, touching, and feeling things.

The development practitioner is usually most interested, and most comfortable, working in the lower level of the worldview. After all, this is the part of the world in which most development activities take place. This is where we dig wells, immunize children, improve agricultural practices, and carry out micro-enterprise activities. The problem arises when this is the only part of the community's story that we listen to or ask about. The community's formal and folk religious views also have important information that we need to hear. Whether we agree or not, these domains of the unseen spiritual world are where the community will tend to locate the cause of its problems and the hope for their solutions. If we are unwilling to view the world from the community's perspective, and begin from there, then we are top-down development practitioners after all.

They know how to survive

The community already has a survival strategy. The community has well-established patterns for making sense out of its world and staying alive in it. Only in disaster situations will we find such severe dislocations that its people are unable to cope and survive. This already existing survival strategy is that part of the community's story that we call the present. Understanding this survival strategy is critical to any attempt to create a vision for a better future. There are two reasons why this is true.

First, we need to see the world the way the community sees it. Helping the community describe its survival strategy is also a way for us to see what the community considers important as well as the community's understanding of what causes things to happen or not happen. The community's survival strategy reveals its capabilities, resources, skills, and knowledge as well as its vulnerabilities, those areas of life over which the community feels it has little or no control. Capabilities are assets around which future development can be planned. Vulnerabilities are the things for which alternatives or mitigating strategies are needed.

Second, allowing a community to describe its survival strategy reinforces in the minds of the community members the idea that they have skills, local knowledge, and ways of working that are good and worth building on. Not everyone in the community is uneducated and ineffective. Enabling people to discover and declare their survival strategy is part of healing the marred identity of the poor.

Ravi Jayakaran has created a framework for "wholistic worldview analysis" in order to aid development workers to understand the community's description of its survival strategy (2007). The part of the world the community feels it can control represents the seen or material world of nature where material cause and effect hold sway, the inside of the circle (Figure 7–3). The community members believe they can make things change, for good or ill, as a result of their own actions. This part of their survival strategy does not invoke religious or spiritual cause and effect.

The other part of their survival strategy, the part outside the circle in Figure 7–3, deals with what the community believes is outside its direct control. This is the world of spirits, gods, demons, and ancestors—the inhabitants of Hiebert's excluded middle. Only spiritual explanations work in this part of their world. (Interestingly, we do not tend to find the gods of formal religion here. Vishnu, Krishna, Allah, Ngai, and the other high gods are not to be bothered with the mundane details of everyday life. The Christian God is the exception.) More on this in the section "Letting the spiritual come through" in Chapter 8.

In search of some measure of influence in these areas of vulnerability, the community will assign gods or shrines or sacred places to these areas. The greater the lack of control, or the greater the perceived efficacy of the god, the larger the shrine. The smaller gods who are invoked as the source of cause and effect in this unseen world represent a map of the community's vulnerability. To gain influence over this part of their life, the community turns to shamans and diviners as those who have access to the unseen world and who can work for good or ill on behalf of individuals and the community. At this point the religious system and worldview can prove exploitative, as money is charged for these services.

This unseen world is a challenge for the development practitioner from the West. We must be able to accept talk about sacred places, shrines, and temples where people make offerings, doing the best they can to negotiate with the unpredictable and capricious unseen spirits who can change their lives for better or for worse. The map of its divinities is the one way the community describes its vulnerabilities (Jayakaran 2007).

In Figure 7–3, for example, the health of children lies both within the domain the community can control and outside of it. This represents the uncertainty the community associates with the health of its children. Sometimes the cause of illness is germs or not having enough food. Since this is empirical and certain, people can take action to create change. Therefore, sick children are taken to the health hut or emergency feeding is sought. Other health problems are attributed by the community to the evil eye or an angry ancestor or spirit. For this, divining and sacrifices are the remedy. The survival strategy as the community describes it acknowledges power in both the seen and the unseen world.

This can get confusing. Both elements of the survival strategy are often described in religious language and involve religious institutions. We must be careful to discern the difference between religious language describing a physical process in contrast to religious language describing the unseen world of the spiritual. As an example of the former, the pre-modern water

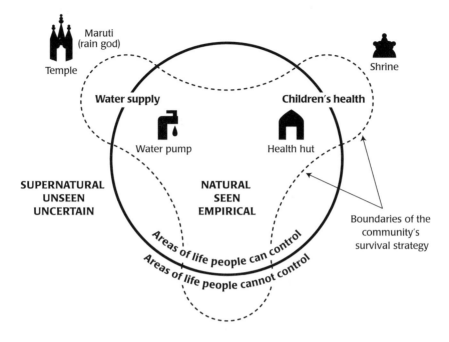

Figure 7–3: The survival strategy of a community.
(Adapted from Jayakaran 1997b, 5)

systems of Bali were linked to a system of temples belonging to a large family of gods. The respective religious rituals associated with each temple served to link all the temples in a way that resulted in a system of water management that ensured that even downstream users got their fair share of water (Lansing 1991, 59). This is an example of spiritual language and ritual providing the framework for a material distribution system.

Bruce Bradshaw (1997) has developed a framework for describing survival systems. He suggests that any survival strategy must describe the sources the community looks to for provision (food and water), peace, justice, healing, guidance, and salvation. Figure 7–4 shows how three tribal groups in Kenya described the sources of these things within the context of their traditional worldview. It is interesting to note that some elements deal with the supernatural, while others connote the recent arrival of Western science and education. The holistic practitioner must work with the community in a way that allows both worlds to be described and understood. This survival strategy is the point of departure for the development journey. To enhance our own understanding of how the community understands cause and effect, we must understand the survival strategy in their categories. The community will work more willingly to participate and take ownership when development interventions resonate with the survival strategy and attempt to enhance it. Then we can ask transformational questions: What are the barriers to the community growing in its ability to survive? Whose interests are served by these barriers?

Figure 7–4: Elements of a Kenyan survival system.
(From Bradshaw 1997)

Respecting indigenous knowledge

One of the more recent discoveries among development professionals is how much local communities actually know that is true and valuable. Traditional medicine is not all superstition and nonsense. In fact, Western pharmaceutical companies are abandoning the random search for drugs in the laboratory in favor of listening to traditional healers and their knowledge of barks, leaves, and grubs.

In Kenya, they still tell the story of Lord Delamare, who "discovered" the rich grasslands north of Nakuru and couldn't understand why the Masai didn't graze their cattle there. He spent a fortune importing English cattle only to discover that the grass in that part of the Rift Valley lacks a key nutrient that results in poor milk production, resulting in the death of most of the calves. This, of course, was something that every Masai boy knew but was never asked.

Olivia Muchena points out that the problem is in the eye of the beholder (Muchena 1996, 179). As long as the facilitator assumes that taboos, myths, and related ethnic values and concepts of the community have no value, they will have nothing to offer the development process. Muchena points out that these "superstitious" ideas are the way communities encode knowledge. If they are taken seriously, important local knowledge, often unavailable to outsiders, can emerge.

In rural India an old man watched a water specialist use a vertical electrical sounding device to determine the best site for an open well. "You don't need that," the old man announced. "Just dig your well under the tallest termite mound. Or dig under those big trees that stay green during the dry season. Everyone knows that is where the water is." And so the modern equipment confirmed.

Respecting and seeking indigenous knowledge "requires a different way of relating to the local community, for they must become partners in the ministry, helping to educate the 'ministers' to the realities from their perspective" (Muchena 1996, 178). We need to listen with an expectation that there are things we can learn.

With a humility that comes from experience, more and more development practitioners and anthropologists are giving the local view of almost everything a more serious hearing. In the arenas of rural development and health, development anthropologists, such as Michael Warren, Johan Pottier, and Paul Sillitoe have been working on methods by which there can be a negotiated translation of both indigenous and Western technological knowledge that allows both to contribute to development programming (Blunt and Warren 1996; Pottier, Bicker, and Sillitoe, 2003).

There are two reasons that we need to seek and value local knowledge. First, as the foregoing illustrations suggest, local knowledge may add to Western knowledge, providing we have the humility to believe that our knowledge system is not complete. Within the African worldview, illness may be the result of material causes, but it may also be the result of broken relationships. The whole person is sick, not just the material body. This kind of thinking is slowly being taken up in the West and is making our approach to medicine both more humane and more relational.

The second reason for respecting indigenous knowledge is more serious. Koyama calls attention to it in an interesting way when he tells his own story as a missionary in rural Thailand, fresh from a seminary in Japan. He describes the angry response of a Thai woman to his conversation about the gospel: "She was annoyed at me for looking at her *in my own terms*. She felt that she was only an object of my religious conquest. I had a message for her, but I did not think of the possibility that she might have a message for me" (Koyama 1974, 90).

Do we believe that the poor have a message for us? When we fail to listen, to see what we can learn, we are in fact telling them that they are without useful information, without contribution. By dismissing what they know, we further mar the identity of the poor. Our good intentions deepen the poverty we seek to alleviate.

Even when indigenous knowledge seems to be wrong, we need to take care. In a Tanzanian village the local people told a development worker that no motor vehicle was allowed to drive around their one-and-only spring. If this should happen, they said, the spirit who lived in the spring would cause the spring to go dry. Wishing to show the villagers that angry spirits do not stop springs from functioning, the development worker drove his four-wheel-drive vehicle by the spring. The water promptly ceased to flow. While there was a natural explanation for this—small physical disturbances in the soil can cause certain kinds of soil to compact temporarily—it is nonetheless true that the development worker created several barriers to any hope he may have had for change. On the one hand, he had shown no respect for the view of the community, and on the other hand, he had reinforced their traditional worldview, something that may hinder development in the future.

From participation to empowerment

If the development story belongs to the community, then local participation is an unavoidable requirement. If poverty is in part a reflection of the marred identity of the poor, then participation is essential to any effort to restore a better sense of identity. If we agree that there are already resources within the community, then participation is the logical means by which this knowledge can be discovered and part of the development process. If we have the humility to know that we do not know enough to do someone else's development for them, then seeking local participation is the only safeguard against our doing unwitting damage. By any measure, local participation is a critical success factor for transformational development.

Quality of participation

The quality of participation matters, however. Norman Uphoff, a development practitioner and scholar at Cornell University, claims that "the value of participation depends upon what kind it is, under what circumstances it is taking place and by and for whom" (Uphoff, Cohen, and Goldsmith 1979, 281). Uphoff goes on to suggest that we should assess the quality of participation in three ways: Who is participating? What kind of participation? How is the participation occurring?

If participation is limited to local leaders, government personnel, and agency staff, then participation is limited to the non-poor and their input will necessarily be flawed because of their desire to sustain their privilege. They are easily tempted to play god in the lives of the poor.

These are Chambers's "uppers," people whose place and circumstances of birth, education, and professional training result in an unspoken (sometimes) sense of superiority that greatly interferes with their hearing and seeing (1997, 58–60). Development with them will be "top-down" and will almost always fail to change any social power relationships. Chambers quips:

> All powerful uppers think they know
> What is right and real for those below.
> At least each upper so believes
> But all are wrong; all power deceives. (1997, 101)

But even if community residents are involved, care needs to be taken that the group includes all social groups—men and women, non-Christian and Christian, young and old—or that there are ways to hear from these various sub-groups. Sometimes we invoke the label *community* as if it were something real and homogeneous. It is not. In an important correction to the literature on participatory methods, Irene Guijt and Meera Kaul Shah's brought this issue to light in *The Myth of Community* (1998). Communities and contexts are complex, dynamic, and fluid. By speaking casually about "listening to the community," we can miss important information about divisions and conflicts as well as winners and losers in terms of power and control. The largest group that is frequently not heard from is women. Even when participatory methodologies are used to minimize biases, the voice of women is too often lost. "Again and again, women are excluded by factors like time and place of meetings, composition of groups, [social] conventions that only men speak in public, outsiders usually being men and men talking to men" (Guijt and Shah 1998, xviii). This, of course, takes us to issues of power and control, of whose voices we hear and whose we don't. Failure to listen to this complex range of voices within a community sews the seeds for future injustice and strife. More on this in Chapter 8.

Participation can also be flawed in terms of the level of participation. Having an opportunity to hear someone else present a plan for you is a very limited form of participation. Participation is meaningful when it means ownership of the process, all the process: research and analysis, planning, implementing, and evaluating.

Finally, we need to be concerned with how participation is occurring. For its impact to be significant, the basis of participation must be as genuine partners, even senior partners. The form of participation must be integral and central, not occasional and formalistic. The extent of participation must be complete and without limit. Finally, the effect of participation must be empowerment. Empowerment is, after all, one of the means of transformation.

Said another way, this kind of full and complete participation is a form of making systematic local autonomy or self-direction real. Communities discover that it is indeed *their* development process that is under way and that they are capable of exercising choice and becoming capable of managing their own development. The following guidelines for effective participation are adapted from a set proposed by Sam Voorhies (1996, 129–35):

- Participation begins at the beginning, with the community's story and analysis.
- Start small, in a manner that the community can manage largely on its own.
- Use a process or learning approach, not a blueprint. Help the community learn how to learn.
- Encourage the community to mobilize its own resources. Get community members to invest.
- Encourage community members to run the program and experience the joy of their successes and learn from their mistakes.
- Build capacity. Participation that empowers needs to be learned; help community members succeed.
- Invest in organizing; help them find new ways of working together.
- Have a bias toward peace. Participation means power, and power tends to divide. Be very inclusive.
- Communicate, communicate, communicate.

A word of caution has emerged from recent studies on the effectiveness and even legitimacy of participation as empowerment. Sometimes participation finds expression as a ritualistic charade that hides the demand for rapid assessment and program design (Cooke and Kothari 2001). Some Filipino friends of mine coined the word *facipulation* to capture the temptation for facilitation to become manipulation. There are powerful pressures that can cause this distortion. The limits of time to meet and be with the poor and pressures for rapid development of program design tend to minimize the potential impact of participation as empowerment. Powerful local elites often work to coopt the participative process for their own ends. The program guidelines of donors tend to trump the emerging programming ideas of the poor. The professional competence of the holistic practitioner creates a hard to resist temptation to "cut to the chase" and get on with the "right" answers for program design. The bottom line is that we must acknowledge that power asymmetries often interfere with and sometimes disable participation as empowerment.

In addition, we must be careful not to take an overly romantic view of participation; that is, that the poor are always right and their views should always trump those of an outsider. The limitations of this view are clear. When local people assert that girls going to school is not a priority or that female genital mutilation is a necessary rite of passage, we are hard pressed to be supportive. The simple fact is that both the poor and the development workers must be actors and have agency.

Jean-Pierre Olivier de Sardan, a French professor of development anthropology, encourages setting aside the "poor are always right" frame of participatory development work in favor of a methodologically informed practice of participation (2005, 9–11). The methodological view places its focus on the tools of anthropology that go beyond the insider-outsider polarity and seek to understand the complex processes by which knowledge and proposals for change are negotiated among the local people themselves and between the local people and outsiders. In other words, amend the focus of participatory methods from just generating local knowledge—most of which is for the benefit of the development worker—to uncovering local processes of negotiation and bargaining—knowledge that may benefit both and in particular truly validate the voice of the poor. Understanding such processes would position the development worker—if properly trained and self-disciplined—to become a broker or translator between two different systems of knowledge: local indigenous knowledge and Western technical knowledge (Lewis and Mosse 2006). The outsider becomes more an intermediary and less an extractor of knowledge needed for program design.

Fortunately, advances in thinking and practice of participatory methodologies in the last decade have provided some remedies for these concerns as well as uncovering new avenues for the use of participatory approaches. Participation became an element of social capital in the mid-1990s and was transformed into concerns for and actions to encourage participatory governance and engaged citizenship by end of the 1990s. "We believe . . . that understanding the ways in which participation relates to existing power structure and political systems provides the basis for moving toward a more transformatory approach to development, which is rooted in the exercise of a broadly defined citizenship" (Hickey and Mohan 2004, 5).

Changing people changes history

There is a more important reason that authentic participation is critical, more important than enhancing dignity or acting out our egalitarian values, as good as these reasons are. It can be argued that empowerment through participation is the single most critical element of transformation.

James Rosenau, in his analysis of change and continuity in the West in the twentieth century, argues that, of the five basic forces at work at the end

---

[1] Rosenau's other four basic forces are (1) changing technology; (2) cross-border threats like AIDS, pollution, and the drug trade; (3) the reduced capability of governments to solve social issues; and (4) sub-groupism, that is, the tendency of people to resist globalism and seek identity in ethnic and religious groupings.

of the century, the most powerful one is that people have changed.[1] Ordinary people in the West now have a set of analytical skills and an awareness of their agency that allows them to understand why things are happening to them and an orientation toward authority that is more self-conscious. "Today's persons on the street are no longer as uninvolved, ignorant and manipulable with respect to world affairs as their forebears" (1990, 13). If this kind of change—the ability to understand why things are as they are and the conviction that we can exert some level of influence over what happens to us—is one of the keys to social change in the West, then empowering participation must be at the core of transformational development among the poor. Only changed people can change history. If people do not change, little else changes in the long term.

Empowerment tends to take on a wide variety of meanings. It is often used to refer to *processes* such as enabling, motivating, and promoting and increasing capability, but it is also used to refer to the *means* of empowerment, which can include participation, education, community organizing, and enabling political voice. The essence of empowerment is that there is some kind of process of social change directed by the people themselves by which people—as individuals and groups—are able to shape their own lives in ways that they choose. This understanding closely connects to Chambers's concerns for "handing over the stick" and Sen's affirmation of development as increasing the freedom or agency of the poor.

Building community

As we bring our story to the story of the community, we face a challenge. How do we merge these stories so that they enhance each other and everyone learns and grows? The key is becoming community to each other. This is one of the reasons we respect all the elements of their story, that we take a social-learning approach to working together, and that we encourage genuine participation. Building community is what good neighbors do.

One of Kosuke Koyama's endearing contributions to missiology is what he calls "neighborology" (1974, 89ff.). He reminds us that people need good neighbors much more than they need good theology or, I would add, good development theory and practice. Our work is about people before it is about ideas, about relationships before development programs. Development workers, who use being good neighbors as their metaphor for working alongside the poor, will be more effective than those who see themselves as problem solvers or answer givers.

By listening to the stories of the poor, our new neighbors, and by sharing our stories with them, we become neighbors to each other. To have community we must have good neighboring. This takes time. Loving neighbors is not something that can be rushed. Something gets lost when we hurry.

Taking our neighbor's questions into account is so time consuming that it is better to forget about time. It is better to learn to be patient. We must learn to speak our neighbor's language and understand our neighbor's memberships in overlapping communities. We must come to know what makes our neighbor laugh and cry. Once we come to love our neighbor, we realize that our love is rooted in the pain of God, the pain God feels when our neighbor is not loved. (Erickson 1996, 154)

If we cannot genuinely love our neighbor, how can development begin?

THE PRACTITIONERS

Ultimately, the effectiveness of transformational development comes down, not to theory, principles, or tools, but to people. Transformation is about transforming relationships, and relationships are transformed by people. Techniques and programs only fulfill their promise when holistic practitioners use them with the right attitude, the right mindset, and professionalism. When development promoters have made the theory and values of transformational development their own, when they live them out in the real world of development practice, then good things can happen.

This section explores the attitudes to which holistic practitioners must aspire, the profile of those who tend to be effective practitioners, and a few words on the formation of holistic practitioners.

The attitude of the holistic practitioner

The profile of the holistic practitioner is deduced from our understanding of the goals of transformation and the ten principles of transformation already described (Chapter 6). With this framework of theory, we can ask what the attributes of a Christian development promoter should be. What kind of attitudes of mind and heart might a holistic practitioner aspire to?

Be a good neighbor. The requirement that we have the attitude of a good neighbor has its roots in the commandment that we are to love God and our neighbor. Chambers puts it simply, "The bottom line is be nice to people" (1997, 233). But being nice is only the beginning. We have to do more to be a true neighbor. Miraslav Volf, in his struggle to create a Christian understanding of reconciliation in the context of modern Croatia and the Bosnian War of the early 1990s, says that "we must have the will to give ourselves to others and 'welcome' them by readjusting our identities to make space for them" (1996, 29). Being a good neighbor requires our willingness to change who we are.

Be patient. Take as much time as it takes. Development does not work on a time table. Getting activities done on time may make donors happy, but it is unlikely to enhance transformation or sustainability. Remember that God is willing to walk at three miles an hour because that's the best that human beings can do (Koyama 1979).

Be humble before the facts. We don't know as much as we wish we did. The other person always knows more than we expect. Besides, we are both going to have to change our minds on things, anyway, as soon as new facts emerge.

Everyone is learning. It is obvious that without learning no transformation is taking place. Sometimes we forget, however, that if *everyone*—the poor, the non-poor, and the holistic practitioner—is not learning, then only limited transformation is taking place.

Everywhere is holy. We need to show respect for the poor. After all, God was in the community before us, working there since the beginning of time.

Every moment and every action is potentially transforming. We will never know what God uses for change until God creates a change. Everything we do carries a message. The only question is what that message is. Every action can heal or harm, can mar identity or heal it. In this sense, every action is a silent offering to God, a potentially transforming moment.

An example might help. In a personal interview in 1997 Ravi Jayakaran reported on a participatory evaluation in a village in India. When he arrived with a colleague, the village brought out chairs for the visitors, while the villagers sat on mats. Ravi and his friend respectfully set the chairs aside and sat alongside the villagers on the dusty mats. They listened to the stories about the well and the school and the other things the project had accomplished. Finally, at the end of the conversation, Ravi asked them: What was the most important change? An older man said, "You are sitting on the same mat, looking me in the eye, and talking to us as equals. That's the biggest change." Sharing the same mat had more transformative power than digging the well or repairing the school.

Love the people, not the program. We always need to remember who our "customer" is. We are here to serve people, not programs. Donors sometimes create environments in which we forget this basic fact.

Love the churches too. In many cases we have brothers and sisters already present in the community. They are a product of what God has already done before we came. These people are our family there. We need to be sure to stop by and introduce ourselves. They are there for our well-being as well as for the well-being of the community. Even if the churches are not all they might be, we need to remember that they are the single most critical element of any eventual spiritual sustainability. God has put gifts in these local communities of faith that are for the whole community, and they need to be identified and developed.

Cultivate a repentant spirit. We will make mistakes. We will do or say things we regret. Part of loving our neighbors includes the willingness to go to them, repent of our mistakes, and seek their forgiveness. Nothing removes the mystery surrounding our professionalism as well as a repentant spirit that shows that we are accountable to God and to those whom we seek to serve.

Act like dependent people. We need to show daily that we are a people who are dependent on God and not on our professional skills, our development technology, or our financial resources. People will see for themselves in whom we most truly place our trust. We need to be sure that our actions and our lives communicate that our trust is in the God of the Bible and nowhere else.

Whose reality counts? We must guard daily against the power of our education and experience. There is always a temptation to assume our view of reality is correct in a way that adds to the poverty of the poor. Chambers poses the critical questions:

> Whose knowledge counts?
> Whose values?
> Whose criteria and preferences?
> Whose appraisal, analysis and planning?
> Whose action?
> Whose monitoring and evaluation?
> Whose learning?
> Whose empowerment?
> Whose reality counts?
> Ours or theirs? (1997, 101)

The characteristics of a holistic practitioner

The characteristics of a holistic practitioner are drawn from the framework for transformational development (Chapter 6) and the understanding of Christian witness in the context of transformational development (Chapter 10). This framework views the world as a seamless spiritual-physical whole. The goals of transformation for the development worker and for the community are the recovery of true identity and discovery of true vocation. These goals are material and spiritual at the same time. This adds up to an absolute demand for holism in the programming, and there is no way to create holism without holistic practitioners. After all, holism is first and foremost in the development promoter or community organizer, not in the program. For this reason, we must pay special attention to the characteristics of the holistic practitioner.

Being Christian

We cannot witness to something that we are not. Holistic practitioners must be committed Christians. This is obvious, but it is not enough. Holistic practitioners also must be holistic disciples. We must love God with all our heart, mind, soul, and spirit, and we must love our neighbors as they love themselves. We must understand that God's rule extends to all of life—our relationship with God, ourselves, our neighbors, and our environment. We must be committed to being obedient to God's call to live out that rule in all areas of life. We must understand the bias of the gospel in favor of the lost, the poor, the forgotten, the ignored, and the exploited. We must live lives that announce the best news that we have—that living transformation is made possible by belief in Jesus Christ.

Being Christian means even more. Holistic practitioners must have a passion for developing a truly biblical way of looking at and making sense of the world, of ourselves and others. This means becoming increasingly aware of the modern (or sometimes traditional) worldview to which education and socialization makes us captive. This means understanding how our non-biblical worldviews influence our understanding of poverty and our view of the better future we desire for ourselves and the communities with whom we work. This means working hard to re-create a genuinely biblical way of viewing the world that is truly holistic, including the supernatural and all that is good in modern science.

Part of being Christian means that seeking true identity and vocation must also be the personal goal of development workers. We are just as susceptible to a web of lies as the non-poor or the poor. We are constantly tempted to play god in the lives of the poor, thus marring their identity and ours. An agent of transformation who is not also being transformed is capable of doing more harm than good.

Being Christian also means maintaining clarity of our mission at the same time that we love people as they are and appreciate their culture. We need to be able to begin where people are without forgetting who we are and our purpose for being there. Shenk reminds us that

> the ministry of Jesus is notable for its clarity of focus and flexibility of response. Jesus responds to people in that way, Jesus allowed people to set the agenda. But, Jesus always responded out of who he was and what he represented. We know that Jesus both announced the Kingdom of God and embodied that reality, God's new order. (1993)

Finally, being Christian means being part of the body of Christ by being a living part of a local fellowship of believers. A Christian apart from a church is ultimately a contradiction in terms. No matter how comfortable the fellowship within a Christian charitable institution may be, an NGO is not and cannot be a church in the biblical sense of the word. We must guard against becoming a sanctuary for those Christians whose pain or disappointment with the church tempts them to try to approximate the church through their work in a para-church agency. Though Christian relief and development agencies do devotions, study the Bible, and worship together, the church is the only community that God has chosen to be the home and family for God's people. A local church is God's choice for the community of the Word, the place where the sacraments and local accountability are to be found.

A word of caution. While it is true that holistic practitioners must be Christian, there is need for some humility. There are agents of transformation within and outside the community whose gifts and skills should be sought out and encouraged. Everyone has a contribution to make, Christian or not. To ignore or devalue such gifts is to devalue what God has created and is offering to us and to the community.

Having Christian character

Holistic practitioners need Christian character, one that causes us to think more highly of others than ourselves. We must have a love for the poor and a call to serve those on society's margin. We must be able to see the image of God in even the most desperate or despicable of human beings and believe that this image is the truth about this person. We must believe that God has given gifts to the poor that can be called out and used by the poor for their own transformation. We must have a passion for helping people, both poor and non-poor, recover their true identity and discover their true vocation. We must believe that the poor are entitled to the same voice and dignity the holistic practitioner wishes for himself or herself. Holistic practitioners must believe that, when all is said and done, poor people have as much potential and can be as effective as any other human beings.

Holistic practitioners must live like Christians. We must be reliable and honest, demonstrating the fruit of the Spirit. We must believe in the transformative power of good relationships and seek to become friends with those we serve. We must be transparent, ever willing to speak of our strengths and our weaknesses, always bearing witness to God as the source of our strengths and the means by which our weaknesses are forgiven and overcome. We must live simply—and this means more than just self-denial. Francis of Assisi understood that "he had to enter into the space of the poor of his day, because only in this space of the poor could he approach the condition God assumed in the Incarnation" (Motte 1996, 71). We must live openly and invitingly, creating no barriers to being a good neighbor or to living an eloquent life.

Holistic practitioners must act like Christians, having that genuine humility that being in Christ allows. We need the balanced humility that affirms the worth and gifts that God has given us and also own the weaknesses and sin that work to undermine our Christian life. We need a humility that allows us to set aside all we know, save our knowledge of Christ, so that in our weakness the poor may find strength (1 Cor 2:1–3). We must understand ourselves as stewards, stewards of the gifts God has given us, stewards of our relationship with the poor, stewards of the resources we bring to the community and that the community already has.

Being professional

When God finished creating this world, God applied only one standard: it was good. God likes good work, and so must we. We should never believe or act as if being a Christian is an excuse to be amateurish in our work. There should be no dichotomy between being Christian and being professional.

Sadly, too many Christians, hearts broken by the suffering of the poor, simply rush out to help. While simple charity is always in order, a desire to extend one's efforts to transformational development uncovers a serious flaw. Wishing to do well is not the same as being competent to do well. Doing development is a profession that requires technical training and constant learning enabled by keeping up with development studies and development research. Every year new things are being learned about what works and what does not. Doing good work means being skillful and continually refining one's skills. The poor need more from us than broken hearts; they need professional skills and knowledge, too.

The starting point for being professional is the challenge to become truly holistic. I've said before that holism is much more in the mind and heart of the practitioner than it is in the program. Without a profound commitment to developing a holistic worldview based on the Bible, the very work of becoming a professional can turn the Christian development worker into a functional atheist when he or she is doing professional work. The social sciences and, sadly, even much mission theology reflect the modern scientific worldview in which the spiritual and the material are unrelated realms, each with its own discipline. It would be a great pity if, in the name of becoming professional, we became less Christian.

Holistic practitioners need to develop a deep understanding of the complexity of poverty and its many dimensions and expressions. They need to be able to use the lessons of the social sciences and of Scripture to understand the causes of poverty—material, spiritual, psychological, cultural, and sociopolitical. They need to be able to develop sophisticated understandings of the local social-political-economic-religious context and how this context works for and against the well-being of the poor. All of this needs to be done with the profound understanding that the community understands its reality in ways that are often deeper and more accurate than those of any outsider. Balancing the need to learn from the community and to take its indigenous knowledge seriously with the equally true fact that the holistic practitioner brings information and knowledge the community needs is a serious and continuing challenge. This is where a truly Christian character is so important. We come with gifts God gave us to add to the gifts God has already placed in the community; there is no room for superiority or pride.

Holistic practitioners need to develop skills for working with communities in ways that empower and liberate. They need to learn how to learn what the community already knows. They need to understand the basics of community-based healthcare, sustainable agriculture, water management, micro-enterprise development. They need to understand and be able to develop sustainable development systems linking families and communities with local government, business, and religious institutions so that life-enhancing relationships are formed. They need to understand the principles and skills of popular education that enable learning to take place at the direction and pace of the community.

Holistic practitioners need to understand and appreciate the importance of culture and its impact on development. They need to understand cultural values and how values are formed and changed. They must understand how the community understands cause and effect and how to help the community move from its traditional and/or modern worldview toward a more biblical one. This is very difficult work because the worldview of the holistic practitioner is itself often not biblical. Suffering from a modern worldview while trying to help people move beyond the unhelpful elements of their traditional worldview is a formula for imposing the former. Both the practitioner and the community are in need of a worldview that has the God of the Bible at its center. This implies that each has something to learn from the other, and that both need to change.

To be professional, holistic practitioners need more than a good understanding of theology and social science. They also need to be "street smart." The Evil One is at work, and there are people who act in evil ways. Part of professionalism is being able to read the social-economic-political-religious context and answer three strategic questions: Who's who in the zoo? Who's doing what to whom? Where is the money going? The price for our naiveté in this regard will be paid by the poor. We need to be sophisticated enough to know that even aid is not neutral and that we are responsible for doing no harm (see Anderson 1996b; Slim 1997). There are hard ethical choices that will need to be made, and we must be equipped and prepared to make these moral choices "on the fly."

Yet the call to professionalism is not a call to pride. Everything we have, we have been given. Every transformation is an act of God, especially our own transformation. We must always remember that we are the servants of the master. John V. Taylor's admonition to missionaries is just as relevant to development professionals:

> We need to come off our religious high horse and get our feet on the lowly, earthy ground of God's primary activity as creator and sustainer

of life. We must relinquish our missionary presuppositions and begin in the beginning with the Holy Spirit. This means humbly watching in any situation in which we find ourselves in order to learn what God is trying to do here, and then doing it with him. (1972, 39)

Chambers suggests that development professionals need to develop an attitude of seeking reversals as an antidote for professionalism becoming an impediment to the poor finding their identity, voice, and place (see Figure 7–5).

	Normal tendencies	Needed reversals
Behavior	Dominating Lecturing Extracting	Facilitating Listening Empowering
Professionalism	Things first Men before women Professionals set priorities Transfers of technology Simplify	People first Women and men Poor people set priorities Choice of technology Complicate
Organizational style	Centralize Standardize Control	Decentralize Diversify Enable
Modes of learning	From above Rural development Tourism	From below Relaxed, participatory appraisal
Analysis and action by	Professionals, outsiders	Local people, insiders

Figure 7–5: Seeking reversals.
(Adapted from Chambers 1997, 204)

Always learning

Holistic practitioners must know that they don't know all they need to know. They must be learners who are always seeking new insights from Scripture, from the community, and from development research. They must be people who document, who ask questions, who listen to the stories of the people, and who spend time with the people in reflection. There must be a passion for discovering meaning. What have we learned? What worked? What did not? What did we miss? What is God saying to us in all this?

The formation of a holistic practitioner

Now we have to get real for a moment. Where does one find these paragons of virtue? Who can meet these standards? Of course, the answer is obvious: no one can. The holistic practitioner just described is a composite of the best that we can imagine based on what our experience and Scripture teach us. No individual will be what I have described. This is why formation is so important.

Formation begins with developing a clear understanding of what is desired in a holistic practitioner. Our description of the holistic practitioner earlier in this chapter suggests that formation needs to be thought of as a kind of disciple-making—developing mature Christians with the best professional skills possible. Only holistic disciples can participate in holistic transformation. With this in mind, we need to define the attitudes, behaviors, and skills that are needed. Then two things must be done.

First, we must be very careful to select people with the right gifts and character. We cannot make something out of nothing. The fruits of the Spirit—love, joy, peace, patience, kindness, goodness, faithfulness, gentleness, and self-control (Gal 5:22)—are a pretty good summary of the attitudes we seek in the holistic practitioner. Use them as part of the screening criteria, alongside the criteria for technical knowledge and experience.

Second, we have to provide intentionally and systematically for training and formation through formal training, hands-on experience, and mentoring, both within the agency and, if at all possible, through the churches that agency staff attend.

In designing this approach to continuing formation, care must be taken to avoid the temptation to think of spiritual formation and professional training as two unrelated activities. Both are inseparable parts of developing the holistic practitioner. This means that spiritual formation, learning the spiritual disciplines, becoming competent in popular education, and doing PLAs and Appreciative Inquiry are all part of the formation of the holistic practitioner. We need to integrate being Christian with being professional.

Knowing who we are

In the chapter on poverty we discovered the importance of being ruthlessly self-aware. All practitioners come with "baggage" that can hurt or help them as practitioners. We need to become conscious of our assumptions about the poor and about poverty and why poverty exists. We need to become aware of these assumptions and seek out every manifestation that reflects the modern flaw of separating the material and the spiritual.

We need to discover why we wish to do development in the first place. What is our goal? Are we ourselves seeking what we wish the poor to seek? Are we on the same journey, or are we really imposing our story on others? Kwame Bediako, when speaking about the importance of holism in the practitioner, reminds us of the importance of Paul's insight in 1 Corinthians 15:1–11. Bediako writes: "Part of every genuinely pure motivation in Christian service is also the Christian worker's own sense of need for the same gospel he or she seeks to incarnate and to impart to others" (1996b, 189).

Even our professionalism can be a liability if we do not ruthlessly explore its underpinnings. Vinay Samuel reminds us that every holistic practitioner is shaped by some particular understanding of progress, health, family life, participation, decision-making, market reality, economic principles, ethics, and spirituality (1995, 153). All inform the practitioner's understanding of the process and desired outcomes of transformational development. These assumptions and presuppositions about how the world works, and how the world can be changed, need to be made explicit and subjected to dialogue with the community and with the Bible.

Finally, we need to examine our deepest motivations. Why are we in the development business? Whose needs are we serving when we serve the poor? There is undoubtedly more than one answer to these difficult questions. Yet we need to discipline ourselves to struggle for self-understanding lest we succumb to the temptation to play god in the lives of the poor, thus adding to their captivity to the god complexes of the non-poor.

Becoming holistic disciples

Holistic practitioners must be holistic disciples themselves. Part of formation is being discipled in a holistic sense. The goal of discipling is to discover in God our own true identity and our own true vocation.

Holistic discipling must address all three levels of Hiebert's worldview framework. We must know the truth of God and the truth contained in God's word. This is why biblical literacy and doing theology are important. We must also know the power of God, the power that is greater than our temptations and greater than the power of the many devils in this world, who are working against what we do. This is where fasting and prayer are important. Finally, we must know the love of God in the real world of space and time, including modern science, with God as part of the explanation, and the important work of ethics and moral choices. The truth of God must become the justice and peace of God in the real world of our relationships.

In seeking holistic discipling we must explore our assumptions about where discipling takes place. When discipling is treated solely as a spiritual activity, we tend to locate discipling in the church as a spiritual exercise. While it is this, it is also much more. Remember that Jesus confirmed his true identity at his baptism in the Jordan River and clarified his true vocation arguing with the devil in the wilderness. Discipleship often happens on the periphery, the most frequent location of the risen Christ. A great number of my Christian friends testify to the fact that they learned far more about the true meaning of their faith and their Scripture working in dusty villages and squalid slums among the poor than they did in their comfortable churches.

In forming holistic disciples we will be helped if we overcome the traditional view of the whole "armor of God" (Eph 6:13–18) as being solely spiritual resources that are needed for the protection of our souls. They are also quite useful in the real world of doing transformational development. Paul's encouragement concerning the armor of God immediately follows his description of our struggle, "not against flesh and blood, but against the rulers, against the authorities, against the powers of this dark world" (Eph 6:12). Walter Wink and Jayakumar Christian make the case that Paul is referring in part to the structures and systems of power and oppression that play such a deadly, godlike role in the lives of the poor. Understanding spiritual warfare as relevant to the material world of social systems releases prayer and fasting to be tools for transformational development.

Since discipleship is about crossing our own transformational frontiers, we need to determine where these frontiers are. I found the work of Peter Kreef particularly helpful here. Kreef identifies our transformational frontiers by comparing the seven deadly sins with the qualities Jesus celebrates in the Sermon on the Mount (see Figure 7–6).

Seven deadly sins		Sermon on the Mount	
Pride	Self-assertion	Poverty of Spirit	Self-giving
Avarice	To have	Mercy	To give
Envy	Resents another's happiness	Mourning	Shares another's happiness
Wrath	Destructive	Meekness and peacemaking	Saves and preserves
Sloth	Refuses to exert will toward good	Hunger and thirst for righteousness	Exerts will toward good
Lust	Dissipates and divides the soul	Purity of heart	Unifies the soul toward God
Gluttony	Consumes the world's things	Being persecuted	Accepts being deprived of the world's things

Figure 7–6: The transformational frontiers inside us.
(Based on Kreef 1986)

One final word on discipleship. Melba Maggay, a veteran of the Marcos era and the People Power movement in the Philippines, describes discipleship as a "dance of death" (1994, 79). She is reminding us that in the kingdom of God dying is always productive. Maggay sees this kind of dying as being productive in two ways. First, we cannot really love our neighbor and be in solidarity unless we are willing to die in some sense to ourselves. This is what Volf means when he says we need to change our identity to make space for the other. Self-emptying is the only way to genuine incarnation. Second, dying is the way to fertility. Each of us had to die to ourselves in order to be alive in Christ. Getting to Easter Sunday always requires suffering through Good Friday, at least in kingdom business. Technical power can come from good training and good experience. Spiritual power comes only this harder way.

Acting theologically

Christians in mission have two sources of help that others do not have: the Holy Spirit, and the word of God. The Holy Spirit is the agent of discipleship, and the Bible is that unique and unusual book that reads us, even when we think we are reading it (Weber 1995). As soon as we make the claim that the Bible speaks to the whole of human life and is the most important source of a holistic Christian way of viewing and making sense of the world, then holistic disciples have to be "acting theologically" all the time. Teaching them how, and how not to do, theology in a way that shapes action is part of formation.

Everyone will agree that holistic disciples must be biblically literate, and of course, they must. They must be theologically literate as well, able to handle the grand themes of the Bible. Their theological and biblical literacy must begin in Genesis and end in Revelation. As shown in the third chapter of this book, understanding the whole biblical story and applying it to the theory and practice of transformational development are essential to professional practice that is truly holistic and Christian. But we need to go farther than this.

Holistic disciples also need to be taught to let the Bible handle them and to avoid spending all their time trying to handle the text. We need to give the living word of God the freedom to have the final say. We need to live with the expectation that the gospel will never be exhausted, that there is always more if we are humble enough to be silent before the text from time to time. This allows us to have a transformational hermeneutic, "a theological response that transforms us before we involve ourselves in mission in the world" (Bosch 1991, 189).

Acting theologically also means doing theology ourselves at the same time that we are willing to assist others in doing their own theology. Holistic practitioners who are able to think and act theologically will be more comfortable helping the community act on its own theology, beginning with the truth of God that it already knows. This kind of theology takes special understanding on the part of the practitioner. Koyama, in his discussion of "neighborology," says that Christian workers are sandwiched between Christ's saving reality, which they have already experienced, and their experience of their neighbor as someone they love:

By submitting and committing himself to the Word of God, [the development worker] tries to communicate the message of the real Christ to his real neighbors. . . . He now moves on to see that his neighbor asks the questions and he seeks the answers in Christ. (Koyama 1974, 91)

Doing theology is also the key to solving the most serious problem that is part of the training of holistic practitioners. Most technical training, even in Christian institutions, is functionally atheistic. We in the West have largely forgotten the origins of our science—it was developed by Christians seeking to understand nature, God's other book—and no longer ask how it is that the world is understandable to us (since we did not create it) or how it is that we have been able to keep figuring out how it works. The result is that our development technology too often carries a message that is not Christian. Unless holistic practitioners can do theology, there is little chance that they can provide the explanation for their effectiveness in finding water or saving children's lives in a way that points to the activity and character of a loving and concerned God. Once we begin to understand the words that must accompany our development technology, every technical professional will need help in becoming aware of his or her functional atheism and then receive training in how to rejoin word and deed so that credit is given to God, the only one to whom credit is due.

An incarnational spirituality
(Written with Lisa Myers)

Christian spirituality is the way in which the invisible heart of God is made visible in the world.

—GROODY 2007, 241

Having talked about the relational nature of poverty and transformational development and about the principles and practice necessary for the holistic practitioner, it must now be clear that a particular kind of spirituality is also required of the holistic practitioner. We need more than technical eyes and empowering assessment methodologies. Our vision needs to see beyond clean water and children in school. Groody reminds us that spirituality is supposed to "transfigure one's vision, enabling one to see with the 'eyes of the heart'" (2007, 240). While discipleship takes us into the world of injustice, we also need to ascend to the mountain of God (ibid., 241ff.) if we are to be truly Christian in our work.

The ability to recognize the fingerprints of God and to hear the small still voice that is quietly uttered among and by the poor requires something Christians call discernment. We need to see through the things, ideas, and noise of this world to recognize what is true. There is a reason that Jesus spent so much time in his work talking about the importance of "eyes that see and ears that hear."

A genuinely Christian spirituality alive and at work in the daily life of holistic practitioners is the key to seeing what is true and what is not. Charles Elliot, dean of Trinity Hall at Cambridge and co-founder of the Institute of Contemporary Spirituality, called for the development of a spirituality that enables us to see the world through the lens of the kingdom of God (1985). It is only when we see as Jesus sees that we are able to recognize marred identity and what is marring it or to detect god complexes and their sources. Only through the lens of the kingdom can we see inadequacies in our worldview and the worldview of the people with whom we work. Only kingdom people view the world as a seamless material-spiritual whole. Only kingdom eyes can discern the presence and deception of the powers in the institutions of this world. We need to help holistic practitioners develop a prophetic view of the world that accurately interprets current social-economic-religious realities while still pointing to the future God is preparing for God's people (Bediako 1996b, 183). As important as this kind of discernment is, our spirituality must go much deeper than this somewhat cognitive view suggests.

A relational understanding of poverty and transformation that affirms that God is already at present among the poor, and that the poor are made in the image of God and thus must be the actors in their own development, demands a spirituality modeled after the incarnation. An incarnational spirituality is one that draws near and listens before it speaks, one that loves before it acts. An incarnational spirituality is a self-emptying spirituality that accompanies the other while making no demands for itself (Phil 2). This kind of spirituality believes that God is always present in the world and among the poor and that this reality can be recognized by discerning eyes and ears. These kinds of people listen and love and are curious about what God and the poor may have to say. They wait, look, and listen. This kind of spirituality is based on being present—present to God, present to the poor, and present to ourselves.

> Praying for the Kingdom, then, begins with a psychic, spiritual opening to the poor, which is likely to be dialectically related to an actual process of becoming acquainted with the poor. This inward opening to the poor is held in counterpoint to an inward opening to God, to his infinite love and his infinite power of transformation. It is thus a simultaneous standing in the presence of the poor and of God; a baring of the deepest parts of one's being to the stuff of the Kingdom and the King. (Elliot 1985, 30)

More than anything else, the poor need to be accompanied by holistic practitioners who know how to be present to them and to God in the fullest sense of the word. From the language of spiritual direction, being present has a family of important meanings. Being present is being with God and the poor, not being isolated and autonomous, waiting to get on with your work. Being present means being open and willing, not willful or controlling. Being present means letting things unfold as they will, not making things happen. Being present is being responsive, not responsible; trusting, not grasping. Most important for the development worker, being present means being open to the unexpected, to mystery, not looking for the expected or being compelled to mastery (Myers 2002, 6–7). Being present is not something we do easily or well without a lot of practice. This is why it is called a discipline.

The historic church has a lot of experience with the formation of people who are able to be present and to look and listen to God and to one another. The resulting spiritual disciplines were not just for quiet times; they were for living life daily. They represent a spirituality for every day, not just for Sunday. These practices enshrine what Christians and the church have learned over time are most helpful in forming the ability to be present, to see, and to hear. Living the disciplines turns us into holistic practitioners who can discern as well as diagnose, who can see the fingerprints of grace as well as the evidence of malnutrition. Many of these practices are associated with the orders of the Roman Catholic Church—Franciscan, Dominican, Jesuit, and so forth. In the last quarter century some such as Charles Elliot, Richard Foster, and Jane Vennard have been working to recover and reintegrate this formation into the Protestant tradition.

One final word on this spirituality. An incarnational spirituality understands that a Christian person is part of the presence of God in a particular situation. We need to understand that the spirit of Christ is in us and can be experienced by others if we are living a life that allows this to happen. We are not engaging in this way when we are bound up in solving problems and planning programs. Then, another kind of spirit is in play, and it is not very attractive.

One of the consequences of healing the dichotomy between the physical and spiritual realms is that prayer can be released to be more than just a tool for personal piety; it is now freed to be a tool for social action. And so it must be. We have already built the case for the causes of poverty being fundamentally spiritual. We have taken note of the role of pervasive evil and the deception of the principalities and powers as key elements in creating and sustaining poverty. Wink reminds us that "intercession is spiritual defiance of what is, in the name of what God has promised. Intercessions visualize an alternative future. . . . History belongs to the intercessors, who believe the future into being" (Wink 1992, 298–99).

Charles Elliot has devoted considerable effort to helping us understand this kind of prayer. In *Praying the Kingdom* he examines the role of prayer in the emergence of the kingdom of God in the world and then provides a series of meditation exercises from the Old and New Testaments that help the practitioner bring praying for the kingdom to the real world of working with the poor (Elliot 1985).

Praying the kingdom means praying for restored identity and for recovered vocation, knowing that at the most fundamental level these are things that only God can do. Praying the kingdom means asking God's action in exposing the god complexes of the non-poor, and for the even more difficult challenge of repentance by the non-poor for having assumed roles that only God should play. Praying the kingdom means remembering that bringing the kingdom is God's business and recalling that, at the end of the day, the kingdom comes from heaven to earth when Jesus comes. We must not assume the burden for something we cannot do. When we do, we are suffering from a god complex of our own, and it will crush us.

A spirituality that sustains

Holistic practitioners need a spirituality for the whole of life, a spirituality that is robust enough to keep them going in the very hard and dangerous conditions in which the poor live today. In the 1980s a number of liberation theologians of Latin America made what may prove to be their most long-lasting contribution to the struggle for justice among the poor. They did so by turning their attention to the critical issue of what sustains holistic disciples for the long haul (Beltrans 1986; Galilea 1984; Gutiérrez 1984; and Green 1979).

The beginning is the realization that we cannot love our neighbor, or even ourselves, if we do not love God with all our heart, soul, and mind. We've already noted that the disciples were called first to *be with* Jesus, and only then to preach the gospel, heal the sick, and cast out demons. Being comes before doing. We cannot share what we do not have. We cannot live eloquent lives that provoke questions to which the gospel is the answer unless our lives are made alive by the Spirit of the living God.

Protecting our inner self

Melba Maggay has given us a very helpful framework for protecting our inner life. She begins by noting something we all know yet too often ignore: "There is something about the daily exposure to poverty and other ills of society which tends to tear away faith and make agents of change some of the most cynical people around" (1994, 92). The daily grind of poverty can mar our identity, too.

One of the keys, according to Maggay, is to keep a rein on our expectations. When we seek after transformation and justice with too much zeal, we can turn into fanatics who love the struggle so much that we forget to love God, our neighbors, and ourselves. When only total victory will do, we are always bitterly disappointed. The key is to teach ourselves and our people how to handle failure and to understand it as Christians. When Paul lists his failures and struggles, he talks about how this enables him to manifest the life of Jesus in his body (2 Cor 4). Maggay interprets this to mean that we need to be ready to "carry in our bodies, the marks of the cross, but also the hope and power of Jesus' risen life" (ibid., 93).

The other side of keeping a rein on our expectations is to release holistic practitioners from the demand, either from us or from within themselves, that they be successful. Following Jesus is about obedience, not success. Ultimately, transforming people and society is something only God can do. All we can do is discern what God is doing and obediently join in. This means that holistic practitioners who give up everything—themselves, their marriages, the well-being of their children—to be successful among the poor, are not doing the work of God. They are making idols of either their work or of the poor. We have a responsibility to help holistic practitioners free themselves in a way that allows them to make a gift of themselves, their character, and their skills, to all their relationships, beginning at home.

Searching for a balance between dedication and being driven is what Reinhold Niebuhr was trying to describe in his well-known Serenity Prayer, the prayer that every holistic practitioner must keep close to his or her heart:

> God,
> grant me serenity to accept the things I cannot change,
> courage to change the things I can, and the wisdom to
>   know the difference:
> Living one day at a time,
> accepting hardship as the pathway to peace,
> taking, as Jesus did,
> this sinful world as it is, not as I would have it;
> trusting that you will make all things right,
> if I surrender to your will, so that,
> I may be reasonably happy in this life and
> supremely happy with you forever in the next.

Maggay also says that we can protect our inner lives if we practice a certain amount of detachment. She quotes a contemplative who said that "the best way to care about the world is not to care." By this she means that from time to time we need to check out mentally and psychologically, pursuing flights of fantasy, using our imaginations to visit a world that we can only hope for, the world where the dragon is slain and where there are no more tears. The visions of Isaiah 65 and John's revelation are invitations to use our imaginations as a resource for renewal. Maggay says that such a "sanity escape" is actually the longing for a Sabbath. We need to withdraw from our work from time to time and sit back and look for what is good.

Doing so allows us to see the seasons in our work, the times of success and the times of failure, the times of struggle and the times of breakthrough.

Finally, staying well for the journey has its roots in our prayer life. First, our prayer is how we declare that God is with us. Wink writes, "Prayer is the ultimate act of partnership with God." He goes on to exhort us, "Unprotected by prayer, our social action runs the danger of becoming self-justifying good works, as our inner resources atrophy, the wells of love run dry, and we are slowly changed into the likeness of the Beast" (1992, 312, 298). Without a vibrant prayer life we not only have nothing to offer, but we may become what we are trying to change.

Caring for the holistic practitioner

Before concluding this section on the formation of the holistic practitioner, a word needs to be said about caring for holistic practitioners. Working for transformation among the poor and non-poor is very hard work, and it is very hard on the people who do it. Jesus did not send the disciples out in pairs by accident. He knew that he was sending them like lambs among the wolves.

The organization that sends people out onto the transformational development front lines needs to take responsibility for creating the environment in which holistic practitioners can thrive. Such institutions need to remember Christ's final admonition to Peter: "Feed my sheep" (Jn 21:17). He did not say, "Manage my sheep," or "Lead my sheep," or "Get the best out of my sheep."

People who work on the front lines need time on the sidelines. A day in the office once in a while is not what I mean. Holistic practitioners need time for physical and psychological rest and for spiritual retreat. They need to have the time and to be in a place where they can be reminded that God's world has beauty, quiet, and peace, not just ugliness, poverty, and conflict. They need to be able to hear the music, listen to the silence, pray, and sit quietly before the Word. Smelling the flowers, walking on the beach, and reading a good book are essential to sustaining our humanity and spirituality.

People who work on the front lines need time on the sidelines for something else. They need a chance to learn from their experience. People need the time and the place to be able to sort out what has happened to them and to make sense of it. They need to figure out what more they need to know or to be, and have the opportunity to learn or develop. We have said repeatedly that holistic practitioners need to be learners all their lives, that their being is as important as their doing. Institutions that send holistic practitioners out need strategies and resources for their periodic rest and renewal.

A great deal has been learned in recent years about how people respond when faced with tragic events in their ministry—the deaths of children or people in whom they have invested or other innocent victims. Such events—"critical incidents"—can mar the identity of the holistic practitioner in the same way that it mars the identity of the poor family. Psychological First Aid is a recent approach for early response to traumatic events that focuses on providing both physical and psychological safety in a way that does not require advanced professional psychological training (Brymer et al. 2006; Gray and Litz 2005). For practitioners who develop emotional distress that interferes with their work and relationships, resources for professional interventions should be offered (Bryant 2007; McNally, Bryant, and Ehlers 2003). Institutions that send significant numbers of people to work in difficult places need to develop the strategies and resources to provide this kind of assistance to those who have made the sacrifice to go where conditions are very hard and harsh.

The bottom line test for a development spirituality and strategy for staff care is simple. Jayakumar Christian (1998b) argues that if a holistic practitioner cannot say of his or her ministry among the poor, "My love of Christ and my understanding of my faith have been deepened," then something is seriously amiss. What is the state of your soul?

HELPFUL RESOURCES

Indigenous knowledge

Pottier, Johan, Alan Bicker, and Paul Sillitoe, eds. 2003. *Negotiating Local Knowledge: Power and Identity in Development*. London: Pluto Press.

Warren, D. Michael, L. Jan Slikkerveer, and David Brokensha. 1995. *The Cultural Dimension of Development: Indigenous Knowledge Systems*. London: Intermediate Technology Publications.

Spirituality

Beltrans, Benigno, SVD. 1986. *Journey into Solitude: A Manual for Retreats and Recollections*. Manila, Philippines: Arnoldus Press.

Callahan, William. 1994. *Noisy Contemplation: Deep Prayer for Busy People*. Hyattsville, MD: Quixote Center.

Famonure, 'Bayo. 1989. *Training to Die: A Manual on Discipleship*. Jos, Nigeria: Capro Media Services.

Galilea, Segundo. 1984. *The Beatitudes: To Evangelize as Jesus Did*. Maryknoll, NY: Orbis Books.

Green, Thomas, SJ. 1979. *When the Well Runs Dry*. Notre Dame, IN: Ave Maria Press.

Gutiérrez, Gustavo. 1984. *We Drink from Our Own Wells: The Spiritual Journey of a People*. Maryknoll, NY: Orbis Books.

Jayakaran, Ravi. 2007. "Wholistic Worldview Analysis: Understanding Community Realities." *PLA Notes* 56, no. 1:41–48. Available on the planotes.org website.

Nouwen, Henri. 1986. *Reaching Out: Three Movements of the Spiritual Life.* Garden City, NY: Image Books.

Rieser, William. 1997. *To Hear God's Word, Listen to the World.* Mahwah, NJ: Paulist Press.

Vennard, Jane E. 2003. *Embracing the World: Praying for Justice and Peace.* San Francisco: Jossey-Bass.

Trauma and psychological first aid

Brymer, Melissa, Christopher Layne, Anne Jacobs, Robert Pynoos, Josef Ruzek, Alan Steinberg, Patricia Watson. 2006. *Psychological First Aid: Field Operations Guide for Community Religious Professionals.* Los Angeles: National Child Traumatic Stress Network and National Center for PTSD. Available on the nctsnet.org website.

Headington Institute Website: Psychological and Spiritual Support for Humanitarian Relief and Development Workers. www.headington-institute.org.

8

Designing programs for transformation

With these principles for development practice always before us, it is time to turn to the design of a transformational development program. First, I introduce the standard approach for designing a development program and then explore its assumptions and subsequent weaknesses. Second, I describe a parallel way of thinking about program design that insists that the *process* by which a program is designed is often more important than creating the development *plan* itself. Then I introduce a variety of participatory tools that can be used to enable communities to tell their own story and examine their own reality as a prelude to their deciding what kind of program they wish to pursue. After a few observations on how to think about the final stages of the development program, I address a few other issues critical to good program design such as the role of women and children and the importance of letting the spiritual peek through.

DESIGNING A DEVELOPMENT PROGRAM

Planning the way to a better future

Every development organization has a framework for the design, monitoring, and evaluation (DME) of a development program. While the exact language and definitions vary, this process of program design is fundamentally the same everywhere. World Vision's version is called Learning through Evaluation with Accountability and Planning (LEAP) and is pictured in Figure 8–1. The design process is assumed to be a straightforward problem-solving process.

Assessment of community assets and needs is done in order to provide the information necessary to set the stage for the *design* of the program. The design of the program includes identifying the indicators of hoped-for results. *Implementation* of the development program is accompanied by an

239

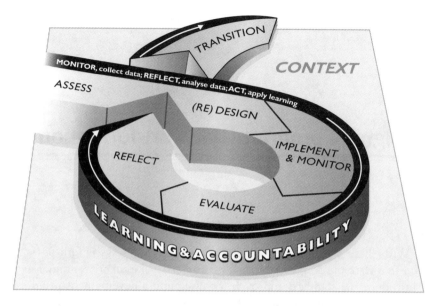

Figure 8–1: Learning through Evaluation with
Accountability and Planning (LEAP).
(World Vision International)

ongoing process of *monitoring* previously identified indicators. At regular intervals, there are *evaluations* that focus on the program's higher-level goals, and periodically there is a process of *reflection* to ensure that the overall purpose and goals of the program do not need to be adjusted and that there are no unintended consequences that need attention. The results of evaluation and reflection then combine with an updated assessment to support the periodic *redesign* of the program. This cyclical process of assessment, planning, implementation, evaluation, and planning again continues until the formal program ends and, it is hoped, the community continues on its own and the results are sustained.

The result of this process is a program design that is carefully thought through from the beginning to the end of the program. This thinking is organized in a Logical Framework (Log Frame).

The Logical Framework

The Logical Framework is a program-planning instrument that has been in use for almost forty years. The results of the DME process just described are organized into a hierarchy of objectives linked together using a logic of cause and effect. *Inputs*, such as money, technical skills, and training, are combined in a logical way to create *outputs*, such as wells dug, water systems installed, schools built, and farmers trained. *Outputs* combine to produce *outcomes or goals*, such as reduced water-borne disease, improved primary-school graduation rates, or increased food production accompanied by reduced malnutrition. Finally, *outcomes* combine to produce the *purpose* of the program expressed as some measure of human or community well-being (see Figure 8–2).

HIERARCHY OF OBJECTIVES	VERIFIABLE INDICATORS	MEANS OF VERIFICATION	RISKS AND ASSUMPTIONS
Purpose			
Outcomes			
Outputs			
Activity			

Figure 8–2: Logical Framework.

The Log Frame assists the development planner in establishing a coherent set of program elements linked by cause and effect along with a set of indicators of success (or not) and a means by which those indicators will be measured. The indicators and means of verification are the foundation of the monitoring and evaluation processes, thus introducing both rigor and accountability into the program.

Also important, the Log Frame requires the development planner to articulate the critical assumptions for each step in the causal chain of program activities. For example, the project may assume that provision of clean water and a staffed and provisioned health hut will lead to improved health outcomes, but it is also assumed that the people will use the new water supply and that the government will provide the staff and medicines for the health hut. Declaring the assumptions helps with redesign when things do not turn out as planned.

The attraction of the Log Frame is obvious. It is hard to imagine any kind of planning activity directed at a clear purpose that is not based on the idea of cause and effect, on inputs ultimately leading to a good purpose if all goes well. Being logically coherent seems to be a good thing, and it is. But experience in actual development programs informs us that this frame has a number of limitations.

First, the Log Frame is a temptation for those who think that good management or good problem solving alone leads to effective development. Just do a good rapid assessment and create an action plan in response. A thirty-minute walk through a poor village or slum provides the experienced outsider with a list of things that need to change to improve people's lives. Clean up the water supply; it is clearly polluted. Improve the housing that is so clearly inadequate for health and safety. The list forms effortlessly. And it is important to note that these things do need to be done. The problem is that the outsider is doing all the learning and the problem solving. A powerful temptation to simply play god raises its seductive head.

Second, the Log Frame focuses primarily on the hardware side of development—schools, wells, immunizations, and other things that are material and measurable. Yet, as we've already seen in earlier chapters, the process or "software" side of development is as important, if not more so. The Log Frame, with its narrow focus on problem solving, logical design, and measurability does not insist on or require good processes or good relationships. The key to mitigating both these potential weaknesses of the Log Frame is to focus first and foremost on the goals of transformation— changed people and changed relationships. This forces us to begin with planning for the *process* part of transformational development and then allowing the process to develop the formal program *plan* as illustrated in Figure 8–3. Process planning is done using the tools of participation, community organization, empowerment, and community ownership. Only when a transformational process is firmly in place can one safely shift attention to designing the program and its focus on inputs, outputs, outcomes, and impact.

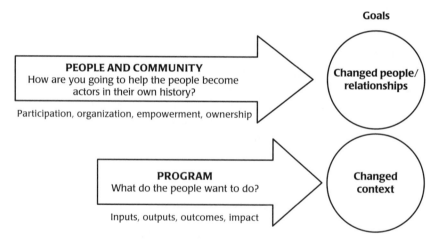

Figure 8–3: People first, then program design.

A second way to correct for the top-down and hardware-only temptations of the Log Frame is to think of development as having an inner dimension and an outer dimension (Williamson 2000). The inner dimension begins with the self-concept of the poor and then expands to issues relating to local skills for development and finally organizational development among the poor. The tools for this inner dimension or software of development are participation, organization, empowerment, and ownership. Only when this process planning is done and resourced should the outer development work be planned in the form of a program. The Log Frame comes second, and its rationality is subordinate to the inner dimensions of the development program (see Figure 8–4).

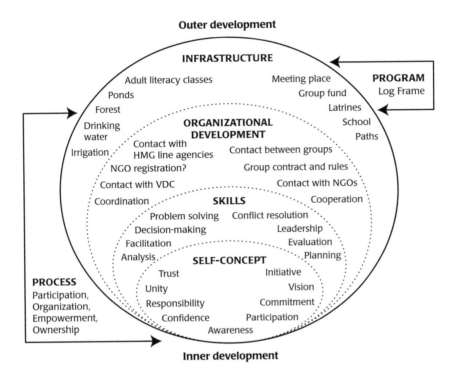

Figure 8–4: Communities first, then program design.
(Adapted from Williamson 2000)

Social change is neither linear nor logical

While the issues of being top down or too focused on hardware can be overcome, there is a deeper issue with the rationality of the Log Frame that needs our attention. The most important weakness of the Log Frame is its underlying assumption that the problem of poverty is mechanical in nature and, as a consequence, that solutions to poverty can be provided by a linear, logical, rational, problem-solving approach. This assumption leads us to believe that the better future of a community can be defined in advance and that it is possible to create a meaningful plan to get to that better future. The Log Frame rests on the modern assumption that all the moving parts of poverty—a mechanical metaphor—are or will be understood well enough so that eradicating poverty is simply the application of problem-solving skills, technology, and money. The temptation is to "treat projects as closed, controllable, and unchanging (mechanical) systems" (Mosse 2001). There are strong echoes of this in the modernist frame of Jeffrey Sachs's *End of Poverty*.

To be sure, there are certain kinds of development work for which this approach is a proven methodology that works. Building a school, running an immunization campaign, and digging a well all lend themselves quite nicely to this kind of rationality because they are essentially mechanical or technical problems. Sand, cement, and water have to behave in a certain way when they are mixed. Immunizations protect children from disease regardless of the vagaries of culture and the unpredictable decisions of human beings. Sadly, social systems, such as a community of poor people, do not work the same way mechanical systems do. Unlike atoms, people have minds of their own, feel emotions, and thus behave unpredictably. Understanding this difference between mechanical and social systems is important to the development practitioner. If development were solely about the hardware or mechanical side of development, the rationality of the Log Frame makes a lot of sense. The problem is that every development practitioner knows that there is a lot more to the development process than just hardware.

Learning our way to a better future

There are a lot of systems in life that are not mechanical at all. These dynamic or complex systems are nonlinear and are consequently counterintuitive. Said another way, they are not predictable. Examples include the weather, stock markets, and much of nature; all are complex or dynamic systems that do not lend themselves to forecasting, much less planning. Social systems—systems of unpredictable people who change their minds and have their own reasons for doing things—are not only complex, but they adapt to changing conditions, hence the phrase "complex adaptive systems" (Pascale, Millemann, and Gioja 2000, 19–20).

For example, think of the challenge of feeding the millions of people who live in New York City. Every day millions of people live and go to work with little or no knowledge about who is going to bring the tomatoes, flour, meat, milk, and thousands of other food stuffs into the city that day. Tens of thousands of New Yorkers and people from outside the city, working with no master plan or central coordination, solve this daily logistical nightmare. Some who are supposed to deliver food get sick. Some farms suffer crop failure and planned-for food is no longer on the way. Trucks break down, and restaurants close. Yet for the most part, every restaurant and home in New York City has the food that it prefers on its table every day. The result is neither perfect nor just. It fails too many people, and there is a lot of waste. But the fact remains that this enormously complex logistical challenge is not master planned or coordinated centrally, yet it happens every day. This is an example of what is called the emergence of deep order from within a complex adaptive social system.

Development is fundamentally an attempt to create sustainable change in adaptive social systems made up of poor communities and the social, political, and economic systems in which they are embedded. The development of poor communities can no more be master planned than the feeding of the people of New York every day.

For complex adaptive systems two ideas are critical: emergence and self-organization (Pascale, Sternin, and Sternin 2010, 113–14). Adaptive social systems do contain order, but it is an order that emerges from within the system at a time that cannot be predicted. The story of bringing the daily food to New York above is an example. The hard news is that this emergent social order, and how it comes into being, can only be understood in retrospect. If one had the time, energy, and information, one could figure out where the food for the millions in New York City came from and how all of it was delivered last month. But this analysis would not predict with any useful certainty how this will happen next month. The system will change; it is dynamic and adaptive. In other words, we can look back in time and piece together a narrative to describe what happened and how, but this offers little help when we look to the future. Development projects are like this.

The bottom line is that the self-ordering of a social system cannot be predicted or managed into being. Said another way, social systems, and this most certainly applies to communities of poor people, are self-organizing; transformation cannot be programmed with any certainty over the long term. For dynamic social systems, the only thing we can safely predict is that the future will consist of outcomes other than what we expected. Even the things we planned for may be accomplished by means we did not anticipate. Unintended consequences are normal and are thus more important to social transformation than careful planning. (See more on the implications of this in the following chapter.)

Among the first to alert us to the unexpected and unpredictable nature of development was David Korten (1980). In a study of five successful development programs in Asia, Korten found that these programs succeeded because they made continuing adjustments to their program design based on information that arose from a continuous process of monitoring and observation. The program purposes remained unchanged, but the inputs, outputs, and outcomes underwent many adjustments over time. Korten encouraged development practitioners to move away from a blueprint model of development. Drawing on the social learning theory of the 1970s, Korten called for a "learning process approach" in which all actors are more in a learning mode than a programming mode (Korten and Klauss 1984).

At the turn of the 1990s, both Korten (1989), reflecting on his work in the Philippines, and Uphoff (1996, 388ff.), reflecting on his work in Sri Lanka, linked the "dynamic, unpredictable and idiosyncratic elements of development programmes; those things that are not easily amenable to planning and management control, but which are nonetheless central to success or failure" (Mosse 2001) to the then-emerging discovery of dynamic or complex systems. Aware of this conversation, Chambers was confirmed in his call to listen to the poor and allow them to "take over the stick" in a more people-centered approach (shown in Figure 8–5). Chambers also mentions complexity theory briefly (1997, 194ff.).

Point of departure	Things	People
Mode	Blueprint	Process
Key word	Planning	Participation
Goals	Preset	Evolving
Decision-making	Centralized	Decentralized
Analytical assumptions	Reductionist	Whole systems
Professional mindset	Instructing	Enabling
	Motivating	Empowering
Local people as	Beneficiaries	Partners, actors

Figure 8–5: From things to people.

What does this mean to development planning? While the mechanical, linear, and logical model of planning fits certain kinds of activities, there are others for which this is the wrong tool. To build a school, use a Log Frame. To transform the way a poor community functions as a social system, we need a different way of working. David Mosse, an anthropologist at the School of Oriental and African Studies at the University of London, concludes that "development 'solutions' often evolve out of experimentation and practice rather than design" (2001, 6). This leads us to two adjustments to take into account the dynamic nature of the communities where we work

First, we need to adjust the way we plan our programs. While keeping the program purpose—our vision of the better human future the people have articulated for themselves—as a lodestar on the horizon, we must relinquish our desire for control and manage the program. We must be much more tentative with all the other elements of the Log Frame—the inputs, outputs, and outcomes—so that we can quickly adjust and redirect our energies and resources as the fruits or threats of unpredictability arise. We have to "learn our way" into the future. In spite of the adulation that donors pour out on Log Frames and results-based management, practitioners know that for social development, linear planning alone simply won't do. The Positive Deviance approach that I will introduce shortly is the best example of adjusting to this reality, but both PLA and Appreciative Inquiry (AI) can also be used to support this approach to learning the way, rather than planning the way, into the future.

Second, because unintended consequences are the norm in adaptive social systems, we need to make monitoring much more frequent and pay much more attention to anything that changes, not focus only on the indicators we set early on. The program plan needs frequent assessment, but so does the social environment of the program. The program may be on track with its plan, but the social environment may be changing. If we are not regularly monitoring the program context, we may miss something important. We need to increase the frequency and our effort in observing and responding to the process side of development.

Spirituality and program design
(Written with Lisa Myers)

There is one last observation about planning a program. There is a temptation to limit our assessments, and thus our design work, to those things we can observe. Because we can only observe material things, our observations are too limited by definition. Not only do we exclude the community's view of the excluded middle (we'll pick up on this later in this chapter), we also exclude God and the Holy Spirit from the process. We must remember that we do not naturally see as God sees; we may not notice what God deems to be most important. After all, in the prophetic literature of the Bible, we learn that while the rulers of Israel were feeling good about the size, success, and influence of the nation of Israel, God viewed the lack of well-being of the widow, orphan, and alien as evidence of false worship (Is 1:4, 16–17; 2:8; 3:13; 58:6; Ez 22:12). God's focus was on the treatment of the poor as the evidence of Israel's well-being. We need to immerse our work of assessment and design in a covering of prayer that asks that we may have eyes to see and ears to hear.

A truly Christian approach to designing a transformational development program also needs to be open and attentive to what God has to say to us. Even more important, the community needs to be invited to be open and attentive to what God has to say to it. Together we need to be quiet and listen in the midst of the all the information we have gathered and be open to God leading us to the information and conclusions that God deems most important.

We need to use the Bible, as the living word of God, as a tool in our planning process (see Chapter 10). What might we hear from the word that is relevant to determining what change really matters? What is God's best future for this community? Where is there evidence of God already being active?

Said another way, the process by which we work with the community is not just a problem-solving or appreciative exercise. It must be a spiritual exercise, an exercise in discernment. We need to integrate the methods of the spiritual disciplines into our development activities and use them as part of the development process. We must learn to be as spiritually discerning as we are professionally discerning.

One final word. If the social systems in poor communities are as unpredictable, unmanageable, and self-directing as I have described, and that Korten, Uphoff, and Mosse report, then our faith in God and God's redemptive work in the world is not just a spiritual affirmation. We need to act and pray that our program design will by God's grace turn out to be part of God's ongoing work in the world. Our prayer needs to be that our program will become part of God's program, a program of transformation on which God has been working for all of human history. The unavoidable uncertainty of development work should drive us to continuing prayer as we realize that any transformational efforts in this fallen and chaotic world are an offering of our faith, hope, and love.

HELPING THE COMMUNITY TELL ITS STORY

From needs analysis to social analysis

Development practice traditionally began with identifying the community's needs or a needs analysis. Rooted in a problem-solving approach, the task is to identify what is not working or is absent and plan to remedy the problem. This approach has some weaknesses.

First, it sees the poor community as a place full of problems, a negative point of departure. While this is understandable for those of us who tend to be a little messianic and see ourselves as God's problem solvers, it tends to obscure the importance of looking for what works and what brings life. I will return to this theme when I discuss Appreciative Inquiry, a development framework that seeks to begin work with a community from a more positive perspective.

Second, as we saw in Chapters 4 and 6, our understanding of the causes of poverty changes depending on the level at which we examine any given situation. As we dig deeper, both our understanding of poverty and the nature of our response changes. This means that needs analysis needs to evolve into a deeper social analysis. We must use the tools of social science in addition to the tools of empirical observation. If we do not, we limit our response primarily to social welfare (see Figure 8–6).

Problem	Level	Response
Hungry children	Need food	Social welfare
Nutrition knowledge Agricultural skills	Immediate causes	Community development
Land tenure Access to markets	Underlying causes	Advocacy
I have a right to the wealth I create	Worldview causes	Value change

Figure 8–6: Level of analysis tends to govern form of the response.

If we employ the tools of social analysis, we need to do it in a way that empowers the community. Its members are the ones who need to develop the skills of social analysis if they are to become active participants in the transformational process. It is their history, and so they need to tell it. It is also their social structure, their context; allow them to describe it and analyze it. Finally, they are the ones who need to figure out who is doing what to whom and where the money goes, so help them analyze and interpret the results. They need to learn the skills that allow them to figure out how things work, who benefits, who's left out, who has the power and all the other things that enable them to work for sustainable change. Too often we do this analysis and thinking for them, assuming that this kind of work is too sophisticated for "uneducated" people. Such a decision is paternalistic and disempowering.

Helping people learn how to decode and demystify their social systems in which they live is hard work because our own culture and worldview keep getting in the way. We are subtly tempted to help them see *our* view of *their* situation. This is how the spiritual side of their understanding of cause and effect often gets lost. We are trained to see the world in material terms and to locate causes solely in this material world. Our Western anthropology and sociology are loaded with assumptions that a non-Western community may not share.

This brings us back to the importance of knowing ourselves. This is an issue in at least three ways. First, we must be aware of our own cultural assumptions about how the world works and about what is good and bad. We must understand how our view of what is ethical is shaped by our culture. Bernard T. Adeney's book *Strange Virtues: Ethics in a Multicultural World* provides a very helpful overview of this complex challenge (1995).

Second, we need to understand how our Christian tradition shapes our view of spirituality and thus our acting in the world. We need to know what our own view of a better future—human flourishing or well-being—is and what process of change toward that future we take for granted is best.

Finally, we need to understand our own development needs. Without this self-understanding our view of the world will seep into our efforts to help the poor do their own social analysis. We will also fail to recognize when we need to learn from them.

One last comment on social analysis and knowing ourselves. We need to be sure we have an adequate understanding of how systems fit together. What do I mean?

There are three ways to think about complex systems. The first is *stratiographic.* This view sees systems as parallel but not connected. There are multiple views of the world: yours, mine, theirs; the sociologist's, the evangelist's, and the economist's. But these views don't touch or influence each other. This understanding is inadequate because the dominant feature of a complex social system is the interaction and feedback among these varying views. This stratiographic view also tends to reinforce the modern view that the spiritual and material are completely distinct from one another.

The second view of complex systems sees all social systems as part of a *comprehensive,* over-arching single system. This view assumes there is a grand unified view of all systems—God's view, if you will. This is what modernity posits: a unified theory for everything. The weakness of this view, many argue, is that if it exists at all, it can only exist for God and is inaccessible to human beings. Furthermore, if a flaw is found in one system, then the entire view fails with it. Too much depends on knowing everything about all the systems.

A third, more helpful view sees systems as *complementary,* such as the plumbing, electrical, and heating systems of a building. Each system is different, but they are interrelated. They must make sense when put together because they function in the same building. There are specialists for each system, but the critical view is that of the architect, who must be sure that the systems all fit together. When we help a community make sense of the social systems in which it is immersed, this view is more helpful than the first two (see Figure 8–7).

A community needs to develop a family of social maps describing its social systems. If we do not understand the whole family of systems—social, personal/psychological, spiritual, and cultural—our assessment of cause and response is limited. A point of view is a view from a point.

Sub-System	Problem	Cause	Response
Biophysical	Illness	Germs	Immunization
Social	Marginalization	Ostracism	Reconciliation
Psychological	Crazy behavior	Unresolved past	Counseling
Spiritual	Possessed	Evil spirit	Exorcism
Cultural	Negative self-view	Worldview	Value change

Figure 8–7: Links among problem, cause, and response.

Capacities and vulnerabilities approach

In the evolution of development practice, needs and social analysis turned to a more sophisticated way of describing the community. Struggling to find ways to work developmentally in the aftermath of disasters, Mary Anderson and Peter Woodrow, then co-directors of the International Relief and Development Project at Harvard University, defined development as "the process by which vulnerabilities are reduced and capacities are increased" (1989, 12). They proposed a framework for analyzing these capacities and vulnerabilities of communities (ibid., 7–9).

Vulnerabilities are long-term factors that affect how the community is able to respond to shocks and disasters as well as how it is able to direct its own development. We explore vulnerabilities to understand why the current situation exists and why it has affected those who are most affected. This helps us in two ways. First, it invites an understanding of why things are as they are, thus directing us to underlying causes. Second, it helps us be sure that our development plans do not actually increase vulnerabilities. Mud schoolhouses in earthquake zones provide schools, but they also create a risk to children's lives. Fertilizers increase agricultural production but also stress the soil and increase the vulnerability of farmers to moneylenders.

Capacities are long-term strengths within a society. Identifying them is one antidote to a purely problem-oriented approach to development and increases the capacity of the community to believe that it is capable of managing its own development.

Anderson and Woodrow divide the vulnerability-capacity analysis into three domains: physical and material, social and organizational, and motivational and attitudinal. The physical-material is where most of us tend to focus—no clean water, poor land use, and so forth. The social-organizational helps disclose the social organization, and helps identify internal conflicts and how the community manages them. The motivational-attitudinal gets at issues like the marred identity of the poor, the god complexes of the non-poor, and an inadequate worldview.

Anderson and Woodrow suggest that the analysis of vulnerabilities and capacities be disaggregated for men and women, and for the rich, middle-class, and poor. Analysis by gender and economic class reveals important things that are obscured by broad generalizations. Taking this next step forces us to get beyond the bias that often results in our analysis when we talk only to community leaders, who are often men and among the non-poor.

Sustainable Livelihoods approach

The vulnerability and capacity assessment framework was adapted as the development conversation moved beyond the narrow focus on food security in the 1970s and 1980s to a broader view that recognized that families can be food secure if they can produce enough food, but also if they have a secure livelihood that permits them to buy food. Food security became a sub-heading under livelihood security. Robert Chambers and Gordon Conway provide the most widely accepted definition of livelihood security: "A livelihood comprises the capabilities, assets (including both material and social resources) and activities required for a means of living" (1992).

The change in thinking led to the development of the Sustainable Livelihoods approach by CARE in 1992 and a later variation by DFID in 2002. This framework rests on an expanded understanding of capital. With apologies to economists, five different forms of capital were identified for assessment. The level of these different kinds of "capital" provides for a more nuanced assessment of capabilities and vulnerabilities. In addition to *financial capital* (money and savings), the poor also possess *human capital* (the things that make them productive) such as their physical strength (work), their health, and their level of education. The poor also may have *physical capital* (if they can prove they own it) in the form of a dwelling, animals, a bicycle, a sewing machine, and so forth. There is *natural capital* if they have access to arable land or water where they can fish. *Social capital* refers to social cohesion (or lack thereof), community organization, and reciprocal social relations such as the extended family. To this, I add *spiritual capital*, which takes the form of prayer and faith as well as the churches, mosques, and temples that aspire to form character and infuse values into the life of the community. The goal of development is to increase these assets and protect or mitigate against those things that would undermine them.

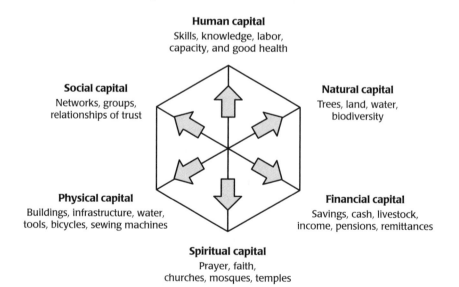

Human capital
Skills, knowledge, labor, capacity, and good health

Social capital
Networks, groups, relationships of trust

Natural capital
Trees, land, water, biodiversity

Physical capital
Buildings, infrastructure, water, tools, bicycles, sewing machines

Financial capital
Savings, cash, livestock, income, pensions, remittances

Spiritual capital
Prayer, faith, churches, mosques, temples

Figure 8–8: Six forms of community capital.

The asset framework expands the ideas of capabilities beyond the personal and individual and assesses the variety of assets the poor have to work with (capabilities) in addition to identifying deficits in or threats to the various forms of capital (vulnerabilities). The assessment of capabilities and vulnerabilities is thus expanded and more comprehensive, with both the social sphere and the environmental context now more clearly in view.

In addition to assessing the different forms of livelihood assets, the Sustainable Livelihoods approach also calls for an assessment of the vulnerabilities that are external to the community. What kinds of periodic natural disasters, such as droughts or floods, occasionally threaten the community's assets? What kinds of seasonal variations threaten livelihood security? What external trends in things like prices may lead to diminished assets? These questions ensure that environmental issues are clearly in view. In addition, assessing possible shocks allows us to add disaster mitigation to the development program plan.

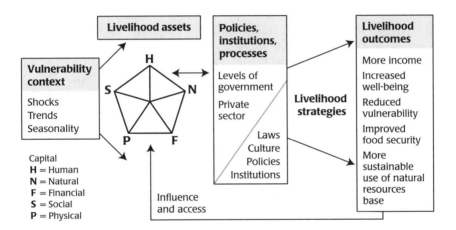

Figure 8–9: Sustainable Livelihoods approach.
(DFID 2003)

The final part of the Sustainable Livelihoods approach examines the community's capital (capabilities) and vulnerabilities in terms of public policies, social institutions, and institutional processes. How do these parts of the community's context help or hinder the building of the various forms of community capital? The potential impact of social, political, and economic systems on the community's assets is now firmly in view. In light of this expanded assessment of assets and context, livelihood strategies are then formed and articulated in the form of livelihood outcomes. The goal of the Sustainable Livelihood approach to assessing capabilities and vulnerabilities is to increase and/or protect the asset base of the poor in all asset areas.

Community organizing

Community organizing emerged in the 1960s in Chicago as Saul Alinsky searched for tools to empower poor people in the inner city to take an active role in their own transformation. Community organizing is a process by which people in a particular area learn to take charge of their situation and develop a sense of the power they have as a group. Community organizing helps the urban poor organize themselves into an action community focused on a shared issue or concern and then create an approach to challenge the political and economic structures that contribute to their poverty. The process of community organizing employs a continuous process of action-reflection-action. The community diagnoses its problems, seeks to understand their causes—including the people and systems that are contributing to their problems, and then organizes an action to confront those responsible.

According to Robert Linthicum, the five steps of the community organizing include:

- *Networking:* Building relationships, identifying issues, and building trust.
- *Coalition building:* Gathering people and organizations together to address community needs identified by the people.
- *Action-reflection-action:* Using a dynamic, continuing learning process to examine why things are as they are and how earlier actions worked or did not work.
- *Leadership empowerment:* Forming locally led networks and coalitions. As local leaders emerge and gain the respect of the community, they must be trained.
- *Birth of a community:* Working together and experiencing success builds trust, and a sense of community emerges for those who share common issues. (1991, 25–26)

While simple needs tend to be addressed in the earlier stages of community organizing, the continuous learning resulting from the reflection process tends to deepen the community's understanding of the causes of its poverty and the necessary steps toward solutions. More substantive issues tend to emerge, and systems and structures become the subject of examination and then action.

Community organizing has proven effective in creating community participation and ownership and has been particularly successful in dealing with inaction on the part of local government bodies. Community organization has also been helpful in urban settings in which the idea of "the community" is hard, if not impossible, to define in a geographical or cultural sense. Organizing around a shared issue or concern creates a community of sorts for a period of time.

Community organizing also suffers from some important weaknesses. First, community organizing contains a temptation to reduce the purpose of development to the creation of power alone. While power for the powerless is good and necessary, it cannot be the final end of development. Ultimately, all power belongs to God. Thus the slogan "Power to the people" is not a biblical concept for either the poor or the non-poor (Christian 1994, 327). This focus on power leads to the most serious weakness of community organizing; that is, its effectiveness is derived from setting one group within a community over and against another group. This confrontational, win-lose approach, while often successful in the short term, can work against sustainability, reconciliation, and peacebuilding.

Participatory Learning and Action

In the early 1990s, a development-planning tool emerged that held great promise in terms of allowing the community to describe itself and interpret the workings of its social systems. The Rapid Rural Appraisal (RRA) methodology of the 1980s, used by technical professionals to design programs rapidly during short field visits, was reinvented as a result of participatory action-reflection research advances, learnings from applied anthropology, and field research in rural agricultural development. The result was called the Participatory Rural Appraisal (PRA). The PRA has gone through several name changes as it has found application in cities and refugee work in addition to development. Today, many call it Participatory Learning and Action (PLA). Figure 8–10 illustrates the nature of this reinvention that put participation at the center of assessment work.

The evolution of the RRA into the PLA represents not so much a change in the tools as a change in the ways the tools are used. There has been a reversal in power and expertise. As outsiders help the local people to pose the questions and then find ways to answer their own questions, the local people are the ones who learn, who are empowered. This is in contrast to the development practice of the 1980s, when the poor were more passive sources of information and the outsider tended to be the one who did most of the learning. In a telephone interview in 1997 Jayakumar Christian spoke straightforwardly about this: "It is demonic to reduce the poor to a source of information."

A wide variety of tools and exercises have been developed as part of the toolkit for the PLA (see Figure 8–11). Their common purpose is to allow the poor to articulate what they already know in a way that invites them to assess and analyze what is working and what is not.

Done properly, the PLA is a helpful set of tools that can be used to allow the poor to describe their reality, including their social systems, using their own categories. After watching and listening to the community as it carries

	RRA	PLA
Mode	Finding out, extracting	Empowering, facilitating
Outsider's role	Investigator	Facilitator
Owner of process	Outsiders	Local people
Methods used	Secondary data	Handing over the stick
	Observing directly	Do-it-yourself research
	Interviews	Local analysis of secondary sources
	Seeking out experts	Mapping by the people
	Probing questions	Time lines by the people
	Case studies and stories	Trend analysis by the people
	Transect walks[*]	Causal linkage diagrams by the people
		Wealth and power rankings by the people
		Seasonal diagrams by the people

[*] A walk through a community noting everything and understanding its meaning.

Figure 8–10: Comparing the RRA and the PLA.
(Based on Chambers 1997, 115)

out the various exercises, one can develop a fairly clear picture of the context in which the community is struggling to survive, thus setting the stage for an analysis of capabilities and vulnerabilities. The development strategy calls for building on capacities and reducing vulnerabilities.

But there is more, and it is as important as creating capacity/vulnerability analyses. From the results of a properly done PLA exercise the poor can discover how much they know, what resources and skills they already have, and how resourceful they have been in the past. Helping the poor discover that what they already know goes a long way toward helping them overcome their marred identity. One old man, after hearing the community describe its local reality in substantial depth as a result of a three-day set of PLA exercises, stood up and exclaimed: "Hey! We really are quite smart, aren't we?" This radical transformation from his prior view that they were ignorant people who need outsiders to help them with their superior knowledge is a small piece of evidence for recovering identity.

Now we need to revisit the work of Amartya Sen for a minute. One of the major consequences of Sen's idea of development as expanding human

Tool	Purpose	Outcome
Time lines	Describe key events in the community history.	Help the community own its own history. What effected change in the past?
Family line	Describe things that have changed in key families.	Demonstrate past coping strategies.
Trends analysis	Describe trajectories of change in the community.	Create a sense of direction and possibility of change.
Seasons diagram	See community life in a seasonal perspective.	Create a climate of dialogue on a wide range of issues. Good for planning purposes.
Resource mapping	Describe social, economic, and demographic resources.	Good for needs analysis and resource allocation.
Transects	Cartoon-like map of community key points, problems, and resources.	Good as an inventory of resources. Good for needs analysis. Also shows resource distribution.
Matrix mapping	Determine community preferences.	Understand rationale for community choices and preferences.
Venn diagram (Chappati diagram)	Describe institutions or people who are important actors in the life of the community.	Understand perceptions of power and relationships among powerful people or institutions. Can identify institutions that need strengthening.
Wealth ranking	Describe local economic system and its players.	Identify the poorest of the poor. Help community think about why non-poor are non-poor.
Causal diagrams	Describe local view of causally related events and actors.	Identify major development opportunities or barriers. Disclose survival strategy.
A typical day	Describe pattern of a typical day.	Identify roles, especially for women and children. Helpful for planning activities.
Conflict analysis	Describe dynamics of conflict.	Reveal major players and causes of conflict. Basis for exploring reconciliation.
Ten-seed technique	Measuring attitudes, ranking things.	An easy way to get to comparative percentages.

Figure 8–11: PLA toolkit.
(Adapted from Jayakaran 1996)

freedom is the emergence of the human capability movement in the form of the Human Development and Capability Association. This network has produced a wide range of participatory methods that support expanding human capabilities (White and Petitt 2007; White 2009) along with a great deal of research on those methods in different contexts (Deneulin and Shahani 2009). Any practitioner would be well advised to follow the work of the human capabilities network closely.

Recent work has shown that PLA methodologies can also be used effectively to enable a community to complete its own policy analysis, thus empowering the community to become its own advocate in addressing the political and economic structures that are contributing to or sustaining its poverty (Holland and Blackburn 1998).

Appreciative Inquiry

AI is a postmodern entry in the field of action research. It represents an attempt to move away from the rationalist, mechanistic, problem-solving frame that is characteristic of most research and seeks an alternative that better fits self-organizing social systems. If reality is socially constructed, as our postmodern friends tell us, then why not allow the community to construct its own reality and take ownership of it?

The starting point for Appreciative Inquiry is the belief that a community that is alive and functioning represents a miracle that can never be fully understood. There is always more to any social organization than we can discover by studying and analyzing its parts or its past. It follows, then, that we can never create or improve a social organization solely by pursuing rationally determined linear processes. David Cooperrider and Suresh Srivastva, the earliest champions of this innovation, describe it this way:

> The appreciative mode of inquiry is a way of living with, being with and directly participating in the varieties of social organization we are compelled to study. Serious consideration and reflection on the ultimate mystery of being engenders a reverence for life that draws the researcher to inquire beyond superficial appearances to deeper levels of the life-generating essentials and potentials for social existence. That is, the action-researcher is drawn to affirm, and thereby illuminate, the factors and forces involved in organizing that serve to nourish the human spirit. (1987, 129)

The appreciative approach to social change posits that social organizations can be imagined and then made by beginning with what is already creating value. If we can determine what is for life and what is generating well-being, we can imagine its expansion. Having done so, the organization or the community will tend to move in this direction. "The more an organization experiments with the conscious evolution of positive imagery, the better it will become. There is an observable self-reinforcing, educative effect of affirmation. Affirmative competence is the key to the self-organizing system" (Cooperrider et al. 1995, 5).

In the development context, AI begins with the general goal of furthering an already existing, even if limited, life-giving, cooperative social reality by asking the question: How did such a social positive phenomenon emerge in the first place? Setting aside the metaphor of a machine and a problem-solving approach, AI begins not with analysis but with a holistic view of what already is and seeks answers to a new set of questions: What made social organization possible here? What allows the community to function at its best? What possibilities await the community that will allow it to reach for higher levels of health, vitality, and well-being? The focus of the appreciative approach is the discovery of what gives or enriches life, of what creates energy and enthusiasm.

In essence, AI is more than a method; it is a way of viewing the world. "It is an intentional posture of continuous affirmation of life, of joy, of beauty, of excellence, of innovation" (Johnson and Ludema 1997, 72). This should remind us of Paul's admonition in Philippians 4:8–9:

> Whatever is true, whatever is noble, whatever is right, whatever is pure, whatever is lovely, whatever is admirable—if anything is excellent or praiseworthy—think about such things. Whatever you have learned or received or heard from me, or seen in me—put it into practice. And the God of peace will be with you.

The underlying theological frame is that God has created a good and life-giving social world; wherever we find good in our world, we are seeing evidence of God's work and gifts. The biblical story is the account of God's project to restore the lives of individuals and communities, marred by sin, so that they can be good, just, and peaceful once again. An appreciative perspective encourages transformational development promoters to find God's redemptive work in the life of the community, and within themselves, and to seek to become more intentionally part of it. At a more personal level, the appreciative frame also fits the gospel account: in spite of our sin, God looks through our brokenness and, recognizing God's image in us, works to restore that image to its fullness.

Appreciative Inquiry stands in contrast to the problem-solving framework of most development research and planning methodologies. Instead of looking for what is wrong or missing and then developing problem-solving responses, it looks for what is working, successful, and life-giving, and attempts to see additional possibilities. The belief is that an organization's single-minded "commitment to a problem-solving view of the world acts as a primary constraint on its imagination and contribution to knowledge"

(Cooperrider and Srivastva 1987, 129). Figure 8–12 contrasts the two frameworks.

	Problem solving	Appreciative Inquiry
Underlying assumption	Organizing is a problem to be solved	Organizing is a mystery to be embraced
Focus	Search for problems	Search for possibilities
Planning metaphor	A problem-solving tree	A possibility tree
Methods	Identify the problems	Valuing the best
	What are the felt needs?	What already is here that's good?
	Analysis of causes	
	Analysis of possible solutions	Envisioning what might be
	Action planning	Dialoguing about what should be
		Innovating what will be

Figure 8–12: Comparing problem-solving approach
to Appreciative Inquiry.

Appreciative visioning begins with the discovery of what is working and creating life and value. This leads to dreaming about what might be if the good of today or the past were expanded or built upon. The next step is a dialogical one about what should be. What is best for us? This is the place where the view of the promoter comes in as he or she participates in this step of the co-construction of a vision. Asking about the ideal also opens the door to ethical considerations. Is this right for us? Is it fair? Will we be proud of ourselves if we are successful? Finally, as a development vision is pursued, the evaluative step, often called *valuing*, inquires into what is working. What is surprising us that we like? How might we enhance these positive things? (see Figure 8–13).

This alternative mindset for development planning uses a very different kind of interviewing methodology than that used for a problem-solving interview. The key characteristics of the appreciative interview include the following:

- An assumption of health and vitality
- A desire to connect through empathy
- A sense of personal excitement, commitment, and concern
- An intense focus to listen with the right side of the brain
- Generative questioning, pointing toward clues, and guiding

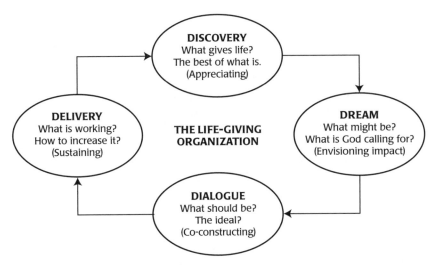

Figure 8–13: Visioning through Appreciative Inquiry.
(Johnson and Ludema 1997, 75)

- Belief in the community and its story (in contrast to doubt)
- Tolerance for ambiguity, generalization, and dreams
- A passion for dialogue and a dislike of monologue (Cooperrider et al. 1995, 9)

This list makes clear the contrast between the appreciative approach and problem solving, but we should also note that the distinction is not absolute. The last four characteristics of the appreciative interview are also typical of the mindset of many who use the PLA methodology. This correctly suggests that an AI mindset might prove entirely compatible with doing PLAs.

The appreciative bias can also be extended to evaluation. Rather than determining what went wrong and seeking solutions, the evaluation questions are different. What went right? What created energy and excitement? What emerged that people affirm as good? The response to such an evaluation exercise is to nurture and add energy to what is working. By focusing resources on what is working, we get an additional benefit. It helps us avoid the problem of retrying things that are not working, a favorite pastime of many social engineers in the West. Resources enhance what is working rather than what is not working.

Two notes of clarification. First, while the appreciative approach begins with the positive and the successful, it does not sweep the negative under the rug. In the light generated by Appreciative Inquiry, darkness no longer obscures identification of problems. Problems can be faced squarely, but within a psycho-social environment that allows them to be addressed with a maximum of energy and good will.

Second, while an appreciative frame will undoubtedly surface information that a problem-solving frame may not, and while it may also prove more helpful in allowing the community to recover its true identity and vocation, the problem-solving frame must not be discarded in the development practitioner's love of the most recent fad. The problem-solving framework has proven highly effective in the development of the West and suits certain kinds of developmental issues very well. Professional development practitioners will not force a choice that does not have to be made. They will do what can be done to incorporate the appreciative frame into existing development-planning tools and will continue to use both frames in a way that helps the community take control of its own development.

World Vision Tanzania has been very creative in adapting and using the appreciative approach (Booy and Sena 1999). Typically, a community welcomes a development NGO with hospitality and presents it with a list of things the community would like done. Getting the community to become its own agent of change is a challenge. Insisting on a discussion focusing on what has worked and on when and how the community has been successful in the past is very helpful in getting past the initial view of the NGO as the giver of good things. Through community meetings and focus groups, World Vision Tanzania works with the community using an appreciative framework to hear the community's answers to questions like the following:

- What life-giving, life-enhancing forces do you have in your community? What gives you the energy and power to change and to cope with adversity?
- Thinking back on the last one hundred years of your community, what has happened that you are proud of, that makes you feel you have been successful?
- What are your best religious and cultural practices? Those that make you feel good about your culture? That has helped you when times were tough?
- What do you value that makes you feel good about yourselves?
- What in your geographical area and in your local political and economic systems has helped you do things of which you are proud?
- What skills or resources have enabled you to do things your children will remember you for having done?
- How have your relationships, both within and without the community, worked for you and helped you do things that you believe were good for the community?

The net result of such an inquiry is often spectacular. The laundry list of problems the community would like the NGO to fix is lost in the enthusiasm of describing what is already working. The community comes to view its past and itself in a new light. We do know things. We do have resources.

We have a lot to be proud of. We are already on the journey. God has been good to us. We can do something. We are not god-forsaken. This is a major step toward recovering the community's true identity and discovering its true vocation. With these discoveries a major transformational frontier has been crossed.

Charles Elliot, in *Locating the Energy for Change: An Introduction to Appreciative Inquiry*, develops the theory of AI as it pertains to development and then presents five case studies in which AI was used as the primary tool for assessment, implementation, and evaluation (1999). In his conclusions he finds that AI has the capacity to overcome cynicism resulting from past failed attempts and even from various expressions of what we are calling marred identity. Elliot is less sure about the sustainability of programs enabled by AI. What happens when the energy and passion for a new vision of a better future meets resistance from those who prefer things as they are? Can the energy released by an appreciative process sustain itself in the face of powerful resistance? (1999, 283).

Positive Deviance

In the late 1990s another approach arose to letting the community tell its own story and choose its preferred solutions. This was a result of some creative work done by Drs. Jerry and Monique Sternin of Save the Children while working on the malnutrition of children in Vietnam.

After completing a community-based nutrition assessment, the Sternins noticed that a small portion of the "very, very poor" in the community had children who were not malnourished. Instead of proceeding to the next PLA step in the conversation with the community—what might be done about malnutrition—they decided to encourage the community to talk to these outliers or "positive deviants" to see if they were doing something for their children that others might do. The community discovered that these few families were harvesting tiny shrimp and crabs that lived in the rice paddies and were adding them, along with some green tops from sweet potatoes, to their children's daily meals of rice. At first the larger community argued that people weren't supposed to eat shrimp, crabs, and sweet potato tops, but the fact that this was being done by some of their own eventually wore down the resistance. Finally, some agreed to adopt this change, and by the program's end three-quarters of the children had put on weight and more and more people had adopted the innovation (Pascale, Sternin, and Sternin 2010, 19–20). The Sternins called this the Positive Deviance (PD) approach.

Before exploring the principles and practice of the PD approach, a few words about diffusion of innovation in communities are needed. Everett Rogers is a sociologist who focused his career on the challenge of "diffusion of innovation" (2003). In the 1960s and 1970s diffusion of innovation theory became the mainstay of rural sociology and primary focus for supporting the Green Revolution and the adoption of its new seeds and techniques around the world.

Rogers discovered that in any community there are always a small number of people whom he called "early adopters"; they will try almost anything new. The communication challenge is to move this innovation on to the rest of the community. Rogers focused on communication channels, formal and informal, within the community and the challenges of communicating across varying educational and income levels. Rogers argued that the rate of diffusion needs serious attention; the pace is determined by processes and realities within the communities, including how they make decisions and traditional values. The rate of adoption tends to follow an S-shaped curve—slow to start, more rapid as the innovation spreads, and then slow at the end as one encounters what Rogers called the laggards (see Figure 8-14). Rogers's major focus ended up on the social system of the community. Social structure matters and is usually not well understood by outsiders. Social norms and taboos matter. Fear of spirits and sacred places matter. The power structure of the community matters. Managing change is a complicated process (2003, 11–21).

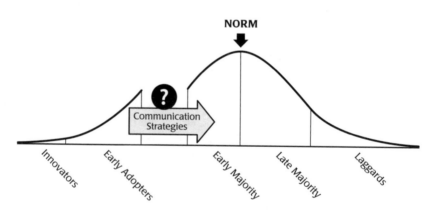

Figure 8–14: Diffusion of innovation in communities.
(Adapted from Rogers 2003, 281)

This is a common experience among development practitioners. We promote something like boiling water to prevent water-borne diseases and a few brave souls start boiling their water immediately. Those whose age, social situation, or personality make them part of the early majority watch the early adopters closely and often adopt the change if things work out. The rest of the community tends to focus on all the reasons why this innovation is a bad idea—culture or value contradictions, worldview threats, risk to survival, the threat to those in power, resistance to things from the outside, and so on. This is why, even if the results from early adopters show that boiling water reduces the disease incidence for their children, adoption of the innovation moves slowly and often never moves into the mainstream of community life at all. Success and repeated attempts to explain why the innovation is a good idea or the science undergirding the innovation help little.

The PD approach draws on diffusion of innovation theory and extends it. PD posits three additional principles of social change. First, PD takes note of psychological research that confirms that telling, educating, or convincing people to change their behavior is not often effective. Communication or education does not often lead to behavior change. Most of the time, it is the other way around. Changing our practice can change how we think and feel about something. Telling ourselves that the Bible says we should love our obnoxious neighbor seldom results in feeling love for our neighbor. But carrying out a series of kind and decent actions toward our neighbor will often change how we feel about our neighbor. Sadly, this is no guarantee that our neighbor will change his or her behavior, but that is a separate issue. PD argues that new practices will change the way we think and feel.

Second, PD focuses on the observable exceptions instead of the norm or majority that is suffering from a problem. PD argues that in every community there are individuals whose uncommon practices or behaviors enable them to find better solutions to problems than neighbors who have access to the same resources. Therefore, rather than introduce a new practice or behavior from the outside, a great temptation of development facilitators, the PD approach searches for the outliers, the ones who are not following the normal behavior patterns of the community and hence have already discovered solutions to the problem the development program seeks to solve.

Finally, the PD approach understands and takes advantage of our earlier observation that dynamic social systems are not susceptible to engineered change from the outside. PD assumes that a community is a dynamic social system for whom change is nonlinear and unpredictable; it is thus unsuited for the linear planning of logical frameworks and "outside-in" direction. PD assumes that social change is an emergent phenomenon or deep order that surfaces from within the community and thus must be discovered or deciphered, not manufactured (Pascale, Millemann, and Gioja 2000, 175).

In terms of process, the PD approach uses the full PLA toolkit, with one critical difference. Once the presenting problem is assessed, described, and defined by the community, the next step is not problem solving. Instead, the community is encouraged to look for those few within the community who either do not suffer from the problem or who are mitigating its effects. This seeking out the exceptions, or "positive deviance," is an extension of

Appreciative Inquiry. Normally, AI focuses on the common view of the community or the norm, just as PLA does. But PD focuses the appreciative lens on the outliers who may have good news that the others have not noticed.

Then the community, not the development practitioner, is encouraged to listen to these outliers or innovators and see if the community can discover and understand why these few are free from the problem under study. In this step taboos or culturally sensitive issues often arise. The response from the majority is often that "we don't do that kind of thing." Cultural and social power issues may also surface as barriers to change. The appreciative engagement between the traditions and social systems of the community, represented in the majority of the community and the change already present in the community, must be encouraged and not shortchanged. This is the place that the early majority folks have to decide for themselves that they want to try out the new behavior. Those in power or authority need to decide that if they will support this change. All of this takes time and sensitive professional facilitation, which often includes peacemaking and reconciliation skills. The goal of PD is to invite social change driven from within and among the people. Contrary to our modern expectations, it is not important that they understand the rationality behind the new behavior or even feel positive about it. Many early adopters have no idea about the underlying science of immunizations or improved seeds. But, PD argues, if they change their behavior and it works for them, their hearts and minds will follow.

The PD approach is highly dependent on skilled facilitation. There are three guidelines. The first is to *design, not engineer*. Facilitating the PD approach "has the feel of a dance and a courtship as opposed to a march and an invasion." The second guideline is to *discover, not dictate*. "The wisdom to solve problems exists and needs to be discovered within each and every community." The third design guideline is to *decipher, not presuppose*. As technically educated development facilitators the temptation is to jump quickly to conclusions based on our knowledge and experience from somewhere else, and thus local knowledge and initiative are squelched. This temptation needs to be resisted. "I am not in charge of anything. My role is to create mirrors that show the whole what the parts are doing. . . . I seek out the positive deviants and support and amplify them" (Pascale, Millemann, and Gioja 2000, 175–81).

This approach to program planning has proven successful in increasing child protection in a situation rife with sex trafficking of young girls in Indonesia (Singhal and Dura 2009, 74–75), in reducing the incident of female genital mutilation in Egypt (Pascale, Sternin, and Sternin 2010, 53–54), and in helping former girl child soldiers reintegrate into society in Uganda (Singhal and Dura 2009, 32–33). It has also been used effectively in a variety of public health programs. (More information is available on the website of the Positive Deviance Initiative at Tufts University.)

The strengths of the PD approach include empowerment as a result of the community discovering an innovation within itself. There is the promise of healing marred identity. The approach creates new behaviors in a way that is more consistent with what psychological research on behavioral change has learned. The approach also protects the development process from the problems that outside-in facilitators create because of their limited knowledge of local language, culture, and other contextual specifics. The solutions are always situated locally. Finally, the PD approach is appropriate for working to change complex social systems; it is a great way to learn our way toward a better future.

There are some limits to the approach that need to be kept in mind. It takes a lot of time, something the community and the holistic practitioner have in short supply. Furthermore, donors may not be willing to invest money in what they perceive as a time-consuming process in contrast to results. PD requires patient and skilled facilitation; it is not an approach for well-intentioned amateurs. The conversation between the many and the few can create fear, resistance, and even violence; the facilitator is encouraging local folk to mess with their social systems and relationships. Finally, PD is not suitable for every development situation. Protecting children against polio only comes through use of the Salk vaccine, for example; there is no local solution awaiting discovery.

As the program ends

As we conclude our thinking about development practice, we need to think a little about what happens when a transformational development program ends. A number of years ago I visited a twelve-year-old area development program in Tanzania that was within a two years of what was then called "phasing out." I was pleased that everyone in the community, including all the community development committees, were clear that a program phase out was in the offing. Each committee reported on its plans for sustaining the water systems, primary schools, agricultural cooperatives, and the like. When I congratulated the community on its phase-out planning, an old man stood up and corrected me: "Phasing out the project is no problem; we have been planning for this for a long time. We are ready. But when my son left home and got married, we were glad for him. But we did not phase him out of our family. Is World Vision phasing out of our relationship?"

This experience prompted World Vision to begin to think more deeply about the end of programs. The development program can and should end, but ending a relationship of almost fifteen years was something else altogether. Based on this work and additional research in Ethiopia, World Vision used the metaphor of the growth of a tree to describe the life cycle of its programs. Programs went from a seedling or start-up stage to a growing or program phase. Then, rather than phasing out the program at this point, a new phase was added that focuses on propagation or sharing. This strategic relationship phase (see Figure 8–15) is the answer to the old man's question.

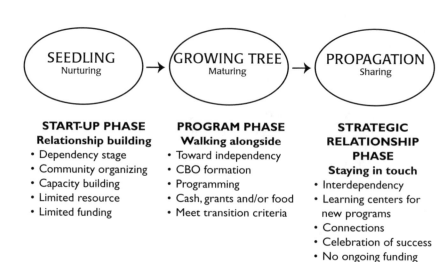

Figure 8–15: Evolution of a development program.

The program begins, as one would expect, with relationship building. This is the getting acquainted, community organizing, assessment, and discovery phase. World Vision has learned to invest people and time, but not very much money, in this phase. Too quick a move to funding a program tends to distort the key elements of the development process. One critical element of this phase is the news that the program and its funding will end at some point. Planning for the final transition must be part of the planning at the beginning of the program.

The program phase is a walking alongside phase as community-based organizations emerge to design and run program elements like the building and staffing of schools, building a water supply, and the like. This is the phase where the formal program design is created in the form of a Logical Framework derived from the DME process (see the next chapter for details). This is the phase with the greatest financial investment and, having been planned with the end in sight, also the time when work is done to create local organizations, mobilize local government departments, and develop local or alternative funding sources for a sustainable future.

The final phase is no longer a program phase but an ongoing strategic relationship. When the community in Tanzania was asked what kinds of things World Vision might include in an ongoing strategic relationship, a variety of suggestions had merit. The community talked about its need for new ideas and new technologies that are hard for it to discover on its own because of its geographic isolation. The community wanted encouragement from time to time, maybe even advice. It wanted World Vision to join in celebrating its successes and to provide accompaniment as it grieved and learned from its failures. The community members offered their community as a place where new World Vision programs might come to visit and learn from their experience. They could teach others what they had learned. This is propagation or sharing and is a sign of interdependence and giving back.

A second contribution to understanding sustainability of programs comes from Norman Uphoff, who carried out a study of an irrigation scheme in Sri Lanka that proved to be sustainable seven years after the outsiders left to go back to their universities and NGOs. Uphoff posed this question: Where does the social energy for sustainability come from? His research pointed to three things: ideas, ideals, and friendship (1996, 375–78). Ideas have the power to shape how we view and respond to our world. Ideals tend to set our sights high and cause us to work together. Friendship means working together, valuing one another's well-being. Together, ideas, ideals, and friendships (relationships) release social energy—energy needed to overcome resistance to change that lives within the poor and non-poor alike. This finding confirms that relationships and vision matter a lot to successful program transitions; they are the software or process side of development that is critical to sustainability.

Finally, there is another set of lessons from mature programs that needs to be part of the planning for transition. In the research into mature area development programs in Tanzania and Ethiopia in the late 1990s, World Vision determined that there were four critical elements relevant to program transitions. Each needs attention as the planning for the formal development program moves toward its mature phase.

First, there needs to be a plan for developing the capacity to be sustainable. The mindset of the people in the community needs to move from that of beneficiaries to that of active and responsible owners of the development program. Community organizations need to be developed that are able to assess, design, and ultimately fund community priorities on their own. Microfinance institutions and other forms of micro-enterprise development will be needed to sustain available credit and insurance. Planning for this needs to begin at the very beginning of program planning.

Second, the community must plan how it will mitigate possible shocks or disasters that could undo years of development work. (Remember the Livelihood Security approach.) The community members know what kinds of natural disasters visit them regularly. Disaster mitigation plans are needed for these. Efforts to develop community resilience and coping mechanisms are necessary (see Figure 8–16).

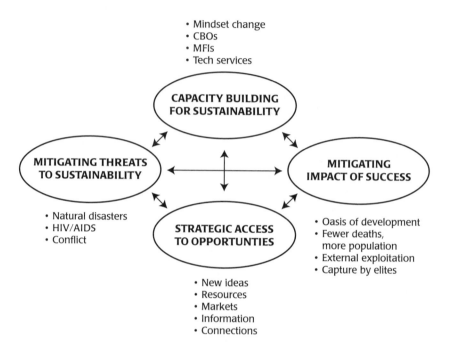

• Mindset change
• CBOs
• MFIs
• Tech services

CAPACITY BUILDING FOR SUSTAINABILITY

MITIGATING THREATS TO SUSTAINABILITY

MITIGATING IMPACT OF SUCCESS

• Natural disasters
• HIV/AIDS
• Conflict

STRATEGIC ACCESS TO OPPORTUNTIES

• Oasis of development
• Fewer deaths, more population
• External exploitation
• Capture by elites

• New ideas
• Resources
• Markets
• Information
• Connections

Figure 8–16: Strategic elements of a program transition.

Just as important as planning for potential problems is planning to mitigate the impact of a successful program. Improving health and nutrition means fewer deaths and thus an increasing population. Fewer children dying under the age of five means increased demand for schools and teachers and eventually jobs. Poor people from surrounding communities will move into a successful program area and thus threaten to overwhelm the benefits the community has worked so hard to create. Surplus agricultural produce or rumors of savings or better livelihoods will attract those who wish to exploit these improvements for their own benefit. Success can create new problems, and these need to be anticipated as much as possible.

Finally, some thinking needs to be done about what might come next for a community and its successful program. What strategic opportunities might it face and how might it plan to take advantage of them. Where will new ideas and innovation come from? Where will the resources for taking advantage of them come from?

Advocacy, citizenship, and good governance

Most development programs begin with the immediate and the obvious—building schools, installing water systems, improving agricultural production, providing health interventions. As these programs pass their five-year mark, many of these good and necessary actions have been taken and a new set of issues arises. The government is not providing competent teachers for the school, or there are no nurses for the health hut. There is no way to get a fair price for the new agricultural surplus because there is no access to regional markets except through unscrupulous middle men (sadly, they are usually men). The non-poor begin to find ways to redirect the benefits of the program to themselves or actively resist or undermine the changes that threaten their continuing power over the community. In other words, development interventions alone are not enough. The social systems within which the poor live must now become the focus of transformational change.

Take, for example, the good idea of providing primary school education for children in a poor village. The assumption is that this is a significant step in transformational development. This would be true if a whole set of additional assumptions about the educational system were also true. Will children, especially girls, be allowed to go to school, or do parents have other priorities? Are school fees affordable for all? Are the teachers capable, and are they being paid enough so that they do not have to ask students for bribes? What does the community do when male teachers seek sexual favors from girl students? Are the curriculum and teaching materials relevant to today's educational needs? Does the Ministry of Education have enough money to sustain this change? Is funding getting through to the teachers and the schools? These issues cannot be addressed by the development program and its technical expertise alone. Effecting the systemic change that will make the change of the development program sustainable usually requires effective policy and advocacy work. Said another way, good development work generates the need for policy and advocacy work.

As I pointed out in Chapter 5 in the section on Amartya Sen, the conversations about human rights and development converged in the first decade of the twenty-first century. The emergence of a rights-based approach to development resulted. Rights-based development integrates traditional development work with advocacy and rights promotion at the grassroots with the new goal of helping the poor become effective, informed, and active citizens (Uvin 2004).

Development programs have a number of ways to integrate rights-based policy and advocacy work into the development program. One assessment tool—ARVIN—helps poor communities evaluate their local context in terms of how it supports or does not support citizen participation and activism. A second tool, community based performance monitoring (CBPM), provides a method by which communities can hold local governments and institutions accountable. A third framework provides a way of determining how advocacy efforts can support a community's livelihood security.

ARVIN is a tool that allows the poor and the development practitioner to assess the degree to which a local context is an enabling environment for citizenship engagement and participation. Developed for the World Bank by Alan Fowler, ARVIN is an analytical framework that assesses the conditions that affect the ability of local community-based organizations to engage in public debate and participate in systems of social accountability. The freedom of citizens to associate (A), the resources (R) citizens can mobilize to fulfill their objectives, their ability to formulate and voice (V) their opinions, their access to critical information (I), and their ability to negotiate (N) to meet their needs make up the five major elements of this diagnostic tool. ARVIN can be used to identify weaknesses or problems as well as strengths and resources.

CBPM was developed in the early 2000s in a CARE health program in Malawi (Shah 2003) and then was further developed by the Social Development Department of the World Bank for use in Sierra Leone and the Gambia (Thindwa, Edgerton, and Forster 2005). Using focus groups and participatory methodologies this tool allows communities to understand the nature and quality of services they should be able to expect from the local government and other service providers and to monitor those services in an open and transparent way. The findings allow the community to give feedback to the government and other social institutions in an immediate and concrete way. The goal of the process is to empower the community to negotiate reforms as they are needed. For example, the community is asked to develop indicators of what makes for a good school (see Figure 8–17). Then periodically the students, in groups to ensure confidentiality, are asked to rate the current level of performance against these indicators. The results are then shared at a community meeting which is attended by local government officials and perhaps even by district educational officers. Gaps in performance are discussed and remedies are explored together. The reform that is identified is then recorded in a new scorecard.

In another example in Uganda there is a chalkboard by the road outside the schoolyard. Everyday the students draw a "happy face" on the board if their teacher is there and teaching or a sad face if the teacher did not show up. Since many in the community walk that road every day, the community quickly learns if and when the teacher is a "no show," and it reacts accordingly.

The final way in which local advocacy can support development comes from working with the Sustainable Livelihoods approach that was described

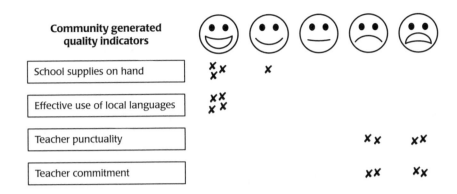

Figure 8–17: Student assessment of a primary school.
(Adapted from Thindwa, Edgerton, and Forster 2005, 9)

earlier in this chapter. Advocacy in the context of development should aspire to create or support any local processes or institutions that increase any form of local capital as a way of increasing livelihood security. Conversely, plans should be made to work against or at least mitigate the impact of processes, cultural values, or institutions that diminish or remove any one of these forms of capital. CBPM or advocacy efforts to improve the quality of local policing are examples of the former. Advocacy against the local practice of female genital mutilation or corrupt practices of local officials are examples of the latter (see Figure 8–18).

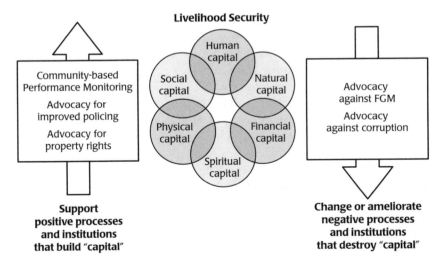

Figure 8–18: Advocacy and livelihood security.

One final caution on the practice of policy analysis and advocacy in the context of development. Too often agencies do the policy research and analysis with professionals and then presume to speak for those whom they claim have no voice. This implies that the poor are unable to diagnose their own situation and that they, in truth, have no voice. This does not have to be the case and, in ensuring that it is not the case, a transformational frontier can be crossed. The poor will be less poor when they learn to do their own research and analysis and find their own voice. This will require help and support, especially in addressing international structures, but this is no excuse for doing their advocacy work for them. At the end of the day, the problem is not that the poor have no voice; it is that no one is listening.

OTHER CRITICAL PROGRAM DESIGN ISSUES

Program design is a complex task especially when working with poor communities which by definition are complex adaptive social systems. The result is that the process of program design is more critical than the actual program design itself. Thus participatory tools, used in both a problem-solving mode and an appreciative mode, can help make the process of program design a transformational event in itself. As they help the community tell its story, recover its true identity and vocation, and take another step in its pilgrimage of transformation, change is taking place. This is not enough, however. There are other blind spots to which we must turn attention.

What is "the community"?

One of the major weaknesses of the discussion thus far is the use of "the community" as if a poor community were homogeneous and uniform. Most of the time this is not the case. While we have alluded to the poor and the non-poor within a community, there are other groups that need our attention when we seek the well-being of whole communities. Communities are made up of men, women, children, and old people, and these groups do not all have the same voice or concerns. There are sometimes groups who are kept out of sight, such as people with handicaps or a shunned ethnic group. There can be differences with regard to religion, caste, and ethnicity. Assuming that those who speak are speaking for everyone can and often does obscure differences in power and voice.

This issue is of particular importance as we employ participatory methods to help us hear the voice of "the community" in order to empower "the community" to take responsibility for its own development. In *The Myth of Community*, Irene Guijt and Meera Kaul Shah point out:

Looking back, it is apparent that "community" has often been viewed naively, or in practice dealt with, as a harmonious and internally

equitable collective. Too often here has been an inadequate understanding of the internal dynamics and differences, that are so crucial
to positive outcomes. This mythical notion of community cohesion
continues to permeate much participatory work, hiding a bias that
favours the opinions and priorities of those with more power and the
ability to voice themselves publically. (1998, 1)

This requires that we examine our participatory methods and how they are
carried out with some care. Ways must be created to assure that a multi-
plicity of voices and perspectives can be heard.

More important, these differences within the community often mean
there is conflict—open or passive aggressive—between and among these
groups. Participatory methods that manage to give voice to these different
groups may result in conflict and power struggles being openly declared.
Those employing participatory methodologies need to be prepared with
strategies for conflict management and resolution. Damage can be done if
participatory methods "are treated uncritically as one-off cheap option, facilitated by inexperienced (action) researchers mainly as a tool for mobilization without a clear strategy for negotiating conflicting interests" (Mayoux
1997).

Listening to women

There are always voices that are not easily heard. Among the most important is that of women. A great deal of gender research has been done in
the last thirty years, and it is now understood that the roles and contributions of men and women in the life of a community are different. It is commonly agreed that, in addition to doing the reproductive work on behalf of
the family and the community, women often carry out a disproportionate
share of the productive work as well and thus are critically involved in areas
that are key to development change. Encouraging change only through
men leaves enormous areas of community life untouched.

Women not only have information that needs to be part of the development process, but research shows that a lot of positive social change is cor-
related with the education and involvement of women. When women become literate, fertility rates and infant mortality rates decline and girls marry
later. Microfinance institutions are widely known to favor women for loans
over men. Women are vital providers of health care and are critical to the
education of children, especially girl children. If women are not involved
and engaged, any development effort is limited.

Because many cultures insist that women be silent, especially in front of
outsiders, their voice is hard to hear. Deliberate and creative efforts need to
be made so that their views and their stories are allowed to be heard. This is
why Anderson and Woodrow encourage the capabilities and vulnerabilities
analysis being done separately for men and women. Participatory tools of

both PLA and AI processes must be adapted to ensure that the voice of women can emerge (Williams, Seed, and Mwau 1994, 250). Often women have knowledge that will not surface any other way.

The current challenge in gender and development is how to go beyond the important objective of empowering women and also find ways to encourage men to change their views and practices with regard to women in their home and community. Simply haranguing or pressuring men about gender equality is not enough. After all, men learned their social roles in the same way women learned theirs—simply by growing up in a particular culture, time, and place. Changing the view of one and not the other makes little sense.

As a result of gender and development research done in the last ten years, we have learned that men often have had their own experiences with marginalization and disempowerment, usually in relationships with those outside the household, that are similar to the disempowering experiences of women (Chant and Gutmann 2002, 271). The current discussions on gender and development are focused on how to help women and men understand their current power relationships, both as the one having power and the one who feels disempowered, and then begin to build a new framework for life and living that begins to overcome oppression and marginalization within gendered relationships. The bottom line is that women and men have to learn their way into a new view of gender together. Sadly, this is a process of culture change, and such processes take a long time—as evidenced by gender change in the West. What is even less clear is how outside groups, such as a development agency, can help this kind of culture change happen.

Listening to children

If women do not always have a voice, children are usually only images of suffering and pain or simply kept out of sight. Although much rhetoric has been invested in stating our concern for children and their well-being, our actions tell another story. "We deem children highly in emotional terms, but deem them 'useless' in any formal sense, excluding their contributions from measurements of work and production, and making them invisible in statistics, debate and policymaking" (Edwards 1996, 814).

Children tend to be seen as passive recipients of development aid. They are portrayed as sad, hungry, and desperately in need of assistance. This image dominates development planning and evaluation process as well. The result is that children are fed and educated but not taken seriously. Chambers has wondered what development entry point could be "more powerful in the long term than changing the way we treat children." He finds it odd that parents' treatment of children is not a "matter of massive global public concern, analysis, critical learning and sharing" (1997, 233). We should extend Chambers's concern to the way relief and development organizations sometimes treat children.

Why should children and their role be more important to us? First, as Michael Edwards, formerly of Save the Children UK points out, children are the future of the community. Childhood is where strength, stamina, health, and brain power are developed and when values are formed. In a sense, any better future begins with better children. Malnourished and poorly educated children are hardly a good harbinger of a better future (Edwards 1996, 820). Second, children and youth are important since there are so many of them in the developing world, making up as much as 40 percent of the population in the Third World.

Yet Ravi Jayakaran reports that in very poor communities adults, even mothers, often lose sight of the well-being of their children when times are hard (Jayakaran 2003). Responding to a severe crisis, in which it is certain that some will die, the focus shifts to saving adults. The future, and hence the children, are sacrificed in order for adults to survive the present circumstances. This leads Jayakaran to note that when the community shifts its attention to the well-being of the children, this is a sign of positive transformation. The community is healthy enough to invest in its children.

We need, however, to take our concern for children one step further. We need a change in thinking that allows us to see children as potential agents of transformation. Just as women in families are in a position to influence the other family members, so too are children. In a personal communication in 1994 Nora Avarientos, a development practitioner in the Philippines, reported that "children can provide the message of hope in a poor community."

In a number of World Vision projects around the world, children have formed committees on issues that are important to them. Some help with the education of younger children through tutoring. Others work on children's rights, especially the right to be free from violence. Children suffering from family violence come to the children's committee for help. In a barrio in Barranquilla, Colombia, children painted a series of "posters" on the mud wall on the side of the road leading into the village, each illustrating one of the rights of the child. This was their way of educating their parents. In the Philippines, children's groups have organized to work against drinking and other addictions. Children sometimes say things adults cannot. In one case in the Philippines, a group of children stood up at a public meeting and told the local politicians, the honored guests of the meeting, that they needed to stop being corrupt.

Sarone Ole Sena, a friend and colleague of World Vision Tanzania, includes children in AI exercises (Booy and Sena 1999). He helps them articulate their dreams as they begin to go to school for the first time. He insists that children see themselves as part of the community's dream. He has found that children's dreams for a community are often bigger, more stretching. In a remote area of Tanzania the children in a village articulated a dream for 2020 in which every child was able to go to school; no children died because of diarrhea, measles, or the flu; men, women, and children worked together for the good of the community; and the community had healthy children for the next generation.

Getting the pace right

The problem with plans and logical frameworks is that every activity is accompanied by a date. This is a useful discipline, but it can lead to anti-developmental activity. Deadlines sometimes become more important than the event associated with the date. This is where an African view of time is more helpful than the Western view. In Africa, the time is marked when something is finished; being "on time" is less important. Things are done when they are done. A view of time that measures the completion of an event rather than chronological time is better suited to sustainable development processes. Why?

We need to begin by asking whose development needs measuring. Too often projects are run on the time table of the development agency or the donor who provides the development funding. This makes no sense. It is the community that is on the transformational journey, and only God knows when the critical events will take place. This becomes even clearer when we remind ourselves what the goals of development are. If development performance is measured by when the wells are dug and when kids graduate from school, a Western chronology can be helpful. If the goals of development are the discovery of true identity and vocation, then these things are discovered when they are discovered. Chronology and deadlines are not very helpful when it comes to process or the software side of development. For this reason many development agencies are seeking longer and longer time frames for their programming, although public funding sources are proving quite unhelpful in this regard.

There is a deeper reason for taking great care in getting the pace right. Koyama reminds us that straightness is not a natural thing (1979, 30). Nature and social systems are made up of curves, of inefficiencies, of surprises. Only technology is straight and efficient. When Koyama says that "technological life makes us straight-minded," he is saying that technology can create a conflict between efficiency and meaning.

> The technologist has an inner drive to control and systematize. This is the point at which technology and the holy conflict. That which is controlled cannot be holy. The holy, in its dignity, rejects being controlled and scheduled. . . . How can we enjoy the fruits of technology yet retain the meaningful experience with the holy? (Koyama 1985, 135)

Empowering processes also resist the technological. They cannot be controlled or scheduled. Human development is not a straight line. As agents of transformation we must be willing to lay down our worship of the well-planned and the timely in favor of what is really important—the discoveries and insights that will come when they will come. Koyama concludes:

> Community building cannot be achieved by such efficient confrontation. It must be guided by the patient spirituality which is ready to accept inefficiency as it deals with a human being not as a "target." This sense of living with inefficiency opposes the spirit of imperialism. (1985, 250)

Letting the spiritual come through

There is a tendency for development practitioners to tune out the spiritual. Even those deeply committed to letting the poor speak for themselves tend to edit the spiritual out of the conversation by dismissing it as superstition or ignorance or by recomposing it as psychology. As a result we end up with large amounts of information about the material world and little or none about the spiritual realities of people's lives. Our information is about family size, incidence of disease, agricultural productivity, and water contamination. This material analysis tends to lead to material solutions: family planning, immunization, introduction of improved seeds, and bore holes.

Our lack of knowledge about values, religious practices, spiritual oppression, and the like limits our development response as Christians. If we truly understand the world as a seamless spiritual-material reality, then the scope of our development research must include both the fear of demons and the quality of drinking water, the impact both of witchcraft and poor soil.

For example, few PLAs or Logical Frameworks in the literature contain descriptions of the spiritual side of the community's life, even though most third-world communities have a deeply religious worldview and describe the life of their communities in spiritual and religious terms. How many causal diagrams refer to spirits, demons, curses, ancestors, and gods? How many transect-walk diagrams show shrines, sacred trees, and places no one will go to at night? The work of Ravi Jayakaran is an exception to this generalization.

Sometimes this information is missing because the community thoughtfully edits it out of its story. The members of the community may have learned that educated outsiders are not interested in or are critical of such information. Everyone knows that Western folk don't believe in this kind of thing. Other times, it is missing because we never ask.

When we allow this side of community life to emerge, we learn some interesting and important things. Ravi Jayakaran has done some very creative work to try and overcome this blind spot. He uses the Ten Seed technique out of the PLA toolkit to create what he calls a Wholistic Worldview Analysis (2007). A tribal group in India identified eight areas in which it would like to see its members' lives improve. The community members were then asked to divide ten seeds among three possible sources of power and control over those eight areas: (1) the tribal group itself; (2) others (meaning outsiders like the government, people from neighboring towns, and NGOs); and (3) gods and spirits. As we can see in Figure 8–19, this tribal group sees itself with limited power. This sense that "we cannot control much" is empirical evidence of its marred identity and forgotten vocation.

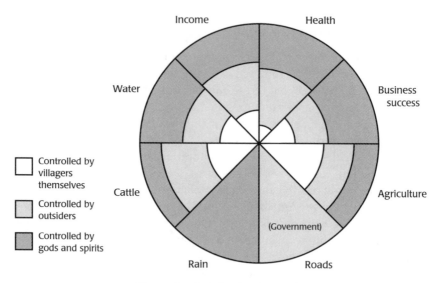

Figure 8–19: Who has control?
(Adapted from Jayakaran 1999)

The community believes that outsiders have considerable power. In the case of improving roads, the government is perceived to have *all* the power; not even the gods can help. This perceived power of outsiders is a window into the community's social, economic, and political systems. Helping the village residents explore, map, and name this outside reality can be helpful to them in recapturing some of this external control for themselves, pushing out the boundary of what they believe they can control. This should remind of Friedmann's understanding of development as extending the boundaries of social power.

The part of the conversation that tends to go unsaid by the community or is usually ignored by the development promoter is the amount of control the tribal group ascribes to the unseen world of the gods and spirits. Yet, according to the villages, the gods and spirits have significant levels of control in seven of the eight areas of their life in which they would like to see improvement.

This perceived power of the gods, spirits, and ancestors explains why technical development interventions are sometimes rejected; the community cannot afford to risk offending what or who they perceive to be the true power behind what is to us simply a material reality. What we see as a straightforward material intervention—perhaps a well or improved seeds—is perceived by the villagers as a spiritual challenge to the gods and spirits they believe are responsible for these areas of life. Since the daily life of traditional cultures is devoted to managing the power and control of the unseen spirit world, they are quite sensibly weighing the cost of innovation (see Figure 8–20).

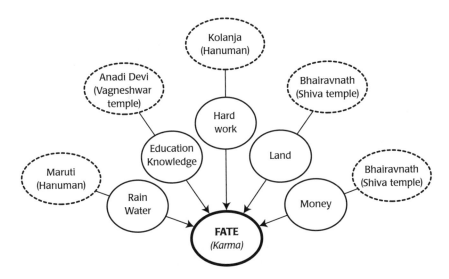

Figure 8–20: What influences fate? Material and spiritual causes.
(Adapted from World Vision India 1995)

In another example, when inhabitants of an Indian village were asked to brainstorm together on the things they would most like to change, they kept coming back to the importance of *karma* or fate. When asked what kinds of things influenced fate, they mentioned water, education, hard work, land, and money. Normally, a PLA exercise would end at this point, and the conversation would shift to helping the community decide how it wanted to improve these areas of material life. Considering the holistic nature of the local worldview, however, another question was asked: What influences these areas of your life? The answers listed the names of local gods and their association with various temples. In the villagers' worldview there are spiritual forces behind the material changes that change one's *karma*. If the development practitioner does not share and seek this view, the PLA exercise too often ends before the full story is told.

Understanding the local view of cause and effect by letting the spiritual come to light in our development learning processes is very important. This is the only way that our understanding of the community's survival strategy (see Chapter 7) is complete. If we tune out the spiritual, we will only be able to describe those parts of the survival strategy that lay "inside the circle" (see Figure 7–3). By editing out the spiritual means we will have ignored a significant part of the community's story, imposing our modern, scientific worldview in its place.

A community's belief that some causes are located in the spiritual realm also influences how it participates in the program. If the development intervention addresses something community members believe is largely controlled by the spirits, then, in their eyes, we are doing spiritual work, even though we outsiders may be oblivious to this, assuming we are working in the concrete, real world of technology and science. This presents the community with a serious problem: Who is more powerful, the development facilitator or the spirit world? Not knowing the answer, community members sensibly step back and watch to see what happens. When we experience high participation in research and planning and then low participation in implementation, this lack of certainty as to who is more powerful may be the explanation.

Letting the spiritual side come through is only the beginning, of course. If we are sensitive enough to let this part of the community's experience and belief surface, we learn important things, but it is far less clear what we should do about what we have learned. Our modern selves tell us that this is superstition, not really real, and that the antidote is a good dose of modern science education. Indeed, education tends to be modernity's answer for every social ill, even when the social problem persists in the face of our education. To make things more complicated, our postmodern selves argue that traditional views must be respected as equally valid ways to believe and should not be challenged. Finally, our religious selves as Christians say that all of this is demonic and needs to be subjected to the transforming power of Christ and the Holy Spirit. Our Christian selves want to go straight to a power encounter. I must confess that I suffer from all the foregoing illnesses and thus have few answers to these painful questions. One of the frontiers in transformational development done by Christians is going to be figuring out how to do responsible transforming development that takes seriously the worldview of people whose worldview is largely religious without (1) validating expressions of the local culture that are anti-life, (2) ignoring the benefits of modern science, or (3) surrendering the tenets and the power of our Christian faith.

Whatever our reservations, we must have the courage and discipline to let the whole story of the people emerge. If the key to development is allowing people to tell their own story and then direct their own process of development, then we have no other choice. The development tools I have described—analysis of capacities and vulnerabilities, PLA, and AI—are not the problem. They do not automatically exclude the spiritual or religious side of life. It is the people who use the tools who are the problem. As good professionals they suffer from a modern bias that takes for granted that the spiritual is not relevant to the material world and hence is not needed when doing development work. This blind spot results in people inadvertently using development learning tools in a way that imposes a Western, materialistic worldview on local people. This is wrong.

HELPFUL RESOURCES

Complex social systems and development

Mosse, David. 2001. "Process-Oriented Approaches to Development Practice and Social Research." In *Development as Process: Concepts and Methods for Working with Complexity*, ed. D. Mosse, John Farrington, and Alan Rew. New Delhi: India Research Press.

Ramalingam, Ben, Harry Jones, Reba Toussaint, and John Young. 2008. "Exploring the Science of Complexity: Ideas and Implications for Development and Humanitarian Efforts." *Working Paper* no. 285. London: Overseas Development Institute.

Participatory Learning and Action

Brock, Karen, and Jethro Pettit. 2007. *Springs of Participation: Creating and Evolving Methods for Participatory Development*. Rugby, UK: Practical Action.

Center for International Development and Environment of the World Resources Institute. 1990. *Participatory Rural Appraisal Handbook: Conducting PRAs in Kenya*. Prepared jointly with the National Environment Secretariat of the Government of Kenya, Egerton University, and Clark University (February).

Jayakaran, Ravi. 2008. "New Participatory Tools for Measuring Attitude, Behavior, Perception, and Change." In *Evaluation South Asia*, ed. M. Sankar and B. Williams. Kathmandu, Nepal: UNICEF South Asia.

———. 2007. "Wholistic Worldview Analysis: Understanding Community Realities." *PLA Notes* 56, no. 1:41–48. Available on the planotes.org website.

————. 2003. *Participatory Poverty Alleviation and Development: A Comprehensive Manual for Development Professionals*. Hong Kong: World Vision China.

Kumar, Somesh. 2002. *Methods for Community Participation: A Complete Guide for Practitioners*. London: ITDG.

Pretty, Jules N. 1995. *A Trainer's Guide for Participatory Learning and Action*. London: International Institute for Environment and Development

PLA Notes. Electronic newsletter available on the planotes.org website.

White, Sarah, and Jethro Pettit. 2007. "Participatory Approaches and Measurement of Well-Being." In *Human Well-being: Concept and Measurement*, ed. M. McGillivray. New York: Palgrave and United Nations University.

Appreciative Inquiry

Elliot, Charles. 1999. *Locating the Energy for Change: An Introduction to Appreciative Inquiry*. Winnipeg, Canada: International Institute for Sustainable Development.

Green, Mike, John O'Brien, Henry Moore, and Dan Duncan. 2006. *When People Care Enough to Act: ABCD in Action*. Toronto: Inclusion Press.

Kretzmann, John P., and John L. McKnight. 1993. *Building Communities from the Inside Out: A Path toward Finding and Mobilizing a Community's Assets*. Evanston, IL: The Asset-Based Community Development Institute.

Positive Deviance

Pascale, Richard T., Jerry Sternin, and Monique Sternin. 2010. *The Power of Positive Deviance: How Improbable Innovators Solve the World's Toughest Problems*. Boston: Harvard Business. The final section contains a basic field guide to the use of the Positive Deviance approach.

Positive Deviance Initiative. http://www.positivedeviance.org.

Singhal, Arvind, and Lucia Dura. 2009. *Protecting Children from Exploitation and Trafficking: Using the Positive Deviance Approach in Uganda and Indonesia*. El Paso: University of Texas.

Gender and development

Guijt, Irene, and Meera Kaul Shah, eds. 1998. *The Myth of Community: Gender Issues in Participatory Development*. London: Intermediate Technology Publications.

Momsen, Janet. 2009. *Gender and Development*. 2d ed. New York: Routledge.

Williams, Suzanne, Janet Seed, and Adelina Mwau. 1994. *Oxfam Gender Training Manual*. Oxford, UK: Oxfam.

Human capabilities movement

Human Development and Capability Association (HDCA). http:// www.capabilityapproach.com/index.php. HDCA also has an electronic newsletter.

Narayan-Parker, Deepa, ed. 2005. *Measuring Empowerment: Cross-disciplinary Perspectives*. Washington DC: World Bank.

White, Sarah. 2009. "Bringing Well-being into Development Practice." WeD Working Paper 09/05. Bath, UK: University of Bath.

Advocacy, citizenship, and good governance

"The ARVIN Framework: A Way to Assess the Enabling Environment for Civil Engagagement." Available on the the Participation and Civic Engagement website of the World Bank.

Gaventa, John, and Anne Marie Goetz. 2001. "Bringing Citizen Voice and Client Focus into Service Delivery." IDS Working Paper no. 138. Brighton: Institute of Development Studies.

Ravindra, Adikeshavalu. 2004. "An Assessment of the Impact of Bangalore Citizen Report Cards on the Performance of Public Agencies." ECD Working Paper Series no. 12. Washington DC: World Bank Operations Evaluation Department.

Thindwa, Jeff, James Edgerton, and Riener Forster. 2005. "Community Based Performance Monitoring (CBPM): Empowering and Giving Voice to Local Communities." Paper read at International Conference on Engaging Communities, August 14–17, Brisbane, Australia.

VeneKlasen, Lisa, Valerie Miller, Debbie Budlender, and Cindy Clark. 2007. *A New Weave of Power, People, and Politics: The Action Guide for Advocacy and Citizen Participation*. Bourton-on-Dunsmore, Warwickshire, UK: Practical Action.

9

Learning toward transformation

If change in complex social systems is unpredictable and beyond management by objectives, then keeping track of what is actually happening becomes very important. Unpredictability can be managed if one gets used to making frequent course adjustments. Thus monitoring, evaluating, and reflecting become more critical than the actual development plan itself. This chapter explores monitoring, evaluating, and reflecting as key tools for learning our way to a better future.

MONITORING, EVALUATING, AND REFLECTING

Learning our way to a better future

Before we come to the important subject of monitoring, evaluating, and reflecting, we need to revisit the unusual nature of working with social systems of poor communities that was introduced in the last chapter. As explained earlier, social systems do not lend themselves to the same kind of linear planning or mechanical metaphors that we use to build a house or dig a well. So how do things unfold when we attempt to work in these kinds of systems? Figure 9–1 illustrates the difference between mechanical and social systems in terms of trying to get to some form of better future.

First, an important clarification. Moving toward a better future in a dynamic and adaptive social system made up of opinionated human actors does not mean that we do not know where we are trying to go. A clear articulation of the better future we seek is critical. It is the process for getting there that is problematic.

This chapter was written with Dr. Frank C. Cookingham, chief evaluation officer, World Vision International.

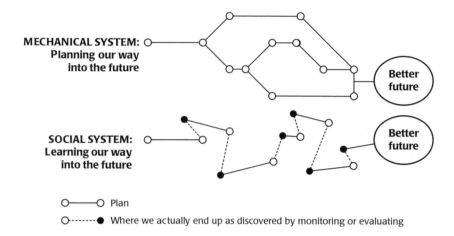

Figure 9–1: Planning for mechanical *vs.* complex social systems.

The adaptation that is required when working to change social systems is to limit action planning to small steps followed by regular monitoring and reflecting. It is only frequent monitoring of the program *and* its context that allows the community to identify things that are not working or that it did not expect to happen or change. Once the community is clear on where it actually is after a period of action, it is empowered to reorient itself to the better future it seeks and then plan a new modest step in that direction. The track to the better future is irregular, uneven, and unpredictable, but with a mindset of continuous assessment and adjustment—social learning—the development planner and the community can move toward the agreed goal. The bottom line is that we have to learn our way toward transformation. A social learning approach—what is or has happened to us and why—and adaptive planning are essential to effectiveness.

With this important qualification in place, we need to clarify the differences among monitoring, evaluating, and reflecting. We then examine a series of critical questions whose answers will inform the practice of these three elements of learning our way toward transformation.

Defining monitoring, evaluating, and reflecting

Monitoring, evaluating, and reflecting are different forms of thinking about the results of a transformational development program. Among development practitioners the value of monitoring has been undersold, the value of evaluating has been oversold, and the value of reflecting has been ignored.

Monitoring is the routine collection of information that shows what has been accomplished (or not accomplished) over some limited period of time.

The community and the holistic practitioner use the information from a monitoring exercise to make adjustments to program plans, budgets, and time lines. If a monitoring report shows cumulative progress, evolution of perceived significant change (see the Most Significant Change technique later in this chapter) and a financial report, the accountability requirements of most donors have been met.

Evaluating program impact as a tool of accountability to donors tends to be oversold. While donors today are enamored with results-based management, it is simply unrealistic to expect that short-term development programs (two to five years) can affect the behavior, attitudes, or circumstances of a community. In most contexts the change envisioned by impact evaluations takes place over decades and sometimes generations. As a result, funding for impact evaluations may be an added value for evaluation consultants, but not so much for programs per se.

One important exception to the idea of minimizing evaluations is the need for a development agency to learn from its experience. This often requires collecting evaluations for a sample of programs and listening to the expectations of donors and even the agency staff. Agencies have made promises. An agency's understanding of the nature and causes of poverty and its response in the form of transformational development constitute a promise to the poor and its donors. Evaluating the degree to which these implied promises are being kept or need to be modified is important. The agency also makes promises to its staff through its statements of mission, vision, values, and transformational development policies and standards. Assessing a sample of programs in light of these commitments is important.

Reflecting is the most important contribution to learning our way toward transformation. Monitoring and evaluating provide information. Reflecting turns information into knowledge and wisdom. Reflecting is a process of stepping back and thinking deeply about what the results from monitoring and evaluating might mean. Reflection enhances the learning potential from a monitoring report or an evaluation. Reflection is a dialogical activity through which a group works to make common discoveries about what is important to it.

Facilitating a reflection event is more than chairing a meeting. Mutual trust and respect among the participants are necessary, which usually means that the participants have had positive interactions together in the past. Such an event is usually best facilitated by someone who has not been involved with the program itself.

The questions for a reflection exercise go beyond the program design and its results. The goal of reflecting is to invite the community to explore higher-level questions and concerns that relate to its theory of poverty and development. What evidence do we see of restoration of the marred image of the poor? Are there examples of the community beginning to deal with the god complexes and webs of lies that ensnare poor and non-poor alike?

Are there stories of exposing deceptions by the principalities and powers? How might inadequacies in worldview and cultural values be changing?

In addition, this is a time for theological reflection and the spiritual disciplines. What is God saying to us? What has happened that is pleasing to God? Not pleasing? What are we learning about God? What have we learned about who God has created us to be and what we are to do? Where is God leading us in the future?

More than monitoring or evaluating, reflecting is itself transformational. People are treated as if they are competent, smart, and able to make sense out of their lives, thus enhancing dignity and contributing to restoring identity and vocation.

What is monitoring and evaluation for?

The traditional approach to monitoring and evaluation—based on a linear view of development change—is to determine if what was planned actually took place. Did inputs become the outputs that were planned? Did the outputs create the outcomes that were planned? Was it done within budget and on time? The purpose is to locate problems so they can be solved or to assess progress so another phase can be planned. This is all good and necessary. It is hard to talk about how to continue the journey to where we want to go if we do not know where we are.

But we are learning that there are other ways to enrich the process of monitoring and evaluation. I've already pointed to the possibility of creating a process of social learning and adaptive planning. In addition, practitioners of AI suggest that inclusion of an appreciative frame may also reveal useful information. What worked and why? What created energy and enthusiasm among the people? An appreciative angle on evaluation seeks expressions of life creation, growth, and change in order to enhance them by allocating money, time, and energy to furthering positive change. The evaluative frame from an appreciative perspective calls for shifting resources to what is working and taking them away from what is not.

Feeding the best and starving the rest can be done another way. In *The White Man's Burden* William Easterly insists on moving monitoring and evaluation to the center of the development stage. As I pointed out in Chapter 2, Easterly is not convinced that we actually know what makes for a successful development effort. He calls for shifting the strategic question from How do we get more development aid and projects? to What is the best use of development aid? This question shifts the focus from churning out more and more projects and insists on a central role for evaluation as the tool for deciding what is actually working and what is not (2006, 374–76). Easterly then calls our attention to the work of Esther Duflo of the MIT Poverty Action Lab, who is encouraging development programmers not to bet on a single solution to any one development problem (Easterly 2008; Duflo and Kremer 2008, 93; Banerjee and Duflo 2011).

For example, if the poor in a valley with a number of villages decided that they wanted to provide primary schools for their children as a way of increasing primary-school graduation rates, the traditional development plan would figure out a common way to do this for all villages. As an alternative, Duflo suggests trying at least two different approaches in parallel (see Figure 9–2) and then using evaluation as the key to learning one's way to effectiveness.

Village 1

Outcome: Increased primary school graduation

Outputs ⟹ Pay teachers for showing up
Repair school
Homes for teachers
Government provides books

⟹**Inputs**   money, materials, training

Village 2

Outcome: Increased primary school graduation

Outputs ⟹ Community-based monitoring of teachers
Repair school
Homes for teachers
Government provides books

⟹**Inputs**   money, materials, training

Figure 9–2: Comparing two approaches for success.

In this example we have the same outcome (primary school graduation), the same inputs, but a variation in method when it comes to creating outputs. One set of villages will pay their teachers to ensure they show up. The second set of villages will not pay their teachers to show up but instead will employ a CBPM approach to ensure the presence of teachers in the classroom. Which approach is best? The one that leads to the highest percentage of primary-school graduates.

Thus the answer to the question What is monitoring and evaluation for? is not ultimately about program efficiency as much as it is about effectiveness, which includes both the hoped for and the unanticipated. Evaluation that serves the poor is about learning our way into the future. Quality reports to donors on inputs, outputs, and outcomes are necessary and are part of being accountable as good stewards. But from a transformational perspective, a stance of learning and discovery is more important to the poor.

Whom is monitoring and evaluation for?

Too often monitoring and evaluation are done for the donor. While accountability to donors is important, the kind of evaluation donors seek may not be same as that which would help the community and its learning process. Sometimes the evaluation is for the development agency, since it desires, quite correctly, to be professional, and professionals test the impact and effectiveness of their work. But the most important audiences for continuous learning must be the communities. It is their development; they need to develop their capacity to assess, learn, and adjust. Every development activity, from the simple to the complex, is an opportunity for the communities to learn.

A lot of work has been done to develop a truly participatory approach to evaluation. But first, it is useful to contrast conventional evaluation and participatory evaluation, as shown in figure 9–3 (Narayan 1993). This "reversal" should remind us of Chambers and his call to "turn over the stick." More on this shortly.

	Conventional evaluation	Participatory evaluation
Who?	External experts	Community members, facilitator
What?	Predetermined indicators, often costs and outputs	Community-identified indicators, which may include process indicators
How?	Focus on objectivity, Distancing evaluator from people, Uniform and often complex procedures, Delayed report, not always accessible to people	Self-evaluation, Simple methods, Open-ended, Immediate sharing of results
When?	Usually at end of project	Frequently monitoring and evaluation blurred, Lots of small learning events
Why?	Accountability to donors	Empowerment enabling local people to learn, adapt, and control

Figure 9–3: Comparing conventional and
participatory evaluation.
(Narayan 1993)

What changed?

This seems a simple question. If development programming were rational and linear, it would be. Did the program achieve the outcomes and purpose for which it was designed? But since we know that this is not the case, answering questions about impact and change is more complex. We have to speak to the change we hoped for as well as the changes we did not anticipate. We have to be clear about the changes that are attributable to our program alone and which are not.

To make things even more complex, our understanding of the fundamental nature and causes of poverty requires that we are concerned about both how people have changed and how their relationships have changed. If our understanding of the best human future is one that points to the kingdom of God, then we are interested in the change in terms of kingdom values as well.

Long-term impact

For too long development practitioners measured the degree to which inputs and activity resulted in planned outputs and assumed this was evaluation. How many wells were dug? How many farmers were trained? How much did the incidence of water-borne diseases decrease? While these determinations are important, they are not sufficient. There are too many programs with a portfolio of successful outputs that would nonetheless be judged as less than successful because of failure to achieve higher-level program purpose, goals, impact, or sustainability.

Many are now calling for the development NGO community to take a harder look at the long-term impact of what it does. There are too many assumptions between inputs and impact to allow us to take for granted that good things will happen if we get the initial conditions right and proceed according to plan. Figure 9–4, provides an example of the linkage of inputs, intermediate outcomes, and the lasting outcomes that need to be assessed. While this is important, the weakness is that the focus is on the program and its impact alone. What about the unintended consequences? How do we take into account the dynamical, unpredictable nature of the work we are trying to do?

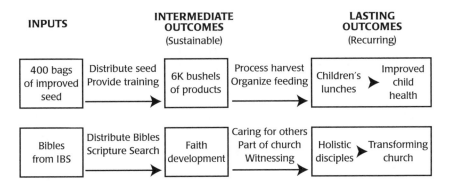

Figure 9–4: Changing the focus of evaluation to lasting outcomes.
(Shared by Frank Cookingham)

There are three recent innovations that widen the evaluative view for assessing impact and that also take into account the non-predictive nature of trying to do development in the dynamic, adaptive social systems of poor communities. These innovations are called Participatory Impact Evaluations, Outcome Mapping, and the Most Significant Change technique.

Participatory Impact Evaluations enlarge the focus of the program—its plans, activities, and outcomes—to include a concern for impact on the people who experience the program (Catley et al. 2007). The focus is now on people and not just the program. This shift has three important consequences. First, it opens up the evaluation to the unexpected both inside and outside the community. Second, by using participatory methodologies, the evaluation itself becomes transformative and empowering. Third, concerns for qualitative issues like changes in a person's sense of dignity, social status, just and peaceful relationships, and general well-being now find a natural home at the center of the investigation of impact.

Recent work by the International Development Research Centre in Canada extended the impact conversation with an innovation called Outcome Mapping. Outcomes are defined as "changes in behavior, relationships, activities and actions *of people* with whom a program works directly" (Earl, Carden, and Smutylo 2001, 1). Like the Participative Impact Evaluation, the evaluative focus is shifted from what the program did to how the people changed, but Outcome Mapping moves beyond changed values and perceptions to focus especially on how people changed their behavior and actions. An increase in their sense of well-being or dignity is very good indeed, but the deeper question is how this changes how they behave or act in life.

By shifting its focus away from the program alone, Outcome Mapping, like Participatory Impact Evaluations, also shifts the evaluative focus to the border between the program and the larger context in which the program takes place. Programs are now treated as socially, politically, and economically embedded, and the evaluative view now includes all the actors and structures within the social, political, and economic context in which the program operates. The concern of Outcome Mapping, in particular, is how the behavior and actions of the people have changed as they operate within or in response to these wider systems. Is there evidence that the people are more empowered as actors? Has human agency and freedom increased?

One result of this shift in focus is that it is less possible to determine if positive change can be causally related to the program activities, something donors are keen to know. The wider-than-the-program and non-causal perspective is a necessary adjustment to the reality that development programs work within adaptive and hence unpredictable social systems, but it is harder to claim that the program alone changed the world.

Another recent innovation shifts the monitoring and evaluation focus and process completely to the people, placing the program plan firmly in the background. The Most Significant Change (MSC) technique is a form of participatory monitoring and evaluation that focuses on collecting stories as opposed to data or information per se (Davies and Dart 2005). The evaluative question is simple: Over the last *(month, quarter, year, etc.),* what do you think was the most significant change in *(name some domain of change such as health, relationships, etc.)*? Everyone provides an answer by telling the story of the change he or she thinks was most important. Then the community discusses the stories of significant change and answers the question, What is the most significant change of all?

The participants are the people, the information comes in the form of their stories, and their communal view is the only one that counts. This simple, open-ended question helps identify unexpected changes and makes clear the values the community uses to assess change. The MSC technique does not require any special professional skills and can be managed locally. While this kind of tool is unnecessary for simple technical programs for which quantitative data is sufficient, such as an immunization campaign, it is ideal for complex programs with diverse and emergent outcomes (Davies and Dart 2005, 12).

Recovering identity and vocation

As we explored the nature of poverty, we concluded that at the most fundamental level the poor suffer from a marred sense of identity and vocation and therefore the development process and the resulting program need to be done in ways that enable God to help the poor recover their true identity and discover their true vocation. Our questions for relection must include the following: Has their marred identity shown signs of liberating recovery? How has their view of themselves changed? Do they feel that God and the world around them view and treat them more positively? Have they begun to discover the gifts that God has placed in their culture and in them as people? Are they beginning to act like stewards who have something to contribute? Are they seeking ways to make that contribution? Do the poor see themselves increasingly as actors and agents of their own development?

For the non-poor the issue is also identity and vocation, but the questions are different. Have the non-poor begun to act like people who care and share? Are they less willing to play god in the lives of the poor? Are they becoming aware of the real identity of the poor as children of God? Are they recognizing that the poor have been given gifts to use for their own development and to contribute to the development of their community? Do the non-poor see increasing the human dignity and agency of the poor as a central concern of development?

The bottom line is simple and needs assessment: Have they all—poor and non-poor—learned better to love God and love their neighbor?

Just and peaceful relationships

Our conversation about the cause of poverty ended with the conclusion that, at the most fundamental level, the cause of poverty is relationships that do not work for human well-being, that do not allow everyone to flourish. Flawed relationships—with self, others, the environment, and God—result in violence, conflict, greed, racism, poverty, oppression, and marginalization. This means that the key element of transformative reflection is to assess these various relationships and how they are changing. Fortunately, the more recent monitoring and evaluation tools we just looked at make this level of assessment easier to do because they have shifted from a single-minded focus on the impact of the project to include a concern for how people have changed.

There is another way to seek information regarding this kind of change. Relationships that don't work are reflected through the distortion of what are normally positive relational values. People may believe in values like loyalty and compassion but in a distorted way that undermines their social good. Examination of relational values and value change can thus be an important indicator of whether the community is moving toward the kingdom of God or not.

The Evangelical Fellowship of India Committee on Relief (EFICOR) created a community-based process that assesses value change in terms of movement from what is today toward values that are more kingdom focused. This can be a useful tool in a Christian context (see Figure 9–5).

Value	Today's distorted version	More kingdom-like version
Loyalty	Only to our family	To all in our community
View of person	Only powerful matter	All men, women, and children matter
Compassion	For those who can help us	For those who are in need
Repentance	Only if caught	Personal responsibility for wrong
Forgiveness	Only to our equals	To all who injure us
Sharing	Only with our family	With all who are in need
Equality	For those who own land	For all men and women
Justice	Only for the powerful	For all, even the weakest
Peacemaking	Within the family	Within the community and world

Figure 9–5: Values moving toward the kingdom.

Ravi Jayakaran has developed a Ten Seeds exercise that allows a community to explore the extent of value change in terms of relationships. First, the community identifies the relational values to which it aspires. Then the community is allowed to develop and use its own criteria for assessing these values. Finally, the community decides how to allocate ten seeds to each of the areas of hoped-for relational change. Seeds are put inside the large overlapping circle if the community decides that the particular desired change is becoming visible in community life. The number of seeds represents the community's estimate of the percentage of the community population that exhibits this change (see Figure 9–6).

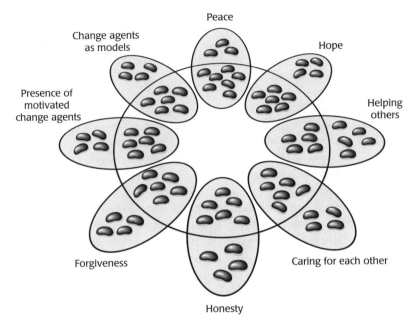

Figure 9–6: Estimating change in relationships.
(Adapted from Jayakaran 2007, 58)

We have also said that the cause of poverty is fundamentally spiritual. Therefore, transformative reflection must allow the community to assess the way its belief systems are changing. Are there elements of its worldview that are against life or that diminish life being changed? Has it encountered the true author of its story? Is there a new, transformative story at work in the community? Is fear of the spirit world diminishing? Are its social and religious practices doing more to release and empower people for growth and change? Are people better able to unmask the deceptions that diminish or reduce life? I will say more on the issue of worldview change in the next chapter.

Social institutions

If the god complexes of the non-poor are expressed through systems and structures by those who inhabit the seats of power, then another test of sustainable change must be the degree to which the social systems and structures are changing. The process of reflection must ask the question: Do systems and structures point outside themselves or have they turned inward, concerned only with serving themselves? Have they begun to support and enhance life? Do they show evidence of turning aside from the lure of what Wink calls "delusional assumptions?" Is there evidence that the non-poor are allowing the poor to become actors and to define their own history and future? Is there evidence of repentance and a willingness to cease playing god in the lives of others?

Who changed?

In addition to what has changed, we need to pay attention to who has changed and in what way. This has two dimensions. The first has to do with the people and their view of who they truly are and what they believe their purpose is as human beings. This is the identity and vocation issue. I will say more on this in the next chapter.

The second dimension has to do with which groups within the community have changed and how. General evaluations describe the changes in the community as a whole. This often means change in terms of those who have a voice, usually the men and the non-poor. We need to expand our evaluative process so that we hear from other actors, such as women and children. Furthermore, the kinds of questions we ask will change depending on which group we are listening to.

For the non-poor occupying structures of power, the set of reflection questions has to do with values and use of gifts. Who do they believe is the source of their wealth and position? What does it mean to be a productive steward of gifts and position? To whom does the social, economic, and political power belong, and what is it for? How are they using their resources of money, position, and privilege?

If there is integrity in a transformative relationship, all parties must experience transformation. This means that we must find ways to assess how the development practitioner and the development agency are changing. What have we learned? What have we failed to learn that the community wishes we would learn?

We need to give the people the responsibility for evaluating our performance as well. Did we do what we said we would do? Did we do it in ways that empowered or that created dependency? Imagine a meeting where we told the community members what we thought we were doing to be helpful to them and then were willing to let them tell us how well we had done. What would happen if we spelled out our understanding of transformation, our vision of a better future, our version of kingdom values, and let the community tell us how well we lived up to all this and to what degree its members shared our vision and values?

This concern for the development agency—its views and biases—and how they are changing reflects Korten's assertion that it is important for development agencies to make their views on poverty and development explicit (1990). The poor have a right to know what is driving and shaping the way practitioners work with them. I suspect a lot of learning would take place.

What do we observe and measure?

What is observed and measured is determined by what the community has set out to do. It begins with the vision of the better future and the values to which the community aspires. The discussion thus far focuses on this people-centered, community-based evaluative focus. The centrality of the community must never be set aside, but it need not be the only evaluative perspective we investigate.

Agencies can use their framework for understanding poverty and development as a framework for program assessment as well. For example, Jayakumar Christian, using his framework for understanding poverty as a disempowering system (Figure 4–6), developed a holistic evaluation framework in the late 1990s for use in the programs in North India that he was facilitating (see Figure 9–7).

Development agencies often create organizational impact measures based on their mission, vision, and values. They apply these to all of their programming as a rough gauge of the overall effectiveness of their work. As an agency focused on the well-being of children in the context of a developmental approach, Christian Children's Fund developed the following evaluative framework in the 1990s:

- Immunization coverage
- Malnutrition, with emphasis on moderate and severe
- Knowledge of oral rehydration therapy for management of diarrhea
- Acute respiratory illness management
- Access to safe water
- Safe sanitation practice
- Literacy, with an emphasis on female literacy
- Formal and non-formal education enrollment, with emphasis on pre-primary and primary education (CCF 1996)

In the same vein of attempting to match the aspirations of the community and the agency, World Vision International has developed a set of transformational development indicators to apply to its programs worldwide. The purpose of these indicators is to help the community assess the trajectory of its change by measuring what matters most: change in the quality of life. Said another way, the impact of the program can be assessed in terms of what has changed—as a direct result of the program or as a result of something else altogether—in the overall quality of community life (see Figure 9–8).

Does the transformational development program show a conscious attempt to ...

Heal the marred image of the poor?
- Affirm consistently that the poor are made in the image of God?
- Clarify the identity of the poor as God's children with gifts and skills?
- Enable the poor to see God in their history?
- Initiate hope-based action for change?
- Enable the poor to deal with structures, systems, values, and interiorities?

Deal with the god complexes that ensnare poor and non-poor alike?
- Reverse the god complexes that keep the poor in their poverty?
- Transform power relationships?
- Prophetically proclaim the truth that power is God's?
- Reorder the relationship between truth and power (power does not equal truth)?

Counteract the deception by principalities and powers?
- Establish the rule of God; announce that Jesus is Lord?
- Declare the deceptions of the principalities and powers?
- Unmask the ultimate powerlessness of the principalities and powers in the face of God's rule?

Change inadequacies in worldview?
- Analyze the worldview of the poor and non-poor?
- Challenge the various aspects of reality that perpetuate poverty?
- Enable the poor to imagine a different future?
- Create hope in the midst of despair?
- Redefine power?
- Teach from the word; link the word to the context; allow the word to critique worldview?

Restore just and peaceful relationships?
- Proclaim the truth within poverty relationships?
- Establish the truth in public life?
- Build covenant communities?
- Develop win-win relationships?
- Promote reconciliation; heal broken relationships?

Use Christian development practices?
- Be highly professional?
- Use prayer and fasting as tools of social action?
- Use the gifts of the Spirit as tools for development action?
- Enable staff to wear the full armor of God?

Figure 9–7: One approach to holistic evaluation.
(Adapted from Christian 1998b)

Well-being of boys, girls and their families in the community

Nutrition	Percent of boys and percent of girls, aged 6-59 months, *stunted*.
Water	Percent of households who have year round access to an improved water source.
Education	Percent of boys and percent of girls who are *enrolled* in or have *completed* the first six years of formal education.
Diarrhea management	Percent of children 0–59 months with *diarrhea* in the past two weeks, whose disease was *acceptably managed*.
Immunization	Percent of children aged 12-23 months *fully immunized*.
Poorest households	Percent of *poorest households*.
Household resilience	Percent of household adopting *coping strategies to mitigate risk* of external shocks and/or environmental stress factors within the past year.

Transformed relationships

Caring for others	Men, women, boys and girls perceive that they care for others and others care for them in their community regarding use of community resources, gender relations, valuing and protection of children, well-being of vulnerable persons and conflict prevention/resolutions.
Emergence of hope	Men, women, boys and girls perceive and demonstrate hope in their future with regard to perceptions of the past and present, attitude towards the future, self-esteem and spirituality.
Christian impact	Christian capacity and intentionality of program teams.

Empowered and interdependent communities

Community participation	Men, women, boys and girls perceive they actively participate in all aspects of their development, with particular focus on program planning, implementation, monitoring and evaluation.
Social sustainability	The capacity within local community/organizations to sustain the long-term viability and impact of development processes.
Citizenship/ governance	Ability to act out citizenship roles and work for effective governance.

Figure 9–8: Transformational Development Indicators.
(Adapted from World Vision International 2003)

WILL IT LAST?

I have already addressed the four dimensions of sustainability in Chapter 5: physical, mental, social, and spiritual. Continuous development learning must assess the issue of sustainability on all four fronts from time to time. Too often evidence of physical sustainability is taken as reassurance that everything is on track. This is naive. We need to evaluate the other three as well.

Mental sustainability

In the area of mental sustainability we need to know whether people are changing their view of themselves, of their worth, of their ability to make change permanent. What are the people learning about themselves? How have their views of themselves and their future changed? What changes can be seen in their understanding of who they are, where they have come from, and what they are here for? How has their worldview changed? What or whom do they fear? To whom do they pray? Has the way they explain cause and effect changed? To what or to whom do they attribute success? Is there any evidence that they are recomposing their story?

Social sustainability

In the area of social sustainability we must find ways to test the emergence of a socially sustainable environment, including transformed power relationships, effective civil society participation, strengthened local institutions, effective citizenship, and the like. Tools like ARVIN, CBPM, and Outcome Mapping help explore these kinds of changes.

Spiritual sustainability

Finally, the spiritual side of sustainability is often overlooked or reduced to a narrow interest in whether people are coming to faith or not. While this is a valid concern, there is danger here. Only the Holy Spirit has the power to call people to repent and turn to a relationship with Jesus Christ and thus become part of the church. Any human efforts, especially development programs, cannot cause conversion and thus should not be evaluated on this basis. But if the programming is done by Christians in a Christian way, there are some things that may change that can be measured for which the holistic practitioners can assume some degree of responsibility.

For example, we can listen to the people we serve concerning how their experience with us and our development program has had an impact in terms of how they understand and/or feel about the gospel (Jayakaran 2007). One way to explore these issues is to use the Ten Seeds technique to allow the community to assess how its attitude toward the gospel or Christ has changed over the course of the program (see Figure 9–9). On the left half of Figure 9–9, for example, the community's self-assessment concerning its change in attitude about Christ is ambiguous. Over the course of the program part of the community is more negative about Christ, while another part of the community is less negative. This result provides an opportunity to dialogue with the community on what this assessment means. How does the community explain this puzzling result? The answers should be valuable in terms of amending the Christian witness strategy.

An assessment of knowledge of the gospel can also be helpful. In the right half of Figure 9–9 the community's knowledge about Christ and the gospel shows signs of improvement. One would hope that a regular contact with Christians who act and think in a Christian manner might have this result. If a community that started with some severe misunderstandings about the gospel was judged not to have experienced any change, some prayer and change in strategy would be in order.

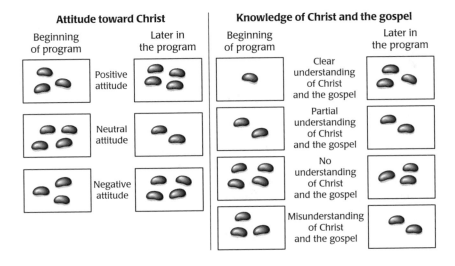

Figure 9–9: Attitude and knowledge about the gospel.
(Results of a Ten Seeds exercise)

Ultimately, the church is of value to the poor only if it tells them the truth that allows them to become less poor. The church has good news when it contributes to relationships being healed and to the emergence of truth, justice, peace, and righteousness. If Christians are not living and sharing the whole gospel for the whole person, then the message of the gospel is truncated and flawed. We need to know whether the Christians in the community are becoming truly holistic disciples: loving God and loving their neighbor, and declaring a gospel of truth, power, and material transformation.

One way to get an indirect indication of whether or not this is the case is to use a Ten Seeds technique to determine the community's attitude toward local Christians or local churches and whether it has changed over the course of the program. Looking at the example in Figure 9–10, the attitude of the community toward both local Christians and local churches has improved. These diagrams provide a focal point for a conversation with the community about why this change has taken place. Understanding what community members think is the reason for this change is an important thing for us to know.

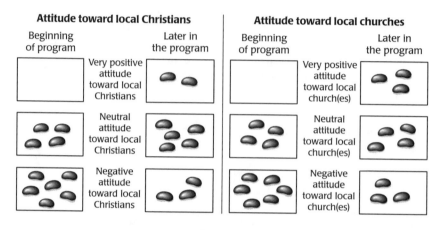

Figure 9–10: Attitude about Christians and the church(es).
(Results of a Ten Seeds exercise)

There are three other areas in which evaluation concerning spiritual sustainability might be helpful: view of God, change in worldview, and who gets the credit for positive change. Focus groups could be used to determine if people are experiencing any change in terms of their experience with God in their daily lives. Are they more or less aware of the activity of God? How has their view of God changed? Has our view of God changed?

Focus groups and the Ten Seeds technique can also be used to explore worldview and value change. Is the local worldview changing in ways that enhance life and turn away from practices that diminish life or disempower people? Is a web of positive relational behavior emerging that will support ongoing, positive change (see Figure 9–6). Is there a values-forming mechanism in the community that is working for the life and the good of the community?

Seeking meaning together

Finally, there is the issue of creating meaning when change takes place. When things change that have never changed before, human beings seek an explanation. Upon completion of an immunization campaign, we must not limit our evaluation to the extent of the immunization coverage. We must also ask how the local people understand immunizations and the cause of their effectiveness. When children no longer get sick and die from the six childhood diseases, what reason is offered? If the answer is either powerful magic or modern science, recalling the worldview issues I raised in Chapter 1, then the community has received effective protection against disease and at the same time created an explanation that is either pre-modern or modern, but not fully Christian. This alerts us to an interesting question. When the community examines the impact of a program, to whom or to what does it attribute the change? To whom does it give credit?

A Ten Seeds exercise can help us understand what the community is thinking (see Figure 9–11). In this case the answer is mixed. Some community members attribute the change to outside interventions—the development worker, the development agency, or the agency's technology. The rest attribute the change to their local gods and spirits. None attributes the change to the God of the Bible. So the program was technically effective and yet fails to connect the God of the Bible with the effectiveness of modern medicine, something that has been a continuing concern for us in this book.

Remember that our goal in this kind of evaluation is seeking understanding so that we may become more effective. Thus we may ask why the diagram appears as it does, but we must not challenge their choices. If it comes out as we'd like, we can praise God. If it does not, as is the case in Figure 9–11, we need to examine our own actions and the implicit and explicit messages we may have been sending that contributed to answers that disappoint us.

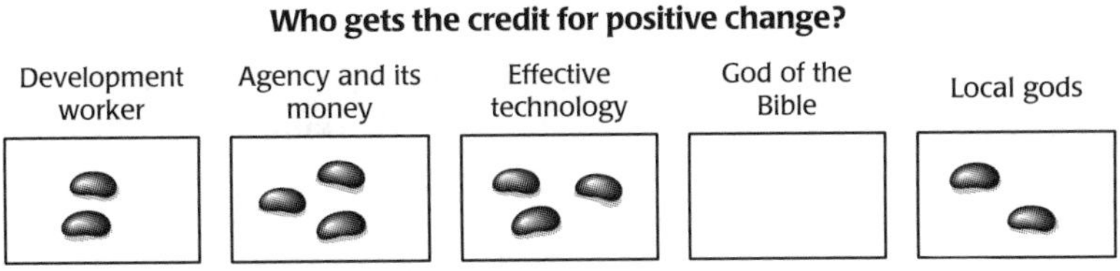

Who gets the credit for positive change?

Figure 9–11: Who gets the credit for positive change?
(Results of a Ten Seeds exercise)

SPIRITUALITY AND PROGRAM ASSESSMENT
(Written with Lisa Myers)

There is one last observation about monitoring, evaluating, and reflecting that needs to be mentioned. There is a temptation, even when monitoring and evaluating spiritual factors like the community's attitude toward the church or the gospel, of which we need to be aware. The temptation is to limit our measurement to those things we can observe and think we have all the information we need to make a judgment. To make this assumption tends to rule God and God's word to us out of the evaluation.

A truly Christian approach to monitoring, evaluating, and reflecting needs to be open and attentive to what God has to say to us. We need to look at what we can see and ask God to help us see the fingerprints of God's work among us and the poor so that credit goes to whom credit is due.

We need to be quiet and listen in the midst of all the information we have gathered to see if God has anything so say, if there is anything in particular to which God might want to call our attention. We need to immerse our work of development and evaluation in a covering of prayer that asks that we may have eyes to see and ears to hear. We need a stance that is open to God leading us to the information and conclusions that God deems to be important. We need to use the Bible, as the living word of God, in our monitoring, evaluating, and reflecting. What might we hear from the word that is relevant to determining what change really matters?

Said another way, monitoring, evaluating, and reflecting compose a spiritual exercise every bit as much as they create a concrete assessment of actions and their consequences. Furthermore, it is a group spiritual exercise, not just a lonely one for the practitioner. Thus, the spirituality of the holistic practitioner and the local Christians needs to be released from its normal captivity to the private and internal and find expression in the work and practice of monitoring, evaluating, and reflecting.

HELPFUL RESOURCES

Advocacy, citizenship, and good governance

Gaventa, John, and Anne Marie Goetz. 2001. "Bringing Citizen Voice and Client Focus into Service Delivery." IDS Working Paper no. 138. Brighton: Institute of Development Studies.

Ravindra, Adikeshavalu. 2004. "An Assessment of the Impact of Bangalore Citizen Report Cards on the Performance of Public Agencies." ECD Working Paper Series no. 12. Washington DC: World Bank Operations Evaluation Department.

Thindwa, Jeff, James Edgerton, and Riener Forster. 2005. "Community-based Performance Monitoring (CBPM): Empowering and Giving Voice to Local Communities." Paper read at the International Conference on Engaging Communities, August 14-17, Brisbane, Australia.

VeneKlasen, Lisa, Valerie Miller, Debbie Budlender, and Cindy Clark. 2007. *A New Weave of Power, People, and Politics: The Action Guide for Advocacy and Citizen Participation*. Bourton-on-Dunsmore, Warwickshire, UK: Practical Action.

"The ARVIN Framework: A Way to Assess the Enabling Environment for Civil Engagagement." Available on the Participation and Civic Engagement website of the World Bank.

Monitoring and evaluation

Bamberger, Michael, Jim Rugh, and Linda Mabry. 2006. *RealWorld Evaluation: Working under Budget, Time, Data, and Political Constraints.* Thousand Oaks, CA: Sage.

Catley, Andrew, John Burns, Dawit Abebe, and Omeno Suji. 2007. *Participatory Impact Assessment: A Guide for Practitioners.* Feinstein International Center, Tufts University. PDF available on the Feinstein Center website.

Davies, Rich, and Jess Dart. 2005. *The "Most Significant Change" (MSC) Technique: A Guide to Its Use.* Available on the mande.co.uk website.

Duflo, Esther. Poverty Action Lab. See her videos on Ted Talks.

Earl, Sarah, Fred Carden, and Terry Smutylo. 2001. *Outcome Mapping: Building Learning and Reflection into Development Programs.* Ottawa: International Development Research Centre.

Marsden, David, Peter Oakley, and Brian Pratt. 1994. *Measuring the Process: Guidelines for Evaluating Social Development.* Oxford, UK: INTRAC.

Mertens, Donna M. 2009. *Transformative Research and Evaluation.* New York: Guilford Press.

10

Christian witness
and transformational development

THE NECESSITY AND CHALLENGE OF CHRISTIAN WITNESS

Why we must witness

Since the Christian faith is a missionary faith, then being a Christian means being a witness. The word *gospel* means "message" or "good news," and messages are not messages unless they are announced. The word *evangelism* means "to announce the news."

When Christians say that they accept Jesus as their Lord and Savior, they are also saying that they intend to announce this fact in every facet of their lives and by every means available to them: by life, deed, word, and sign. For Christians, being a witness is integral to who we are and what we believe. But there are other reasons why we must witness to Christ in the context of doing transformational development.

First, the need to proclaim the good news of Christ is directly related to a Christian understanding of transformation. For Christians, belief is the beginning of knowing. Athanasius said that the gospel provided a new *arche*, a new starting point for the way we understand and make sense of our world. Augustine of Hippo took the biblical story as the point of departure for his radical reconstruction of his former ways of thinking, following the dictum *Credo ut intelligam*—I believe in order to know (quoted in Newbigin 1995, 9).

In this sense Christian witness is the beginning of transformation. Melba Maggay reminds us, "Social change is primarily what happens to people in that level of being where the Spirit alone has access" (1994, 72).

Newbigin explains this further by saying that by proclaiming Christ we offer people the possibility of understanding what God is doing in history. By sharing God's good news with people, we offer the beginning of the process of recovering identity and vocation.

309

[They receive] a vision of the goal of human history . . . a vision which makes it possible to act hopefully when there is no earthly hope, to find the way when everything is dark and there are no earthly land marks. (1989, 129)

I have already said that every development program represents a convergence of stories: ours, the community's, and God's. God's story is the only one that has the power to redirect and make sense out of all our stories. The best human future is one that moves toward the kingdom of God. Thus witnessing to God's story is the beginning of hope and the promise of a new story.

Second, we need to bring the best that we have. In our best moments our development processes are empowering and our development technology can make short work of dirty water, parasites, malnutrition, and poor agricultural production. Yet as good as all these things are, they are not the best news that we have. Because our own experience tells us that Christ has the power to seek, to save, and to recompose our stories into stories of hope and purpose, we can hardly help sharing this very best of our good news with others.

Finally, Jesus gave us two simple commandments. We are to love God with all we have and to love our neighbors as ourselves. This is the motivation that takes us to the poor in the first place. How can we say we love our neighbors if we limit our work to improving their material lives in the here and now and never share the news that holds the promise of transforming their lives now and forever?

For Christians, therefore, our thinking and practice of transforming development must have an evangelistic intent, although this needs to be understood with some care. This is not a call for proselytism; neither is it a call to coercive, manipulative, or culturally insensitive evangelism. It is not even a call for all development practitioners to become evangelists. After all, no one knows the moment when someone is ready for faith, nor is God limited to the staff of a particular Christian development agency in bringing God's good news. Rather, it is a call to be sure we do our development with an attitude that prays and yearns for people to know Jesus Christ.

Understanding evangelism

It may be helpful for me to say a little about the meaning of the word *evangelism*. Evangelism is the verbal sharing of the good news of Jesus Christ and his offer to fallen human beings, but we need to work a little harder to be clear on what we mean by this. Too often the gospel message is presented as a set of propositional statements. While this is true, it is not enough—and it can be misleading.

Tim Dearborn points out that evangelism is good news about a person, not just a set of propositions. The gospel invitation is to a relationship, not just intellectual assent or agreement to a set of ideas. In this sense, the gospel is not against other religions; it is simply true (1997, 37).

William Abraham, a Methodist theologian, clarifies this further when he reminds us that evangelism is not simply speaking about something that we believe or that we feel compelled to share. Evangelism is announcing something that has happened in the world about which everyone has a right to know.

> What makes proclamation evangelism is not the proclamation *per se*, but the message being proclaimed: the coming rule of God. . . . Without this announcement, people will not know about its arrival, nor will they have a clear view of what it means for the kingdom of God to come now in the present or in the future. (1989, 59)

Walter Brueggemann, the Presbyterian Old Testament scholar, defines evangelism as an invitation to choose a new story, employing the biblical story as the "definitional story of our life, and thereby authorizing people to give up, abandon and renounce other stories that have shaped their lives in false and distorting ways" (1993a, 10). Brueggemann describes the act of evangelism as drama, a story with a beginning, a middle, and an end. The first scene is about the conflict between two powerful forces that battle for control of the future. The second scene presents the witness who gives testimony, telling the outcome of the conflict that he or she has already experienced. In the third and final scene, the listener must make an appropriate response to this witness.

It also may be useful to say a few things about what evangelism is not. Evangelism is not about sales. The gospel must never be treated as a marketable product that we entice people to "buy." "We are not purveyors of a commodity . . . but facilitators of a people's own discovery of their heritage as the children of Abraham" (Bediako 1996b, 187). Nor is evangelism about sales effectiveness. Vinay Samuel is fond of saying that evangelism is a commitment to sharing, not an announcement of expected outcomes. Finally, the greatest danger to wrong-headed thinking about evangelism is that we will use evangelism as a way to play god in the lives of other people, believing we know the state of their soul, when they need to say yes to God, or that we know something about their future that they do not.

We are witnessing anyway

Sometimes we don't think hard enough about this business of being witnesses. Sometimes we think there are two choices: being witnesses or not being witnesses. This is not true. We are always witnesses to something. The only question is to what or to whom?

Augustine Musopole, the Malawian theologian, reports that the more successful the development intervention, the greater the reinforcement of traditional religion. "The more education, the better the job, the larger the house, the more you have to protect and the greater the temptation of witchcraft" (Musopole 1997).

In a well-drilling project on the edge of the Sahara, a community watched a soil scientist and a hydrologist converse in highly technical language as they did soil chemistry and studied a hydrological survey. When asked what these two men were doing, the community replied that they were witch doctors. One was consulting the spirit of the earth and asking it where the spirit of the water lived. The other was reading magic texts in the search of power, just as their marabouts did with the Qur'an. Asked if these witch doctors were any good, the villagers replied that they were very good, better than their own witch doctors. "After all, they always find the water."

When confronted with this interpretation of their actions, the men decided to go back the next day and explain the science behind their work in simple terms the village could understand. Explaining the miracle of finding water in the desert as "just science," however, is a witness, only this time to the efficiency of modern science and technology.

Development technology continually creates this problem in traditional cultures (Bradshaw 1993; Myers 1993). Whether water is found in the desert or children do not die that normally would die, an explanation is demanded. With no explanation, the traditional worldview provides its animist explanation. Or, if the modern development professional reduces the good news to "just science," the explanation is a secular one. Either way, a witness is made that is not Christian and an invitation to idolatry has been extended.

To make it harder, it is not even enough to announce that we are Christians, as if this will somehow change how the community understands the success of our development interventions. In Vietnam, when villagers were asked why a Christian NGO was helping them reconstruct their dikes, they explained that Christians care about the poor. When asked why Christians care about the poor, they responded that Christians were earning merit for their next life, a Buddhist explanation. When Muslims in Mauritania were asked the same kind of question, two responses predominated. Either Christians were earning their way into paradise, a Muslim understanding of charity, or they were getting rich by working in the aid business, a secular understanding of why expatriates serve overseas.

Finally, to make things even more complicated, explaining that the intervention is made possible because the Christian God is a powerful God and the source of technology is not enough. If this is all that is said, Paul Hiebert estimated that within three generations the people will be secularized (Hiebert 1997). It is a an example of Ockham's Razor: As soon as the people figure out, as we in the West have, that technology works without God as part of the explanation, God is dropped from the explanation.

The bottom line is that we need to be concerned about who gets worshiped at the end of the development program. Jayakumar Christian reminds us that whatever we put at the center of the program during its lifetime will tend to be what the community worships in the end (1998b). As we have just seen, if development technology is perceived as the source of change, technology will be worshiped as the source of transformation. If the development agency and its expertise and resources are the central feature of the program, the agency will become the object of worship. In one case in India it was discovered that World Vision had been added to a tribal community's list of gurus—those who have answers the community does not have—and prayers and sacrifices had been instituted to ensure that this new guru kept helping the community. If money is the focus, then money is perceived to be the key to transformation.

What we put at the center of our program is our witness. We must always ask if we are acting as a dependent people, looking to God for every good thing. We want people to observe us and say, "Theirs must be a living God!"

The twin challenge

Christian witness presents an interesting pair of challenges to the development worker. I've just described the first part of the challenge. Every development effort witnesses to something. The only question is, To what is it witnessing?

The second part of the challenge has to do with the traditional framework of Christian witness. Too often Christian witness is pursued in a way that is contradictory to the community-driven development framework proposed in this book. In the spiritual arena, the community is assumed to have a problem of which it is not aware. The evangelist assumes the role of answer-giver to those who do not to know the answer. Finally, there is an assumption that the evangelist knows something about the future of the audience that the audience does not know, namely, their ultimate destination if they do not believe.

At the most fundamental level, these claims are true. Christians do have a truth that the non-Christians do not have, and there is an obligation for us to share this news, even if people are not aware they need it. And Christians do believe that eternal life is only possible by believing in Jesus Christ as Lord and Savior. Yet there is a fine line between being faithful to these beliefs and crossing over the line and assuming a smug arrogance, playing god in the lives of those who do not yet believe. There is always the danger that we may act, not as undeserving recipients of a gift, but as people with a sense of superiority, expressing the "teacher complex" that Koyama feels damages the attractiveness of the gospel.

I doubt strongly whether the idea that the "people over there are enemies of God" is central to the Spirit of Christ. The Spirit of Christ
does not support the spirit of greed to conquer others and self-righ-
teousness to demonstrate our superior piety. (1993, 293)

If done sensitively and without arrogance, the "go and tell" frame for
Christian witness may be appropriate for a church or traditional mission
agency, but it is not a good fit for a development agency for the simple
reason that it is anti-developmental. It cuts across the idea that the community is the owner of its own development. It works against the notion of
beginning where the community is and helping it find answers to its own
questions. The initiative is with the outsider; the position of power and
control is external. Since we don't do "go and tell" development, we should
do what we can to avoid "go and tell" evangelism.

The second challenge of Christian witness in the context of doing transformational development is whether or not an alternative framework for
Christian witness can be found that allows Christians to be faithful to their
belief that the gospel must be shared and, at the same time, allows the kind
of transformative development process I described in the earlier chapters.
Is there a developmental approach to Christian witness? I believe there is.

PROVOKING THE QUESTION: WITNESS AS THE SECOND ACT

The book of Acts describes the growth of the early church. Examining
these stories Newbigin calls our attention to an interesting pattern that
helps us with the dilemma I have just posed (1989, 132–33). Evangelism,
the saying of the gospel, is often the second act of the story. What do I
mean?

When Peter gives his first public statement of the gospel, we are told
that three thousand believers were added that day. Yet his sermon was spon-
taneous, unplanned. He begins his message by saying, "Let me explain this
to you." What was the "this" that needed explaining? The people of Jerusalem had gathered and heard the disciples praising God. Incredibly, each
observer heard this in his or her own language. This powerful act of the
Holy Spirit made the people utterly amazed, and they created their own
explanation: the disciples must be drunk. Peter's message was in response
to this amazement and was intended to correct an inaccurate explanation.
Peter's evangelistic sermon answered a question being asked by the crowd.

The second articulation of the gospel in Acts follows a similar pattern.
After healing the crippled beggar at the temple gate, the crowd gathers,
astonished at the sight of the former cripple walking around and praising
God. Peter once again finds himself needing to clarify the situation. "Men
of Israel, why does this surprise you? Why do you stare at us as if by our

own power or godliness we have made this man to walk? The God of Abraham, Isaac and Jacob, the God of our fathers, has glorified his servant Jesus" (Acts 3:12–13). Peter's speech is in response to a question from the crowd, provoked by evidence of the activity of God.

The same pattern emerges in the story of Stephen. His opportunity to share the gospel's recomposition of the history of Israel took place, not by plan, but as a result of his being falsely accused because he "did great wonders and miraculous signs among the people" (Acts 6:8). As a result of Stephen's preaching in front of the Sanhedrin, a Pharisee named Saul heard the gospel for the first time.

Do you see the pattern? In each case, the gospel is proclaimed, not by intent or plan, but in response to a question provoked by the activity of God in the community. There is an action that demands an explanation, and the gospel was the explanation. "Something has happened which makes people aware of a new reality, and therefore the question arises: What is this reality? The communication of the gospel is the answering of that question" (Newbigin 1989, 132).

This framework suggests that, in addition to the "go and tell" framework, we can also think of evangelism as the work the Christian community does—or better, that God does through the Christian community—that provokes questions to which the good news of Jesus Christ is the answer (Newbigin 1989, 133; Myers 1992b).

The idea of living and doing development in a way that evokes questions to which the gospel is the answer addresses the second of my twin challenges for Christian witness in the context of transformational development. When water is found in the desert, when children no longer die, when water no longer makes people sick, something has happened that needs an explanation. When trained professionals live in poor villages and everyone there knows they could be making more money and their children could go to better schools in the city, this odd behavior provokes a question. The explanation is the gospel. The answer to the question Who witnesses? is that development facilitators do through the life that they lead, how they treat the poor, and how they promote transformational development.

There is much to commend this framework for Christian witness in the context of doing transformational development. First, the questions are asked by the people when they witness something they do not expect or understand. The initiative lies with them. This avoids Tillich's complaint that "it is wrong to throw answers, like stones, at the heads of those who haven't even asked a question." Second, the burden for response is on the Christians, not the people. If the people do not ask questions to which the gospel is the answer, we can no longer just say, "Their hearts were hardened," and walk away feeling good that we have witnessed to the gospel. Instead, we need to get down on our knees and ask God why our life and our work are so unremarkable that neither result in a question relating to what we believe and whom we worship.

There is evidence that the framework of living in hopes that the Holy Spirit will provoke questions to which the gospel is the answer is a valid approach. After four years of sacrificially working alongside the poor in a village in India, adhering strictly to a promise not to do overt evangelism, local political leaders came to the humble house of the Christian development worker, asking him and his family to leave. When asked for the reason, the response was, "The way you live is disturbing our people, causing them to ask questions about your God." In an interview in 1997, Sarone Ole Sena commented that, as Appreciative Inquiry gives voice to how the local religious and spiritual views have given strength and life to the community, the question invariably comes back: "What do you believe? What gives you strength and life?" In Mali, a mullah watched every week when the Christian nurse came to hold a clinic. When she had offered to begin her work in his village, he had told her that he was aware that Christians used health care as a mask for doing evangelism. She promised him she would never abuse her profession in this way. After a year he told her that, in addition to keeping her word, he had observed that she truly loved his people and cared about them. He then asked her to tell him more about Issa (the Arabic name for Jesus).

TRANSFORMATIONAL WITNESS

As we develop our thinking about Christian witness in the context of transformational development, we must be sure that our understanding of witness is as transformational as our understanding of development. We must be clear as to the goals for transformational witness. We must understand the organic nature of the gospel message. We need to overcome the dichotomy between evangelism and discipleship. Finally, we must be sure that our Christian witness shares the whole biblical story.

The goals of Christian witness

The goals of Christian witness are the same as the goals of transformational development: changed people and changed relationships. We desire that all people—the poor, the non-poor, and ourselves—be able to experience the lifelong process of recovering our true identity as children of God and the restoration of our true vocation as productive stewards in God's creation. This comes about only by restoring the family of relationships of which we are a part.

The only difference between the goals for transformational development and the goals for Christian witness is that Christian witness focuses more, but not exclusively, on our relationship with God through Jesus Christ, while the goals of transformational development focus more, but not exclusively, on the other four critical relationships: with self, community, others, and our environment. Because the focus of Christian witness is more on our relationship with God, witness-by-word moves to center stage alongside witness-by-life and witness-by-deed. The fact that the goals for Christian witness and the goals for transformational development are the same, except for focus, should be reassuring. They can only be the same if we have overcome the dichotomy between the physical (development) and the spiritual (Christian witness), the modern problem with which this book has been struggling throughout.

One final word on the need to verbalize the good news of the gospel. The motive to invite people to faith is not a form of imperialism or a messianic desire to make everyone over in our image, although I must admit with sadness that some Christians have acted out of these motivations. In our best moments the motive is much less selfish. We want others to know the good news about the Lord. The gospel of Jesus Christ is the best news that we have, better than community mobilization or development technology. As Christians, we have experienced the most fundamental of discoveries: "Ultimately, any social transformation happens in our deepest level of being, that part where God alone can go" (Maggay 1994, 71).

Gospel as life, deed, word, and sign

In Chapter 1, I discussed how the modern worldview of the West has encouraged us to separate gospel-as-word, gospel-as-sign, and gospel-as-deed. Any holistic understanding of Christian witness must reunite these three aspects of what is really a single gospel message. But there is a fourth aspect of the message that must be included in this reunification. The gospel is not a disembodied message; it is carried and communicated in the life of Christian people. Therefore, a holistic understanding of the gospel begins with life, a life that is then lived out by deed and word and sign.

When Jesus selected the twelve disciples, they were appointed so that "they might be with him and that he might send them out to preach and to have the authority to drive out demons" (Mk 3:14–15). When they returned from being sent out for the first time, we are told that they "went out and preached that people should repent. They drove out demons and anointed many sick people with oil and healed them" (Mk 6:12–13). The activist is eager to get to the sending and acting part, gladly taking note of the threefold nature of the gospel: preaching words, healing deeds, and demon-sending signs.

What activists too often miss, however, is the *reason* for the appointing of the disciples in the first place: so the disciples would *be with* Jesus. Being with Jesus is the beginning of any biblical ministry. Yet being with Jesus means more than simply being a Christian. As the disciples learned, it also means traveling with Jesus, listening and learning from Jesus, being rebuked by Jesus—truly being with Jesus all the time.

This is the key to Christian witness that provokes questions to which the gospel is the answer. We will live eloquent lives only if we are being with Jesus, following Jesus, and seeking, by his grace, to become more like Jesus. The leading edge of witnessing to the whole gospel is being with Jesus. Only then do gospel words, deeds, and signs follow. Transformation is fundamentally about relationships, remember? Our ability to facilitate transformation depends on our being transformed, and this depends on our life, our relationship with our Lord.

We must also remember that the gospel message is an organic whole. Life, deed, word, and sign must all find expression for us to encounter and comprehend the whole of the good news of Jesus Christ. Life alone is too solitary. Word, deed, and sign alone are all ambiguous. Words alone can be posturing, positioning, even selling. Deeds alone do not declare identity or indicate in whom one has placed his or her faith. Signs can be done by demons and spirits or by the Holy Spirit. It is only when life, deed, word, and sign are expressed in a consistent and coherent whole that the gospel of the Son of God is clear (see Figure 3–6).

This organic relationship of life, word, deed, and sign creates an interesting ability for Christian witness to begin where people are. We can start with whichever part of the gospel message most closely relates to the needs of those to whom we wish to witness.

> The ministry of Jesus is notable for its clarity of focus and the flexibility of its response. In that way, Jesus allowed the other person to set the agenda. But Jesus always responded out of who he was and what he represented. (Shenk 1993, 73)

For those afraid of spirits, we pray for the Holy Spirit to do the signs that show that God is more powerful. For those who are seeking intellectual truth, we begin with words. For those who are empirically inclined or seeking evidence that God is concerned for the material world, we begin with gospel as deed. For those who seek meaning in their relationships, we begin with gospel as life.

While we can begin with any aspect of the gospel message, we must never stop there. Any Christian understanding of transformation must find expression for all elements of the gospel message—life, deed, word, and sign—each in God's time. Everyone needs to encounter and engage the gospel message in its wholeness. To stop short is to truncate the gospel.

One final clarification. Having asserted the inseparability of life, deed, word, and sign, we must not overlook the question, How do people come to faith? Romans 10 points to the unique role of gospel-as-word. Neither gospel-as-sign nor gospel-as-deed is sufficient. In other words, the gospel message points people in a direction and toward a decision. The direction is toward the kingdom of God, and the decision is whether or not to accept Jesus as Savior and Lord and thereby enter God's kingdom. So, while we must recover a gospel message that is inseparably word, deed, and sign, we must also understand that its purpose is to invite people to reconciliation with God and with each other through Jesus Christ.

Evangelism and discipleship

In carrying out holistic Christian witness, it is helpful to remember that evangelism is not different from or unrelated to discipleship. Another of the inadvertent and unhelpful impacts of modernity and its separation of the physical and the spiritual is that discipleship is too often reduced to developing one's relationship with God, with little or no attention to developing one's relationship with one's community and the environment. This mental separation results in reducing prayer, reading the Bible, and worship to spiritual activities, obscuring their relevance to work and act in the "real" world. This is the explanation for how some Christians spiritualize and privatize the Bible, and thus have trouble believing it speaks to the physical realms of politics, economics, and issues of race and culture. If the "real" world of Christians is solely the spiritual world, then discipleship is necessarily limited solely to spiritual things. This is an artificial limitation with tragic consequences.

Cesar Molebatsi, a Christian leader in South Africa, wrote the following to me in 1991: "My deepest pain is that, in the very continent where the Christian church is growing the fastest and where so many countries are mostly inhabited by Christians, we see rampant racism, ethnic violence, AIDS, corruption and increasing poverty. What kind of Christians are we creating?" I must ask the same question of my American culture, which claims the label Christian in the midst of racism, gang warfare, deserted inner cities, pornography, abortion on demand, drug use, and rampant consumerism. When evangelism is separated from discipleship, we tend to move on once someone accepts Jesus as Savior; there is the real risk that he or she will never know him as Lord. Catholic theologian Avery Dulles reminds us that evangelism is not complete with the first proclamation of the gospel: "It is a lifelong process of letting the gospel permeate and transform all our ideas and attitudes" (1996, 28).

William Abraham has defined *evangelism* as the "set of intentional activities which is governed by the goal of initiating people into the kingdom of God for the first time" (1989, 95). Defining evangelism this way, brings evangelism and discipleship into a unified whole. Using initiation as a metaphor for evangelism, Abraham goes beyond baptism, the traditional end-point of evangelism, and adds five elements to his understanding of the work of evangelism:

- Owning the intellectual claims of the Christian tradition, without which understanding the kingdom of God is impossible.
- Appropriating the very particular moral vision that serves as the bedrock of moral action in the Christian community and the world. At its heart this vision is about loving God and loving one's neighbor as oneself.
- Experiencing in one's inner life the kind of assurance that only the Holy Spirit can give.
- Receiving and developing gifts that equip one to serve as an agent of God.
- Appropriating those spiritual disciplines that are essential for responsible obedience to the joys of the kingdom. (Abraham 1989, 95–103)

Abraham's frame does something else that is worth noting. Evangelism always involves proclamation, but, if done with intent, may now include working for peace and justice, prayer, acts of mercy, patient conversation, caring for the poor, and even stern rebuke. "What makes actions evangelism is that they are part of a process that is governed by the goal of initiating people into the kingdom of God" (ibid., 104).

Telling the whole story

Finally, a holistic view of Christian witness requires that we tell our whole story. We must not reduce the good news simply to the account of Jesus in the gospels. We must avoid the risk that the central part of the story will be unintelligible because we do not share the biblical story as a whole. To link the gospel to the process of development, the people need to hear about the God who created the world and their culture; the God who wants human beings to worship God and love their neighbor; and the God who wants and will enable them to be productive stewards in creation. Furthermore, in many traditional cultures people find it easier to recognize themselves and make an identity link with the Old Testament stories. The Masai quickly identified with the Old Testament accounts of nomads, cattle, and God's dislike of sin and then responded eagerly to the unexpected good news that the God of the Old Testament is also a God who forgives. We need to tell the whole story so that the gospel account makes full sense.

There is a second sense in which we need to tell the whole story. Too often the gospel is reduced to a personal gospel that restores an individual's relationship with God. And this is true. Yet the whole gospel is more than this. More on the role of the Bible and the whole biblical story later.

HOW WE MUST WITNESS?

Living eloquent lives

The Christian witness framework of provoking the question depends on the winsomeness of the life, lifestyle, and management style of the development facilitator. For the development practitioner, the challenge is serious indeed. We need to do our work and live our lives in a way that calls attention to the new Spirit that lives within us and who is changing us. We need to relate to people and promote our development technology in ways that create a sense of wonder. We must seek a spirituality that makes our lives eloquent. Dorothy Day is reported to have admonished us to "live a life so mysterious that the only adequate explanation is the presence of a living, loving God."

A crucified mind

Our attitude in Christian witness is worthy of attention. I've already alluded to the temptation to slip into an unwitting attitude of superiority. This temptation comes in a variety of subtle forms. Sometimes we are sure we know best because we are development professionals. Sometimes it is because we are educated or come from what we feel is a more sophisticated culture. Sometimes we fall into the trap of unknowingly judging another culture as not quite as good as our own because of its fear of the spirits and its belief in the unseen. Sometimes it is because we have gotten caught up in the fact that we are Christians and the others are not. Whatever the reason, this kind of attitude acts like a corrosive acid, eating away at our effectiveness in transformational development and Christian witness.

Koyama has called over the years for Christians to set aside their often crusading mind in favor of what he calls the crucified mind, the mind of Christ. If anyone had the right to feel superior, it was the Son of God. Yet we know from the second chapter of Philippians that Christ chose to set this prerogative aside, even to the point of death on a cross. And so must we. Whatever we have was given to us.

There is another reason for humility in our Christian witness. We are the carriers of the message, not the actor who compels a response. When Paul preaches the gospel to Lydia in Philippi, Luke reports that "the Lord opened her heart to respond to Paul's message" (Acts 16:14). The evangelist was the Holy Spirit; Paul was merely the messenger. Newbigin reminds us that "the mission is not, first of all, an action of ours. It is the action of God." He later says, "The gospel has a sovereignty of its own and is never an instrument in the hands of the evangelist" (1989, 135, 153). The good news is not ours to feel superior about or to use as a tool or a weapon. It is not our story; it is God's story.

The beginning of the crucified mind is the unconditional embrace of the other, just as Jesus unconditionally embraced us. Without regard for history or ethnicity, wisdom or folly, sin or saintliness, Christ embraced us and showed us the way to life. And so we must embrace the poor, accepting them as God presents them to us. Our professionalism and our faith were gifts to us in order that we might share them with others. "This is how God loves every person, and the one who is a messenger about the good news of God's love cannot limit the gift of God. The embrace itself becomes the message" (Motte 1996, 81).

Recognizing the fingerprints of God

I've already made the case that we are witnessing all the time, in everything we say and do. The only question is to whom or to what are we witnessing. We also need to remember that God has been witnessing as well: "He was in the world, and though the world was made through him, the world did not recognize him" (Jn 1:10). The problem is that we are not always good witnesses and human beings are not very good at recognizing God, even in God's self-revelation.

The key, then, is to work harder at recognizing God's fingerprints in daily life as part of our daily practice of Christian witness. We need to use every conversation, every program activity, as an opportunity to point to the work of God. This is one of the strengths of Appreciative Inquiry and its demand that we focus on things that are "excellent or praiseworthy" (Phil 4:8). All of these good things are linked to "whatever you have learned or received or heard from me, or seen in me" (Phil 4:9). We need to get away from the idea that development is a process in which God periodically intervenes and realize that God has a development process already underway in which the community and the development agency periodically co-operates.

Loving people toward recognition

The way we do development can be a source of witness. The way we treat the poor can be a way of announcing that a different spirit is at work in us and in the community. When we treat the poor as equals, as having wisdom that we wish to hear, they have a chance to begin the recovery of their true identity and the discovery of their true vocation. Remember my earlier story, "[The most important thing that has changed as a result of this project is that] you are sitting on the same mat, looking me in the eye, and talking to us as equals." Every time hope and vision emerge, we can stop to give thanks to its true source. AI and PLA exercises can be used to celebrate the work of God in the past of the community if we use them well. Every time we challenge the web of lies with the truth we can speak of one who is Truth and whose truth we proclaim. Even the very process of evaluating and reflection, and our ability to learn, could point us to God. Where does this ability come from other than from a gracious God who does not insist on determinism? (Leupp 1996, 85).

Recognizing God in history

God works in every community's history determining times set for them and the exact places where they should live. God did this so that men and women "would seek him and perhaps reach out for him and find him" (Acts 17:27). The history of a people is a sign pointing to God, if we have eyes to see.

This directly contradicts the way history is normally perceived by the poor. They see themselves as being on the sidelines of both the making of history and the telling of history's story. Helping the poor to learn to read their own history and to find their place and that of God in it is a transformational frontier and an opportunity for Christian witness. We need to teach them "to re-read their history with God as the point of reference" (Christian 1998a, 9). Christian calls this "drawing the portrait of Christ in their history."

Thus we can use our development processes as a way to help people draw closer to God by recognizing God's work in their past. One of the results of tools like Appreciative Inquiry and PLA is that people can come to recognize the successes and the life-creating occurrences in their history. It is a short step to connect these instances with the activity and character of a loving and involved God: "In the past God spoke to our forefathers through the prophets at many times and in various ways" (Heb 1:1).

Recognizing God in creation

Psalm 104 provides a magnificent metaphor for helping us recognize God's work in creation. All the verbs relating to God are active: he stretches out the heavens, makes the winds, and covers the earth with water, setting its boundaries. God speaks and directs while the creation responds. This activity results in an ecosystem in which water is provided to the beasts of the field and birds have habitation. And all of this is so that human beings may thrive:

> He makes grass grow for the cattle,
> and plants for man to cultivate—
> bringing forth food from the earth,
> wine that gladdens the heart of man,
> oil to make his face shine
> and bread that sustains his heart. (Ps 104:14–15)

Sadly, much of the Western world—and most development profession-als—do not use this kind of a lens when we read nature. We assign the creative part to evolution, the ecosystem to science, and take over the re-sponsibility for the parts about being glad, having shining faces, and pro-ducing the bread. We no longer need God as part of the explanation.

It does not have to be this way. Christians could work to recover this kind of metaphor for making sense out of the world. We might get some help from traditional cultures if we had the humility to listen. Their worldview is very close to Psalm 104. The only issue of difference is the name of the God who is active in creation and whether or not he had a son who died on a hill in Palestine over two thousand years ago.

Recomposing the program

One way to enhance the range of our witness is to reexamine all those parts of development programming that we may have assumed were with-out spiritual character. Once we begin to look for biblical metaphors and values in the routine, we will be surprised at the opportunities that we have overlooked.

For example, most programs call for a program agreement, stating what the agency will do and what the community will do—a simple, normal part of development administration. Loc Le Chau, an inspired program man-ager in Senegal, realized there was potentially something more. He real-ized that both Muslims and Christians are familiar with the biblical con-cept of covenant. The program agreement was transformed into a covenant between the people, the agency, and God. Old Testament language was deliberately employed, and a covenant was written to say that the village would bring what it had, the agency what it had, and, when and if the well drilling was successful, God would be thanked. A simple piece of paper had been transformed. It was not just culturally more appropriate. God's activ-ity and an occasion for praising God had been uncovered. There was now space to recognize the glory of God active in the world.

There is a wide range of other possibilities. The Greek words for salva-tion and healing are the same. This creates opportunities to reinterpret health-care interventions. Creation theology, agricultural practices, and environmental friendliness make natural partners. The same is true of mi-cro-enterprise development and the biblical idea of being productive stew-ards; the prophetic literature even adds the social responsibility element that the worshipers of the unfettered free market cannot provide.

Seeking meaning together

Why are things this way? How do we explain success? Failure? Unex-pected outcomes? What does this mean? These questions always take us to heart issues. They move us beyond the surface of PLA results and capability and vulnerability exercises and raise the truly transformational issues of meaning and purpose.

When the results were posted of the Ten Seeds exercise I described in Chapter 9, the tribal people had shown how little power they felt they had over income, health, roads, and food. They felt that most of the control over these areas of their lives belonged to outsiders and the spirit world. While this was very helpful to know, the more important question was *why* they believe this is the way things are. What explanation could they give for why they had so little control over their world? They responded with the epic story of their origins as a people.

It seems that Krishna was undertaking a meditative process by which he hoped to surrender all desire. A rival god was concerned that, were Krishna successful, he would gain favor. So he sent a beautiful woman to distract Krishna. The ploy worked, and the result was a dark-skinned son with thick lips, the iconic image of this tribal group. A reminder of a failed spiritual exercise, the son remained in Krishna's household. Then this unwanted son accidentally caused the death of Krishna's favorite bull. Furious, Krishna banished the child. This, the tribal group explained, was why they had left the Himalayas and moved into what is now India.

The tribal group understood itself as a cursed people. This was the story of their origins. They had always been cursed. This was why the gods and spirits were so unkind. This was why the government was not interested in them and would not rebuild the road. This was why they were poor, marginalized, and frequently oppressed. This was why the tribal group believed it was less than human. It had been ordained from the time of the first member of their race (Jayakaran 1997a).

Once again we encounter poverty of being and the deception of a distorted view of history. The very mythic origins of the people, the core of their self-understanding and worldview, validates, even mandates, their continuing poverty. Even their successes are co-opted by this story. When asked why good things happen, they explained that their sacrifices and prayers occasionally worked, but that the curse held sway most of the time.

This discovery—triggered by asking questions about meaning—changed the development conversation in a radical way. While wells, improved agriculture, immunizations, and schools were still needed, they were not enough. Why? Doing development without understanding this story would lead to development that is neither sustainable nor Christian. Every success will be interpreted as the result of effective prayers or sacrifices. Every setback will confirm the truth of the curse account. The fact that we are Christian is irrelevant to their explanation of the events. We are simply incorporated into the tribal group's view of how the world works.

This kind of discovery demands an engagement about stories. This tribal group will only be transformed if it is able or is enabled to recompose the story of its origins. How do stories get recomposed? It is the right question, but it is a hard one to answer.

We get a hint in the story of every personal conversion. My story was recomposed when I became a Christian. From the day Jesus became my Lord, I told my personal story in a different way. The facts did not change, of course. I was born on the same date, had the same parents, and went to the same schools. But the meaning I give to the events in my life was transformed by my encounter with the gospel. I now tell my story in a different way.

An encounter with the true Author of everyone's story is the only answer I can think of for the tribal group. Only the transforming power of the God who created the tribal group can empower it by rewriting its story. Its story, as its members now understand it, has truth in it. But it is still fundamentally a lie. The tribal group has been deceived, and this deception is the most fundamental cause of the people's poverty. At this level the tribal group's material and spiritual poverty have the same foundational cause: deception, the work of the devil. The truth and power of the gospel are the only way to transformation.

This is easy to say and yet seems very hard to bring about. Too often evangelism and Christian discipleship result in the Christian story being laid on top of the traditional story of a culture. As long as it is possible to live the Christian story and the traditional story at the same time, everything is fine. The problem comes when the two stories come into conflict. Too often, it seems, the traditional story wins out.

The United States is a good example. The great majority of people identify themselves as Christian. Over 40 percent say they attend church regularly. Yet, research shows that in behavioral terms, Christian social behavior—cheating on taxes, divorce rate, and so on—is indistinguishable from that of non-Christians. As long as the Christian story and the American story are consistent, people are good Christians (and good Americans). When they are in conflict, they tend to act like good Americans.

This hierarchy of stories is reflected widely. African Christian leaders have complained that their congregations go to doctors (the modern story) and ask for prayers of healing (the Christian story), and, if these are not effective, consult traditional shamans (the African story) at night. In Bosnia the ethnic story is more powerful than the religious story of the Orthodox, Catholics, and Muslims. In Rwanda the tribal story won out over the Christian story when the ethnic card was callously played by those seeking power.

Interpreting technology with God as part of the explanation

Development technology carries a message. When children cease to die or agricultural production doubles, these "miracles" demand an explanation. The explanation usually comes either from the traditional worldview of the people or from the scientific worldview of the development facilitator. Neither points to the God of the Bible.

This is not a new problem. Acts 14 recounts that while preaching, Paul sees a man who had been lame from birth. Paul directs the man to stand up, and the man is healed. There are no words from Paul to explain how the healing took place. So the people provide their own explanation and announce that "the gods have come down to us in human form" (Acts 14:11). The people then, quite appropriately, set out to organize the required sacrifices and worship. Only then does Paul realize the mistake he has made and scrambles to explain that "we too are only men, human like you" (Acts 14:15), going on to explain whose miracle it really is.

Lesslie Newbigin has alerted us to an interesting pattern in the gospels. In the long sections of teaching in the gospel of John, most of his teaching is explanatory of something Jesus has done: healing the paralytic, feeding the multitude, giving sight to the blind man, raising a man from the dead. This link between words and deeds is also evident in the sending of the twelve in Matthew. The disciples were sent to cast out demons and heal every disease, and only then, Jesus said, were they to say that the kingdom of heaven is at hand. The preaching of the good news is an explanation of the healings. Newbigin observes that, as marvelous as they were, healings do not explain themselves. They could be misinterpreted—as in fact they were by Jesus' enemies, who attributed his works to Satanic power. "Healings, even the most wonderful, do not call this present world radically into question; the gospel does, and this has to be made explicit" (Newbigin 1989, 132).

The critical question is how to interpret development technology so that it is understood as evidence of the work and character of a loving, engaged God rather than setting itself up as the explanation of its own success. To answer this question, we need to understand what technology is for and whence it comes.

Technology is a good, but a limited good. While technology has made things efficient and has greatly sped up the rate of change in the material world, there are too many things that technology cannot do. Wolterstorff, in his discussion of shalom, points out that technology does help us toward shalom in terms of our relationship with nature, but it cannot help us create shalom within ourselves, with God, or between ourselves and our neighbors. Even when technology works in our relationship with nature, technology is a double-edged sword; it can make life easier or it can be used to kill our neighbor (Wolterstorff 1983, 71). Science cannot create and does not operate within a vision of what ought to be (Shenk 1993, 67).

So what is technology for? Lynn White points out that in the twelfth century Hugh of St. Victor described tools as a search for a remedy, a kind of penitential activity, to make the effects of sin a little less unpleasant by reducing cold, hunger, and weakness (White 1978, 13). By the end of the Middle Ages this understanding of technology found its full expression:

The chief glory of the later Middle Ages was not its cathedrals or its epics or its scholasticism: it was the building for the first time in human history of a complex civilization which rested not on the backs of sweating slaves and coolies but primarily on non-human power. (ibid., 22)

Francis Bacon, who challenged Scholasticism in the early seventeenth century and opened the door for the era of the natural sciences, criticized Scholasticism precisely because of its lack of interest in improving the lives of ordinary people. In its origins, science and technology were understood as human centered and life enhancing, characteristics of the grace of God in human history (Anderson 1960, 23, 78).

It is only in more recent times that this understanding of technology has become distorted and is now deceiving us. Technology has become self-justifying and claims to be an end in itself. Today, technology speaks only of power, of offering convenience, efficiency, and prosperity. Yet technology is a jealous god. Those who follow it must "shape their needs and aspirations to the possibilities of technology" (Postman 1997, 31). This modern technological god is a false god and worshiping it is idolatry. "Idolatry defrauds God, denying him of his proper honors and conferring them upon others" (Koyama 1985, 48). And this is precisely what we have seen happen when development technology works its "magic" in poor communities. Therefore, when we share development technology with poor communities, we must insist on asking if we are inadvertently promoting idolatry. Are we guilty of helping people exchange "their Glory [God] for an image of a bull, which eats grass" (Ps 106:20)?

The Christian interpretative words for explaining technology's good deeds begin with the obvious: "What do you have that you did not receive? And if you did receive it, why do you boast as though you did not?" (1 Cor 4:7). The human discovery of tools and technology is a direct result of an order-making God, who made a universe that operates within a framework of physical and moral laws. Furthermore, this God made human beings in God's own image, thus enabling them to discover how God made the physical processes of the world work. God granted us the ability to be creative, just as God was and is.

The issue of explaining God at work in nature has proven to be a difficult one. The intellectual challenge is to balance the need to acknowledge God's sovereignty with the fact that an object must fall to the ground every time unless something prevents it. God must be God, and gravity must be gravity. Both must be true at the same time.

This creates two dilemmas. First, if the laws of science are laws, then God must keep them, and this seems to limit God's sovereignty and preclude miracles. This places God outside God's creation, with no room to act within created processes. Second, and equally serious, we cannot postulate that God is in control of every outcome since this (a) denies the possibility of human freedom, (b) provides no explanation for randomness or complexity, and (c) makes God responsible for evil, pain, and injustice.

Nancey Murphy, a theologian at Fuller Theological Seminary, has struggled with the issue of creating an account of divine action in nature that is consistent with Christian doctrines and yet also consistent with what we know about science (Murphy 1995). She is seeking an account for top-down causality (God and human beings as actors) that does not contradict bottom-up causality (gravity, DNA, and the movement of the basic particles of nature) (Murphy and Brown 2009). Nature functions in the way we learned in science class. God sustains creation, governs nature, and cooperates with nature. Yet God does this non-coercively, granting human freedom even if it means rejecting God or ignoring science.

Murphy accounts for this by noting the difference between physics at the human level in contrast to physics at the quantum level. Physics at the macro level is governed by deterministic laws. If one drops a ball, it will fall to the earth every time. At the quantum level, however, physics works differently; probabilities rule. This upset Einstein so much that he fought quantum physics for years: "God does not play dice," he asserted. Einstein was right—and wrong.

The absence of determinism at the quantum level does not mean complete randomness or that nature is not governed by mathematical equations. The way out of this seeming dilemma arose with the new work on dynamical systems, popularly referred to as chaos theory, that demonstrates that we can have deep order without determinism. We examined the impact of dynamical systems on social change in Chapter 8. It is at the quantum level that Murphy postulates that we are free to make the claim that "all events are a result of God's causal influence" without having to set aside the determinism of the macro-physical world (1995, 354). At the quantum level, divine will and natural causation are no longer opposing acts.

By analogy we can apply this to the real world of human beings. Joseph acknowledges God's intentions when he recomposes his story on the occasion of confessing his identity to his brothers. He gives the historical account—the choice his brothers made to get rid of him—and the divine account—God sent me here to save lives (Gn 50:19).

Say what you believe

In his captivating account of his work among the Masai, Vincent Donovan tells the story of the Catholic mission in Tanzania, with its school, mission hospital, and work to improve Masai cattle. By caring for the Masai in concrete terms, mission by deed, it was hoped that some would come to faith in time. The longtime Masai resistance to verbal proclamation of the gospel was cited as evident that the Masai were not to ready for direct verbal witness.

After several years of seeing no results, Donovan wrote to his Bishop, announcing his intention to go out to Masai villages and do nothing but talk to them about his faith. Upon arrival at his first village, a Masai elder asked Donovan his reason for wanting to talk to the elders. "You know us for our work among you in schools and the hospital. But I no longer want to talk about schools and hospitals, but about God in the life of the Masai." The response was immediate, "If this is why you came, why did you wait so long to tell us about this" (Donovan 1978, 22)?

Sometimes Christians doing the work of transformational development are hesitant to talk about their Christian beliefs. Even people committed to Christian witness are reluctant witnesses for good reasons. Respecting the development process is important to them, and they do not want to witness in a way that undermines this important value. In addition, there is the danger of taking advantage of the implicit power relationship that invariably accompanies attempts to help the poor.

Sensitivity is a good thing, but making ourselves silent is not. In West Africa local Muslims criticized Christian facilitators for lacking spirituality because they were so reluctant to talk about their faith. In a personal interview in 1997 Nora Avarientos wisely counseled, "Don't put up your own ghosts. Speak what you believe!" This is a call for conversation, not monologues. The story of Jesus and the woman in John 4 suggests that treating people as equals and having provocative, stretching, engaging conversations about ultimate things are often valued and transformational.

THE BIBLE AND TRANSFORMATIONAL DEVELOPMENT

Why the Bible is important

I have proposed that the narrative context of transformational development is the convergence of stories. The story of the community is joined by the story of the development facilitator and, for the duration of the program, they share a story. God has been and is at work in both stories, and God is offering to both a better future story. This means that the biblical story must become an integral part of the transformational development process.

Furthermore, the goals of transformation that I have suggested—recovering true identity and discovering true vocation—are derived from the biblical story and are the goals for both the community and the development facilitator. Seeking the truth from the biblical story is the beginning of transformation in our lives and our relationships. Therefore, engaging the biblical story must be central to the practice of transformational development done by Christians. This claim deserves a few clarifications.

First, as the word of God the Bible is the only true and unbiased source of guidance to the goals and means of human transformation. The Bible calls into account every other account of the human story—our account, the account of ideologies, of science and modernity, of every culture. The Bible is the one normative source that stands on its own and speaks for itself, as long as we let it. People do not have to believe Christians. God has spoken, and God's word is available to everyone.

Second, the Bible is not simply a book. It is a living word. An encounter with the Bible provides the possibility of an encounter with the One who knows us, the One who knows our past, our present, and our future. An engagement with the Bible sheds its own light, celebrating life and resisting anti-life, regardless of its location. Andrew Walls reminds us that the Bible is "a dynamic, developing, growing, creative factor in the mind; ever fresh, ever bringing out new things, never getting stuck in the past, never getting stale or out of date" (1996, 50).

The Bible is the only book that Christians believe stands in a privileged position over every human being. Hans-Ruedi Weber tells the story of a village woman in East Africa who walked around her village carrying a Bible. "Why always the Bible?" her neighbors asked teasingly. "There are lots of other books you could read." Speaking with authority, the woman replied, "Yes, of course, there are many books which I could read. But there is only one book which reads me" (Weber 1995, ix).

Third, the word of God is a creative word. God's word brought order to chaos, according to Genesis. Thus we must release God's creative word to bring order into our lives and the life of the community. Hope is found in the fact that the word of God is not constrained by the context in which it is heard.

Fourth, the word of God is the birthplace of our identity. We can be children of God "through the living and enduring word of God" (1 Pt 1:23). And the word of God gives us our place in our community (1 Pt 2:10).

Finally, for the Christian, the Bible is universal history (Newbigin 1989, 89). Unlike any other sacred book, the Bible speaks of human life in the context of cosmic history from creation to consummation. In spite of the particularity of Israel, and the even greater particularity of Jesus, the Bible is the account of everyone's past and everyone's future. To those who live within its story in faith, the Bible will create what Peter Berger calls a "plausibility structure," the biblical frame that provides a coherent and consistent framework for creating meaning in and providing explanation about the world in which we live.

How the Bible must be used

In order for the biblical story to be what I have just described, we must take note of some important conditions in terms of how the story is used. The challenge is the same as the one I described earlier in this chapter about matching our approach to Christian witness to the principles we've established for the transformational development process. "Go and tell" evangelism and participatory, grassroots-driven development simply are not consistent methodologies. This drove us to the "provoking the question" framework for Christian witness as a better fit.

The same is true for how we use the Bible. The "study, preach, and teach" frameworks of the expository preacher or the theological teacher are "outside-in" methodologies through which experts provide the knowledge that the non-experts do not have. Like "go and tell" Christian witness, this "go and preach the Bible" approach contradicts the principles of local own-ership, local direction, and the idea that the responsibility for development, including spiritual development, belongs to the people and not to us. The challenge is to find ways of using the Bible in human and social transforma-tion that place the responsibility for asking questions of and seeking an-swers from the Bible within the community itself.

I hasten to add that I am not saying that expository preachers or theol-ogy teachers are using inappropriate methods. In fact, exposition and for-mal teaching methods are ideal for church and classroom settings. I *am* saying that community development is very different and thus makes dif-ferent requirements of us when it comes to using the Bible.

There are two ways to think about using the Bible in a way that better suits the bottom-up framework of transformational development. The first is a product of what I have said about the ownership of the development process, and the second is a reaction to the way some Christians use (or misuse) the biblical story.

First, the issue of ownership. Since the development process must be-long to and be controlled and directed by those who are seeking transfor-mation, it follows that they are the ones who must engage and find their own answers and place in the biblical story. They need to discover for them-selves that God has made them in God's image and that they have been given gifts and are expected to be productive stewards. They need to find for themselves the story that explains relationships that do not work for life and learn that God has provided a means for their restoration. After all, the Bible needs to be their story, not just ours.

Second, there is the issue of how some Christians use the Bible. We need to be aware of and work against some serious shortcomings. The first is the tendency of some Christians to assume that, since the Bible is about spiri-tual things, then the domain to which the Bible speaks is only the spiritual realm. This results in the Bible being used solely for personal discipleship, worship, and nurture of the soul. While this is good and proper, it unwit-tingly precludes the Bible from speaking to the material world of science and development. The Bible lies trapped in Sunday Schools, churches, and Bible study groups, where Christians use it for spiritual development. Our first challenge is to free the Bible from its spiritual captivity and allow it to engage and speak to the whole of human life.

The second limitation in terms of how Christians use the Bible is our temptation to use it in a way that "handles" or domesticates the Bible, thus making it our word instead of God's word. Especially in this modern world, we tend to assume the vantage point of the evaluator, the one who always does the examining. We too often speak for the Bible rather than letting it speak for itself. We must always ask whether we are being the servants or the lords of scripture.

The third limitation is our tendency to treat the Bible solely as a text of inestimable utilitarian value. Such a view objectifies the text and works against the idea of the Bible being the living word of a living God, a God who might like to have a word with us. Engaging God's word in the right way with the right spirit might lead to a personal encounter with the One whose word it is.

Part of the answer to overcoming these limitations is to avoid understanding the biblical text in the same way we would a textbook. We must learn to go beyond studying the Bible solely in order to report what we have learned to others, since this is speaking for the text. We need to be willing to go beyond studying the Bible in order to select what we think is useful for what we want to do, since this is using and almost certainly limiting the text. When we stand outside the text and look into it as a resource from which we pick and choose, we are putting ourselves above the text. This stance is exemplified both by historical criticism and by those who favor proof-texting as a tool of persuasion.

The East African village lady is right. We must live within the text, allowing it to read us, to examine us, to bring life to us, perhaps even to personally encounter us. We must learn, and the people with whom we work must learn, to use the biblical text as an interpretive lens and as a possible meeting place with God.

Newbigin talks of "indwelling" the biblical story. When we dwell within the story, the story has the final say and the storyteller has an opportunity to say hello to us. Indwelling the story means living with the text in such a way that we, and those with whom we work, come to experience the story as fundamentally about us, about the poor and the non-poor.

> *We* are the people whom God liberated from Egypt and led through the Red Sea; *we* are the people languishing in exile and crying out for release; *we* are the disciples whom Jesus rebuked for misunderstanding his mission and to whom he appeared after his resurrection; *we* are the newly formed church who received the outpouring of the Spirit at Pentecost. (Middleton and Walsh 1995, 175)

This framework of living within the biblical story and letting it speak for itself is the key to releasing the transformative power of the Bible as the normative story, the story that makes sense out of all other stories.

This is a whole new kind of Bible for many of us. We have to learn to set aside our own understanding of scripture and allow the living word of the living God to say what God will, to us as well as to the community. Brueggemann says that "our situation needs to be submitted to the text for fresh discernment. . . . In every generation, this text subverts all our old readings of reality and forces us to new, dangerous, obedient reading" (1993b, 18–25). It is in this sense of letting the word of God speak its own word of transformation that I believe that the Bible must be applied within a Christian understanding of transformational development.

Experiences with the Bible and transformational development

Using the Bible as a tool for transformation in the development process is a fairly recent experience for Protestants. Allowing lay leaders to lead open-ended inquiries into the biblical story as it applies the practical questions of the real issues of our lives and that of our community is something new. We are often more comfortable with the experts telling us what the Bible says or means. Even the phrase *Bible study* is assumed often to mean that someone, who is trained, leads us, who have not been trained. We have delegated the responsibility for our own learning to pastors and the theologically trained, becoming passive recipients of their view of what the Bible says.

Catholic social activists Joe Holland and Peter Henriot proposed an approach to social action that embeds scripture as a critical part of the process of determining a course of action among the poor (1983). They call it the Pastoral Circle, and it has four elements: insertion, social analysis, theological reflection, and action.

Insertion is becoming part of the community and building relationships. *Social analysis* is the work the community does of analyzing and making sense out of its own reality. *Theological reflection* is the step in which the community is encouraged to think theologically about what it has learned about its situation and its social, political, and economic context. *Action* is the step in which the community acts on its theology (see Figure 10–1).

Working within this Pastoral Circle the Bible is used to illumine the past as well as guide the future. The Bible is used as a resource for the community's ongoing dialogue regarding commitments, values, beliefs, and traditions, all of which affect the possibilities of the development program in positive or negative ways. The goal of the process is to take action and then assess what actually happens. Then the circle continues: re-action, theological reflection, and action again.

New ways to use the Bible in the process of transformational development allow God and the Bible to speak for themselves. Two ways that illustrate this are the Scripture Search methodology of World Vision Philippines and the Seven Steps method of the Lumko Institute, a Roman Catholic

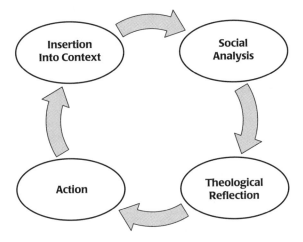

Figure 10–1: Pastoral Circle.
(Adapted from Holland and Henriot 1983)

lay institute in South Africa. This method has been implemented in some World Vision programs in Latin America. I will close with a brief description of the Storying the Gospel approach of New Tribes Mission, which has the potential, if made more holistic, to contribute to the use of the Bible in Christian witness in the context of transformational development.

Scripture Search

The Scripture Search use of the Bible in transformational development is largely the work of Rev. Malcolm Bradshaw, a longtime World Vision staff member in the Philippines, who came across a different methodology for using the Bible in his personal encounter with the Catholic Renewal Movement in the Philippines. Bradshaw then adapted it for use in the context of doing development. Scripture Search is a life-to-Bible approach for using the Bible in a community setting (see Figure 10–2).

Scripture Search assumes the Bible is less a source of rules or a conceptual foundation and more a creative encounter with God and the story that God has chosen to tell us. If we will let it, "scripture breathes hope, life, dynamism and immense possibilities beyond human imagination" (Alvarez, Avarientos, and McAlpine 1999). The Scripture Search process is intended to help get past the spiritual captivity of the Bible that I described earlier. It allows the Bible to speak to issues of private and public morality, to Monday through Saturday as well as Sunday, and to the work of the church as well as the work of the NGO.

Traditional Protestant use of the Bible	Scripture Search use of the Bible
Primarily addressed to the individual	Primarily addressed to the community
Primarily about spiritual things	About all spheres of life, including the spiritual
Primarily about the world to come	Primarily about this world, and by extension, the world to come
Primarily written from the divine point of view	Primarily written from the divine point of view, but includes the view of the "least of these"

Figure 10–2: Scripture Search use of the Bible.
(Developed from Alvarez, Avarientos, and McAlpine 1999)

In using the Bible in the communities, World Vision Philippines operates under the following assumptions:

- God is already at work in the community.
- Members of the community have accumulated a great deal of wisdom about all areas of life, including spiritual perspectives on life.
- The community is solely responsible for its own spiritual pilgrimage.
- People in community are capable of making their own application of spiritual truth to their local situation.
- The local churches have the major responsibility for contributing to the spiritual nurture of the community and hence Scripture Search is non-proselytizing.

Scripture Search is done as part of an action-reflection-action process à la Holland and Henriot by which the community guides its own development.

The Scripture Search methodology is a simple two-step process. First, a facilitator comes to a community meeting having selected a scripture reading, usually a story or a parable, for use during the reflection period when experience-sharing is at a high point. (A listing of Scripture Search Bible passages and their related themes can be found in Appendix 1 at the end of this chapter). The selection is determined by the nature of some critical issue the community is facing. The story or verses are handled like a case study, with open-ended questions. Preaching or teaching from the text is discouraged.

Second, it is up to the people themselves to discover the relevance of the text to their lives in light of the issues with which the group is struggling. Facilitators use a variety of non-directive methods to encourage wide participation and to draw out insights. Three questions apply in most settings:

- What are the similarities between what is happening in this text and your experience now? (This encourages contextualization.)
- What light does this text and the experience of the people in it shed on your experience today? (This leads to prayerful reflection.)
- What do you think you should do about these insights as a group and personally? (This leads to actualization and results in a contribution to new plans that trigger the next action-reflection-action process.)

World Vision Philippines reported seeing both personal and social change emerge as a result of this approach to biblical reflection. People report that their relationship with God has deepened, that their relationships with their spouse and children have improved, and that they are more deeply committed to serving their community than before. Community leaders report gaining confidence in leading the community. Because this process is done in community by lay people, it has proven highly effective in allowing Protestants and Roman Catholics to develop relationships and work together. This has translated into formal cooperation between Protestant World Vision and a variety of Catholic institutions concerned for spiritual formation.

As a result of their experience with Scripture Search, World Vision Philippines and the communities with which it works report discovering the Bible in a whole new way. "We have rediscovered the Bible as a powerful story explaining the meaning and purpose of life, full of cases that model abundance, reconciliation, forgiveness, transformation of persons, communities, nations and nature itself" (Alvarez, Avarientos, and McAlpine 1999).

The Seven Steps

Seven Steps has it roots in the creative work of the Lumko Institute, the pastoral institute of the Southern African Catholic Bishops' Conference, which has been developing tools for the pastoral use of the Bible since the 1960s.

The Seven Steps approach has a Bible-to-life orientation and is an adaptation of an ancient approach to praying the scriptures called *Lectio Divina*. In the first centuries of the Christian church the Bible was experienced as the spoken word in four movements: reading aloud, meditation (reflection), prayer, and contemplation (God's presence beyond the words).

The Seven Steps is more a method of Bible reading, and less one of Bible study (Alvarez, Avarientos, and McAlpine 1999). The emphasis is on group listening and receiving, not on the left-brain work of determining the meaning of the text. The focus is on what God is saying to me (or us)— on sharing and hearing, not discussing and deciding. While this may sound open-ended in the extreme, the practice of patient listening can translate into increasing the capacity for people to address program concerns within a climate of peace and receptivity. Thus Seven Steps is a counterpoint to Scripture Search, not simply a variation.

The Seven Steps takes place in small groups, usually the groups that are part of the development process or one of Holland and Henriot's Pastoral Circles. Its effectiveness is enhanced when the same people are at each meeting. Because it is based on listening to the spoken word, it can be used with people who cannot read. The texts that seem to work best are taken from the gospels and the psalms.

The facilitator of the Seven Steps process follows the outline shown in Figure 10–3. Each of the steps is carried out in a particular way. When the text is *read* aloud, the facilitator waits until people have found the text, because participation of every person is important. *View with wonder* means letting the word or phrase come to us. We are listening for God's word to us. *Listen* means just that, silent listening, enjoying Christ's presence with us. This is not a time for active prayer. *Share* is when people may speak,

---

The Seven Steps

1. Invite
We remind ourselves that the Risen Lord is with us. Would someone like to welcome Jesus in a prayer?

2. Read
Let us open our Bibles to . . .

3. View with wonder
We pick our word or short phrases, read them aloud prayerfully, allowing enough silence between them to say the words three times in our hearts.

4. Listen
We keep silence for ___ minutes and allow God to speak to us.

5. Share
Which word or phrase has touched us personally?
(Do not discuss any contribution.)

6. Group tasks
Now we discuss any task or work our group is called to do and report back on our previous task. What new task needs to be done? Who will do what and when?

7. Pray
Anyone who wishes may pray spontaneously. We close with a hymn, chorus, or prayer that everyone knows.

Figure 10–3: The Seven Steps.

saying the word or phrase that has come to them and briefly sharing how it has illumined their life. The group listens and does not respond. This is not a time for discussion, teaching, or preaching. During *group tasks* the group becomes more verbal, moving from the Bible to life. Any issue relating to the work of the group or the program may arise. This is the reflection step of an action-reflection-action cycle, reporting back and planning ahead. While the text read aloud most often will not be linked thematically to the work at hand, "the practice of careful listening in the previous steps characteristically influences the way the participants approach their tasks and their relationships with each other" (Alvarez, Avarientos, and McAlpine 1999).

The results have been encouraging. Better team work, more inclusive participation in project work, and reconciliation, especially between Catholics and Protestants, have been reported. Many report deepening of their relationships with God and increased participation in local churches.

There have been some challenges to using this method, largely because listening to the text rather than mining it for meaning is a significant change for many Protestants. In many contexts the normative way of using the Bible is authoritarian. Someone in authority, a pastor or the development facilitator, tells everyone else what the text says and means. This tends to cause the group to rush through to step 5, when the talking can begin, and to step 6, when the reporting and planning take place. But the effectiveness of this method comes down to the skill of the facilitator and the willingness of the group to open itself to something new. It is very hard to shift from a framework of how we can use scripture to one that allows scripture to use us.

Anne Hope and Sally Timmel, longtime field workers in Zimbabwe, have developed a four-volume series called *Tools for Transformation* based on the liberation education principles of Paolo Freire, which applies scripture in a way similar to Scripture Search. A list of the scriptures they use in volume 1 of that series is listed in Appendix 2 at the end of this chapter.

Storying the gospel

Scripture Search and the Seven Steps are helpful tools for engaging the Bible in relationship to life issues, values, priorities, and the ordering of relationships. Because they focus on a single text, however, they are less helpful in communicating the biblical story as a whole. Yet, as I have attempted to make clear in this book, engaging the whole biblical story is foundational to how the story of the community and our story come under the transforming power of God's only true story. Storying the Gospel is an approach that, if modified to fit better the context of transformational development, holds promise in this regard.

Storying the Gospel was developed by Trevor McIlwain of New Tribes Mission as an evangelism tool for preliterate people. McIlwain noted that traditional people had trouble understanding and relating to the gospel story. The problem was more than simply unfamiliar geography and unusual cultural practices. Preliterate people rely on epic stories and poems to tell the story of their culture and pass on its values. They rely on their story as a people to create meaning for today. Hearing the Jesus story disconnected from the whole story of the biblical people proved hard for them to understand. When told out of context, without reference to its origins or its future, there is no foundation to enable understanding the Jesus story. Without hearing the whole of the biblical story, the listener may not know that there is only one God or understand the character of the God about whom we are talking. Without the whole story, how can people understand what God intends or how everything came to be as we experience it today? Obedience, sin, grace, and faith are hard to understand apart from the story that gives them their particular Christian meaning.

McIlwain decided to resequence the Bible chronologically so that it could be told as an epic story, beginning with creation in Genesis and ending with the second coming of Christ in Revelation. The result is a chronological teaching outline that tells the whole salvation story so that it builds a foundation on which a person, who has never heard of Jesus or of Israel or been to a city, can say with understanding, "Yes, I believe." McIlwain understood that it is the whole of our story as Christians that reveals the character and activity of the God of the Bible in human history. "The story of Christ begins in the first verse in Genesis" (McIlwain 1991, 32). If telling the whole biblical story is foundational to understanding the Jesus story and making an informed faith decision, no one should be invited to make such a decision until he or she has heard the whole story. In this sense, discipleship begins before the evangelistic act itself.

This approach is attractive to the transformational development process. As techniques like PLA and AI give the community the opportunity to share its story and to articulate what gives it life and meaning, the question often comes back: "And you? What do you believe? What gives you life?" McIlwain's framework suggests a different response than simply saying that we are Christian or followers of Jesus Christ. We could, instead, share the epic story of our people, the biblical story. Sharing the whole story puts us in the position of addressing many of the issues that are contributing to the poverty we wish to transform—marred identity, inadequate worldview, oppressive relationships, fear of the spirit world, god complexes, and the like. By telling our whole story we can address the issues of all human beings: Who are we? What are we for?

As I introduced Storying the Gospel, I alluded to a need for modification. As presented in the training materials and books, this method focuses solely on the issue of personal salvation and the Bible as the story of God's salvific work in history. While this is certainly true, it is not enough. Part of the story is left out. After all, God's story is about more than saving souls.

The biblical account has a more holistic view of salvation, seeking the restoration by grace alone of our relationships with God, with each other, and with God's creation. While personal salvation through faith in Christ is the center of God's concern, it is not the limit of God's concern. If the chronological story of the Bible were made less narrow, so that God's concern for people as productive stewards living in just and peaceful relationships could emerge alongside God's concern for people living in right relationship with God, then we would have the full story in play.

THE EVALUATION OF CHRISTIAN WITNESS

As we think about Christian witness in the context of transformational development, we need to remind ourselves of what the scope of that witness entails. We need to keep our goals for transformation clearly in mind so that the way we witness, the content of our witness, and the way we use the Bible address these important transformational frontiers.

This is important to how we approach evaluation and the need to make evaluations genuinely holistic. In Chapter 9 we saw how a concern for Christian witness leads us to expand the number of program indicators beyond a simple focus on the material aspects of the program. The standards and indicators for Christian witness in Appendix 3, developed by Frank Cookingham and myself, include many from Chapter 9 and a new set of indicators related to the character of the holistic practitioner developed in Chapter 7.

But the key focus of evaluating Christian witness must come back to our understanding of the nature of poverty—marred identity and vocation, and the causes of poverty—relationships that do not work for the well-being of all, as well as the underlying importance of changing values and worldview.

Recovering identity and vocation

Recovering identity and discovering vocation are the twin goals of transformation. Everything else follows. Therefore, our Christian witness must address the issues of identity and vocation. This is not always easy, since one of the outcomes of poverty is an identity so marred that believing one is a child of God is like being asked to believe that one can fly. The first step is to treat people as if we believe they are made in the image of God and are as worthy of respect as anyone. How we treat and listen to the poor can be the beginning of recovering identity.

Another non-directive way to encourage recovery of identity and discovery of vocation is to encourage people to pursue their own investigation of the biblical story. Allow them to find themselves in the story and to hear the good news that their current story is not wholly true and that there is an

Evil One who wants them to believe that they are god-forsaken. In a small Assemblies of God school in Central America, a boy was asked what he liked best about the school schedule. "The Bible study," he replied. Surprised, the researcher asked about the meals, sports, and leather craft. "No, the best is the Bible study." When asked why, the little boy replied, "I am no longer a thief or someone who begs in the street. I am a child of God" (Dyrness 1998, 39). Learning who we really are is good news!

We can also help people recover their history and tell their own story as a way of recovering identity. Using PLA and AI can help people name what has been successful and what has created value in their past. Reading this positive side of their history alongside the Bible can lead to people linking their story to the biblical story, seeing where their account is true and where it is false. This way their chronological past becomes their "ontological" past (Bediako 1992, 4). Remember the story of the tribal people who believe they have always been cursed by God? We can barely imagine the joy and release of energy they would experience if they were able to discover for themselves that their story is true, in the sense that all people live under the curse of sin, but false in that this curse does not have the final say. In Jesus, God has provided for the lifting of their curse. The statement that they are a cursed people is a lie.

We must also witness to the non-poor concerning identity and vocation. We need to help the non-poor explore and identify their own poverty, to get in touch with what happens when one confuses being with having, or serving with power and control. The non-poor also need to read their story against the story of the Bible. The Bible has good news for them, too, even though they tend to find this hard to believe. The problem for the non-poor is that the cost of being who they really are and doing what they were meant to do is too high. Surrendering god complexes and using human skill, the power of position, and financial resources like a servant is very hard indeed. This is why the rich young man walked away (Mt 19:16–22).

Just and peaceful relationships

True transformation occurs when people know their identity and their vocation and live in just and peaceful relationships. I have already explained the fivefold nature of these relationships: relationship with God, self, community, "other," and the environment. Christian witness within the context of transformational development must witness to Christ's lordship over all of these relationships and to his intention that being part of his kingdom means seeking justice and peace.

For the poor, our witness will include helping them find their voice and place. Once the poor begin to discover their true identity and vocation, they need to give expression to each. This change takes place at several levels. First, within the household. In Latin America, it is well known that spiritually changed lives lead to the reduction of alcohol consumption, treating drug addicts, reestablishing released prisoners, and kindling the imagination of students (Maldonado 1993, 196). When women believe the gospel in Colombia, the way they act and witness leads to the erosion of the *machismo* culture of the men. This means less drinking and womanizing, which in turn means more surplus cash. The women invest this surplus in micro-enterprise, and the household income increases (Brusco 1986). This is transformational development at its best; we cannot tell where the spiritual and material change begin and end.

The second level is the social system. People who have discovered that they are children of God, with value and voice, are less likely to be passive in the face of political structures that see the poor only as votes. Evidence from area development programs in Tanzania, India, and elsewhere suggests that such people begin to demand that services due them are delivered and that politicians take them and their views more seriously. When people change, everything else comes under pressure to change (Rosenau 1990). In these ways holistic Christian witness addresses social, political, economic, and cultural relationships, calling into account those that inhibit life or limit the participation of the poor.

For the non-poor, Christian witness must include an invitation to lay down their god complexes and to turn over to God those roles that are rightfully God's. Christian witness means a call to exercise leadership as stewards who think more highly of others than themselves. Leaders with a biblical worldview know that all power belongs to God and that they exercise power only as stewards, not as owners or masters. Of those who have more, more is expected.

Changing worldview

One of the sources of the web of lies that disempower the poor and entices the non-poor to play god in the lives of the poor is worldview (see Figure 4–14). This is why changing worldview must be one of the foci of Christian witness. However, to say that changing worldview is hard is not to say enough. Allowing the biblical story to truly transform any cultural story is difficult in the extreme. Getting a tribal group that believes it is cursed to transform that belief and view itself as a group of people whom God wants to bless is the most difficult of transformational frontiers.

Changing worldview means more than changing behavior. It is even more than changing beliefs or values. Changing a worldview means changing a people's entire story so that the community adopts a new story. This can be only done by a people, not by individuals. While changing the worldview of a people must be a goal of discipleship, it is the work of the Holy Spirit of God.

Some have argued that no culture can evangelize or change its own story. The community cannot see its flat spots and idolatries, and neither can we. Both have the need to see and correct inadequacies in worldview; this is their common task. Another way of saying this is to note that there is no difference between the evangelist and the disciple when it comes to worldview. Both are learning the gospel at the foot of the cross (Koyama 1985, 245). This is why it is so important that the development facilitator be open to and undergoing transformation even as he or she works to help the community experience transformation (see Figure 10–4).

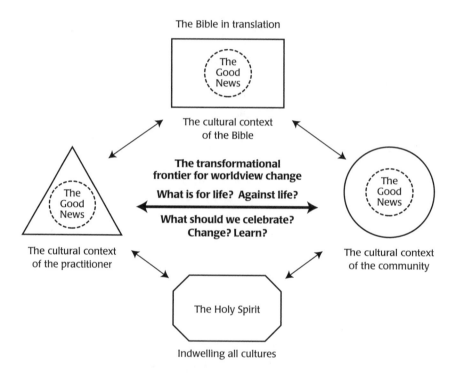

Figure 10–4: Helping each other change our worldview.

Worldview change requires a two-way dialogue between the two cultures, with both open to the prompting and teaching of the Holy Spirit and the will to surrender themselves to the worldview contained in the Bible. The fact that the Bible is translated into both the language of the facilitator and the language of the community is significant. Translation of the Bible means that the word of God can find expression in all cultures. Sanneh points out that "translation relativizes culture by denying that there is only one normative expression of the gospel. It opens culture up to the demand and need for change" (1987, 332). This opens the door to a conversation between our culture and that of the community on the goals and process of transformation. Each carrier of a culture brings to the table the ability to help the other culture see what needs changing. Each has things in its own culture that need changing.

Christian witness and changing worldview take us to the basic beliefs that create meaning and explain why things are as they are. This is where we address the issue of which God we are talking about. Who is being worshiped? This is an important question. The Bible is the account of God working on this question with God's people over the centuries (Hiebert 1998). Abraham began by worshiping El, the high god of traditional cultures. This God, whom Abraham called El, then taught Abraham that God was also El Shaddai, El Elyon, and El Olam. In the following centuries this same God told Moses his name and taught Israel that theirs was a personal God, the God of the descendants of Abraham, Isaac, and Jacob. Today, God's people know that the Christian God is one God—Father, Son, and Holy Spirit. Changing worldview has to do with getting to know the name of the true God, becoming clear on whom we must worship to be truly human.

Worldviews are also the source of answers to the question of who human beings are and what they are for. Because of the importance I have attached to the issue of identity and vocation in this book, it is obvious that this is another area of worldview that must be addressed with the goal of seeking a biblical view.

A third issue of importance when thinking about Christian witness and worldview is to consider what happens to traditional cultures when our Christian witness is not holistic. The effect of only witnessing to the spiritual truth of the gospel is a serious distortion of the gospel. In response to hearing the gospel only as word addressing spiritual need, people may experience only a conversion at the level of formal religion and begin to go to church, read their Bible, and identify themselves as Christians. Yet, the other two dimensions of their worldview remain untouched by the gospel. In fact, people may not even realize that there is good news for these parts of their worldview. The consequences can be serious (see Figure 10–5).

If the folk religion part of their worldview has not experienced conversion, animist beliefs continue to hold sway. Or they develop into a kind of folk Christianity, marked by a Christianized view of magic. If the folk science part of their worldview has not been addressed by Christian witness, then the power of development may have converted this part of their worldview into a belief in modern science and technology, just as we in the West believe. This fragmentation of worldview, each part owing allegiance to a different story, creates psychological and intellectual incoherence and a kind of multiple personality. People try to live as Christians in their spiritual life and be like good moderns in their material life, while still being bound to their animism. This explains the actions of some Christians who

THE TRADITIONAL WORLDVIEW   A PARTIAL CHRISTIAN WORLDVIEW

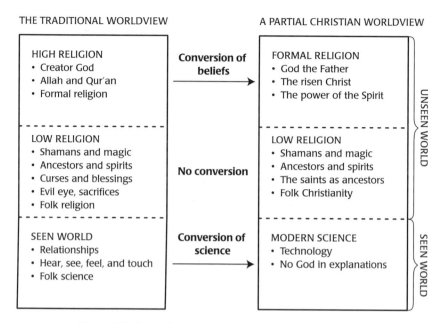

Figure 10–5: An incomplete conversion of worldview.

go to the doctor for medical advice, ask the church to pray for healing, and visit the shaman at night. The bottom line is that our Christian witness must address and engage every level of worldview.

Another area of focus for Christian witness is the cultural system and its contribution to the web of lies that disempowers the poor and validates the god complexes of the non-poor. Changing cultural systems is hard, but is too important a part of transformation to be ignored. Economic and political structures that are validated by the cultural system cannot be changed unless the undergirding validation is called into question. For example, the poverty-creating nature of caste cannot be adequately dealt with apart from the underlying religious beliefs that establish caste. Changing a dowry system that leads to children becoming bonded laborers, or altering the practice of saints or angel days that take away from productive time and require the poor to spend what little they have on alcohol and food cannot be done apart from changing worldview.

The how of changing worldview involves two points of action. First, as I pointed out earlier, the role of the biblical story must come into play. This is the normative story for all cultures and, as the living word of God, it is the source of possible worldview change. Andrew Walls explains the power of the living word to transform the worldview:

> The Word is to pass into all those distinctive ways of thought, those networks of kinship, those special ways of doing things, that give a

nation its commonality, its coherence, its identity. It [the Word] has to travel through the shared mental and moral processes of a community, the way decisions are made in the community. (1996, 50)

The second point of action centers in the Christian development facilitator. Working for worldview change requires sensitivity, skill, and openness to change on both sides. In one sense the work of worldview change is a form of spiritual discernment. Prayer and fasting are important tools as preparation. Changing worldview presupposes relationships of trust in which all parties believe the others are sharing in this process of discovery and are open to letting the Spirit speak a word of truth to any and all. The first step is an appreciative effort to identify local values that are kingdom values so that we celebrate what is already in the culture that enhances or supports life. At this point, in a spirit of dialogue, it is acceptable to ask prophetic questions about practices and beliefs that seem anti-life. Does this value make you proud? Does this value enable you to enhance life in your community? Even better, is this value something that you want your children to inherit?

An example might help. In a Tanzanian tribal context, one traditional belief held that to be the best, a true warrior, a young man had to go to another tribe and bring back a head. Then the whole village celebrated. Challenging this anti-life practice began with a meeting at which men and women, young and old, attended. The starting point was trying to understand why this practice was celebrated. Why is it important? Why does it make the village proud? "It is our tradition," they answered. Then the prophetic questions came. "How do you think the other community felt? What was its reaction?" "They prepare for war," was the response. The prophetic questions continued. "Does going to war make you feel exceptionally good about yourselves? Is this one of the 'prouds' that you would like your children to inherit?" At the end of long discussions, the answer came back that this is something they would like to change. They began to rethink their history in order to move toward a different future. The key was shifting the conversation from a past practice to the future they wish for their children.

I want to emphasize the point that the beginning of worldview change must be listening and learning with no rush to judgment. Often an anti-life practice has a cause behind it that must be addressed before the people can even consider doing something different. In southern India a group of villages had a tradition of female infanticide. Instead of simply announcing the evil of this practice, the development facilitators began a quiet dialogue about how this cultural practice came into being. It turned out that these people were gypsies, a group with no standing in Hindu India. Because gypsies were associated with thievery, the police insisted that the men come to the police station to be locked up every evening. While the men were in jail, the police took advantage of the gypsy women. The village explained that its practice of killing girl children began with the fact that every girl child is a permanent memory of this humiliation. Remember Jayakaran's limitations to growth? Behind every limitation, such as female infanticide, we must look for a stakeholder who has a vested interest in the limitation. Until the issue of the police and their abuse of women are addressed, changing the practice of female infanticide will be an uphill battle in the extreme.

Who changes?

Everyone

I have said several times that everyone who is part of the process must be open to transformational change. This is especially true in Christian witness. Even though we share the gospel, we must never assume we understand or express it fully. We must always be listening to the prompting of the Spirit, even in the voices of those to whom we witness.

Vincent Donovan tells a story that illustrates this wonderfully. After affirming the religious devotion of the Masai toward their High God, Engai, he challenged the Masai with the idea that unwittingly they had trapped or limited Engai when they made him their tribal god. He encouraged them to free Engai, thus allowing him to be the High God of all the tribes, even of the whole world. There was a prolonged silence and Donovan wondered if he had gone too far. Finally, the silence was broken by a question: "This story of Abraham's God, does it speak only to the Masai? Or does it speak to you? Has your tribe found this High God?"

Donovan admits that he almost gave a glib answer, until Joan of Arc inexplicably came to mind and he thought about the French and their tendency to associate God with France's quest for glory. Then he thought of the Americans and their belief that God blesses their side in wars. And then he thought of Hitler, who never failed to call on *Gott, der Allmächtige*, in his speeches. Vincent found himself silent with his thoughts for a long time. Finally, he said, "No, we have not found the High God. My tribe has not known him. For us, too, he is the unknown God. But we are searching for him. I have come a long, long distance to invite you to search for him with us. Let us search for him together. Maybe, together, we can find him" (Donovan 1978, 46).

Christian witness in the context of transformational development is a two-way conversation with the culture of the facilitator and the culture of the community both open to the word of God in the biblical account and to the activity of the Holy Spirit, who indwells both cultures. Christian witness is not negative campaigning. We do not have to speak positively about our faith by speaking negatively about theirs. We do not need the crusading mind that "exposes all their unclean spirits and promotes our own clean spirits" (Koyama 1993, 292).

John V. Taylor said it well:

> Ruthlessness has had a long run in Africa, and so long as the missionary encounter is conceived as a dialogue one will have to "cede to the other." But may it not be truer to see it as a meeting of three, in which Christ has drawn together the witness who proclaims Him and the other who does not know His name, so that in their slow discovery of one another, each may discern more of Him. (1963, 34–35)

Governments

There is one other often-unidentified area in which we must be willing to witness. Most Western governments are adamant that spiritual things and religion must not be part of the development process. This is more than a nonbiblical position. There is a deep irony here.

Governments in the West are worried about Christians being involved in development because they are afraid Christians will use their aid as a tool to encourage people to change their faith. To use aid to promote a particular religion is not appropriate, they say. And, of course, they are right. Any Christian would agree.

But Western governments go a step further and make a bad mistake. In the name of separation of church and state, a logical extension of the modern separation of the spiritual and the material, they require that the programming they fund can never include anything remotely religious in nature. This demand for purely materialistic programming is at complete odds with the holistic worldview of most of the people who are the recipients of development aid. Whether the poor are animists, Muslims, Buddhists, Christians, or Hindus, they believe in an integrated spiritual-physical universe. Western governments are guilty of the same sin they are concerned Christian agencies may commit: By the limitations they place on what is and is not appropriate in programs they pay for, they are using their money to promote a belief system, a faith, that is radically different from the people they are trying to help. Western governments are insisting on a particular worldview—secular liberal democratic—and imposing it, in the form of their funding choices and consultants, on people who do not accept this worldview. This is neo-imperialism.

The attitude of governments to religion in the context of development is flawed in another way as well. William van Geest (1993) has argued persuasively in a Canadian church and development dialogue that there is no such thing as development without value change, and that value change has to do with religion. The argument for this is unassailable. When a community is taught that clean water from pipes is better than muddy water from a stream, we are also challenging its belief that the water in the stream comes or does not come because of a water spirit who must be kept happy. When we challenge the acceptability of female circumcision or the insistence by village males that women have no place in the development dialogue, we are engaged in value change. I've already made the case that the cause of poverty is fundamentally spiritual. Development by definition is about changing culture and changing culture *is* about changing values and worldviews. By denying the role of religion in development, Western governments are setting aside one of the most critical factors to the success of any development initiative.

This is an area in which Christian NGOs need to make their witness in the public square. This stance by Western governments is wrong and harmful. We cannot be who we are and do what we do best unless we are willing to witness to this need for change.

SUMMARY

In an evaluation study from an area development program in Agua Blanca, near Cali, Colombia, a sociologist and a development professional, both Christians, spent an extended period of time allowing the women in the program to explain what had been most helpful and why in terms of spiritual nurture. Most of these women were Roman Catholic and had initially been more than a little suspicious of the work of an evangelical agency like World Vision in their area. As soon as their experience told them that the agenda was about deepening faith experience, not changing churches, the women became enthusiastic participants. Using open-ended interviews and a variety of group exercises derived from the popular education movement in Latin America, the study empirically developed the following indicators of impact in terms of spiritual nurture:

- A change in worldview, including a new view of life, death, poverty, and justice as well as of past, present, and future.
- The development of a devotional life, including prayer, a life based on the Bible and hope in the future.
- A vocation of service, including community leadership, community organization, and solidarity.
- A change in their understanding of God to one who is near, loving, and just.
- A new ethical dimension to life, both private and communal.
- A development that was holistic, including character formation, better self-image, and improved family and community relationships.

Also interesting in light of the framework for Christian witness I have presented in this chapter, the study concluded that the following were key elements of transformation in Agua Blanca:

- The lifestyle of the facilitators.
- The central role of the Bible in the lives of the facilitators and as a "training tool" for the community.
- The development of a devotional stance in daily institutional work. "Every intervention, every contact, provided a spirituality in which God is present and is the center of all activities. We can speak here of a spirituality as the basis for sustainable transformational development."
- The verbalization of the gospel. (Atiencia and Guzman 1997, 12)

Ultimately, the best of transformational development deeds are ambiguous. Good development is being done every day by Buddhists, Muslims, and atheists. The driving force for Christian witness in the context of transformational development is to be sure that credit is given where credit is due. We must take great care that we point, not to our own sacrifices or professionalism, and not to the effectiveness of our development technology, but to the fact that the good deeds that create and enhance life in the community are evidence of the character and activity of the God of the Bible, the God whose Son makes a continuing invitation to new life and whose Spirit is daily at work in our world.

APPENDIX 1:
SCRIPTURE SEARCH TEXTS FOR BIBLICAL REFLECTION
(Taken from Alvarez, Avarientos, and McAlpine 1999)

Jb 29:7–17	Advocacy
Eccl 11:1–6	Agriculture. Dealing with uncertainties
Ps 104	Agriculture. God's blessing
Ps 72	Agriculture. God's blessing, fertility, and justice
Jl 1	Agriculture. Land and desolation
1 Kgs 21:1–19	Agriculture. Land and justice
Gn 1:1–2:3	Agriculture. Land and life
Acts 2	Christian witness: Life, word, deed, sign
Acts 14:5–23	Christian witness: Life, word, deed, sign
Acts 16:11–40	Christian witness: Life, word, deed, sign
Mt 20:1–16	Development. Compare assistance received
Lk 6:1–5	Development. People and institutions
Lk 13:10–21	Development. People and institutions
Acts 16:11–24	Economics. Christian witness
Lk 12:13–21	Economics. Practices. Avarice
Prv 6:6–11	Economics. Practices. Diligence
Dt 15:12–18	Economics. Practices. Generosity
Lv 25	Economics. Practices. Justice. Jubilee
Gn 1	Economics. Practices. Justice. Stewardship, right, and responsibility
Dt 24:10–15	Economics. Practices. Justice. Treatment of weak
Am 8:4–8	Economics. Practices. Justice. Treatment of weak
Jas 5:1–6	Economics. Practices. Justice. Treatment of weak
1 Sm 17:34–37	Economics. Practices. Manual work
Acts 18:1–4	Economics. Practices. Manual work
Prv 1:8–19	Economics. Practices. Prudence
1 Thes 4:9–12	Economics. Practices. Self–sufficiency
2 Thes 3:6–15	Economics. Practices. Self–sufficiency
Mt 6:19–34	Economics. Practices. Trust in God
Mk 5:1–20	Economics. Practices. What is a human being worth?
Ex 31:1–11	Economics. Work. Expression of God-given gifts
Lk 3:21–22	Group. Foundations. Baptism
Jn 3:1–21	Group. Foundations. Conversion
Lk 22:15–34	Group. Foundations. Jesus
Jn 15	Group. Foundations. Jesus
Lk 1:39–56	Group. Foundations. Kingdom of God (personal/ group)
Jn 4:1–42	Group. Practices. Transformation
Rom 12:1–8	Group. Practices. Transformation (ongoing)
Phlm 1	Group. Practices. Transformation of relationships
Lk 12:22–34	Group. Practices. Trust for physical needs
Mt 8:23–27	Group. Practices. Trust in crises

Gn 1:26–27	Group. Self–image
Lk 5:17–26	Health. Committee. Motivate, mobilize, and strengthen
Ps 127	Health. Family
Sg 4:1–5:1	Health. Family
Ex 15:22–27	Health. God's blessing
Ps 139	Health. God's blessing
Mk 2:1–12	Health. God's blessing
Rv 21:1–4	Health. God's blessing
Mt 10:5–15	Health. God's healing and prayer
Jas 5:13–18	Health. God's healing and prayer
2 Kgs 2:19–22	Health. Indigenous medicine
2 Kgs 4:38–41	Health. Indigenous medicine
2 Kgs 20:1–7	Health. Indigenous medicine
Jn 4:1–42	Health. Installation/monitoring of water pumps
Lk 13:10–17	Health. Justice
Lk 4:16–30	Holistic mission. Elements
Lk 24:36–53	Holistic mission. Elements
1 Cor 4:1–5	Management. Evaluation
Neh	Management. Evaluation and monitoring
Neh	Management. Implementation
Lk 9:10–17	Management. Implementation. Inadequate resources?
Neh	Management. Planning
Nm 13—14	Management. Planning. Baseline
Mt 13:31–32	Management. Planning. Membership expansion and why?
Gn 12:1–3	Management. Planning. Vision
Is 2:1–4	Management. Planning. Vision
Is 65:17–25	Management. Planning. Vision
Hos 2:14–23	Management. Planning. Vision
Gn 1:1–2.3	Management. Planning/Evaluation
Neh 5:1–13	Public awareness
Lv 20:1–5	Sponsorship. Importance of children
Lk 15:1–7	Sponsorship. Monitoring
1 Cor 12:12–31	Group. Identification of roles and responsibilities
Ex 18:13–27	Group. Leadership. Delegation of responsibility
Jn 4:1–42	Group. Leadership. Facilitating skills
Acts 18:1–4, 24–28	Group. Leadership. Men and women
Gal 3:23–29	Group. Leadership. Men and women
Acts 8:14–24	Group. Leadership. Money
2 Sm 11—12	Group. Leadership. Power
Mt 6:1–18	Group. Leadership. Reality and appearances
Mt 23:1–12	Group. Leadership. Reality and appearances
Mk 9:33–37	Group. Leadership. Servant
Lk 22:15–34	Group. Leadership. Servant
Jn 13:1–17	Group. Leadership. Servant
Ex 3—4	Group. Leadership. Vocation
Mt 5:21–48	Group. Practices
Lk 10:25–42	Group. Practices
Lk 18:15–30	Group. Practices
Lk 19:1–10	Group. Practices. Behavior

Lk 8:40–56	Group. Practices. Choosing beneficiaries
Ex 1:8–22	Group. Practices. Civil disobedience
Gn 13:1–13	Group. Practices. Dealing with conflict
Acts 6:1–7	Group. Practices. Dealing with conflict
Mt 18:21–35	Group. Practices. Forgiveness
Lk 21:1–4	Group. Practices. Giving out of poverty
Lk 1:26–38	Group. Practices. Hearing and consenting
Mt 7:24–27	Group. Practices. Hearing and doing the Word
Lk 8:4–21	Group. Practices. Hearing and doing the Word
Lk 3:1–20	Group. Practices. Justice
Lk 12:13–21	Group. Practices. Money
1 Tim 6:3–10	Group. Practices. Money
Lk 4:1–13	Group. Practices. Power
Mk 11:20–25	Group. Practices. Prayer
Lk 18:1–14	Group. Practices. Prayer
Lk 10:25–37	Group. Practices. Responsiveness
Lk 15:11–32	Group. Practices. Rules and relationships
Lk 4:1–13	Group. Practices. Scripture
Lk 8:1–3	Group. Practices. Solidarity
Acts 11:27–30	Group. Practices. Solidarity
Jas 2:1–7	Group. Practices. Status
Mt 25:14–30	Group. Practices. Stewardship of gifts
Lk 10:1–12	Group. Practices. Strength and weakness
Jn 4:1–42	Sponsorship. Responding to real needs
Lk 19:1–10	Sponsorship. Treatment of families
Ez 47:1–12	Strategic initiatives
Col 1:15–23	Strategic initiatives. Church and world
1 Pt 2:11–25	Strategic initiatives. Church and world
Acts 2:37–47	Strategic initiatives. Models
Acts 4:32–35	Strategic initiatives. Models
Rv 2—3	Strategic initiatives. Models

APPENDIX 2:
BIBLICAL REFERENCES ON TRANSFORMATION
FOR REFLECTION AND LITURGY
(Hope and Timmel 1984)

Old Testament

Genesis 1:26-29	Creation and human beings as co-creators
4:9-10	Where is your brother Abel?
Exodus 3:1-15	God intervenes on the side of the oppressed
22:25-27	Do not keep the poor man's cloak
Leviticus 25:8-10	The Jubilee Year
25:35-28	Kindness to strangers
19:9-11	Sharing with the poor
19:13-15	Sharing with the poor
Deuteronomy 24:17-11	Leaving some of the harvest
Psalm 72:1-4	God's concern for justice
72:11-17	God's concern for justice
105:22-27	Celebration of the Exodus
Isaiah 1:11-17	I am sick of holocausts
3:13-15	The vineyard
11:1-9	They do not hurt or harm
58:1-12	Worship, poverty, and oppression
65:17-25	New heaven and new earth
Jeremiah 22:16	Is not that what it means to know me?
Amos 5:14-24	Woe to those who feel secure
6:1-6	Woe to those who feel secure
8:4-7	Woe to those who feel secure
Micah 2:1-2	Beat their swords into plowshares
4:1-4	Beat their swords into plowshares
Ruth 1-4	Love and faithfulness

New Testament

Luke 3:2-11	John the Baptist
4:16-21	He sent me to bring the good news to the poor

6:20-25	The beatitudes
19:1-10	Zacchaeus gives away his riches
10:25-37	The good Samaritan
16:19-31	Dives and Lazarus
Matthew 25:31-45	I was hungry and you gave me to eat
John 4:5-42	Woman at the well
8:3-11	Jesus stops the stoning of the woman
20:11-18	Jesus sends a woman to announce the resurrection
Acts 2:42-47	Sharing among the first Christians
4:32-35	Sharing among the first Christians
Galatians 3:26-28	Neither Jew nor Greek
Philippians 2:3-11	He emptied himself
James 2:14-17, 26	Faith without works
1 John 3:14-18	If anyone has the world's goods and sees his brother in need
Revelation 21:1-5	Behold I make all things new
13:1-17	The power of the beast

APPENDIX 3:
STANDARDS AND INDICATORS FOR CHRISTIAN WITNESS
(Developed by Bryant Myers and codified by Frank Cookingham)

Standards	Indicators
Cultural and religious change in project area	
Churches in the project area are active in the political, social, and cultural life of the area communities.	Examples of activities based on interviews with pastors and other church leaders.
	Descriptions of church activities by community members—examples of services provided to the communities.
Development technology is accompanied by an explanation which points to the activity of God.	Examples of explanations based on interviews of staff and project committee members.
The Bible is used in appropriate ways with people in communities as they plan activities, make decisions, and solve problems.	Descriptions of applications discussed during Bible studies in the community.
	Examples based on interviews of staff and project committee members.
Attitudes toward Christians and the gospel message	
Attitudes toward Christians become more positive over the life of the project.	Words used by community members to describe Christians.
People deepen their understanding of the nature of the God of the Bible.	Words used by community members to describe the character of the God of the Bible.
People become more open to listening to the gospel.	Number of people seeking or participating in discussions of spiritual things, attending Bible studies, or attending church services.
	Number of conversations about some aspect of the gospel between staff and community members.

Spiritual powers

	Descriptions of what controls individual lives, based on interviews of community members.
	Descriptions of what people do or whom they turn to when they are afraid of something, based on interviews of community members, pastors, and those who are sought for help.
	Descriptions by community people of who or what they believe controls the lives of World Vision staff.

Quality of witness

Staff learn the local language, are culturally sensitive and show interest in learning and understanding local customs.	Observations of language used as staff converses with community members.
	Comparison of appearance of staff dwelling with typical dwellings in the community.
Staff members are perceived as caring people who love God and neighbor.	Knowledge of local religious beliefs and practices.
	Words used by community members to describe staff.
Staff are perceived as a dependent people, who pray and act as a spiritual people.	Descriptions by community members of prayer experiences with staff.
	Observations of staff as they interact with community members—encouragement to pray, inclusion of prayer in conversations or meetings.

Bibliography

Official documents of the Roman Catholic Church are available on the vatican.va website and are reprinted in numerous books, such as O'Brien and Shannon 2003.

Abraham, William J. 1989. *The Logic of Evangelism.* Grand Rapids, MI: Eerdmans.

Adeney, Bernard T. 1995. *Strange Virtues: Ethics in a Multicultural World.* Downers Grove, IL: InterVarsity Press.

Altieri, Miguel. 1995. *Agroecolog: The Science of Sustainable Agriculture.* Boulder, CO: Westview.

Alvarez, Joy, Nora Avarientos, and Tom McAlpine. 1999. "Our Experience with the Bible and Transformational Development." In Myers 1999.

Anderson, Fulton H. 1960. *The New Organon and Related Writings.* New York: Macmillan.

Anderson, Mary B. 1999. *Do No Harm: How Aid Can Support Peace—or War.* Boulder, CO.: Lynne Rienner.

———. 1996b. *Do No Harm: Supporting Local Capacities for Peace Through Aid.* Cambridge, MA: Collaborative Action for Development.

———. 1996c. "Understanding Difference and Building Solidarity." In *Development and Social Diversity,* ed. Mary B. Anderson. Oxford, UK: Oxfam.

———, and Peter J. Woodrow. 1989. *Rising from the Ashes: Development Strategies in Times of Disaster.* Boulder, CO: Westview Press.

Appadurai, Arjun. 2004. "The Capacity to Aspire and the Terms of Recognition." In Rao and Walton 2004.

Aprodev Rights and Development Group. 2008. "Rights-based Development from a Faith-based Perspective." Joint position paper of the Arprodev Rights and Development Group. Available on the aprodev.eu website.

Atiencia, Jorge, and Agelit Guzman. 1997. "The Impact of Christian Witness in the Agua Blanca ADP." Evaluation Report for World Vision Latin America Region.

Bacon, Francis. 1620. "Aphorisim 28." *Novum Organum, Book 1.* Quoted in Anderson 1960, 29.

Bamford, Christopher, and William Parker March. 1987. *Celtic Christianity: Ecology and Holiness.* Great Barrington, MA: Lindisfarne Press.

Banerjee, Abhijit V., and Esther Duflo. 2011. *Poor Economics: A Radical Rethinking of the Way to Fight Global Poverty.* New York: PublicAffairs.

Banks, Robert. 1993. *Redeeming the Routines: Bringing Theology to Life.* Wheaton, II: Bridgepoint/Victor Books.

Bauckham, Richard. 1993. *The Theology of the Book of Revelation* of *New Testament Theology.* Cambridge: Cambridge University Press.

Bediako, Kwame. 1996a. "Biblical Perspectives on Transformational Development: Some Reflections." Unpublished manuscript presented at the World Vision Development Training and Education Workshop, Lilongwe, Malawi (October 4–9).

———. 1996b. "Theological Reflections." In Yamamori et al. 1996.

———. 1994. "Jesus in African Culture." In *Emerging Voices in Global Christian Theology*, ed. William A. Dyrness. Grand Rapids, MI: Zondervan.

———. 1992. *Theology and Identity: The Impact of Culture of Christian Thought in the Second Century and in Modern Africa*. Oxford, UK: Regnum.

Belshaw, D. G. R., Robert Calderisi, and Chris Sugden. 2001. *Faith in Development: Partnership between the World Bank and the Churches of Africa*. Washington DC: World Bank.

Beltrans, Benigno, S.V.D. 1986. *Journey into Solitude: A Manual for Retreats and Recollections*. Manila, Philippines: Arnoldus Press.

Blunt, Peter, and Michael D. Warren. 1996. *Indigenous Organizations and Development*. London: Intermediate Technology Publications.

Bok, Derek Curtis. 2010. *The Politics of Happiness: What Government Can Learn from the New Research on Well-being*. Princeton, NJ: Princeton University Press.

Bok, Sissela. 2010. *Exploring Happiness: From Aristotle to Brain Science*. New Haven, CT: Yale University Press.

Booy, Dirk, and Sarone Ole Sena. 1999. "Capacity Building Using the Appreciative Inquiry approach." In Myers 1999.

Bosch, David. 1991. *Transforming Mission: Paradigm Shifts in Theology of Mission*. Maryknoll, NY: Orbis Books.

Bradshaw, Bruce. 1997. Christian Witness and Transformational Development Workshop. Developed for internal use by World Vision International.

———. 1993. *Bridging the Gap: Evangelism, Development, and Shalom*. Monrovia, CA: MARC.

Brady, Bernard V. 2008. *Essential Catholic Social Thought*. Maryknoll, NY: Orbis Books.

Bragg, Wayne G. 1983. "Beyond Development." In *The Church in Response to Human Need*, ed. Tom Sine. Monrovia, CA: MARC (1983).

Brock, Karen, and Jethro Pettit. 2007. *Springs of Participation: Creating and Evolving Methods for Participatory Development*. Rugby, UK: Practical Action.

Brueggemann, Walter. 1993a. *Biblical Perspectives on Evangelism: Living in a Three-Storied Universe*. Nashville, TN: Abingdon Press.

———. 1993b. *Texts under Negotiation: The Bible and Post-Modern Imagination*. Minneapolis, MN: Fortress Press.

Brusco, Elizabeth. 1986. "The Household Basis of Evangelical Religion and the Transformation of *Machismo* in Colombia." Ph.D. thesis, City University of New York.

Bryant, Richard. 2007. "Early Intervention for Post-traumatic Stress Disorder." *Early Intervention in Psychiatry* 1, 19–26.

Brymer, Melissa, Christopher Layne, Anne Jacobs, Robert Pynoos, Josef Ruzek, Alan Steinberg, Patricia Watson. 2006. *Psychological First Aid: Field Operations Guide for Community Religious Professionals*. Los Angeles: National Child Traumatic Stress Network and National Center for PTSD. Available on the nctsnet.org website.

Catley, Andrew, John Burns, Dawit Abebe, and Omeno Suji. 2007. *Participatory Impact Assessment: A Guide for Practitioners*. Feinstein International Center, Tufts University. PDF available on the Feinstein Center website.

Center for International Development and Environment of the World Resources Institute. 1990. *Participatory Rural Appraisal Handbook: Conducting PRAs in Kenya*. Prepared jointly with the National Environment Secretariat of the Government of Kenya, Egerton University, and Clark University (February).

Chambers, Robert. 2005. *Ideas for Development*: Sterling, VA: Earthscan.

———. 1997. *Whose Reality Counts? Putting the First Last*. London: Intermediate Technology Publications.

———. 1994. "The Poor and the Environment: Whose Reality Counts?" Working Paper no. 3. Brighton, UK: Institute of Development Studies, University of Sussex (May).

———. 1983. *Rural Development: Putting the Last First*. London: Longman Group.

———, and Gordon Conway. 1992. "Sustainable Rural Livelihoods: Practical Concepts for the Twenty-first Century. Discussion Paper 296. Brighton, UK: Institute of Development Studies.

Chant, Sylvia, and Matthew Gutmann. 2002. "Men-streaming Gender? Questions for Gender and Development." *Gender and Development* 2, no. 4:269–82.

Chester, Tim, ed. 2002. *Justice, Mercy, and Humility: Integral Mission and the Poor*. Carlisle, UK: Paternoster Press.

Christian Children's Fund. 1996. *State of CCF's Children 1996: Annual Impact Monitoring and Evaluation Report*. Richmond, VA: Christian Children's Fund (July).

Christian, Jayakumar. 1999. *God of the Empty-Handed: Poverty, Power, and the Kingdom of God*. Monrovia, CA: MARC.

———. 1998a. "A Different Way to Look at Poverty." *Body and Soul*. London: World Vision UK.

———. 1998b. "Reflections Poverty and Transformation." Lecture series for the WVI Board of Directors (March).

———. 1994. *Powerlessness of the Poor: Toward an Alternative Kingdom of God Paradigm of Response*. Ph.D. thesis, Fuller Theological Seminary, Pasadena, CA.

Clarke, Gerard. 2006. "Faith Matters: Faith-based Organizations, Civil Society and International Development." *Journal of International Development* 18: 835–48.

Collier, Paul. 2007. *The Bottom Billion: Why the Poorest Countries are Failing and What Can Be Done about It*. New York: Oxford University Press.

Cooke, Bill, and Uma Kothari. 2001. *Participation: The New Tyranny?* London: Zed Books.

Cookingham, Frank. 1998. "Ministry Standards Working Group: 1998 Guidelines for Field Testing." World Vision International internal working paper.

Cooperrider, David, Jim Ludema, Suresh Srivastva, and Craig Wishart. 1995. Appreciative Inquiry: A Constructive Approach to Organizational Capacity Building. Workshop for World Vision Relief and Development. Department of Organizational Behavior, Wetherhead School of Management, Case Western Reserve, Cleveland, OH (May).

Cooperrider, David L., and Suresh Srivastva. 1987. "Appreciative Inquiry in Organizational Life." *Research in Organizational Change and Development* 1, 129–69.

Cray, Graham. 1997. "Communications Methods and the Contextualisation of the Gospel." Paper read at the Lausanne Contextualization Revisited Consultation, Haslev, Denmark (June).

Cromartie, Michael. 1995. *The Nine Lives of Population Control*. Grand Rapids, MI: Eerdmans.

Cudd, Ann E. 2006. *Analyzing Oppression*. New York: Oxford University Press.

D'Abreo, Desmond A. 1989. *From Development Worker to Activist: A Case Study in Participatory Training*. 2d ed. Mangalore, India: DEEDS.

Davies, Rich, and Jess Dart. 2005. *The "Most Significant Change" (MSC) Technique: A Guide to Its Use*. Available on the mande.co.uk website.

Dayton, Donald W. 1976. *Discovering an Evangelical Heritage*. New York: Harper Row.

Dearborn, Tim. 1997. *Beyond Duty: A Passion for Christ*. Monrovia, CA: MARC.

De Soto, Hernando. 2000. *The Mystery of Capital: Why Captitalism Triumphs in the West and Fails Everywhere Else*. New York: Basic Books.

———. 1989. *The Other Path: The Invisible Revolution in the Third World*. New York: Harper and Row.

Deneulin, Séverine, and Lila Shahani. 2009. *An Introduction to the Human Development and Capability Approach: Freedom and Agency*. London: Earthscan.

Deneulin, Séverine, and Masooda Bano. 2009. *Religion in Development: Rewriting the Secular Script*. London: Zed.

De Waal, Alex. 1997. *Famine Crisis: Politics and the Disaster Relief Industry in Africa*. Oxford, UK: James Curry.

DFID (Department for International Development). 2003. "Sustainable Livelihood Guidance Sheets." Available online.

Diamond, Jared M. 1997. *Guns, Germs, and Steel: The Fates of Human Societies*. New York: W. W. Norton.

Dilulio, John, Jr. 1995. "The Coming of the Super-Predators." *The Weekly Standard* (November 27).

Donovan, Vincent J. 1978. *Christianity Rediscovered*. Chicago: Fides/Claretian.

Dowla, Asif, and Dipal Barua. 2006. *The Poor Always Pay Back: The Grameen II Story*. Bloomfield, CT: Kumarian Press.

Duflo, Esther, and Mark Kremer. 2008. "Use of Randomization in the Evaluation of Development Effectiveness." In *Reinventing Foreign Aid*, ed. W. Easterly. Cambridge, MA: MIT.

Dulles, Avery. 1996. "Evangelizing Theology," *First Things* 61 (March): 27–32.

Dyrness, Andrea. 1998. "Seeds of Change: NGOs, the Church, and Educational Reform in Central America." Report for the Strachan Foundation.

Dyrness, William A. 2010. *Poetic Theology*. Grand Rapids, MI: Eerdmans.

———, William A. 1997. *The Earth Is God's: A Theology of American Culture*. Maryknoll, NY: Orbis Books.

Earl, Sarah, Fred Carden, and Terry Smutylo. 2001. *Outcome Mapping: Building Learning and Reflection into Development Programs*. Ottawa: International Development Research Centre.

Easterly, William. 2008. *Reinventing Foreign Aid*. Cambridge, MA: MIT.

———. 2006. *The White Man's Burden: Why the West's Efforts to Aid the Rest Have Done So Much Ill and So Little Good*. New York: Penguin Press.

Edwards, Michael. 1996. "New Approaches to Children and Development: Introduction and Overview." *Journal of International Development* 8, no. 6: 813–27.

Elizondo, Virgilio. 2007. "Culture, the Option of the Poor, and Liberation." In *The Option of the Poor in Christian Theology*, ed. D. Groody. Notre Dame, IN: University of Notre Dame Press.

Elliot, Charles. 1999. *Locating the Energy for Change: An Introduction to Appreciative Inquiry*. Winnipeg, Canada: International Institute for Sustainable Development.

———. 1987. *Comfortable Compassion? Poverty, Power, and the Church*. London: Hodder and Stoughton.

———. 1985. *Praying the Kingdom: Towards a Political Spirituality*. London: Darton, Longman, and Todd.

Ellul, Jacques. 1967. *The Presence of the Kingdom*. New York: Seabury.

Erickson, Victoria Lee. 1996. "Neighborology: A Feminist Ethno-missiological Celebration of Kosuke Koyama." In *The Agitated Mind of God*, ed. Dale T. Irvin and Akintude E. Akindade. Maryknoll, NY: Orbis Books.

Escobar, Arturo. 1995. *Encountering Development: The Making and Unmaking of the Third World*. Princeton, NJ: Princeton University Press.

Famonure, Bayo. 1989. *Training to Die: A Manual on Discipleship*. Ibadan, Nigeria: Salem Media.

Felix, Monica. 2009. "Trauma Research and the Chronically Poor: A Cross Disciplinary Dialogue." Paper written for School of Intercultural Studies, Fuller Theological Seminary, Pasadena, CA.

Feuerstein, Marie-Therese. 1986. *Partners in Evaluation: Evaluating Development Programming and Community Programmes with Participants*. London: Macmillan Publishers.

Fondation, Larry, Peter Tufano, and Patricia Walker. 1999. "Collaborating with Congregations: Opportunities for Financial Services in the Inner City." *Harvard Business Review* (July-August).

Fowler, Alan. 1997. *Striking a Balance: A Guide to Enhancing the Effectiveness of Non-Governmental Organizations in International Development*. London: Earthscan Publications.

Freire, Paulo. 1990. *Pedagogy of the Oppressed*. New York: Continuum Books.

Friedmann, John. 1992. *Empowerment: The Politics of Alternative Development*. Cambridge, MA: Blackwell.

Galilea, Segundo. 1984. *The Beatitudes: To Evangelize as Jesus Did*. Maryknoll, NY: Orbis Books.

Gaventa, John, and Anne Marie Goetz. 2001. "Bringing Citizen Voice and Client Focus into Service Delivery." IDS Working Paper no. 138. Brighton: Institute of Development Studies.

Gillespie, Michael Allen. 2008. *The Theological Origins of Modernity*. Chicago: University of Chicago Press.

Goffman, Erving. 1963. *Stigma: Notes on the Management of Spoiled Identity*. New York: Simon and Schuster.

Goizueta, Roberto S. 1995. *Caminemos con Jesus: Toward a Hispanic/Latino Theology of Accompaniment*. Maryknoll, NY: Orbis Books.

Gray, Matt, and Brett Litz. 2005. "Behavioral Interventions for Recent Trauma: Empirically Informed Practice Guidelines." *Behavioral Modification* 29, 189–215.

Green, Mike, John O'Brien, Henry Moore, and Dan Duncan. 2006. *When People Care Enough to Act: ABCD in Action*. Toronto: Inclusion Press.

Green, Thomas, SJ. 1979. *When the Well Runs Dry*. Notre Dame, IN: Ave Maria Press.

Groody, Daniel G. 2007. *Globalization, Spirituality, and Justice: Navigating a Path to Peace*. Maryknoll, NY: Orbis Books.

Guijt, Irene, and Meera Kaul Shah, eds. 1998. *The Myth of Community: Gender Issues in Participatory Development*. London: Intermediate Technology Publications.

Gunton, Colin. 1997. "The Trinity, Natural Theology, and a Theology of Nature." In *The Trinity in a Pluralistic Society*, ed. Kevin J. Vanhoozer. Grand Rapids, MI: Eerdmans.

Gutiérrez, Gustavo. 1984. *We Drink from Our Own Wells: The Spiritual Journey of a People*. Maryknoll, NY: Orbis Books.

Hall, Douglas John. 1985. *The Stewardship of Life in the Kingdom of Death*. New York: Friendship Press.

Harrison, Lawrence E. 1985. *Underdevelopment Is a State of Mind: The Latin American Case*. Lanham, MD: Center for International Affairs, Harvard University.

———, and Samuel P. Huntington, eds. 2000. *Culture Matters: How Values Shape Human Progress*. New York: Basic Books.

Hawtrey, Kim. 1990. "Oxford Declaration on Christian Faith and Economics." *Transformation* 7, no. 2:1–8.

Heilbroner, Robert L. 1999. *The Worldly Philosophers: The Lives, Times, and Ideas of the Great Economic Thinkers*. Rev. 7th ed. New York: Simon and Schuster.

Henry, Carl F. H. 1947. *The Uneasy Conscience of Modern Fundamentalism*. Grand Rapids, MI: Eerdmans.

Hertzke, Allen D. 2004. *Freeing God's Children: The Unlikely Alliance for Global Human Rights*. Lanham, MD: Rowman and Littlefield.

Hickey, Samuel, and Giles Mohan. 2004. *Participation: From Tyranny to Transformation? Exploring New Approaches to Participation in Development*. New York: Zed Books.

Hiebert, Paul G. 1998. *Missiological Implications of Epistemological Shifts*. Valley Forge, PA: Trinity Press International.

———. 1997. "The Excluded Middle." Prepared for Changing the Story: Christian Witness and Transformational Development Consultation, World Vision, Pasadena, CA (May 5–10).

———. 1982. "The Flaw of the Excluded Middle." *Missiology* 10, no. 1: 35–47.

———, Dan Shaw, and Tite Tienou. 1998. *Folk Religions: A Christian Response to Popular Religiosity*. Grand Rapids, MI: Baker Books.

Hoksbergen, Roland, Janel Curry, and Tracy Kuperus. 2009. "International Development: Christian Reflections on Today's Competing Theories." *Christian Scholars Review* 39, no. 1: 11–36.

Holland, Jeremy, with James Blackburn, eds. 1998. *Whose Voice? Participatory Research and Policy Change*. London: Intermediate Technology Publications.

Holland, Joe, and Peter J. Henriot. 1983. *Social Analysis: Linking Faith and Justice*. Maryknoll, NY: Orbis Books.

Holman, Susan R. 2008. *Wealth and Poverty in Early Church and Society*. Grand Rapids, MI: Baker.

Hope, Anne, and Sally Timmel. 1984. *Training for Transformation: A Handbook for Community Workers*. Harare, Zimbabwe: Mambo Press.

Hughes, Dewi Arwel. 2008. *Power and Poverty: Divine and Human Rule in a World of Need*. Downers Grove, IL: InterVarsity Press Academic.

———, with Matthew Bennett. 1998. *God of the Poor*. Carlisle, UK: OM Publishing.

Hunter, James Davison. 2010. *To Change the World: The Irony, Tragedy, and Possibility of Christianity in the Late Modern World*. New York: Oxford University Press.

Janoff-Bulman, Ronnie. 1992. *Shattered Assumptions: Towards a New Psychology of Trauma*. New York: Free Press.

Jayakaran, Ravi. 2008. "New Participatory Tools for Measuring Attitude, Behavior, Perception, and Change." In *Evaluation South Asia*, ed. M. Sankar and B. Williams. Kathmandu, Nepal: UNICEF South Asia.

———. 2007. "Wholistic Worldview Analysis: Understanding Community Realities." *PLA Notes* 56, no. 1:41–48. Available on the planotes.org website.

———. 2003. *Participatory Poverty Alleviation and Development: A Comprehensive Manual for Development Professionals*. Hong Kong: World Vision China.

———. 1999. "Holistic Participatory Learning and Action: Seeing the Spiritual and Whose Reality Counts." In Myers 1999.

———. 1997a. "The Story of the Bhil." Prepared for Changing the Story: Christian Witness and Transformational Development Consultation, World Vision, Pasadena, CA (May 5–10).

———. 1997b. *Wholistic World View Analysis: Seeing Their World as They See It*. Madras, India: World Vision India.

———. 1996. *Participatory Learning and Action: User Guide and Manual*. Madras, India: World Vision India.

Jenson, Robert W. 1993. "How the World Lost Its Story." *First Things* (October).

Johnson, Richard Boyd. 1998. *World View and International Development: A Critical Study of the Idea of Progress in Development Work of World Vision Tanzania*. Ph.D. thesis. Oxford Centre for Mission Studies, Oxford, UK.

Johnson, Scott, and James D. Ludema. 1997. *Partnering to Build and Measure Organizational Capacity: Lessons from NGOs around the World*. Grand Rapids, MI: Christian Reformed World Relief Committee.

Jones, E. Stanley. 1972. *The Unchanging Person and the Unshakable Kingdom*. New York: Abingdon Press.

Kenny, Anthony, and Charles Kenny. 2006. *Life, Liberty, and the Pursuit of Utility: Happiness in Philosophical and Economic Thought*. Exeter: Imprint Academic.

Korten, David C. 1991. "Two Visions of Development." Overhead transparency from People-Centered Development Forum (April 23).

———. 1990. *Getting to the Twenty-first Century: Voluntary Action and the Global Agenda*. West Hartford, CT: Kumarian Press.

———. 1989. "Social Science in the Service of Social Transformation." In *A Decade of Process Documentation Research: Reflections and Synthesis*, ed. C. C. Veneracion. Quezon City, Philippines: Institute of Philippine Culture, Ateneo de Manila University.

———. 1980. "Community Organization and Rural Development: A Learning Process Approach." *Public Administration Review* 40, no. 5:480–511.

———, and Rudi Klauss, eds. 1984. *People-centered Development: Contributions toward Theory and Planning Frameworks*. West Hartford, CT: Kumarian Press.

Koyama, Kosuke. 1993. "'Extend Hospitality to Strangers'—A Missiology of *Theologia Crucis*." *International Review of Mission* 82, no. 327 (October).

———. 1985. *Mt. Fuji and Mt. Sinai: A Critique of Idols*. Maryknoll, NY: Orbis Books.

———. 1979. *Three Mile an Hour God*. Maryknoll, NY: Orbis Books.

———. 1974. *Waterbuffalo Theology*. London: SCM.

Kraybill, Donald B. 1978. *The Upside Down Kingdom*. Scottdale, PA: Herald Press.

Kreef, Peter. 1986. *Back to Virtue: Traditional Moral Wisdom for Modern Moral Confusion*. San Francisco: Ignatius Press.

Kretzmann, John P., and John L. McKnight. 1993. *Building Communities from the Inside Out: A Path toward Finding and Mobilizing a Community's Assets.* Evanston, IL: The Asset-Based Community Development Institute.

Kumar, Somesh. 2002. *Methods for Community Participation: A Complete Guide for Practitioners.* London: ITDG.

LaCugna, Catherine Mowry. 1991. *God for Us: The Trinity and Christian Life.* San Francisco: Harper Collins.

Landes, David S. 1999. *The Wealth and Poverty of Nations: Why Some Are So Rich and Some So Poor.* New York: W. W. Norton.

Lansing, J. Stephen. 1991. *Priests and Programmers: Technologies of Power in the Engineered Landscape of Bali.* Princeton, NJ: Princeton University Press.

Leupp, Roderick T. 1996. *Knowing the Name of God.* Downers Grove, IL: InterVarsity Press.

Lewis, David, and David Mosse, eds. 2006. *Development Brokers and Translators: The Ethnography of Aid and Agencies.* Bloomfield, CT: Kumarian Press.

Lewis, Oscar. 1959. *Five Families: Mexican Case Studies in the Culture of Poverty.* New York: Basic Books.

Linthicum, Robert C. 1991. *Empowering the Poor.* Monrovia, CA: MARC.

Maddison, Angus. 2003. *The World Economy: Historical Statistics.* Paris: OECD.

———. 2001. *The World Economy: A Millennial Perspective.* Paris: OECD.

Maggay, Melba. 1994. *Transforming Society.* London: Regnum.

Malanes, Maurice. 2009. "Dalit's Inner Strength Defeats Caste-based Discrimination." Available on the cbcisite.com website.

Maldonado, Jorge E. 1993. "Evangelicalism and the Family in Latin America." *International Review of Mission* 82, no. 326 (April).

Marsden, David, and Peter Oakley, eds. 1990. *Evaluating Social Development Projects.* Oxford, UK: Oxfam.

Marshall, Katherine. 2001. "Development and Religion: A Different Lens on Development Debates." *Peobody Journal of Education* 76: 339–95.

———, and Marisa Van Saanen. 2007. *Development and Faith: Where Mind, Heart, and Soul Work Together.* Washington DC: World Bank.

Mayoux, Linda. 1997. "Impact Assessment and Women's Empowerment in Microfinance Programmes: Issues for a Participatory and Action Learning Approach." Background paper submitted to the CGAP virtual meeting on impact assessment methodologies in microfinance programs (April 7–19).

McAlpine, Tom. 1995. *By Word, Work, and Wonder.* Monrovia, CA: MARC.

McCloskey, Deirdre. 2010. *Bourgeois Dignity: Why Economics Can't Explain the Modern World.* Chicago: University of Chicago Press.

McIlwain, Trevor. 1991. *Firm Foundations: Creation to Christ.* Sanford, FL: New Tribes Mission.

McNally, Richard, Richard Bryant, and Anke Ehlers. 2003. "Does Early Psychological Intervention Promote Recovery from Post-traumatic Stress?" *Psychological Science in the Public Interest* 4, 45–79.

Middleton, J. Richard. 2005. *The Liberating Image: The Imago Dei in Genesis 1.* Grand Rapids, MI: Brazos Press.

———, and Brian J. Walsh. 1995. *Truth Is Stranger than It Used to Be.* London: SPCK.

Mills, C. Wright. 1993. "The Structure of Power in American Society." In *Power in Modern Societies*, ed. Marvin E. Olsen and Martin N. Marger. Boulder, CO: Westview Press.

Momsen, Janet. 2009. *Gender and Development*. 2d ed. New York: Routledge.

Mosse, David. 2005. *Cultivating Development: An Ethnography of Aid Policy and Practice of Anthropology, Culture, and Society*. London: Pluto Press.

———. 2001. "Process-oriented Approaches to Development Practice and Social Research." In *Development as Process: Concepts and Methods for Working with Complexity*, edited by D. Mosse, John Farrington, John and Alan Rew. New Delhi: India Research Press.

Motte, Mary. 1996. "In the Image of the Crucified God." In *The Agitated Mind of God*, ed. Dale T. Irvin and Akintude E. Akindade. Maryknoll, NY: Orbis Books.

Mouw, Richard J. 1989. "Thinking about the Poor: What Evangelicals Can Learn from the Bishops." In *Prophetic Visions and Economic Realities: Protestants, Jews and Catholics Confront the Bishop's Letter on the Economy*, ed. Charles R. Strain. Grand Rapids, MI: Eerdmans.

Muchena, Olivia. 1996. "Sociological and Anthropological Reflections." In Yamamori et al. 1996.

Murphy, Nancey C. 1995. "Divine Action in the Natural Order: Buridian's Ass and Schroedinger's Cat." In *Chaos and Complexity: Scientific Perspectives on Divine Action*, ed. Robert Russell et al. Berkeley, CA: Center for Theology and the Natural Sciences.

———, and Warren S. Brown. 2009. *Did My Neurons Make Me Do It? Philosophical and Neurobiological Perspectives on Moral Responsibility and Free Will*. Oxford: Oxford University Press.

Musopole, A. C. 1997. "African World View." Prepared for Changing the Story: Christian Witness and Transformational Development Consultation, World Vision, Pasadena, CA (May 5–10).

Mveng, Englebert. 1994. "Impoverishment and Liberation: A Theological Approach for Africa and the Third World." In *Paths of African Theology*, ed. R. Gibellini. Maryknoll, NY: Orbis Books.

Myers, Bryant L. 1999. *Working with the Poor: New Insights and Learnings from Development Practitioners*. Monrovia, CA: World Vision.

———. 1998a. "We Are a Cursed People?" *MARC Newsletter* 98, no. 1 (March).

———. 1998b. "What Makes Development Christian? Recovering from the Impact of Modernity." *Missiology* 26, no. 2 (April): 143–53.

———. 1997. "Changing the Story: Christian Witness and Transformational Development." Notes from Changing the Story: Christian Witness and Transformational Development Consultation, World Vision, Pasadena, CA (May 5–10).

———. 1994. "State of the World's Children." *International Bulletin of Missionary Research* 18, no. 3 (July).

———. 1993. "What Message Did They Hear?" *MARC Newsletter* 93, no. 4 (December).

———. 1992a. "Beyond Management by Objectives." *MARC Newsletter* 92, no. 2 (June).

———. 1992b. "Provoking the Question." *MARC Newsletter* 92, no. 1 (March).

Myers, Lisa. 2002. "Practicing Presence in Community." Retreat handout.

Narayan, Deepa. 1993. "Participatory Evaluation: Tools for Managing Change in Water and Sanitation." World Bank Technical Paper no. 207. Washington DC: The World Bank.

Narayan-Parker, Deepa, ed. 2005. *Measuring Empowerment: Cross-disciplinary Perspectives*. Washington DC: World Bank.

Narayan-Parker, Deepa, Robert Chambers, Meera Shaw, and Patti Petesch. 2000. *Voices of the Poor: Crying Out for Change*. New York: Oxford University Press for the World Bank.

Nelson, Geoffrey B., and Isaac Prilleltensky. 2010. *Community Psychology: In Pursuit of Liberation and Well-being*. 2d ed. New York: Palgrave Macmillan.

Newbigin, Lesslie. 1995. *Proper Confidence: Faith, Doubt, and Certainty in Christian Discipleship*. Grand Rapids, MI: Eerdmans.

———. 1989. *The Gospel in a Pluralist Society*. Geneva: WCC.

———. 1986. *Foolishness to the Greeks: The Gospel and Western Culture*. Grand Rapids, MI: Eerdmans.

———. 1981. *Sign of the Kingdom*. Grand Rapids, MI: Eerdmans.

———. 1954. *The Household of God*. New York: Friendship Press.

Nicholls, Bruce, ed. 1986. *In Word and Deed: Evangelism and Social Responsibility*. Grand Rapids, MI: Eerdmans.

North, Douglass Cecil. 2005. *Understanding the Process of Economic Change*. Princeton, NJ: Princeton University Press.

Nussbaum, Martha Craven, and Amartya Kumar Sen. 1993. *The Quality of Life*. Oxford: Clarendon Press.

Nussbaum, Stan. 1996–98. *The Wisdom of African Proverbs CD-ROM. Rev. 1.03*. Colorado Springs, CO: Global Mapping Int'l.

O'Brien, David J., and Thomas A. Shannon. 2003. *Catholic Social Thought*. Maryknoll, NY: Orbis Books.

Oden, Thomas C. 1986. *Crisis Ministries*. New York: Crossroad.

O'Gorman, Frances. 1992. *Charity and Change: From Bandaid to Beacon*. Melbourne: World Vision Australia.

Okorocha, Cyril. 1994. "The Meaning of Salvation: An African Perspective." In *Emerging Voices in Global Christian Theology*, ed. William A. Dyrness. Grand Rapids, MI: Zondervan.

Olivier de Sardan, Jean-Pierre. 2005. *Anthropology and Development: Understanding Contemporary Social Change*. New York: Zed Books.

O'Reilly, Siobhan. 1998. *The Contribution of Community Development to Peacebuilding: World Vision's Area Development Programs*. Milton Keynes, UK: World Vision UK.

Park, Andrew Sung. 2004. *From Hurt to Healing: A Theology of the Wounded*. Nashville, TN: Abingdon Press.

———, 1993. *The Wounded Heart of God: The Asian Concept of Han and the Christian Doctrine of Sin*. Nashville, TN: Abingdon.

Parker, Cristián. 1996. *Popular Religion and Modernization in Latin America: A Different Logic*. Maryknoll, NY: Orbis Books.

Pascale, Richard, Jerry Sternin, and Monique Sternin. 2010. *The Power of Positive Deviance: How Improbable Innovators Solve the World's Toughest Problems*. Boston: Harvard Business.

Pascale, Richard, Mark Millemann, and Linda Gioja. 2000. *Surfing the Edge of Chaos: The Laws of Nature and the New Laws of Business*. New York: Three Rivers Press.

Paz, Octavio. 1972. *The Other Mexico: Critique of the Pyramid*. Translated by Lysander Kemp. New York: Grove Press.

Phillips, Tommy M. 2007. "A Triarchic Model of Poverty." *Theory and Science* 9, no. 3.

Postman, Neil. 1997. "Science and the Story That We Need." *First Things* (January).

Pottier, Johan, Alan Bicker, and Paul Sillitoe, eds. 2003. *Negotiating Local Knowledge: Power and Identity in Development*. London: Pluto Press.

Pretty, Jules N. 1995. *Regenerating Agriculture*. London: Earthscan.

———, Irene Guijt, John Thompson, and Ian Scoones. 1995. *Participatory Learning and Action: A Trainer's Guide*. London: International Institute for Environment and Development.

Prilleltensky, Isaac. 2003. "Poverty and Power." In *Poverty and Psychology: From Global Perspective to Local Practice*, ed. S. C. Carr and T. S. Sloan. New York: Plenum Publishers.

———, and Geoffrey Nelson. 2002. *Doing Psychology Critically: Making a Difference to Diverse Settings*. New York: Palgrave Macmillan.

Raistrick, Tulo. 2010. "The Local Church: Transforming Community." In *Holistic Mission: God's Plan for God's People*, ed. B. Woolnough and W. Ma. Oxford, UK: Regnum.

Ramalingam, Ben, Harry Jones, Reba Toussaint, and John Young. 2008. "Exploring the Science of Complexity: Ideas and Implications for Development and Humanitarian Efforts." Working Paper no. 285. London: Overseas Development Institute.

Rao, V. R., and M. Walton, eds. 2004. *Culture and Public Action*. Stanford, CA: Stanford University.

Ravindra, Adikeshavalu. 2004. "An Assessment of the Impact of Bangalore Citizen Report Cards on the Performance of Public Agencies." ECD Working Paper Series no. 12. Washington DC: World Bank Operations Evaluation Department.

Robert, L. Dana. 1996. *American Women in Mission: A Social History of Their Thought and Practice*. Macon, GA: Macon University Press.

Rogers, Everett M. 2003. *Diffusion of Innovations*. 5th ed. New York: Free Press.

Rosenau, James N. 1990. *Turbulence and World Politics: A Theory of Change and Continuity*. Princeton, NJ: Princeton University Press.

Rostow, William. W. 1960. *The Stages of Economic Growth: A Non-Communist Manifesto*. Cambridge: Cambridge University Press.

Sachs, Jeffrey. 2005. *The End of Poverty: Economic Possibilities for Our Time*. New York: Penguin Press.

Samuel, Vinay. 1995. "A Theological Perspective." In Yamamori et al. 1995.

———, and Chris Sugden, eds. 1987. *The Church in Response to Human Need*. Grand Rapids, MI: Eerdmans.

Sanneh, Lamin O. 1989. *Translating the Message: The Missionary Impact on Culture*. Maryknoll, NY: Orbis Books.

———. 1987. "Christian Missions and the Western Guilt Complex." *The Christian Century* (April 8).

Save the Children. 1982. *Bridging the Gap: A Participatory Approach to Health and Nutrition Education*. Westport, CT: Save the Children.

Schumacher, E. F. 1973. *Small Is Beautiful: Economics as if People Mattered*. New York: Harper and Row.

Scoones, Ian, and John Thompson. 1994. *Beyond Farmer First: Rural People's Knowledge, Agricultural Research and Extension Practice*. London: Intermediate Technology Publications.

Sen, Amartya. 1999. *Development as Feedom*. New York: Knopf.

Serageldin, Ismail. 1995. *Toward Sustainable Management of Water Resources*. Directions in Development series. Washington DC: World Bank.

Shah, Meera Kaul. 2003. "Using Community Scorecards for Improving Transparency and Accountability in the Delivery of Public Health Services." CARE International.

Shenk, Wilbert R. 1993. "The Whole Is Greater than the Sum of the Parts: Moving beyond Word and Deed." *Missiology* 20 (January).

Sillitoe, Paul. 1998. "The Development of Indigenous Knowledge: A New Applied Anthropology." *Current Anthropology* 19, no. 2: 223–52.

Singhal, Arvind, and Lucia Dura. 2009. *Protecting Children from Exploitation and Trafficking: Using the Positive Deviance Approach in Uganda and Indonesia*. El Paso: University of Texas.

Slim, Hugo. 1997. "Doing the Right Thing: Relief Agencies, Moral Dilemma, and Moral Responsibility in Political Emergencies and War." *Studies on Emergencies and Disaster Relief.* Report no. 6. Uppsala: Nordiska Afrikainstitutet.

Sloan, Tod S. 2003. "Poverty and Psychology: A Call to Arms." In *Poverty and Psychology: From Global Perspective to Local Practice*, ed. S. C. Carr and T. S. Sloan. New York: Plenum Publishers.

Stark, Rodney. 2005. *The Victory of Reason: How Christianity Led to Freedom, Capitalism, and Western Success*. New York: Random House.

Stassen, Glen. 2008. "Human Rights." In *Global Dictionary of Theology: A Resource for the Worldwide Church*, ed. W. A. Dyrness and V. Kärkkäinen. Downers Grove, IL: InterVarsity Press Academic.

Stott, John R. W. 1975. *The Lausanne Covenant: An Exposition and Commentary*. Minneapolis, MN: World Wide Publications.

Sugden, Christopher. 1997. *Seeking the Asian Face of Jesus: The Practice and Theology of Christian Social Witness in Indonesia and India 1974–1996*. Oxford, UK: Regnum.

Swartz, David. 1997. *Culture and Power: The Sociology of Pierre Bourdieu*. Chicago: University of Chicago.

Sznaider, Natan. 1998. "The Sociology of Compassion: A Study in the Sociology of Morals." *Cultural Values* 2, no. 1: 117–39.

Taylor, John V. 1972. *The Go-Between God: The Holy Spirit and Christian Mission*. London: SCM.

———. 1963. *The Primal Vision*. London: SCM.

Thindwa, Jeff, James Edgerton, and Riener Forster. 2005. "Community-based Performance Monitoring (CBPM): Empowering and Giving Voice to Local Communities." Paper read at the International Conference on Engaging Communities, August 14–17, Brisbane, Australia.

Thurman, Howard. 1996. *Jesus and the Disinherited*. 3d ed. Boston: Beacon Press.

Tyndale, Wendy, ed. 2006. *Visions of Development: Faith-based Initiatives*. Burlington, VT: Ashgate.

Uphoff, Norman. 1996. *Learning from Gal Oya: Possibilities for Participatory Development and Post-Newtonian Social Science*. London: Intermediate Technology Publications.

———, J. M. Cohen, and A. A. Goldsmith. 1979. *Feasibility and Application of Rural Development Participation: A State of the Art Paper.* Ithaca, NY: Cornell University, Rural Development Committee, Center for International Studies.

Uvin, Peter. 2004. *Human Rights and Development*. Bloomfield, CT: Kumarian Press.

van Geest, William. 1993. "The Relationship between Development and Other Religious Activities and Objectives." Paper presented at the Churches and

Development Dialogue sponsored by Canadian International Development Assistance (CIDA). Toronto (June).

VeneKlasen, Lisa, Valerie Miller, Debbie Budlender, and Cindy Clark. 2007. *A New Weave of Power, People, and Politics: The Action Guide for Advocacy and Citizen Participation*. Bourton-on-Dunsmore, Warwickshire, UK: Practical Action.

Volf, Miraslav. 2009. "God, Justice, and Love." *Books and Culture* (January/February).

———. 1996. *Exclusion and Embrace: A Theological Exploration of Identity, Otherness, and Reconciliation*. Nashville, TN: Abingdon Press.

Voorhies, Samuel J. 1996. "Community Participation and Holistic Development." In Yamamori et al. 1996.

Wallace, Tina, with Candida March, eds. 1991. *Changing Perceptions: Writings on Gender and Development*. Oxford, UK: Oxfam.

Walls, Andrew. 1996. *The Missionary Movement in Christian History: Studies in the Transmission of the Faith*. Maryknoll, NY: Orbis Books.

———. 1989. "The Significance of Christianity in Africa." Public lecture, St. Colm's Education Centre and College, May 21.

———. 1987. "The Old Age of the Missionary Movement." *International Review of Mission* 66 (January).

Warren, D. Michael, L. Jan Slikkerveer, and David Brokensha. 1995. *The Cultural Dimension of Development: Indigenous Knowledge Systems*. London: Intermediate Technology Publications.

Weaver, James H., Michael T. Rock, and Kenneth Kusterer. 1997. *Achieving Broad-Based Sustainable Development: Governance, Environment, and Growth with Equity*. West Hartford, CT: Kumarian Press.

Weber, Hans-Reudi. 1995. *The Book That Reads Me*. Geneva: WCC.

Weigel, George. 2008. *Against the Grain: Christianity and Democracy, War, and Peace*. New York: Crossroad.

Whaites, Alan. 1996. "Let's Get Civil Society Straight: NGOs and Political Theory." *Development in Practice* 6, no. 3 (August).

White, Lynn Jr. 1978. "The Medieval Roots of Modern Technology and Science." In *Medieval Religion and Technology: Collected Essays*. Berkeley, CA: Center for Medieval and Renaissance Studies.

White, Sarah. 2009. "Bringing Well Being into Development Practice." WeD Working Paper 09/05. Bath, UK: University of Bath.

———, and Jethro Pettit. 2007. "Participatory Approaches and Measurement of Well-being." In *Human Well Being: Concept and Measurement*, ed. M. McGillivray. New York: Palgrave and United Nations University.

Williams, Suzanne, Janet Seed, and Adelina Mwau. 1994. *The Oxfam Gender Training Manual*. Oxford, UK: Oxfam.

Williamson, John. 2000. "Practical Community Empowerment." MCC Occasional Paper, no. 27. Available on the mcc.org website.

Wink, Walter. 1992. *Engaging the Powers: Discernment and Resistance in a World of Domination*. Minneapolis, MN: Fortress Press.

Wolterstorff, Nicholas. 2008. *Justice: Rights and Wrongs*. Princeton, NJ: Princeton University Press.

———. 1983. *Until Justice and Peace Embrace*. Grand Rapids, MI: Eerdmans.

World Bank. 2010. "Regional Aggregation Using 2005 PPP and $1.25/day Poverty Line." Available on the iresearch.worldbank.org website.

———. 2009. *Global Monitoring Report*. Washington DC: World Bank.

————. 2008. "Development Indicators Report." Available on the worldbank.org website.

World Vision India. 1995. "Record of PRA/PLA Walk Through (transcept) Exercise." (November).

World Vision International. 2003. *TDI Field Guide*. Available on the transformational-development.org website.

Wright, Christopher J. H. 1983. *An Eye for an Eye: The Place of Old Testament Ethics Today*. Downers Grove, IL.: InterVarsity Press.

Yamamori, Tetsunao, Bryant L. Myers, and David Conner, eds. 1995. *Serving with the Poor in Asia: Cases in Holistic Ministry*. Monrovia, CA: MARC.

————, Bryant L. Myers, Kwame Bediako, and Larry Reed, eds. 1996. *Serving with the Poor in Africa: Cases in Holistic Ministry*. Monrovia, CA: MARC.

————, Bryant L. Myers, C. René Padilla, and Greg Rake, eds. 1997. *Serving with the Poor in Latin America: Cases in Holistic Ministry*. Monrovia, CA: MARC.

————, Bryant L. Myers, and Kenneth L. Luscombe, eds. 1998. *Serving with the Urban Poor: Cases in Holistic Ministry*. Monrovia, CA: MARC.

Yunus, Muhammad. 2009. *Creating a World without Poverty: Social Business and the Future of Capitalism*. New York: Public Affairs.

Index

Figures and notes are indicated by *f* and *n* following the page number.